14.95

P9-CKU-212

The Ethnic Imperative

305.8
St342

The Ethnic Imperative

Examining the New White Ethnic Movement

Howard F. Stein and
Robert F. Hill

WITHDRAWN

The Pennsylvania State University Press
University Park and London

LIBRARY ST. MARY'S COLLEGE
193548

Library of Congress Cataloging in Publication Data
Stein, Howard F
The ethnic imperative.

Includes bibliographical references and index.
1. Minorities—United States. 2. Ethnicity.
3. United states—Social conditions—1960-
I. Hill, Robert F., joint author. II. Title.
E184.A1S79   301.451   77-1694
ISBN 0-271-00508-4

Copyright © 1977 The Pennsylvania State University
All rights reserved

Designed by Gretl Yeager Magadini

Printed in the United States of America

gift 3/93

TO OTTO VON MERING,
who taught that each of us is a "minority
of one."

Contents

Foreword   ix
Preface   xi
Introduction   1
1 The Changing Meanings of Ethnicity   13
2 American Dreams and American
   Realities   46
3 From Rising Expectations to Unfulfilled
   Ambitions   81
4 The Search for a New Stability and Security:
   Taproots of the New Ethnicity   112
5 The Illusion of Pluralism and the Preservation of
   Caste   139
6 The New Ethnicity As Counterculture   160
7 Transformation of a Personal Identity   213
8 Beyond the Ethnic Imperative   262
Notes   288
Index   303

"The speech of the poet does not stand the test of thorough criticism. Poets are poets, but level-headed men always stand on guard, ready to pour a bucket of cold water on the dreamer."

Alexander Dimitrievich Gradovsky,
in "Illusions and Reality,"
quoted in Hans Kohn, *Pan-Slavism.*

"Generally it is infinitely better to have no history than to keep up in the people the inclination to falsehood. It is a wrong piety to wish to cover up the errors of our fathers; the only means of honoring the memory of our fathers consists of abandoning their mistakes."

Ernest Denis,
La Bohème depuis la Montagne-Blanche.

"It is useless to hate the past; a man can only struggle to recover from it, and to modify as we can what time has made of us. . . . Culture and neurosis are both largely fossil habit. Some other better grounds for belief than habitual *nomos* must be found, some supra-tribal touchstone for truth, and rational argument must be produced concerning why and how *physis,* re-encountered, compels credence in one contingent hypothesis over another. . . . The problem set by our humanity remains. How to accept and how to embody male *authority,* how to express and when to modulate aggressiveness against other men—how, in short, to be father and son, government and citizen—these still remain the towering problems of the oedipal animal. And make no mistake of it: our human nature is built upon volcanoes and the tensions of potential earthquakes, the clear rational mind lies uneasily above archaic Titans fettered beneath in darkness. The relation of fathers and sons is mysterious and terrifying. It has never been rational, nor will it ever be. It is not the only relationship that men must suffer. But father and son form the most critical and dangerous animal relationship on earth, and to suppose otherwise is to invite catastrophe. For it is by no means delivered to us that this species-paradigm will survive annihilation in blind self-slaughter through some displaced pathology of this relationship. No man ever grows beyond the reach of its influence. To maintain that he does is to mask anguish with the coward lie of self-deceiving denial and false indifference. And that anguish is the root of religion, the way we suffer that anguish the secret of who we are."

Weston La Barre,
The Ghost Dance: The Origins of Religion.

Foreword

In the hands of most writers the "new ethnicity" has seemed to many anthropologists no more than the old and familiar "ethnocentrism" dressed up with a modish new cant title, hence the reader's delight in these authors' wry view of the uses of this "ethnicity" in the academic economics of grantsmanship. Again, the ethnicity of hyphenated-Americans appeared to be only decreasing cultural distinctiveness, under increasing acculturation to an implicitly WASP northwest-European ethos—hence mere vanishing ethnography which, better known and in purer form in Europe, was hardly worth fieldwork.

However, this book by Stein and Hill is a stunningly original one, with a biting incisiveness and relentless perceptivity. Whereas other writers have been content to present ethnic groups as, at most, special-interest blocs for political lobbying—and passively to accept or even to augment the ethnics' propagandizing—Stein and Hill *analyze* with stinging insight the uses of "ethnicity" for rationalization and self-deception.

This book is by far the most stimulating I have yet encountered on ethnicity. It is not only well written (what a satisfaction to find the word *ironic* properly used!), but it is also full of intellectual felicities that lead the reader on with mounting interest and enthusiasm. The book is that rare thing: edifying. There is elegance in seeing the Declaration of Independence as eschatological. The Kennedy-Johnson-Nixon sequence is strikingly apposite in the context of their argument (on Vietnam, on target), as is the treatment of Ford and Carter. There is fine discernment of "Galton's problem," and in a freshly perceptive manner. The authors show a sound grasp of regression and other Freudian concepts. They use anthropological theory (Devereux) well; they perceive the "double bind" predicament (Bateson) of diverse ethnicity in parents as shaping individual conflict in identity (Erikson). There is a fair-minded and compassionate analysis of the specific black problem of permanent racial visibility, and a graceful, decent treatment of Novak polemically. The gift of phrase is conspicuous: among my favorites are their scorn at "the normalization of everything" and their shrewdly analytic awareness that ethnics have "pseudo-insight based on shared resistances." And liberals, surely, will enjoy the hyper-rational B. F. Skinner being deftly defrocked to naked irrationality.

One important insight is the core of the book: what does "ethnicity" *do for* ethnic minorities? An authentically ethnic tribe, so to speak, does not need "ethnicity." It already possesses, firmly and complacently, the unquestioned cultural Truth; and any departure from this is manifestly mere ignorance and error. Epistemological strain comes only when a group, functionally a minority, has become permissively acculturated to the potency (and hence suspected "superiority") of a stable and unassailable host culture. In this sense, ethnicity is an "only in America" phenomenon: a pluralistic egalitarian society has freely allowed new minorities to settle among them—a fact all the more impressive since there often has been escape from mutually competitive ethnic groups in a politically hierarchical or more absolutist European nation-state (e.g., Hamtramck is by no means a Russian *shtetl,* nor does American "ethnicity" represent a Walloon-Flamingant in Belgium, a North Ireland, or a Serbo-Croatian conflict).

There are of course aspects of the situation that can be turned into gains, neurotic or otherwise. One may asseverate, out of self-doubt, that "minority is beautiful." Or, like monks contesting that "I am more humble than you are," one may argue that "We're more a minority than you are" (but the ultimate minority here is the individual, whom the American ideal specifically honors already), or even "We're a bigger minority [sc. *less* a one] than you are"—but in either way through perverse one-downsmanship make minority into superiority solely because it is not a majority!

It is in the sure grasp of these dynamic contextual matters that lies the sophisticated quality of Stein and Hill's treatment of ethnicity. It is a basic and permanent accomplishment. But their ideas will have a still wider bearing in the future world village. This is a delightful book, and I hope and predict it will achieve a wide and admiring readership.

WESTON LA BARRE

Duke University

Preface

The Ethnic Imperative is a psychosocial study of the White Ethnic Cultural Movement. It is our belief that culture continuity and change can only be superficially understood if the role of psychodynamic process is omitted. This is not a new idea but one that builds on what we regard as a great tradition in anthropology. At this time we would like to acknowledge those major influences on our thinking that pervade this work. It is not so much a matter of name-dropping as an acknowledgment of indebtedness. Alphabetically: Martin Buber, George Devereux, George De Vos, Erik Erikson, Joshua Fishman, Sigmund Freud, Jules Henry, Harold Isaacs, Clyde Kluckhohn, Heinz Kohut, Weston La Barre, Margaret Mead, Talcott Parsons, Theodore Schwartz, Edward Spicer, and Melford Spiro. Moreover, we would like to single out three books that have decisively influenced our thinking: Erikson's *Childhood and Society* (1950), Devereux's *Reality and Dream* (1951), and La Barre's *The Ghost Dance* (1970). We emphasize, however, that our intellectual ancestors are not held responsible for the errors of their offspring. Contrary to the biblical warning, we realize that the sins of the offspring are often visited on those from whom they claim descent.

It is perhaps not by accident that we are writing a psychocultural grammar of the New Ethnicity. Otto von Mering, our former teacher at the University of Pittsburgh, had written *A Grammar of Human Values* (1961) at a similar stage in his professional development. Unlike many other anthropologists who were locked into static "structural" and formalist thinking, von Mering emphasized that nothing is static and that all is process. Thus the laws of nature are discovered out of the analysis of process.

We are equally indebted to Philip Hallen, president of the Maurice Falk Medical Fund, who supported our graduate training and our fieldwork through far more than a monthly paycheck. His confidence in, and encouragement for, our approach to the study of ethnicity reaffirmed our belief in what was decidedly unconventional, if not anathema.

We would also like to thank two historians: James Clarke at the University of Pittsburgh, and Thomas Spira at the University of Prince Edward Island, who endorsed our analytic framework when it was only an idea which had not yet been systematized.

The gestation, birth, and postnatal survival of this manuscript have been greatly aided by the interest and support of John M. Pickering, editorial director of The Pennsylvania State University Press. We would also like to express our gratitude to our respective institutions, Meharry Medical College and the University of Oklahoma Health Sciences Center. We are especially grateful to Dr. Lloyd Elam, Dr. Ralph Hines, Dr. William Coopwood, and medical student Hagos Habtezghi at Meharry; and to Dr. Thomas Lynn, Dr. Oscar Parsons, and Mr. William Stanhope at Oklahoma.

Our secretaries have done the heroic, if not the impossible: Ms. Loyce Droke, Ms. Marion Morgan, Ms. Lettie Giles, and Ms. Ruth Coleman Garrett. Finally, our greatest debt is to our families, who endured the months of Dr. Jekyll and Mr. Hyde.

Previously published material by the authors, adopted for this work, is acknowledged as follows:

The Canadian Review of Studies in Nationalism, Vol. 1, No. 1, Fall 1973, published at The University of Prince Edward Island.

Published by permission of Transaction, Inc., from *Society,* Vol. 11, No. 6, Copyright © 1974, by Transaction, Inc.

The University of Chicago *School Review,* Vol. 83, No. 2, February 1975.

We would like to express our gratitude to Professor Janet Schreiber and Professor Theodore Schwartz for permission to quote passages from unpublished manuscripts.

Introduction

At a 1974 workshop concerning ethnicity and mental health, a national leader of the White Ethnic Movement, in fact, one of its entrepreneurs, noted with dismay the recent "about-face" that psychoanalyst Erik H. Erikson had made about the concept of identity. In private remarks to Howard Stein, he said: "Tell me, Howard, what's Erikson trying to do? I don't understand him. Here he's been writing all along on how important it is to have an identity, on how a person's identity lies in the core of his group. Now he's going back on everything. What he's putting out now simply flies in the face of fact. Erikson seems unable to accept the fact that human groups project their negative self-images on outgroups, that they consider their way to be the human way, and that ethnic groups are here to stay. I don't understand why Erikson dislikes groups so much. What he calls 'pseudo-species' [races, nationalities, tribes, etc.] is the way human groups have always behaved. Erikson knows better—because he said it himself. He's all caught up in this universalism, and his head is in the clouds. He may want us all to be universalists, but that's not the way people are. That's what was wrong with American culture. It tried to deny that people's basic attachment is to their ethnic culture." This is the ideology and the complaint of the New Ethnicity succinctly stated.

Not long ago Robert Ardrey argued for a human territorial imperative, and Konrad Lorenz persuaded many that a human aggressive instinct required periodic expression in forms of violence and warfare. In *Men in Groups*, Lionel Tiger proposes the existence of an inherent male bonding to other males that derives from our long ancestry as hunters, and in *The Imperial Animal*, Lionel Tiger and Robin Fox argue that dominance/submission, superordinate/subordinate relations are sociobiological givens in the human condition. Finally, Steven Goldberg proposes the inevitability of patriarchy as the dominant principle governing human relationships. Added to these imperatives is yet another, *the ethnic imperative,* which is purported to lie at the core of our very personalities and identities, wherein self and group are inseparable, merged in common identity.[1] Napoleon said that history is destiny; for the new ethnophiles, however, *ethnicity* is destiny.

This book is an analysis of the claims of that new categorical imperative and of the cultural movement in America, the New Ethnicity, that perceives itself to be one of its expressions. While the New White Ethnics, or ethnophiles, speak of ethnicity as a constant *given,* an invariant in the human condition, we shall inquire into the *dynamics of its givenness.* Although the ethnophiles believe that ethnicity is the unquestioned premise of human identity, this study will analyze the cultural, psychological, and historical underpinnings not only of the premises themselves but of their assertion. While ethnicity has certainly come of age as a legitimate subject of inquiry, there has arisen the tendency to see everything as ethnic or, at least, everything nonethnic as counterfeit. Since intellectual fashion, collective obsession (and panic), and funding strangely coincide, ethnicity will be discovered in an abundance proportionate to the availability of capital to support its discovery.[2]

Anthropologists, for instance, now tend to replace tribes and cultures with *ethnic groups,* subsuming the same data under a far more lucrative title[3]—one heretofore the domain of sociology, folklore, and history. We certainly do not disparage the field of ethnic studies in which we number ourselves. One of the main arguments of this book, however, is that the New Ethnicity is a "revitalization movement," a "nativistic movement," and a "crisis cult";[4] it is *something new* and clearly distinguishable from what scholars see as time-honored or timeless cultural units. To borrow and apply the term *ethnic group* or *ethnicity* to the present cultural movement is to miss the entire point of the New Ethnicity, which is a new identity that selectively incorporates cultural content from the past. The key to such use is not the past, however, but current needs. The New Ethnicity offers a sense of descent and of affiliation that confers the illusion of continuity with the chosen past. Furthermore, the New Ethnicity cannot be studied under the old rubric. As the following evolutionary metaphor states: Our present exploration of the New Ethnicity is not the study of a static *species* (as if even a species were ever static), but of the dynamics of *speciation.*

Much of the scholarship of ethnic studies consists of salvage ethnography, an attempt not only to trace origins but to demonstrate the persistence of those origins in the present—and if the origins are not present, to insist that they should be. The past must redeem the present. What was discarded in the past is now avidly sought out and painstakingly collected as sacred relic. What was until recently sent to the weekly trash is now saved, catalogued, and archived. For example, old weekly ethnic newspapers have suddenly become valuable as records of the treasures of ethno-American culture and history. Many New Ethnics lament that even the national ethnic organizations did not make complete and protected archives of their newspapers and annuals. The question might be asked: Why should they? What function were the ethnic newspapers originally designed to perform? Old ethnic newspapers are not intrinsically valuable; indeed, they can be viewed as something of a "projective test." What they mean is what the reader reads into them! Only a new sense of history makes them significant and worthy of pursuit by literary archeology. It is pointless to say that the ethnic organizations did not realize what gold mines of history they possessed, for it is the contemporary sense of history—the selection of facts that are relevant links to the present—that confers immeasurable value on these documents. In this book we shall pay close attention to the *criteria* for such selection. The new historiography not only documents the assumed validity of the new-world view, but is part of it. It is necessary, we suggest, to inquire into the fear of the irretrievable loss of the past, and the need to rescue this particular past from oblivion.

Not the presence of tradition, but the search and scholarly research for it is one of the hallmarks of the New Ethnicity. Recognizing this fundamental misunderstanding about the nature of the White Ethnic Movement, and of the New Ethnicity in general, has offered us insight into the dynamics of contemporary American society and into the American intellectual history of the past several decades. The anthropological concepts of holism and functionalism—the search for interrelationships and networks of meaning and behavior—have made this linkage of the less-than-obvious necessary to the very understanding of meanings and actions that are virtually taken for granted. This study of the ethnic imperative is nothing less than a study in the creation of culture. A clarification of the new meaning of *identity,* in turn, is essential if we are to understand the new culture that is created in its image.

The cult of identity-consciousness in contemporary America is perhaps analogous to the cult of youth in the Weimar culture of the 1920s. The two periods of unrest share an "unbridled romanticism and emotional thinking." In Germany, writes Peter Gay, "the *völkisch,* right-wing groups demanded the 'reawakening of a genuine Germanness—*deutsches Volkstum*—in German lands,' while the left-wing groups called for 'the restoration of a *societas,* a communally constructed society.' Everywhere, amid endless splintering of groups and futile efforts at reunion, there was a certain fixation on the experience of youth itself. . . . Flight into the future through flight into the past, reformation through nostalgia—in the end, such thinking amounted to nothing more than the decision to make adolescence itself into an ideology." Titling the chapter "The Hunger for Wholeness," Gay writes later that "if the Germany of 1927 needed anything, it needed clarity, concreteness, demystification."[5]

In contemporary American culture, the *Volkstum* of the American Right is ethnicity or *ethnitude*, while the radical socialism of the New Left (itself *völkisch*) would tear everything down and rebuild from the bottom up. There is plenty of evidence of the endless splintering of groups and of fragile, temporary alliances. The spectrum ranges in biblical terms from analogues of reformationist Zealots (e.g., the New Left) to parallels with the quietistic Essenes (e.g., The Farm in Tennessee). A culture-wide obsession with identity reflects a fixation on conflicts that are heightened during the *developmental phase* of adolescence. American culture, of course, has from the beginning made an ideology of adolescence in its revolutionary commitment to tentativeness, incompleteness, open-endedness, to youth and idealism. It is the opposite pole of adolescent dynamics that prevails at present: the dread of the future, the wresting of absolutism out of uncertainty, the quest for closure, for a neatly packaged orientation that will solve once and for all the unsettling disorientation. In Erikson's terms, the hunger for "wholeness" is renounced by a demand for "totalistic" coherence that will overcome inner and outer fragmentation. The hunger for finalism is satiated through a flight into the past, through a "nostalgiafication" of reality. An unbridled romanticism and emotional thinking are reflected in the penchant for undisciplined subjectivity, the insistence on the primacy of personal experience, the popularity of anti-intellectualism and antirationalism. Reality becomes reconstituted in accordance with the demands of narcissism.

In our study of the development and consolidation of the identity, ideology, and polity of the White Ethnic Movement, we attempt to explain the cultural and psychological conditions that underlie the embracing of the irrational. An explanation of the role of nostalgia, romanticism, and emotion in generating and preserving—for their adherents at least—a semblance of personal and social stability is also attempted. To explicate, however, is not to legitimate. To apply Peter Gay's prescription for Weimar Germany to the present American context: If the New Ethnicity, or American culture in general, needs anything, it needs clarity, concreteness, and demystification. Meeting that need is the goal of this book: to clarify why for many Americans ethnicity has become an imperative; to make its dynamics concrete or explicit; and thus to demystify it.

The impulse to create culture anew arises from a crisis in the existing culture. The New Ethnicity is one among many diverse expressions or symptoms of the contemporary American malaise and of attempts to resolve it. Prevailing norms and values are questioned, devalued, and inverted by a host of sects and movements: the youth culture, the Black Power Movement, the New Left, the Woman's Movement, the New Ethnicity (white ethnics), Gay Liberation, the American Indian Movement, and the Hispanic Movement. The quest for equality often gives way to the assertion of superiority. For many, ethnicity becomes the new generic category and emblem of recovered status. Ethnicity succeeds where other identities such as "race" for blacks, "religion" for Jews, and "working class" for white ethnics have failed. Celebrating the fact (and the act) of cultural difference, the New Ethnic identity promises for its adherents the completeness of roots, a proud ancestry, peoplehood, solidarity, community, high culture, and the memory or fact of nationhood.

In contemporary America pluralism prevails, legitimating every conceivable kind of difference. Difference itself is glorified, and the insistence on being different from what one is expected to be reflects the oppositional nature of the new identities. To be "different" is an end in itself. Existing differences are not sufficient: it is necessary to *create* difference. One current slogan insists on "the right to be different"; another encourages each person to "do your own thing" and to "tell it like it is." What was yesterday regarded as deviant or abnormal, today is proudly and shamelessly displayed as normal or healthy. In turn, the erstwhile normal is ridiculed and condemned as sick. In a sense, everything has come out of the closets and taken to the streets. There is a slogan for this too: "Let it all hang out." Expressed in the form of the dichotomous health-illness, normal-abnormal model, the new identities, to feel legitimate, must affirm themselves and insist on confirmation from without as normal or healthy. The stigma of sickness, abnormality, or deviance must be removed by having the identity sanctioned as healthy. The New Ethnicity emphasizes that to be ethnic, as opposed to being 100 percent American, is not to be a deviant, a cultural oddity, or even un-American. On the contrary, to be ethnic is to possess "soul," to have an authentic identity, and to be mentally healthy. Thus the New Ethnics are far superior to the rootless Americans.

The new condition of self-conscious ethnicity alters both the condition of research and the response to it. The New Ethnic ideology emphasizes the inscrutability of the subjective, personal experience as well as the ineffability of the imagination and intuition. Ethnicity becomes a matter of internal history. Great stress is placed on *Respect,* an attitude that involves more than acceptance and seems to combine deference and awe. An outside observer, even a participant-observer, cannot possibly fathom the depth of the ethnic bond. Although the New Ethnics overtly stress inaccessibility from the outside, they close themselves off from the inside as a means of protecting their fragile self-esteem. Since only an insider can truly know the meaning of the ethnic experience and can share the common "soul" that contains such knowledge, the abundant literature on American ethnic groups is discounted as irrelevant and foreign. If the outsider was formerly the expert on the natives yet could not possibly understand what they were doing, the insider is now the only expert who knows his or her people from within.

It is beside the point to cite the staggering amount of literature that has been written by American social and behavioral scientists about white ethnic groups. Even anthropology, with its traditional penchant for the "primitive" and the distant, has contributed admirably to white-ethnic literature over the past several decades. The existing literature concerning history, family dynamics, health and illness patterns, religious practices, customs, marriage patterns, and acculturation, is not, however, the *kind* of material that the New Ethnicity seeks. Hence its irrelevance and the declaration that no literature exists. What, then, is *relevant?* The White Ethnic Movement requires a body of literature that will support, sustain, and validate its ideological premises and identity. The old literature simply does not confirm the new image, one that requires visibility without vulnerability. Since ethnic primordiality becomes the new universal arbiter, anything that contradicts the highly self-conscious imagery must be totally rejected. The only literature, therefore, that the movement can accept is pseudo-insight based on shared resistances, confirming the New Ethnic identity, providing a further basis for pride and self-esteem, and demonstrating that American ethnicity is flourishing both culturally and numerically. The politization of research and the ultimate subversion of knowledge follow, unerringly.

Let us be clear. We are not applying these observations to an abstract, nonexistent ethnicity, but to a specific, new identity based on a particular meaning-set that utilizes ethnic symbolism. We are not "enemies of the past," nor do we believe that a sense of time that includes the past is automatically "symptomatic." Our concern is how the past is used, the meanings of a particular sense of history, the conceptualization of time itself. Because *ethnicity* is a psycholinguistic category that encompasses specific time-bound meanings, contexts, and intrapsychic dynamics, it cannot be analyzed apart from these. The relationship between the New Ethnicity and identity process is our ultimate concern in this book. At stake is nothing less than our understanding of human development and the nature of being human.

We agree with De Vos and Romanucci-Ross that "ethnic identity can be a positive affirmation containing a negative potential for becoming a hysterical or paranoid defense. As in all forms of belonging, it can be used to express one's humanness, or to deny the humanness of others; its use depends on collective and individual mental health. It also depends on the reality of external pressure and oppression."[6] We would evaluate ethnic identity, or any expression of identity, by the *quality* of humanness it evinces. With Devereux, we would emphasize that one cannot affirm one's humanness without concurrently confirming the humanness of others. Functional identity is inclusive; dysfunctional identity, which utilizes hysterical, paranoid, and dissociative defenses to maintain rigid boundaries, is exclusive. It is dysfunctional identity which we find at the core of the identity and ideology of the New Ethnicity.

Among the dysfunctional characteristics and consequences of ethnic identity, Devereux includes (1) the reduction of an individual to "one-dimensionality"; (2) the highly ritualized, "insistent, and even obsessive clinging to one's ethnic . . . identity"; (3) hypercathexis of ethnic identity, as a means of shoring up a flawed self; (4) the creation of a closed-system identity; and (5) the "obliteration of individual distinctiveness." For Devereux, "a hypercathecting of one's ethnic identity leads to the annihilation of the individual's real identity." "Yet, man's functionally relevant dissimilarity from all others is what makes him human: similar to others precisely through his high degree of differentiation. It is this which permits him to claim a human identity."[7] Devereux concludes that

> an overriding emphasis on one of a person's several "class" identities, such as ethnic identity, simply seeks to shore up a flawed self and an uncertain awareness of one's identity as a person. The current tendency to stress one's ethnic or class identity, its use as a crutch, is *prima facie* evidence of the impending collapse of the only valid sense of identity: one's differentness, which is replaced by the most archaic pseudo-identity imaginable. I do not think that

the "identity crisis" of our age can be resolved by recourse to the artificial props of collective identities: of ethnic, class, religious, occupational or any other "assistant identity." . . . this can lead only to a renunciation of identity, in order to fend off what is apprehended as a danger of total annihilation. . . . I consider the evolving of any massive and dominant "class" identity as a first step toward such a "protective" renunciation of true identity.[8]

Not the fact of ethnicity, but the defensive quality of the New Ethnic identity is what makes us question the tenet that ethnic belongingness is the only legitimate form of life. Such developmental processes as individuation, differentiation, and separation are anathema to the New Ethnic ideology. What is acclaimed to be the essence of human potential, inherent in the very nature of the human animal, seems, upon closer inspection, to be diagnostic of developmental arrest and regression. It is as though life is not an ongoing developmental process, but something completed in the earliest years (a caricature of Freud, to say the least). Moreover, the seemingly desperate quest for belonging, continuity, linkage with the past, and absorption into selfless timelessness strongly suggests a need to deny and overcome personal mortality. By bridging death, the followers of the New Ethnicity assure themselves of eternal life.

Discussing "The New Pluralists," Harold Isaacs differentiates "between those whose primary commitment is to their membership in their particular group, and those who see their group identity as a threshold from which to look for broader human identification and outcomes."[9] It is precisely the quality of the commitment and identification, of the sense of security and belonging, that differentiates between those who use ethnicity as a defense and those for whom ethnicity is synthesized into an ever-inclusive whole. There is all the difference in the world between "feeling at home" and withdrawing into an enclave mentality, feeling besieged by the world.

If ethnicity must be publicly declared and romanticized, it cannot be authentically lived. We suggest that for the majority of Euro-Americans, ethnicity need not be made into a conspicuously consumed and self-conscious style of life and rhetoric because it is not separate from an integrated life. The New Ethnicity replaces relation with an *ideology* of relation. Authenticity, too, is a casualty of the new identity because people become abstract personifications of categories, insider or outsider. Invidious comparison makes pluralism into a fond illusion, since a doctrine of reconciliation is disqualified by a culturally rationalized separatism. We value human variability or *pluralism* that does not make a forced distinction such as Anglo, American, or ethnic. An ideology of difference, however, is a crypto-conformism, since only specifically sanctioned differences will be tolerated (from Hippies to white ethnics). Difference for the sake of being "different" is a type of narcissism that in group form becomes an insistence on sameness and causes the eradication of genuine difference.

The New Ethnicity, then, is both a symptomatic expression of a disintegrated life and an attempt to cope with this sense of personal disintegration through regression to an earlier stage in individual development. The ambivalence that is reawakened is intensified, and the subsequent fragmentation is resolved by regression. The return to a fictionalized past and to newly idealized kinsmen is an expression of *regression in the service of the archaic superego*. The New Ethnic vogue is a "false consciousness" in a deeply *Freudian* way. The personality dynamics underlying the New Ethnicity do not allow its adherents insight into the very conflicts they are attempting to resolve. The New Ethnics cannot solve their problems because they insist on looking in the wrong places for their solutions: namely, outside themselves. They must defend against the insight that they are in part the sources of their own problems.

The New Ethnicity is an expression of what Weston La Barre has called "institutionalized modes of self-deception," in which a culturally constituted delusional system substitutes for reality. Ironically, what the New Ethnics discover to be the ethnic nature of the human condition is a projection of their own escapism onto reality. Withdrawal from reality can be called "reality" only from a regressed position. A culture does not become psychodynamically normal simply by virtue of being a culture or a cultural movement. For a social scientist to embrace the New Ethnicity is to accept a popularly shared delusion as fact, and to rationalize rather than analyze. We are not antiethnic. We refuse, however, to substitute delusion for reality. "History," writes Weston La Barre, "is what you can't cop out from." So is reality.[10]

Any distinction between authentic and inauthentic identity lies in the extent to which identity is based on genuine relation and insight, or pseudo-relation and self-conning, respectively. With the former goes humility, and with the latter, a terror-ridden arrogant pride. We are cultural relativists to the extent that we look at something in its own context. But one meta-cultural context that cannot be omitted is that of biological and developmental invariants with which all cultures must come to terms. It is this *Anlage* of invariants—with its potentialities, vulnerabilities, and defenses—that compels us to explore the White Ethnic Movement in a context that allows clinical judgment to be made on cultural norms and behavior.

At the outset we should say something about our own approach to research among white-ethnic Americans. Stein researched among Slovak- and Ruthene-Americans, Hill, among Polish-Americans.[11] Beginning our field research in the late 1960s under a Maurice Falk Medical Fund Fellowship in Ethnicity, Racism, and Mental Health, we did not undertake fieldwork expecting to observe firsthand a New Ethnic Movement, although it subsequently became one of our foci. If anything, we expected to do a traditional, though psychologically oriented, study of the old ethnicity by working among three- and four-generation Slavic-American extended families. Specifically, we were interested in deepening the current understanding of cultural continuity and change by studying the identity process over the life cycle of individuals and families. We expected to find ethnicity neither alive and well nor vanishing; furthermore, we were not interested in finding cultural "survivals" or in preserving or vindicating any culture. We were quite aware that one could consciously and unconsciously act upon Polish or Slovak values without regarding them as specifically Polish or Slovak. For the most part, our work was among unselfconscious white ethnics whose ethnicity and Americanness were interwoven into a personal synthesis which was expressed in the routine of their daily lives. Even among highly self-conscious white ethnics who drew specific attention to selected attributes of their ethnicity, we were able to observe the quiet, unobtrusive workings of ethnic personality structure, values, attitudes, and beliefs. Among these New Ethnics, moreover, we were able to observe the tremendous struggle within the same person between the "old" and the "new" ethnic—and the necessary relation of both to the American identity.

It is necessary, then, to reexamine the nature of American culture and the changing meanings of ethnicity. In particular, we must ask how the American identity came to mean so much and then how it came to mean so little. We must also ask how ethnicity changed from an unassuming part integrated within a larger identity, into a voracious and exclusive identity concept that claims only itself to be genuine, and hence demands the discarding of prior elements of the whole.

As we shall see in the second half of *The Ethnic Imperative,* the identity, ideology, and imagery of the New Ethnicity is far from indigenous, but is predicated on opposition to aspects of American culture with which it defines itself by contrast. The identity of the New Ethnicity is not independent of American identity. It requires, however, the externalized enemy to create and perpetuate the new internal solidarity. What is within the personal and group boundary is systematically related to what is outside that boundary. One of our main themes is that what is now excluded was only recently included and was indeed the very basis for identity, including self-esteem, and self-image.

To understand the New Ethnicity, the culture with which it is ineradicably bound must be considered. The point of departure for our itinerary will thus *not* be the movement itself, but the dynamics of American culture history and the role of the changing meaning of ethnicity in that dynamic. The first chapter will discuss the changing meanings and functions of ethnicity in the American context. The second chapter will explore, in broad strokes, the promises and realities of American culture. In the third and fourth chapters we shall delineate what we believe to be the antecedent and causal conditions precipitating and catalyzing the New Ethnic Movement: the World War II era of liberation, culminating in the Kennedy New Frontier, and the subsequent era of restoration with its search for order. The New Ethnicity will be seen as one means among many current attempts to *reorder* personal and social reality based on a pervasive sense of inner and outer *disorder*.

In the fifth chapter we arrive at the White Ethnic Movement, which is analyzed in terms of a variation on a culture-wide American theme: the dichotomy and polarization between black and white. An analysis of the juxtaposed terms *white* and *ethnic* reveals just what the new identity is, and is not. This chapter and subsequent ones will concern the oppositional dynamic of the white ethnic identity in terms of contrast categories most salient to it: black, American, and WASP, in particular. We shall examine the complex psychological dynamics underlying the transformation of identity from American to white ethnic, and relate the new symbolism, imagery, and polity to the needs of the new identity. The analysis of a single revitalization-nativist movement will culminate in the presentation of a succinct model of identity revitalization movements in general, which, in turn, should contribute to our understanding of ethno-nationalist movements and the so-called primitive cults.[12]

In the final chapter we shall look beyond the ethnic imperative for an understanding of human identity, seeing in the New Ethnicity a cultural elaboration based on defense against further development rather than being the measure of human development. Our endeavor is based on the following paradox. While we seek to explain the readiness with which human beings accept delusion as truth, we steadfastly hold with Otto von Mering, our former teacher, that "unwelcome truth is better than cherished error." We do not harbor the naive faith that "truth always wins" in the end. Our commitment to the human species is that it *must*. That is why this book is as much "applied" as it is "ethnographic" and theoretical. Insight is intrinsically a tool for change.

1 The Changing Meanings of Ethnicity

One of the principal tasks of this work is to elucidate the meanings of such widely used and evocative terms as *ethnic identity, ethnicity, identity, cultural pluralism, the New Ethnicity,* and *white ethnic*—all of which are the core concepts of the nativistic movement we are exploring.[1] In one sense, their meanings are evident: how they are used, what those who employ them explicitly refer to. This is what is called the native or folk system or model: what those who use the words consciously believe and intend, how those who are speaking wish to be understood.[2] In another sense, however, the meanings are far from evident, for native explanations *may* be just as misleading from the scientific point of view as they *may* be accurate. In this case, the cultural symbol or representation must be decoded and its multiplicity of unconscious meanings uncovered. In this way, we discover the referents of the symbolism. Decoding or analyzing assumes that it is necessary to look for more satisfactory explanations "below the surface": hence the search for substrate, *Anlage,* precursors, unconscious dynamics, and deep structure.

Until less than a decade ago, American culture was studied to a large extent as though ethnicity no longer existed. There were, however, numerous exceptions to this generalization. Today, those who would correct the error of neglect merely invert it by proposing that ethnic groups can be studied as though American culture hardly existed, except perhaps as an "oppressor." American history *is* ethnic history, the history of groups. Therefore, one set of sins of omission and commission is traded for another. This reversal of the valence of symbols and values represents one among many examples of the oppositional nature of the White Ethnic Movement, that is, what was formerly valued positively is now negated, and conversely.

We deem it necessary to distinguish between the current self-conscious *ideological ethnicity* and what might be called the prior unselfconscious, if not unconscious, *behavioral ethnicity*. George Devereux has recently made the identical distinction, calling the former "ethnic identity" and the latter "ethnic personality."[3] The present study is predominantly an exploration of ideological ethnicity. The intelligentsia of the New Ethnicity, however, wish to merge the two, claiming that the white ethnics simply have become conscious of their ethnicity and that the persistence of behavioral ethnicity confirms the premises of the ideology. In the New Ethnicity, what was private becomes public; what was done for its own sake now takes on the character of performance or staging. It is widely recognized that much of unconscious, behavioral ethnicity persists out of awareness in personality dynamics, values, attitudes, and interpersonal relationships, even into the third or fourth Americanized generation, who may no longer label themselves according to ethnic descent or who may choose their ethnic group from among several alternatives in the parental or grandparental generation. One may think, feel, and act Polish or Irish without being able to apply an ethnic label to one's behavior.

The New Ethnics, however, make an issue out of this fact, use it as the basis of an ideology, rationalize its neglect as a social problem meriting political and economic redress, and flaunt it proudly as evidence that the ethnics have not melted. When one becomes self-conscious of his or her identity, the very quality and character of that identity change, and this is the problem. It is not simply a matter of becoming aware of preexistent identity. Rather, the New Ethnicity is a new identity that selectively incorporates attributes of the old and labels the new synthesis "ethnicity."

Several concepts from the social and behavioral sciences require definition and discussion at this point because they will provide the analytic framework for the study. First, there is the distinction between "surface structure" and "deep structure" made by linguist Noam Chomsky as central to his "transformational grammar."[4] According to Chomsky, the human mind is preadapted for the transformation of overt, particularistic words and phrases, the "surface structure" of a language, into covert, universal, deep structures which provide the basis for meaning and action. Likewise, the structuralist theory of anthropologist Claude Levi-Strauss rests on the assumption of a deep, universal, human, cognitive endowment which guides or transforms the expression of particular social and cultural forms.[5] Levi-Strauss also employs the concept transformation as denoting the insistence on difference, a process involving the redefinition, segregation, inversion, or reversal of cultural elements on either side of a cultural boundary.

Similarly, the "semantic differential," postulated by social psychologist Charles Osgood, rests on the proposition that perception and cognition are grounded in a universal predisposition for bipolar antagonisms.[6] Both Levi-Strauss and Osgood believe that such binary distinctions as "hard" and "soft," "dark" and "light," "up" and "down," "left" and "right," and "north" and "south" provide what might be called the raw perceptual distinctions (surface structures) that form the basis for cognitive classes (deep structures). Osgood's reluctant wedding of his "semantic differential" to learning theory, however, apparently precluded his further exploration of it in terms of deep structure.

Second, there is the concept of "opposition," implicit in the constructs of Chomsky, Levi-Strauss, and Osgood, but explicit in the writings of others. Cultural anthropologist Edward Spicer, for example, speaks of the "oppositional process" underlying a "persistent identity system" in complex society. He states that "a persistent identity system is a product of this [the oppositional] process. Its formation and maintenance are intimately bound up with the conditions of opposition. . . ." Similarly, political scientist Eric Voegelin introduced the term *Gegenidee* (contrast conception) to account for the creation of personal and group boundaries in national conflict. He suggested that differences between opponents become symbols of relative status. Ethnocentrism becomes intensified and the "other" is evaluated in terms of dissociated aspects of one's self. Through bipolarization, one's own group comes to embody the "good" and is purged of what is regarded as "evil." Likewise, Erik Erikson speaks of "negative conversion" (transformation), which is characterized by the totalistic embracing of the negative identity; what was formerly positive becomes negative, and vice versa.[7] What used to be a hidden source of shame becomes a badge of pride that is boldly exhibited. Aspects of one's self that were formerly regarded as evil are now projected onto a disparaged outgroup.

Third, we employ the concept of "ethnos," which we operationally define as the inextricable interlinking of egos in a group or corporate identity. It captures, for us, the essence of the phenomenon whereby individual ego is regarded as only an extension of what might be called "group ego." Personal identity literally becomes embedded in the superorganic. Following this, *ethnitude* is the ideological expression of *ethnos,* and *ethnophile,* one of its *true believers.* We emphasize that the mystical concept of ethnos does not apply to traditional ethnic or tribal units whether in isolation or in complex societies. We use it parsimoniously to denote only the romanticized culture which the nativists believe once existed, and which they wish to restore.

From the point of view of the generative grammar, the ethnos is a form taken by the surface structure to represent and attempt to cope with conflicts residing in the deep structure. From the point of view of adherents to the New Ethnicity, however, this perspective is nonsensical as well as threatening, precisely because the basis of the new identity must be denied. Thus the New Ethnic sees the ethnos as the deep structure generating all that is worthwhile in life. In this book it is our task to understand the New Ethnic Movement both from the participant's point of view *and* from an analytic point of view, whose validity must be denied by the New Ethnics in order to preserve their newly won identity.

The relationship between ethnos and American culture is not merely one of logical opposites but of active opposition. Ethnos and American culture are two poles of an antagonistic system, standing in dialectic relation to one another. One cannot be understood in isolation from the other. In this perspective the ethnophile's insistence on the independence and primordiality of the ethnos is not so much descriptive of reality as it reflects the ethnophile's need to compartmentalize and isolate the ethnos as a defended identity.

This analysis of the White Ethnic Movement also assumes that its symbols, rituals, beliefs, and behaviors are all part of an interdependent system which must be viewed holistically and not only separately. Moreover, this functionally interacting system is not static, but dynamic. Every slice of a lifetime, of an institution, and of time is simply a single "frame" of an ongoing "film." To continue the metaphor of cinematics, in situations of rapid cultural change (the White Ethnic Movement, incidentally, is a response to such a change), there is more difference between adjacent "frames" than in more or less "traditional" and hence more stable conditions.

In our quest for the meaning of current cultural change, we employ both a functional-systems analysis of the dynamics of American culture "at this point in time," and a culture-historic or ethnohistoric perspective, allowing us to discern underlying patterns or themes that transcend the given moment in history and which are present in all cultural process.[8] The "theme" is essential to our understanding of the "variation"; without the former, any interpretation of the latter would be of extremely limited use, if not altogether misleading.

Our emphasis on process necessitates that we perceive the "noun" in terms of the "verb," that is, structure is not independent of structuring and constant restructuring. Cultural difference cannot be intelligibly interpreted apart from the dynamics of differentiation and the maintenance of difference. Identity cannot be understood apart from the psychodynamics of identification and ego process; personal and ethnic boundaries cannot be understood apart from the affective, cognitive, and behavioral process by which they are erected, maintained, and altered.

This dynamic perspective, based simultaneously on attention to emotion, cognition, and action, influences the manner in which we approach such issues as identity, ethnic identity, religiosity, and American identity. Typically, these have been studied on a linear scale and as a matter of degree, in terms of trait lists, presenceabsence, and replacement. They have also been studied quantitatively, in terms of objective criteria from without. Questions generated by this approach include: (1) How *religious* (Jewish, Protestant, Catholic . . .) is such and such person? (2) How *ethnic* (Polish, Jewish, Slovak, Italian . . .) is such and such person? (3) How *American* is such and such person? (4) How *regional* (northern, southern, midwestern . . .) is such and such person? One needed only to formulate questionnaires or conduct interviews that revealed attitudes, values, institutional affiliation and attendance, customs, and language use. The approach assumed beforehand what were salient indices, and these were based on some good criteria and on some commonly held stereotypes.

It seems almost natural to think of the maintenance or disappearance of ethnic identity in terms of, for instance, membership in a fraternal organization, buying life insurance from an ethnic fraternal group,* attending a national ethnic parish in the Roman Catholic church, preferring certain native foods, speaking the native language, intragroup marriage (endogamy), and celebrating ethnoreligious or ethnopolitical festivals. A researcher can set up a scale, write a questionnaire, analyze the data, and demonstrate that the process of Americanization through item-replacement is linear. The only problem (we have set up a straw man intentionally) is that linearity is built

---

*In this work, *ethnic fraternals* will refer to a class of ethnic associations that originally developed for purposes of self-help, mutual assistance, self-defense, death and accident benefits, life insurance, and the purchase of burial tracts. Subsequently, they became sources of financial support for church construction, cultural continuity, and athleticgymnastic activities. They also aided the World War I and postwar era nationalist movements. Their lodges or clubs became the centers of social activities. The *ethnic fraternals* became powerful agents and bridges of Americanization.

into the assumptions about the nature of ethnicity and Americanization and is part of the instrument that is supposed to measure the process. The results are, therefore, prestructured because the researcher has chosen to identify the most tangible indices of ethnicity with the most significant ones (*to the observer*).

So much for what we do not do. The foregoing elements, however, remain salient in a different frame of reference in which linear replacement *may* emerge as one possible organization of the data (but is not preordained by the eliciting techniques). The anthropological emphasis on participant observation, intersubjectivity between ethnographer and informant, and the complex relation between ideal, real, expected, and stated (all of which are themselves situational and not necessarily rigid) requires that we approach ethnicity, identity, religion, and Americanization qualitatively. Thus we ask: (1) What does it mean to this person to be *religious?* How is this person religious? (2) How is this person ethnic? What is the personal meaning of being *ethnic?* (3) How is this person American? What is this person's subjective meaning of being *American?* (4) How is this person *regional-American?* What does being a southerner or midwesterner mean to this person? What we ultimately seek is not merely reported facts, but contexts in which facts emerge and from which they derive and give meaning. The how, why, when, and where are abstracted through a synthesis of data gathered in this way.

As a brief example, consider membership in the Polish Falcons or the First Catholic Slovak Union. What does membership or nonmembership, or the extent and type of participation, if a member, mean to the person? Is it *just* a life insurance company, or is it a means of maintaining ethnic continuity? How does it contribute to such continuity, since the ethnic fraternals are also a major instrument of Americanization? If one left the fraternal, when and why did he leave? Was it after returning from World War II, when he sought a more *American* fraternal affiliation such as the American Legion, the Catholic War Veterans, the Elks, or the Moose? Was it because he resented cleric-controlled organizations that should have been secularized? Did he remain a member of the fraternal because it was the only bastion of ethnicity left in an increasingly secularized world? How does membership or nonmembership in an ethnic fraternal relate to other aspects of his life?

It belabors the obvious to say that one cannot understand a culture or an institution without an intimate understanding of the lives of individuals who derive meaning from, and confer meaning on them. The change in function of the ethnic fraternals, for instance, reflects changes in values, institutions, and orientations during the lifetime of individual members. When we approach the New Ethnicity, we find many adherents who were civil-rights activists and student radicals, socially mobile and highly acculturated only a decade ago. Many of them, however, have undergone a radical life crisis and have converted to the new faith of ethnicity. This fact cannot simply be studied at a distance, for it is intimate history, inaccessible through the study of ideology alone. In our own five years of participant observation among multigeneration Polish- and Slovak-American families, the intersubjectivity of deeply felt relationships provided insight into life histories that culminated in the present search for ethnic identity. A full discussion of this research is provided elsewhere.[9]

It is sufficient to say here that our work included the following: (1) life histories and family histories, (2) ethnohistoric profiles of the European culture areas, (3) documentary analysis, (4) written and oral histories of the ethnic experience in America, (5) the relationship of the ethnic group to the wider community and its institutions, (6) interviews with church and fraternal leaders (local and national), (7) participation in local and national conferences concerning ethnicity, and (8) careful attention to events and publications related to the emergence of the New Ethnicity. Although the present study will explore the relations between ethnicity and American life, our focus is on those features which have been most salient to the development of the present revitalization of ethnic identity.

Perspectives on American Ethnicity

Although we shall not review the extensive literature which defines *ethnicity,* it is necessary to start with a base line. In a recent paper, Wsevolod W. Isajiw carefully analyzed diverse definitions of ethnicity and concluded by offering a generic definition: "an involuntary group of people who share the same culture or . . . descendants of such people who identify themselves and/or are identified as belonging to the same involuntary group." More specifically, an ethnic group is an involuntary group that provides a sense of common origin based on the sharing of cultural traits acquired through socialization. "Ethnicity," states Isajiw, "is a matter of a double boundary, a boundary from within, maintained by the socialization process, and a boundary from without established by the process of intergroup relations." Students of the North American experience tend to define ethnicity in terms of a subgroup or subculture in a larger, complex society. Students of the European experience, on the other hand, see an ethnic group as an actual, or potential, proto-political, territorial group, a "nationality." Thus political scientist Harold R. Isaacs sees membership in an ethnic group as providing a "basic group identity" based on "primordial affinities and attachments" which in turn make a group a potential nation.[10] Anthropology, at least until very recently, has conceptualized the ethnic or tribal group in terms of carefully circumscribed unit-cultures, whose boundaries and integrity are maintained. Fredrik Barth writes:

> Practically all anthropological reasoning rests on the premise that cultural variation is discontinuous. . . . There are discrete groups of people, i.e., ethnic units, to correspond to each culture. . . . It is clear that boundaries persist despite a flow of personnel across them. In other words, categorical ethnic distinctions do not depend on an absence of mobility, contact and information, but do entail social processes of exclusion and incorporation whereby discrete categories are maintained *despite* changing participation and membership in the course of individual life histories. Secondly, one finds that stable, persisting, and often vitally important social relations are maintained across such boundaries, and are based precisely on the dichotomized ethnic statuses. In other words, ethnic distinctions do not depend on the absence of social interaction and acceptance, but are quite to the contrary often the very foundations on which embracing social systems are built. Interaction in such a social system does not lead to its liquidation through change and acculturation; cultural difference can persist despite inter-ethnic contact and interdependence.[11]

From this we are led to wonder how groups and boundaries ever change. Barth's statement is simply too broad because we need to know about the conditions under which boundaries come into being, the dynamics of their persistence, and what leads to change. As we shall see, ethnic boundaries and identity, like ethnic primordial attachments, rapidly become conceptually reified givens, assuming the very nature of the subject of inquiry. Even if Barth is correct, the conditions under which his model corresponds to social reality must be specified and not assumed to represent the entire social universe. The dynamics of the American identity and Americanization will, in subsequent chapters, provide a test of his proposition. Just as once there was no Polish or Slovak ethnic group, and associated symbols of identification, likewise *American* is a very recent social category.

We cannot simply assimilate Barth's model to complex American society and deny change and the possibility of the creation of new social and personal identities and boundaries, and the atrophy of formerly salient ones. If we did this for American culture, then we would be obliged to do it for Polish culture, since *Polish* is only a composite of a host of Slavic tribes gathered in a political system.

There is another difficulty in conceptualizing identity and boundaries in this way, namely, the assumption that an individual views his or her participation in terms of either/or. One goes "out" from one's ethnic group, engages in social relations beyond the ethnic social boundary, and goes "back" to one's primordial group. It is indeed possible that an individual could view his or her behavior in this dichotomous way. Another individual, however, a Slovak-American who became a good friend of Stein's, was simultaneously a member of the Slovak Club, the Swedish Club, the German Club, the Eagles, and the Moose. Consequently, he regarded neither his participation in Slovak activities as "inside," nor his participation in the other clubs as "outside." He did not rank them because he went out drinking or eating with his wife at these various clubs in the same way another person alternates eating out at a handful of favorite restaurants. The neglected *voluntaristic* aspect of ethnicity will be discussed in greater detail later. We only note here that in this informant's life, as in the lives of countless others, ethnicity began as a *comprehensive,* involuntary way of life. Later, however, he selectively incorporated elements of ethnicity into his identity. Ethnicity is not "inside" and American, "outside"; rather, through personal choice—whatever their determinants—ethnic and nonethnic elements are synthesized into a personal whole. Since the above-mentioned informant never "leaves," he has no need to "return."

Ethnicity, then, is no longer a whole way of life. Individuals select symbols of their ethnic identity from their ancestral past based on "needs created perhaps by the specific character of relations in society as a whole." Although Isajiw is perfectly correct in his observation, this statement contradicts his carefully argued thesis that an ethnic group is an involuntary group rooted in socialization. It is essential to recognize that ethnicity, ethnic identity, and ethnic groups undergo a change of function as a consequence of the Americanization process both within a generation over the life cycle and intergenerationally. As Joshua Fishman has noted, this change is not one of "degree," but of "type."

Talcott Parsons's recent discussion of ethnicity offers a model that is closest to our own observation of the changing meanings of ethnicity. Parsons first presents the ethnic group as an "ideal" sociological type: trans-generational, ascriptive, holistic, exclusive, and, to some degree, optional and voluntary. The highly differentiated nature of the ethnic groups that took part in the great migration from southern, central, and eastern Europe (1880–1920) is expressed in the inter-group animosities and avoidances that were rife through World War II and which still linger among many of the immigrants and even second-generation Americans. For example, it was common for children who married outside the ethnic group to be disowned by their parents, even if both families shared the same religion. The sense of siblinghood, of membership in one great family, white ethnic, is considerably new and was nurtured by a common *American* experience, not by primordial pan-ethnic bonds.

Parsons observes, following David Schneider, that although full assimilation in the United States has not taken place, and that individual identification with some ethnic unit or marker is widespread, "ethnic status is conspicuously devoid of 'social content,' " that is, ethnic identity markers are "empty of elaborate social distinctions." The character of ethnicity has changed markedly from that of the immigrants. Ethnic groups have largely been what Schneider calls "desocialized" and "transformed into primarily cultural symbolic groups," one of whose main features is "voluntary selectivity."[12] On the one hand, an individual will choose a grandparent with whom he or she wishes to identify ethnically, thereby "becoming" symbolically a descendant of that group. This does not, however, get translated into social differences and differentiations that are expressed as *us* and *them*. On the other hand, this affiliation and descent is by choice, not tradition.

We might half seriously speak of "dime-store ethnicity" as characterizing the predominant form of ethnicity in contemporary American life.[13] Many attributes of a multitude of ethnic cultures are offered for consumption. One selects, tries, likes or dislikes, and returns for the same "purchase" or an alternate. Ethnicity is assimilated into the syncretic, fluid nature of American culture in general. One could just as easily speak of "dime-store religion." Nevertheless, this does not imply that ethnicity is empty or discardable. Much of what can be called "hidden ethnicity," for instance, food preferences or attitudes toward health and illness based on values and ethnic personality structure, is highly valent in private and public social life. This does not mean that acculturated ethnic Americans are really hiding. The New Ethnic emphasis on visibility, even ethno-exhibitionism, misunderstands those ethnic Americans who are simply being themselves and who are hiding nothing. *Hidden* refers to the fact that the common American culture may not be aware of them, or even that the ethnics, themselves, engage in activities that are in accordance with specific values, without knowing why.

The New Ethnic Movement has returned the concept of ethnicity to being one of differentiation, that is, one which generates social distinctions. The white ethnic identity makes a claim on one's life, not merely a part of it. The new identity is claimed to be coextensive with one's personal identity, thereby creating a clearly defined boundary between *me* and *not me*.

The Emergence of Ethnic Identification

Our starting place for the study of ethnic identification is the preemigrant European base line. The major source of our data is that of Poles, Slovaks, and Ruthenes. These groups are located in east-central Europe, Slovakia being in the northernmost sector of the former Kingdom of Hungary, and Ruthenia, now a part of the Ukraine, being directly east of Slovakia. Both are to the south of Poland. The question of ethnic definition and social distinction must begin in Europe. Over the next several pages we are providing a detailed account of categories and changes in categories of self-reference. We feel that such an exposition is necessary to convey to the reader the hidden subtleties in the very concept of ethnicity, and to contrast these with the facile group labeling indulged in by American ethnophiles who glibly stereotype those whom they champion but do not know.

Our research among Slovak-, Polish-, and Ruthenian-Americans confirms the following point made by Vladimir Nahirny and Joshua Fishman that the original immigrant's self-identification and orientation was not ethnic or national, but rather local, or at most regional. "Many peasant immigrants—whether of Finnish, Slovak, Italian, Ukrainian, Norwegian, or even Polish or German origin—were hardly conscious of the existence of comprehensive categories by means of which they would relate themselves to others." Many a Ukrainian peasant, for example, continued well into this century to inform census officials who appeared in his village that he was of "indigenous" ethnic background. This response was given for the simple reason that he was utterly innocent of the very existence of the terms *Ukraine* and *Ukrainian*. Likewise, the authors cite a study by Bujak (1903) in which many inhabitants of the Prussian-Polish village of Zmaica identify their nationalities as "Catholics," "peasants," or *cysarskimi* ("the Kaiser's people").[14] Slovak, Polish, and Ruthene immigrants, too, identified themselves almost exclusively in terms of village, religion (among Slovaks: Latin-Rite and Byzantine-Rite Catholic; Independent Catholic; Lutheran; and a few Calvinists), economic status (peasant), and geographic administrative unit. Only the relatively wealthy and educated would have a perspective other than parochial and local, in which such terms as *Polak* ("man of the fields") or *Ukraine* ("border, or frontier, lands") would have any meaning. An individual Slovak or Ruthenian peasant identified tenaciously and lovingly with his or her few strips of land; the local village; the church or mission; the local dialect; the administrative district or *župa* ("county"); and the cultural equivalent to social class.

Immigrants and their descendants from the eastern Slovak *župa* of Zemplín would feel superior to those from neighboring counties of Spiš, Gemer, or Šariš, and vice versa. Sentiments attached to districts closely resemble what we would call "ethnic" ones, even though the dialect differences between them would be small. The "hill" people from upland Slovakia-Ruthenia-Galicia would dislike the "valley" people, who were closer to the Hungarian Plain in the south than the Polish east European Plain in the north, regarding them as arrogant like the Magyars or Polish nobility. The "valley" people in turn would think of those in the uplands as "inferior" and "backward." Trading insults and jokes would be an ordinary pastime in conversation between residents or immigrants from different *župy*. Since our fieldwork began in 1970, it should be noted that knowledge of European nations was commonplace even among those immigrants who did not originally think of their places of origin in ethnic or national terms. Paradoxically, it was largely through the efforts of those whose ethnic self-consciousness was created and mobilized in America that many European nation-states were created or re-created in the post-World War I era. Despite such knowledge, however, Slovakia or Ruthenia, except for professional ethnics and intellectuals, was a vague abstraction.

After establishing that one spoke *po slovensky* ("in Slovak") or *po russky* ("in Rusin-Ruthenian"), the most salient category to the speaker was the village, which he or she described in detail. As awareness extended beyond the administrative district, those Slovaks in western Slovakia, with their own dialect, considered themselves more westernized and civilized than those more eastward, and regarded the Slovak inhabitants of eastern Slovakia (the *župy* of

Zemplín, Spiš, and Šariš) as inferior Slovaks, and the inhabitants of
Ruthenia (formerly part of Czechoslovakia) as beyond the pale, oriental, barbarian, Byzantine-Rite "Russians." Eastern Slovakia and Ruthenia are metaphorically and geographically seen as "the tail" of
Slovakia. Historically, the Byzantine Rite within the Roman Catholic
church has always been felt to be a compromise by the church to gain
more adherents to Rome. Its adherents have always felt themselves to
be seen as second-rate Catholics (in Europe and America), who
would eventually be Latinized and absorbed in the "real" church. To
the Roman Catholic church, the accommodation of the Byzantine
Rite was at most a temporary concession, even though it was made to
look like the embracing of *bona fide* Catholics and their inclusion in
the fold. In Europe and America, the Latinization of Byzantine Catholics and the Slovakization of Ruthenes became for clergy and laity a
means of achieving higher social status and mobility.

While we usually think of the acculturation experience of white
ethnics in America as a single process of Americanization, this view
is too simplistic. Not only are Roman Catholic white ethnics mediated
by the Irish-Catholic culture and hierarchy, both locally and nationally, but by other ethno-religious groupings, though not as powerfully
as the former. Byzantine Catholic Ruthenes have complained for a
number of years about the Slovakizing and Latinizing proclivities of
the Archbishoprics of Munhall, Pennsylvania, and Passaic, New
Jersey. However, those Slovaks who seek to Latinize, and those
Ruthenes who seek to become Slovak and Latinized, welcome the
changes. Many Latinized and Slovakized Ruthenes, or Latinized Slovak Byzantine Catholics, take a further step and join a Latin-Rite
Slovak "national parish." One may further acculturate by joining a
"territorial parish" whose influence is predominantly Irish and
American.

We emphasize, however, that the much-discussed Irishization was
in numerous parishes, and for many Slovaks and Ruthenes, a far less
immediate issue than the traditional European-derived conflict over
ethnicity and rite. Latin-Rite Catholics have felt superior to Byzantine-Rite Catholics in Europe and the United States. Slovak Byzantine Catholics have considerable difficulty in convincing the more
westernized and Romanized Slovaks that they are indeed good Slovaks and good Catholics. One Byzantine Catholic Slovak-American,
who literally decided that he was Slovak and not Ruthene (he had
equated Ruthene with religion rather than ethnicity), remarked that
the Latin-Rite Slovaks think of themselves as "Yankees" and look
upon the Byzantine-Rite Slovaks as "Confederates" or "Rebels." As

a child, he remembers that the Latin-Rite Slovaks would not let their children play with the Byzantine-Rite children. Another Byzantine-Rite Slovak-American recalls that in parochial school he was ridiculed and reprimanded by his teacher for crossing himself from right to left, a Byzantine practice, rather than from left to right. The nun said that *this* was the way the Pope did it, and that no other way was right. Finally, many Byzantine-Rite Slovaks and Ruthenes recall the ridicule (and sometimes physical assault) from Latin-Rite Catholics which they experienced in years past on Palm Sunday, when they left their churches with pussy willow branches rather than palm leaves. To be a second-class Slovak, or Catholic, left its mark.

Historically, the Latin-Rite-acculturated or Byzantine-Rite-practicing eastern Slovaks were ethnically Ruthenes (indeed a heterogeneous group), a point which the more westernized Slovaks will not let them live down. These regional and religious variants are reflected in the following ethnic, Slovak, fraternal organizations: the First Catholic Slovak Union (Latin-Rite); the Greek Catholic Union (Byzantine-Rite, lay officers; membership largely Slovak, Ruthene, and some Ukrainian); the United Societies of U.S.A. (Byzantine-Rite; lay and clerical officers; Slovaks and Ruthenes); the National Slovak Society (no religious affiliation; an attempt to crosscut religious schism); the Slovak Lutheran Society (associated with the Zion Lutheran Synod, LCA); and a spectrum of *Sokol,* or Falcon athletic-gymnastic societies.

The complexity hidden in the category *Polish* could be similarly analyzed, although *Polish* is far less fragmented and segmented than the reality within *Slovak* or *Ruthene.* For some thousand years, Polish culture has been tenaciously, almost monolithically, Latin-Rite Catholic as an oppositional defense against the "barbaric" Russians and Orthodoxy to the east, and as a means of asserting its membership in the western European community. Furthermore, this rationale is also voiced by the intelligentsia, the priesthood, and the aristocracy, and is essentially unavailable to the peasantry, for whom the world is the village. However, even the peasants recognize the uneasy boundary and mix between Lithuania and Poland, and the Polonization of Lithuanians beginning in the fifteenth and sixteenth centuries. (A Pole says *Vilna;* a Lithuanian says *Vilnius.*) Moreover, the tripartition of Poland has produced quasi-ethnic divisions of Prussian-Poland, Russian-Poland, and Austrian-Poland; acculturation and assimilation were directed toward those respective empires, despite countervailing efforts at independence and unification. Following World War I, Polish-Americans were more responsible than native Poles for the restoration of the Polish state. In the United States, the Polish National Catholic Church Movement, formed in the late 1880s, spread throughout America and then diffused to Poland, indicating a further revitalization from emigrants abroad. The movement's emphasis on liturgy in the native language, the permission of the clergy to marry, and group (as opposed to individual) confession, found a parallel in the much smaller Slovak National Catholic Church Movement, and was based on a reaction against the denationalization of Polish and Slovak parishes by the Irish-dominated American Catholic church. In short, even within as homogeneous a group as the Polish-Americans, there are considerable differences in dialect, social class, period of arrival in America, and place of settlement. There also exists heterogeneity among many of the *ethnic* homogenizing influences derived from the American experience, previous to which one's ethnic identity was primarily associated with village rather than nation.

Settlement in the United States went remarkably according to village and region. A specific mill town in western Pennsylvania, for example, would be primarily inhabited by immigrants from a number of adjacent or nearby villages in a single *župa*. Larger cities such as McKeesport and Duquesne would have inhabitants from several contiguous *župy*. Even in the largest cities, settlement was not random; rather, different sections would be settled by immigrants from correspondingly different regions of Slovakia or Poland. Settlers always clustered around a kin network who informed compatriots in the homeland of job opportunities, thus enabling them to emigrate. Affiliation was based on concrete, preexisting ties, not on the more abstract and distal notions of ethnicity or nationality. In fact, settlements in America frequently crosscut ethno-national categories, reflecting the frequent heterogeneity of the place of origin. Thus, just as an upland Hungarian village would be composed of Magyars, Slovaks, Ruthenes (with their religious diversity), Jews, and perhaps Germans (from the mining towns), urban-ethnic enclaves would be similarly composed and traditional relationships kept intact. Many Slovak- and Ruthene-Americans in McKeesport spoke fondly of the early "urban village" adjacent to the U.S. Steel mill (National Tube) as an early "Melting Pot" in which Slovaks, Ruthenes, Magyars, Jews, Poles, Croats, and others were members of a single community, despite ethnic particularism and the persistence of many Old World animosities.

It seems tenable to suggest that ethnic group and nationality, as self-conscious categories of self-reference and as corporate identities (given expression through churches, fraternal societies, and nationalist movements), were learned and formed in America and were not strictly imports. The consciousness of ethnic and national *kind* was primarily a product of stereotypes and categories significant to Americans who were already here. Under relentless exclusion, exploitation, harassment, and shaming, the immigrants reversed categories of disparagement and invidious comparison into positive categories of self-affirmation. One became a Pole only after being regarded as a "Polak"; one became a Slovak, Hungarian, or Croat only after being called "Hunkie." This in turn became fertile ground for an early nativist movement catalyzed by World War I and the political exploits and selective empathy of President Woodrow Wilson and his secretary of state. While ethnic personality, values, attitudes, and beliefs were transplanted from the country of origin and resynthesized in accordance with the American experience to facilitate adaptation, the self-conscious sense of ethnic identity developed for the most part in America as a product of social relations in the host country. This latter meaning of ethnicity is anything but aboriginal.

Changing Meanings of Migration

For the Slovaks and Poles, like numerous other European peasants, seasonal agricultural migration to other districts, or beyond the national boundaries to the Hungarian Plain, or to Germany, was a way of life. From approximately 1850, a period marked by the freeing of the serfs, the beginnings of urbanization and industrialization, overpopulation, loosening of extended-family ties, and the pressures of nationalism (e.g., Russification, Magyarization, Germanization), supplemental work was sought in nontraditional settings. Migration to the mines and mills of the urban-industrial east and east-central United States was at first regarded by most workers as an extended "season" away from home. The frequently expressed purpose of migration was economic: to work for a year or two, enduring the hazards and the filth, amassing as much income as possible in order to return home and purchase additional land, or build a better home. Many came to the United States several times, deciding with their second or third return migration to settle in the United States. Only after 1900, however, did the initial migration take place for rapid economic gain *and* settlement. The early immigration was almost exclusively that of males, for there was no reason to bring one's family to America. America meant instant wealth, which would be translated into prosperity and higher social status upon one's return to family, parish, and village.

This socioeconomic argument is stated well by Janet Schreiber, writing about recent southern Italian migrants to Switzerland and Germany. Like the Polish and Slovak migrant workers in America, they regarded their stay in the host country as temporary.

> They left because they had reached a juncture in their life plans where they felt that they could maximize their social and economic benefits by working away from home. . . .
>
> The migrants interviewed define the situation in the host country as a passing state of relative unimportance compared with the benefits it will provide them when they return to their home community. A migrant who is focused upon resolving his status position and demonstrating his personal adequacy in terms of others who are significant to him, i.e., members of his home community, does not plan his goals in terms of the area to which he migrates. He is migrating to maximize his conditions and family status in the place of origin, not the place of immigration, and his actions are consequent to his interpretation. . . . The position of his family and its reputation permeates all other social categories of which he is a member.[15]

The desire to improve one's standard of living, together with the wish to acquire a higher social status in the natal community, and the utilization of "seasonal" migration to America in order to achieve these personal aims, suggest that economic factors are part of a means to an end. This is true even for those who were forced to leave their homes permanently because of paucity of land to be divided up among too many sons (and as part of a daughter's dowry). Many of the younger sons were "bought off" by their fathers, who had no land to further subdivide while still providing a subsistence for a family. The "price" was frequently the cost of a boat ticket to America. This nuclearization was one further extension of the gradual breakup of the patrilineally extended family (joint family) into smaller segments (the stem family) in which older parents and a married son or two worked, owned, and shared the family land and possessions in a variety of innovative ways. The stability of the smaller extended families was very fragile.

Both endogenous and exogenous influences eroded the fragmented vestiges of the feudal order. Simply put, the push of the Old World combined forces with the pull of the New World, and not just in disembodied economics. Dissatisfaction with peasant life—held in check by the feudal system, but now run rife with open resentment—

was increased by the image of America that was eagerly imported. The desire for freedom and the possibility of making new alternatives and choices combined with the disappearance of many traditional restraints from economic to religious to familial. Conflicts over inheritance, responsibilities, obedience to authority, property rights, and the power of the priest led to further fragmentation, nucleation, and emigration. The move to America—from Slovakia and Ruthenia alone over 20 percent of the population migrated—was further catalyzed by news from returning migrants, from the local Jewish tavern, from agents of American factories and steamship lines, and from glowing letters from relatives in America.

It is certainly true that many letters told of squalid living conditions, the loss of life or limb by immigrant workers who were as replaceable as cattle, and the unpredictable fluctuation of periods of work with those of layoff in which all precious savings were spent. Some returned to live better in Slovakia; others returned broken in body or spirit. But most remained—perhaps after a second or third return migration—because of the two words we heard most often to describe what American meant: "a chance." What they could never be in Slovakia, they felt they were free to become in America. Before they set foot on American soil, the immigrants had re-created the American Dream. They were ready for the conversion from the old to the new, and there was considerable preadaptation in their preimmigrant personalities for Americanization. Conflicts in the ethnic personality greatly facilitated the cultural change from ethnic to American, and not merely at the superficial level of personality organization. Eric Hoffer noted that most immigrants to the United States, impoverished and rejected in their homelands, "came here with the ardent desire to shed their old world identity and be reborn to a new life; and they were automatically equipped with an unbounded capacity to imitate and adopt the new."[16]

Conflicts latent in traditional culture surfaced with the decline of feudalism and with the availability of new choices and opportunities. One Slovak-American immigrant, now in his late eighties, recalled coming to America first only to make some money for a few years. Then he planned to return to his family in Slovakia, purchase more land, and improve his home. Upon returning, however, he decided that he had lost his sense of freedom by going home and that neither land, nor home, nor slightly increased status in the village was worth the loss. His wife told Stein: "He came to U.S.—first Chicago, when he was nineteen. Work there three years. Go back home. His mother—I don't know, she was too strict. So he came back here, to get away."

Her husband, sitting at the opposite end of the table, nodded a decisive assent. On numerous occasions we heard stories from Polish and Slovak immigrants of how the men who came over alone had the time of their lives, and how they did not exactly look forward to returning home or to having their wives and families join them. The American migrant experience was a chance to break away from it all, and the immigrants were loathe to relinquish their freedom. Better yet, the very ideology, idealism, and legendary history of this strange land, which the fraternal newspapers described in continuous installments, corresponded to what the immigrants ardently sought: "life, liberty, and the pursuit of happiness," desiderata unattainable in Europe.

In Slovakia, Ruthenia, or Poland, the returning migrant might purchase more land, build a better and larger home, and be able to marry into a respectable family. But the land was still poor, and he would have only more of it. The family would always be able to get by, but would never be wealthy. The effect of the accumulated wages from America was at best temporary. Even if the migrant did become wealthier, he was still regarded by the Polish or Magyar nobility as a peasant. One Magyar expression translates: "A Slovak is not a human being." Even if a Slovak peasant could raise his social class to the level of a Magyar, his status and power would still be less than even a poorer Magyar. So what was the point of trying to improve one's self and one's family in a social system where birth and ascription counted more than any achievement, and where only a few wealthy peasants could "pass"? In America all was not streets paved with gold and other cherished illusions. Nevertheless, the American Dream said that the past did not count, that one's original status is irrelevant to one's future, and that only what one did, not who one was, mattered. The arrogant American dared call a Slovak or Hungarian peasant ignorant and dumb, though the proud American could speak only English, whereas the peasant had command of Slovak, Hungarian, some Yiddish, and even some German. But all this would surely pass because the American Dream promised that any people could become Americans, equal to anyone else.

Even the American language encoded the social equalizer, for the special category of respect, *thou* is absent, and all people are addressed as *you*. We do not overlook the painfully obvious fact that the American English language since the final decades of the nineteenth century also encoded such epithets of disrespect and categories of outsidership as "Dago," "Polak," "Hunkie," and "Kike." What we find most significant for the dynamics of Americanization is that these insults were endured and, in a way, accepted because the immigrants and their children did not believe them to be the permanent features of American culture. America was *not* Hungary or Russia or Italy. Relationships were not unchangeable. The future would eliminate the inequalities and hardships of the present; indeed, it was the belief in the progress of the future that made the present tolerable.

What most distinguished the American experience from the European was the *promise,* and it was this promise that induced the immigrants to think of themselves not as temporary, visiting laborers in a "host" foreign country, but as potential Americans. The identity of *American* gradually became an intrinsic part of the self and was no longer an extrinsic occupational hazard that was the source of a few years' income. Subsequent learning of American history and official legend served only to confirm, through the examples of the past, the identity which the immigrants sought and the means of securing it. They were ready to listen to American history because it enacted on the grand scale their own personal history and provided the paradigm for the relation of past, present, and future that corresponded with their fondest hopes. For this reason, they did not require acculturation in order to wish to become Americans; their own motivation, like that of their predecessors, provided the deep or underlying structure for the acceptance of the cultural-symbolic content of the surface structure. Likewise, it was the premigration and migration experience itself, more than acculturation, that made the immigrants "good Americans." Moreover, this suggests that one cannot radically dichotomize between an initial emigration purely for purposes of finding temporary work and the decision to settle in America. The pull of the American Dream was present from the beginning in preemigrant life, and its force was only increased by the discrepancy between the first experience in America and life in the natal village, which one left or to which one reluctantly returned several times. It is more accurate to say that the most compelling, realistic, and conscious reasons for the initial migration were economic and environmental. Subsequent experiences made more obvious the equally compelling, unconscious, and highly personal factors that had always been present and which finally came to predominate—and to facilitate Americanization.

Voluntary Associations and Americanization

The zealous programs of the ethnic fraternals toward Americanization attest to the pull of the American Dream even in the face of rejection and adversity.[17] The immigrants fervently believed that the barriers between themselves and the Americans would be overcome and that it was only a matter of time, hard work, and monumental patience until one would no longer be seen as foreign, strange, and as a perpetual outsider who remained a threat. The American Dream and Melting Pot promised that *we* and *they* would together fuse into Americans. It was on this promise that the immigrants wagered their futures and those of their future children. The pressures for conformity (what we shall later call "American conformity") provided far less motivation or impetus for Americanization than the American Dream, which was based on hope. Thus, while the fraternals and churches, in their capacity as associations for self-defense, self-help, and security, served as *centripetal* ethnic forces in their capacity as agents of Americanization, modernization, and even secularization, they functioned as *centrifugal* antiethnic forces and as agents of change rather than resistance.

This view is confirmed by the authors as a result of interviews with national officers, local officers, and with members of the Polish Falcons, the Polish National Alliance, the National Slovak Society, the First Catholic Slovak Union, the Greek Catholic Union, United Societies of U.S.A. (*Sobranije*), and the Slovak Evangelical Union. Further confirmation was obtained through a reading of the following fraternal weeklies (now monthlies) and yearbooks dating from the formation of the associations: *GCU Messenger; Jednota; Slovakia; Prosvita; Katolicky Sokol; Sokol U.S.A. Times;* and *Narodne Noviny.*

For example, Stein examined the annual *Kalendar,* or "yearbook," of the Greek Catholic Union spanning the years 1903 through 1972. (Due to the schism within the society, there were considerable gaps in the 1930s and 1940s.) From the GCU's founding in 1892 through the 1930s, there were advertisements in the *Kalendar* for such goods and services as banks, saloons, hotels, liquors, a variety of medicinal cures, boat tickets, home building (financing, mortgages, titles, etc.), and shipping from overseas. Essays were written on such subjects as American history (including praiseworthy accounts of American founding heroes and legendary leaders). The *Kalendar* also contained the following information: an explanation of American government and how to participate in it; why and how to obtain citizenship; descriptions of the nature of the population and geography of the United States; and accounts of farming in America and of technological innovations from the zeppelin through the airplane. Considerable space was also devoted to a description of the Slovak-Ruthene homeland, culture, and religious customs. Although much of the writing through the 1930s was in an eastern Slovak-Ruthene dialect, and written in Cyrillic or Latin characters, English was used in essays concerning American history and government as early as 1905, when the article was printed in both languages. Americanization, more specifically, bridge-building between the insular ethnic world and the more expanding American world, was one of the major purposes of the fraternals.

Americanization was also one of the major points of stress between traditionalists and acculturationists that led to attrition of membership and schism in churches and fraternals alike. On the one hand, the Polish National Catholic church (or Slovak Independent), a variety of independent Ruthene-eastern, Slovak-western, Ukrainian Orthodox churches, and the United Societies of U.S.A. (among others) broke with their Americanizing-Irishizing parent organizations and became guardians of tradition in matters concerning liturgy and customs. Yet this self-defensive, or self-protective, function could be said for all of the ethnic voluntary organizations. In other words, schism was apparently the basis of all ethnic voluntary societies. On the other hand, even the most traditionalist societies urged Americanization by exhortation and by example of its leadership.

With this in mind we return briefly to the history of the Greek Catholic Union, in order to discuss the schism of 1902 that led to the founding of the United Societies of U.S.A. (*Sobranije*). At the convention of the Greek Catholic Union, there was strong debate over whether the largely Hungarian or Magyarized Ruthene-Slovak clergy leadership should be permitted to retain its official position, since the clergymen insisted on remaining citizens of the Kingdom of Hungary. The convention overwhelmingly voted that henceforth all officers of the GCU would have to be American citizens. Moreover, there was a long-standing resentment against domination of Slovak or Ruthene parishioners by a Magyar or Magyarized clergy. In Hungary, the laity obviously could do nothing about it. In America, however, the former peasants could vote out those who were either members of the Hungarian aristocracy or had used the church, as well as ethnic assimilation, as a means of social mobility. The orientation toward a secular leadership became obvious when the Byzantine Catholic laity of the fraternal announced that it would be a strong supporter of the church but would not be its tool. The United Societies of U.S.A., conversely, retained priests among its officials through the present; its birth dates from the time in which a number of delegates walked out of the GCU convention in 1902 and founded the United Societies' first church-affiliated lodge in McKeesport.

Schism, segmentation, and attrition of membership were prominent characteristics of church and fraternal organizations from the beginning. Although we shall discuss the special significance of World War II for accelerating the Americanization process, we note here, from discussions with Latin- and Byzantine-Rite Catholic priests, with Lutheran and Independent-Catholic Slovak-American clergymen, the importance of the war as a catalyst in Americanization within the parishes. We also note the cause of division, even schism, within the parishes. A Slovak-Lutheran minister in his forties who grew up in Johnstown, Pennsylvania, relates his experience there and generalizes from it.

> In my church in Johnstown, there was no English until 1942—at least until 1942, when I left for World War II. When I left, no English had been introduced. But after the war, the young people coming back demanded that English be adopted as a separate service. The effect of the war was to put people of all different backgrounds together, and the common language there was English. The men thought and spoke and felt in English, so that when they got home after the war, their native towns and churches were like a foreign country.

In many Slovak-American Lutheran parishes, the institution of separate services solved part of the problem of the different intergenerational linguistic and cultural orientations. On such occasions as Christmas, Easter Sunday, and Confirmation, joint services are held with roughly half of the liturgy in English and half in Slovak, equally distributed throughout the service; the sermon is usually in English. During the late 1940s and early 1950s, a further attempt at integration of Slovak-American Lutherans within the wider American Lutheran community resulted in the dropping of the name *Slovak* in many churches, and a further shortening of the name of the church. Although a major objective of such acts was to attract new, non-Slovak members into a denominational, American church, an equally important factor was the attempt to retain those Slovak-American members who were becoming dissatisfied with the dominance of the decreasing number of "old timers" within the parish. The traditionalist orientation within the leadership of the Slovak Zion Synod of the Lutheran Church in America also displeased many Slovak-Americans.

World War II and the postwar era further catalyzed the Americanizing trend which was already well in progress. In the 1930s the Slovak Lutheran parish in Duquesne, Pennsylvania, experienced a schism by the more Americanized members who wanted English introduced into the service and who wanted to establish a Sunday school for their children in which English was the language of instruction. The more adamant Slovaks refused to permit any change, and between one-third and one-half of the congregation left the church. They took up membership at the nearby German Lutheran and English Lutheran churches.

Internal change, in contrast with schism, was far less dramatic, but equally significant. For example, in the *Sokol* ("Falcon") or gymnastic/athletic societies, and in the other fraternals, sports in the early period was group rather than individual oriented. Enormous gymnastic exhibitions and displays (*slets*) were held, and continued until the disruption of World War II and the depletion of the organization through induction into the armed services. Following the war, the *Sokols* attempted to revive the *slets*. Their efforts, however, were unsuccessful. In the 1920s a shift had already begun toward more individual-oriented sports, although in a team context (i.e., more American-individual than ethnic-communal). The trend in the fraternals paralleled the national trend: from baseball to football, later to bowling leagues, and finally, in the 1960s, golf leagues. Internally, the organizations became less ethnic and more American.[18]

Marriage, Family Size, and Value Change

The same pattern of change in values, identity, and life-style is reflected in changing patterns of marriage and family size; specifically, there has been an increase in intermarriage and a drastic reduction in the number of offspring over a generation.

One of the principal assumptions of the New Ethnicity is that of background homogeneity among those whom white ethnic leaders choose to speak for. Empirical data from the authors' fieldwork among Polish- and Slovak-Americans suggest that this assumption is without foundation. In fact, the statistics which follow show that white ethnics, even in their most traditional institutions, very quickly adapted the patterns idealized by American culture.

Table 1 shows marriage data from an inner-city Slovak-American church in McKeesport, Pennsylvania. "Mixed" marriages (Catholic/Protestant) were almost nonexistent between 1895 and 1929. After 1930, however, "mixed" marriages increased steadily, reaching a level of more than one in four by 1969.

TABLE 1 Number and Percentage of "Mixed" Marriages at "Slovak" Nationality Parish; 1930–69[19]

Period	Number	Percentage
1930–34	6	4.2
1935–39	18	8.5
1940–44	15	8.5
1945–49	24	10.8
1950–54	16	9.0
1955–59	21	16.2
1960–64	15	12.7
1965–69	26	26.8

Table 2, with data gathered from another inner-city McKeesport church, confirms the pattern of "mixed" religious marriages shown in Table 1 and suggests that nationality "mixing" is even more common—reaching a rate of more than one in three between 1960 and 1970. We would expect that the rate would be considerably higher in a territorial or suburban church. Until about 1965 it was customary for the wedding to be held in the bride's church, thus the most accurate measure of "mixing" is to determine the background of the groom.

TABLE 2 Religion and Nationality Backgrounds of *Husbands* in Marriages at a Slovak-Rusin Byzantine-Rite Church: Number and Percentage by Selected Five-Year Intervals[20]

Religion Background				Nationality Background		
Catholic No. (%)	Protestant No. (%)	Other No. (%)	Period	Slovak-Rusin No. (%)	Other Slovak No. (%)	Other No. (%)
32 (100.0)	—	—	1930	26 (81.3)	2 (6.3)	4 (12.5)
21 (95.5)	1 (4.5)	—	1935	12 (54.5)	1 (4.5)	9 (40.9)
32 (91.4)	3 (8.6)	—	1940	20 (57.1)	2 (5.7)	13 (37.1)
16 (69.6)	7 (30.4)	—	1945	8 (34.8)	4 (17.4)	11 (47.8)
19 (90.5)	2 (9.5)	—	1950	14 (66.7)	2 (9.5)	5 (35.7)
13 (68.4)	3 (15.8)	3 (15.8)	1955	14 (73.7)	1 (5.3)	4 (21.1)
13 (65.0)	6 (30.0)	1 (1.0)	1960	12 (60.0)	—	8 (40.0)
11 (73.3)	3 (20.0)	1 (6.7)	1965	9 (60.0)	—	6 (40.0)
5 (45.5)	6 (54.5)	—	1970	4 (36.4)	—	7 (63.6)
162 (81.8)	31 (15.7)	5 (2.5)		119 (60.1)	12 (6.1)	67 (33.8)

TABLE 3 Number and Percentage of Background Homogeneity among
Students at "Polish" Nationality School; 1969[21]

Background	Number	Percentage
Polish	28	23.0
German	3	2.5
Irish	2	6.6
Croatian	1	0.8
African	1	0.8
"Mixed"	87	71.3
	122	100.0

Table 3 presents data from another inner-city institution, a Pittsburgh Roman Catholic High School, located in a predominantly
Polish-American community. In this case, students from the entire
junior class were asked to identify the nationality background of
their parents. Almost three out of four students were of mixed heritage, the overwhelming proportion of these from Polish intermarriage
with German- and Irish-Americans who emigrated earlier. Thus the
sons and daughters of today's white ethnics, most of them third-,
fourth-, and even fifth-generation Americans, bear little resemblance
to the picture of biological and cultural purity attributed to them by
the purveyors of ethnos. The enclave is remarkably heterogeneous.
The questions then become: Who is Polish? Slovak? Italian? Irish?
If a self-identified enclave is not homogeneous, what is ethnic homogeneity? Additional evidence of Americanization (or modernization)
of white ethnics in their "bounded communities" is presented in
Table 4.

The data collected from fifty Polish-American families in a Pitts-

TABLE 4 Average Number of Children in Polish-American Families of
First and Second Generation[22]

Birth Cohort	Parental First Generation	Informant Second Generation
1900–09	8.6	2.4
1910–19	6.6	2.2
1920–29	5.8	2.8
1900–29 (composite)	6.7	2.4

burgh inner-city enclave show that family size decreased dramatically in only one generation, as parents born between 1900 and 1929 had only about one third as many children as their own parents. Despite religious proscriptions against effective birth-control measures, and traditional peasant culture stressing the value of large families for security, prestige, and to counter a high mortality rate, these Polish-Americans consciously limited the size of their families.

Although "economics" was the most frequently given reason for this change ("people shouldn't have more children than they can support"), it strongly represents a departure from traditional life goals and values, and an identification with the new host culture and reference culture. Economics cannot be separated from values. These new Americans invested their resources differently from the way traditional peasants would. They sought greater personal mobility as a means of overcoming the past; they sought less restricted experiences; and they also sought freedom from the insularity of family, church, and enclave. Not that these new values did not conflict with the still resilient earlier ones, but the new American identity rapidly became a part of a new sense of selfhood and affiliation. White ethnics is a very recent category and the sense of being "siblings" is far greater among the intelligentsia than among the people. For a Pole to marry an Italian or a German, or vice versa, was not to marry one's own kind, but to marry a stranger and invite ostracism from the family, even at the present time. Intermarriage and the desire to have fewer children represent a departure from, if not a rejection of, the past and symbolize, very concretely, Americanness.

The Primordial Bond of Ethnicity

Ethnicity, as we have seen, is hardly a monolith. Understood in terms of Wittgenstein's operational philosophy, ethnicity is what ethnicity does and means. We have thus far discussed the ethnic American experience as a rather *complex* matter. Turning now to the New Ethnic perception of ethnicity, we find that it is remarkably simple, even simplistic. Previously we saw ethnicity engaged in wider worlds of meaning; the New Ethnicity, however, in its alluring parochialism, increasingly retreats into a world of closely circumscribed certitude.

The withdrawal from universalism and the embracing of a radical particularism are fundamental to the dynamics of the New Ethnicity.

We offer a few examples from our own profession. At the 1974 meetings of the American Anthropological Association which were held in
Mexico City, a paper concerning the Italian immigrant in the United
States passionately concluded that we must "hold in abeyance the
onslaught of global culture."[23] The presenting author documented the
distorted and humiliating stereotypes that greeted and pursued Italian-
Americans to the present; accused sociological theory of merely re-
phrasing old prejudices into scientific language, thereby rationalizing
them; and asserted that Italian-Americans had not assimilated. The
last statement was not merely reported as an ethnographic fact, but
was asserted with defiant pride. The author had placed great personal
value on that fact. At another symposium in which one of the present
authors (Stein) was discussant, the same theme was reiterated in relation to research conducted among French-Americans in the South.
The presenting author noted the resurgence of interest in the French
language and culture among the young, and praised their "resistance"
to Americanization.

During the 1974 Distinguished Lecture which took place at the meetings, Miguel Leon-Portilla argued that the preservation of ethnic cultures and the integrity of ethnic identity should be central concerns of
anthropology in the postcolonialist era. According to Leon-Portilla's
following statement, it is the task of anthropologists not only to analyze, but to revitalize, themselves and their own ethnic cultures—cultures they are more familiar with than any outsider could possibly be.

> I am convinced of the necessity that historians and anthropolo-
> gists, who study their own or another culture, be aware of the
> urgent need for endangered societies to delve deeply from the in-
> side into their own cultural legacies. Thus, these societies will be
> able to overcome the threat of *nepantlism* ["being caught in the
> middle" by forced acculturation] by revitalizing their own values,
> symbols, and institutions. In this manner they will be able to enrich
> their own consciousness of identity by contrasting it with the im-
> ages that others have of it. Opinions coming from the outside will
> then be considered more critically, and thus they will not easily
> become vehicles of subtle pressures for induced acculturation.[24]

Finally, George De Vos and Lola Romanucci-Ross conclude their
monumental book *Ethnic Identity: Cultural Continuities and Change*
(1975), suggesting that "ultimately, ethnic identity is the unex-
pressed meaning of anthropology. Anthropologists intellectualize
about human culture, yet they try to preserve in their own modes of
pursuing knowledge the value of man's past, and so to assert that

without a consciousness of the past, the present becomes devoid of meaning.''[25]

The major premise of the New Ethnicity is the *primordiality* of ethnic identity, that is, ethnicity is the core of human identity. According to the New Ethnics, ''only an insider can know'' the meaning of ethnicity; America is a pluralistic ''nation of nations''; and ethnicity will cure all the ills of modernism. Ethnicity provides security and is the strongest tie of affiliation and loyalty. A number of metaphors used in the New Ethnicity evoke the idealized mother, if not intrauterine, prenatal existence: primordial bonds, group identity, corporate identity, cave, tribe, womb, organic community, genuine identity, purity, peoplehood, security, safety, search for roots, recovery of the past, solidarity, group ego, taste, and flavor. Ethnicity is not a matter of voluntary, existential choice; it is an essential given of human existence. Relationships based on it are proximal, deep, and meaningful; other relationships are distal, situational, and tentative. From one's earliest months, one becomes ''conscious of one's kind,''[26] of how one is like others significant to one's self, internalizing in one's self categories and meanings significant to them.

The model of the *onion* is an apt analogy for the way in which the New Ethnic ideology sees human development. What is learned earliest, through gesture and affect, is the most durable part of the human personality, most resistant to change; additional and more remote layers of the onion are less central to the basic personality and more easily removed and replaced. Ethnicity, for instance, is at the center, and American, at the outer skin. Many white ethnics see American culture as the realm of the marketplace and of making a living, an overarching political identity that provides the framework for a mosaic of ethnic communities. One can change jobs, but one cannot change tribes. The fallacy of the onion model, however, is that human development, as we have learned from Freud through Erikson, is not a matter of discrete layers, but of interdependent phases, with each phase having not only its own conflicts and tasks, but reawakening and requiring re-solution for earlier ones. Moreover, the New Ethnicity seems to regard the ethnic core as conflict-free, and the introduction of frustration is located at subsequent, American layers. The ennui will be relieved by the removal of the diseased outer layers. The model, then, is made to conform to identity needs.

Significantly, the New Ethnicity, in its perception of the range from community to childhood, employs an ''equilibrium'' model of life and society, reflecting, as we shall see, a yearning for equilibrium and stability. About two decades ago, anthropology began to realize the severe restrictions and virtual unreality of closed, static models of society and culture, recognizing the ubiquity of process and change even in the most seemingly changeless "traditional" societies. Process models which saw structures as way stations were catalyzed by the seminal work of Edmund Leach on myth and ritual.[27] Persistence and change both required explanation. Studies concerning culture change, contact, acculturation-assimilation, and the life cycle proliferated, influenced by experiences of World War II, the postcolonial era, and the anthropological study of nations. Studies in anthropology and allied behavioral sciences that emphasized the antiquity of primordiality, of inexorable continuities in ethnic identity (then called "tribal"), were increasingly questioned. Margaret Mead's *New Lives for Old* cogently argued the case for the wish of Melanesian "primitives" to be included in the modern world.[28] The "cargo cult" phenomenon was a magical means of attempting to achieve this by the wholesale abandonment and destruction of traditional culture as the arrival of "cargo" was eagerly awaited. The urge to modernity was not a product of oppression or exploitation, but the simple perception of the chasm and discrepancy between what one sought to be and what one traditionally was. Process models were necessary to account for the primordial that could no longer be taken for granted. In *The Social Anthropology of the Nation-State,* Lloyd A. Fallers wrote the following:

> The term "primordial" has been criticized on the ground that the social bonds and cultural unities in question are often not at all ancient, but on the contrary are demonstrably quite recent. For example, several million persons in eastern Nigeria "discovered," with the help of ideologists, ethnographers and colonial administrators, that they were all Ibo only during the British colonial period. This new unity, however, once discovered, became very strong, forming the basis for the Biafran secession movement a few years after independence. "Material interests" of course became involved, as they do in such situations, but this does not alter the fact that the community on behalf of which these interests were asserted *had come to think of itself* as a primordial one. (italics in original)[29]

The renewed emphasis on primordiality which is made by the New Ethnicity and such respected scholars as Clifford Geertz ("primordial attachments," "givens"), Andrew Greeley (American ethnicity), and Harold Isaacs (nationalism, "retribalization") suggests a return to the equilibrium model that reflects the search for security and quietude. One major difference separates the new equilibrists from the old. In the former (for instance, Robert Redfield's study of a Mexican village) harmony was seen as a pervasive element in the culture.[30] Indeed, it was this idyllic picture that Oscar Lewis later challenged in his re-study in which he found conflict and discord endemic to the cultural patterning.[31] The new equilibrists discover harmony and respite *within* the romanticized ethnic group (or pan-ethnic alliance) and dis-cord and conflict between white ethnics, blacks, Anglo-Americans, Jews, and others *outside* the boundaries of the group.

Despite this significant difference, however, both assume the strength of the tribal-ethnic tie. One cannot inquire into how ethnicity fits holistically into an individual's life by presupposing its salience and strength. It is necessary to explain the search for and the renewed vitality of the ethnic imperative. Specifically, the paradox is that the New Ethnicity was created not when traditional *ethnic* culture was threatened, but when the *American Dream* was threatened, that is, when members of various "groups" felt the dream to be unrealizable for them. Many white ethnics, in part, acknowledge this and often point to the Black Power Movement as the cultural event that re-minded them of their own ethnic ties. This, too, is only a half-truth, since the cultural revitalization of the Black Power and Pride Move-ment could only have "diffused" if there existed a basis for receptiv-ity, a readiness for selection. That readiness—a readiness common to all revitalized identities—is based not on the sudden awareness of continuity with an ethnic past, but on the realization of discontinuity with the American future in which one had invested so highly. It is the very romanticization of ethnicity that is the key to the alienation from the past that the New Ethnics redress by the inversion of values and the merger of self with group.

The rejection of Western rationalism, of American culture, and the embracing of the "primitive" can, in part, explain the popularity of Claude Levi-Strauss's structuralist anthropology since 1965, and the justification that many white ethnic writers find in him. Levi-Strauss extended the anthropological premise of the psychic unity of man-kind, exhaustively documenting his proposition that "primitive" sys-tems of thought are as rational, orderly, consistent, and valid as Western ones. A Rousseauian dichotomy between civilization as life denying and artificial, and primitive cultures as natural, was an under-standable result. What was felt to be superior, having undergone de-valuation, was now looked upon as inferior. Each cultural system was to be valued exclusively in terms of itself, marking a return to a radical relativism. The study of culture is a course in aesthetics, and Levi-Strauss is, no doubt, a master aesthetician.

He noted that anthropology was the handmaiden of colonialism and imperialism. Structuralism provided the ideological antidote for the devastations by colonialism: a universal paradigm that restored dignity through relativism. The comparative method yielded a universalism that now makes invidious comparison or cross-cultural judgment impossible. If the "primitives" were vindicated in the 1960s, now the white ethnics similarly find their vindication. With many social scientists turning inward to study their own tribal caves, the ethnics of whatever cave become the new "primitives" to be championed and kept free of Western or American contamination.

If social scientists tend to forswear invidious comparison in order to help preserve vanishing cultures, many "primitives" are not so reluctant. The latter know, as the former seem not to, that the preservation of culture means equally the preservation of status and condition ("life chances"). Social scientists and tribalists look to each other to find what they are lacking. The former refuse to "look down," and, through empathy, regard the latter as equals. The latter, however, do not cease "looking up" because they know they are not equals. The new primordialist relativism subtly preserves colonialism and exploitation by saying, in essence: "You wouldn't like to be like us. You are better off the way you are." *Traditional* is sacred, and *modern* is profane. Traditional primitivists and New Ethnic intelligentsia alike, from their own disenchantment with modernization and secularization, resolve their private conflicts through those they champion. We shall later discuss this issue with respect to the white ethnic leadership, and we shall also see that the "nativist" celebrants of "romantic ethnicity" are barely recognizable as natives at all, and most closely resemble those whom they openly detest.[32]

The following is a brief allegory on the problem of the universality of group differentiation on the basis of primordial bonds. When Americans get together, and strangers are introduced, they often ask (in various forms) such questions as: Where are you from? What do you do (job)? What is your religion? What ethnic group do you belong to? The American search for security through superiority, and through the effort to discern sameness or difference, contrasts with that of the Australian aborigine. Among the latter, two strangers meeting will spend countless hours tracing real and fictitious descent until a common ancestor is found, and they discover themselves to be relatives. The attempt is to establish affinity, a common tie. The primordial bond, if we can speak of one, is negotiated and created rather than perceived as a given. The givenness, however, is thereafter assumed. In a sense, difference is overcome through the creation of a link, a putative relationship, in a situational context. Social interaction becomes a means for establishing affinities (as opposed to differences or hierarchic ranking). One might say that the Australian aboriginal rules for reckoning common descent are more "relative," while American rules are more "absolute"; but that misses the point that the rules are simply different. Primordial ties do not have a universal meaning. To understand what the New Ethnics are saying in using the term *primordial,* we must look not to their aboriginal cultures but to nativist movements, whose common goal is the recovery of the past.

This work will try to answer a number of questions that directly concern the validity of the concept of ethnic primordiality. Among them: What are the psychocultural dynamics underlying the choice and act of migration? If ethnicity is primordial, why was Americanization so readily and eagerly sought and embraced? If ethnicity is primordial, why was World War II felt to be so liberating an experience from the closed world of the ethnic enclave? Where was the doctrine of ethnic primordiality and corporateness in the era of John F. Kennedy and the New Frontier, when the American Dream was expected to be fulfilled for all? What is the significance of the assassination of President Kennedy and other liberal leaders for the subsequent quest of ethnic roots? If ethnicity is ineradicably primordial, why is a strenuous campaign of consciousness-raising, adult socialization, and the preparation of ethnic studies materials for public schools and colleges necessary for the inculcation of the natural?

2 American Dreams and American Realities

Although spokesmen for the White Ethnic Movement often speak as though the New Ethnic identity reflects primordial ties and hence is something *sui generis,* we shall argue in this chapter that the New Ethnicity exists and came into being only through dialectic relation with the American Dream. The New Ethnicity presupposes the very identity of the American Dream that it denounces. Thus in order to understand it, we must understand that "other"—which is now the dissociated "American" part of the self—against which it defines itself, and how the opposition arose. To do this, it is necessary to understand the psychocultural dynamics and patterns underlying American historical process, pervading both past and present. More explicitly, to understand the meaning of *being* and *becoming* a New Ethnic, we must first understand the complex process of being and becoming an American. This chapter is not, however, intended to be a comprehensive study of American culture; rather, it will emphasize a number of main themes that have been systematically explored in scholarly literature. Our goal is to look retrospectively from the New Ethnic Movement and discern themes in American culture which are clearly present in it; we also intend to look prospectively from the perspective of the ongoing and historical dynamics of American culture to discover perennial conflicts in the present movement. The multiplicity of American promises and dilemmas will be discussed, and of equal importance will be a discussion of their relationship to the New Ethnic Movement.

Two decades ago Melford Spiro posed some of the most crucial questions about the relationship between ethnicity and acculturation (Americanization). "If early experiences are of determinative importance, why do most ethnic groups prefer social mobility to ethnic integrity and class- over ethnic-identification? . . . If behavior is determined by one's cultural heritage, then why do ethnics (who desire acculturation) attempt to behave in accordance with norms they do not know rather than in accordance with those they have already learned? But 'cultural determinism' is concerned with psychological phenomena as well. To what extent, for example, is culture a constituent element of the self? And to what degree is ego-identity a function of group identification?"[1]

The New Ethnicity offers very direct, concise answers to these questions: (1) To the extent that social mobility, class identification, and American norms replace ethnicity, to that degree have individuals been desocialized and deculturated by the coerciveness and conformism of American education and society, and resocialized into facsimile replicas of the variation-less "American." (2) Ethnicity is the primary constituent element of the self, whose ego-identity is inextricably bound up with the primordial group through early identification. Anglo-conformist socializers may try to eradicate one's ethnic core, but they succeed only in driving it beneath the surface where it carries on a life of its own, though absent from public inspection. Although the American identity may be superimposed on the ethnic, it cannot replace it. The suppression of ethnicity creates a resistance to acculturation, rather than capitulation. Ethnicity then, according to the New Ethnics, is like the phoenix awaiting the opportunity to rise from the pyre of fallen imperial identities.

Our own answers to Spiro's questions are quite different and more complex. Americanization cannot be reduced to such single-factor concepts as racism, exploitation, oppression, deculturation, cultural imperialism or colonialism, or Anglo-conformity. Nor is the familiar European model of *Kulturkampf,* or culture-struggle, readily transposable to explain the American ethnic experience. Americanization of the white ethnic immigrant is not equivalent, either in dynamics or outcome, to the Magyarization of Slovaks and other Slavs, the Russification of Ukrainians, or the Germanization of Poles in Prussian-Poland. Nor is the European model of ethnic groups as nations or proto-nation states transportable across the Atlantic and adequate as an explanation for the ethnic-American experience. The United States, not only in ideology but in function, may be a "nation of immigrants," brought here by a variety of coercions, but it is not a "nation of nations." It has never established the European or Ottoman social structure of "corporate minorities" with their own special statuses and vulnerabilities. The relation of ethnicity, class, caste, and racism must be understood in the context of American culture—with its multitude of "dreams" and "dilemmas."

To say that the American Dream (and its multitude of individual dreams) is simply an illusion, a false promise, or a myth that has led to disillusionment, demoralization, and frustration, therefore making the defensive ethnic identities of today virtually inevitable, even adaptive strategies of survival, is to oversimplify and fail to answer some important questions and ultimately to misinterpret the nature of American culture. The sense of "relative deprivation," or dissatisfaction, of unfulfilled promises is a chronic American affliction built into the cultural fabric. It is not limited to the present discontent. Millions, not just an isolated and chosen few, have "made it," not spectacularly perhaps, but because they believed in the myth that embodied a sense of the past and provided a paradigm for the future, thus promising a return on their investment in toil and in years. Cultural ideals are abstractions that are rarely fulfilled in splendid completeness. But the compelling myth of "log cabin to White House," or "from rags to riches," inspires as much as it misleads. It does not guarantee that everyone who tries will make it so remarkably, but that everyone has the opportunity to try to succeed. Those few who fulfill the myth are idealized; they vindicate the belief and give reason for others to believe not only in the American Dream, but in themselves. Their lives become legendary and timeless: hence exemplary and paradigmatic.

Today, however, the cultural myth of *success* is replaced with the inverted myth of *failure,* a historical and sociological revisionism that does not complement or balance the earlier history and sociology, but gives a mirror-image distortion of the original. Michael Harrington's *The Other America* (1963) is "rewritten" by the New Ethnicity to include virtually the whole of America, save for the core of "effete snobs" comprised mostly of upper-class WASPs and Jews. At the very least, the New Ethnic professors, despite their penchant for easy contrast categories that make WASPs and Jews "them" and white ethnics "us," are forced to recognize diversity in their neat categories. For instance, there are large numbers of impoverished Jews who defy the American stereotype; and there is economic, status, and political stratification of Jews, with English and German Jews at the top and the "uncultured" Russian Jews at the bottom. Similar stratification can be readily found within each of the white ethnic groups as well. And although WASPs are alleged to run everything, there are of course numerous Anglo-Protestant "blue-blood" ancestries in the working class of American industrial cities and in the poverty belt of Appalachia, who have political influence over nothing. We hear little of those Poles, Italians, Greeks, and Slavs (in Michael Novak's acronym, PIGS) who worked their way to the suburbs, or at least up on the "hill" above the factory (as opposed to living on the flood-plain adjacent to the factory). Rather, from the New Ethnicity, we hear only about those who have been unable to get out, how they defend what little they have, and how their fear of loss and invasion is justified—and hence their hostility.

This reality is not to be denied, although a complete portrait of lived-in, rather than idealized, America is necessary. However, to replace a celebration of victories with a litany of casualties does not do justice to the whole of American culture, historical or contemporary.[2] We would ask, for instance: What is the relation between the victories and the casualties? Is it inherent in the nature of American culture that in order for there to be victories, numerous casualties are necessary? More scientifically: What, if any, is the functional relation between those who succeed and those who fail? This problem, we shall suggest, is both endemic and chronic in American culture history. If this is so, then *why* does the white ethnic nativist movement occur *now?* What is different about the disappointments now and the earlier ones, and why were the earlier ones tolerable and endurable while the present ones are intolerable? Specifically, why the radical questioning of the American Dream now? *Absolutely* speaking, the conditions of the immigrants at the time of their immigration and for the first several decades were infinitely worse than even those of inner-city white ethnics at present. When we look at the problem *relatively,* we may perhaps come closer to answering the question. For instance, many of the *New Immigrants* from eastern and southern Europe initially migrated, and indeed re-migrated several times, for the sole purpose of amassing money from work in the mines and mills. Then they planned to return to their own countries and live better. Thus conditions in America, from filth to ridicule, were tolerable because the host country was not the frame of reference. When they began considering permanent residence, however, the problem of the discrepancy, of relative deprivation, began. Still, this does not adequately answer the question of *Why now?* Or *Why not before?* To answer this question, we must look into the dynamics of American culture, in general, and the era of World War II through the present.

The Last Best Hope of Mankind

Before America was a nation, it was a land; before it was a land, it was an idea, a dream, and a hope. There was an American Dream more than three centuries before the Revolution embodied it in the ideology of a nation; the nation was created in the image of its vision and ideal. The American Dream was born in the decline of feudalism and the Middle Ages, first in England and western Europe, spreading eastward through the nineteenth century, and is now something of a universal model of liberation and modernization.

Accompanying the decline of feudalism was "the inner emancipation of the sons" leading to a host of revolutionary liberation movements whose culture climax and continual source of imitation was the American Revolution.[3] But inner revolutions preceded outer ones. The closed dark world of medieval papacy, feudal fiefdom, church, dogma, and ritual was challenged by a growing individual restlessness and doubt, and by the search for reality and self-realization beyond received truth. *New worlds* were being explored, discovered, and opened before the advent of the *New World*. The Renaissance turned from scholasticism and ritual to realism and empiricism. The Age of Exploration involved more than the search for a water route to the spices of Asia in the aftermath of the Turko-Tatar conquest of the land routes in the thirteenth century. The restless cultural spirit of exploration and inquiry pervaded all facets of urban life during the Italian Renaissance—the source of diffusion of new paths in mathematics, science, art, music, and sculpture. The stagnant, decadent Old World of the medieval papacy was challenged and disobeyed. The Renaissance, Reformation, and Enlightenment were not three separate eras, but developmental phases of the same spirit. Some persons were burned for their heresies; others recanted and repented. Galileo knew he did not have to fight the church and die for science; he publicly recanted and privately went about his research, which became avidly sought and readily available elsewhere in Europe. He did not need to be a martyr.

In France, during Galileo's time, René Descartes heralded the Enlightenment and its emphasis on individual autonomy and thought. He first radically doubted everything received from the past: *Dubitans.* Then the famous: *Cogito ergo sum,* "I think, therefore I am." First, the questioning of all that had been totally accepted from the experienced past; then his self-affirmation as an independent thinker which became the basis of his identity and a paradigm for the cultural identity of the Enlightenment throughout Europe and America. An autonomous, exploring, empirically minded individual dared assert his doubt about everything, which he overcame by further asserting his capacity to search for answers that were not already given. A new method would be a new means toward knowledge, would direct the anxiety of uncertainty, and allow an almost indefinite postponing of resolution because it was the means that counted, rather than the end. The person became a separate member of a community rather than one who was organically fused with the community. One's future would be based on achievement rather than ascription, ability rather than birth, and reason rather than tradition. The image of the social and natural world became one of process and fluidity, instead of fixity.

We hasten to add that the dichotomy between the Dark Ages and succeeding ever-enlightening ones should not be overdrawn. Ideological difference is not the only measure of distance and may, in fact, betray the extent of commonality and conflict between the two. To idealize the enlightened ages and disparage the benighted ones is to indulge in countertransference to the data. Our own enlightened stereotypes tend to obscure and distort the culture history we record. Each age must live with its own past. By understanding a particular sense of the past, we gain insight into its influence on the present (or any present).

We might say that the medieval Age of Faith was a monumental Age of Reason whose scholasticism provided the official underpinnings of faith. The expression "by faith alone" belonged to the Reformation, which in turn produced its own emphasis on works and "right" faith. The eighteenth-century Enlightenment, on the other hand, was an Age of Reason which repudiated the superstitiousness of unquestioning and unevidenced faith, yet which maintained an unquestioned faith in the future, in human progress, and in its own reasonability. Man, not God, became the measure of all things. The Age of Belief placed supreme credibility in that which could not be seen, and the Age of Reason accepted only that which could be empirically demonstrated with the "common sense" of science. (Yet gravity, like God, was perhaps *visibilium et invisibilium omnia*.) Enlightenment rationalists were stylistically medieval and as Thomistic about freedom as the Scholastics were about God. Carl L. Becker more than amply argued this point in *The Heavenly City of the Eighteenth-Century Philosophers*.[4] Whereas medievalists were dedicated to demonstrating Divine mystery in everything, Enlightenment scientists and encyclopedists were dedicated to asserting the human mastery of everything. The former found God everywhere; the latter were unrelentingly intent on proving that God was present nowhere. The Galilean-Newtonian universe was a perfect mechanical device, with everything in its place, running with well-oiled precision. If the period from the Renaissance through the Enlightenment was a time of dynamic change, upheaval, and progress, one of its most compelling images was that of "universe-as-machine," a metaphor of the ordered and the static, inherited from medievalism.

The Reformation and the Renaissance were as much eras of retrenchment as they were of progress. Their liberations and ideologies of individual salvation and personal knowledge were accompanied by new fundamentalisms, conformisms, and nationalisms. Newly liberating sects quickly became coercive denominations. Reformations catalyzed counterreformations not only from without, but from within as well. Martin Luther rebelled against the papacy only to become a wrathful potentate himself. The Enlightenment certainly had its Dogmatics. Was not Montesquieu or Diderot an Aquinas of his age? Each age had its own right belief, heterodoxies, and consuming inquisitions (from the Jesuits to Robespierre). Each age practiced its own brand of fanaticism and intolerance. Each era offered its own overarching universalism: medieval Christendom, Reformationist personal faith, Renaissance individualism, and Enlightenment rationalism. If medieval despotism prepared the way for the Reformation, then Enlightenment despotism (as in *enlightened despotism*) invited the revolutions in North America and continental Europe. Chronological succession explains nothing. Each age lived in dialectical relation to those preceding it, embodying its spirit even as it repudiated it and replaced it with a new, and more pure, spirit. Every present is a way of coping with the past.

This explanation, however, does not diminish the legacy of the Enlightenment and its liberating precursors. Its excesses in the service of autonomy, liberation, freedom, secularism, and individualism were a direct measure of the extent to which those who migrated and rebelled felt the need to rid themselves of the oppressive past. If the Christian legacy was the quest for a utopian perfection, the Enlightenment rationalist Deists sought that perfection in *this* world. Faith undercut by doubt led to a search for a new faith on new premises. If man was nothing in Creation, he was now the measure of all things. If life was based on self-denial, life would now be lived by self-assertion. Obedience to authority was replaced by defiance of authority. Transcendent outer authority (from God to king) was replaced by immanent inner authority. Hubris, not humility, expressed man's sense of place and possibility. Before, omniscience and omnipotence were the jealously guarded prerogatives of God the Father (and His human representatives). Now, these would be taken over by the sons of Europe and the Americas, by migration and escape, and by scientific and political revolution. Man was no longer a mere conduit of the past, but an active planner of his own future. The change in ethos can perhaps be best summed up by rewording Freud's ontogenetic aphorism "Where id is, there shall ego be" into a culture historic one: Where superego is, there shall ego (and, in excess, egotism) be.

The discovery of the New World meant that mankind would have a chance to start all over in an environment that contrasted with the Old World. Rebirth and the opportunity for continual renewal contrasted with old age and decadence. Europe was the land of the father, and America belonged to the son, the perpetual adolescent. America became the new Eden. Explorer Ponce de León sought the ancient orphic "fountain of youth" in Florida. A host of explorers expected to find gold everywhere, and those who did became the first great despoilers in the name of God, king, and avarice. Gold was the universal standard of wealth and was symbolically not unrelated to the cult of youth that lies at the foundation of American mythology, a mythology that, though ancient, seemed *realizable* on American soil. America itself became the alchemist's magic catalyst.

America would become the eternal male adolescent, as well as his dream, the exclusive claim of the son to virgin land and motherland,[5] the escape from dominating and punitive fathers, the success of the son beyond the father, and the escape from the guilt-inducing oedipal family through spatial and interpersonal separation. America as a place quickly embodied what everything else was not, but what one wished it to be. In the New World, man would be refashioned by remaking himself. Unbounded hopes and wishes were matched by boundless frontier. To the newcomers the "empty" land would be filled with their dreams.[6] Geography, therefore, matched their cultural psychology. Even for later immigrants who personally knew only the cities of the East, the most significant geography was the frontier Midwest and West because it was a spatial representation of the psychological character of movement and "room" to move around.

The opportunity to make a new start, to achieve, and the promise of that achievement was the driving force behind migration and the eager Americanization of the immigrant. Five centuries before Adlai Stevenson declared the 1950s to be the "age of rising expectations," the foreign-born imagery of America had already made continuously rising expectations, progressive dissatisfaction, and the need for ever-expanding frontiers (of the imagination, land, and marketplace) part of the American ethos. The New Frontier of the Kennedy days is only a modern variant on this theme. No achievement is final or sufficient; no frontier is ever the last. Each new frontier is a promised land until there arises a vision of a yet more distant, more elusive and challenging land to be explored, conquered, tamed, and defended with ferocity—which in turn becomes yet another dead end. California, of gold-rush days and of the present, symbolizes the hope and the promise of liberty and success, and the danger of perverse shiftlessness and emptiness. Horace Greeley's clarion call to "go West, young man" meant equally to "keep moving" toward ever receding frontiers. Americans, intent on "getting there first," are soon dissatisfied with the limits of what has been gained.[7]

What is *American* is not the product, but the process. If one cannot leave, he feels imprisoned; one must believe that he actively chose to remain and was not compelled by forces beyond himself. If one is to understand the meaning of *social mobility* or even of what Vance Packard speaks of as a temporary society made up of a "nation of strangers,"[8] then we must recognize the special meaning *movement* has and its pervasiveness in language and culture. For example, the expressions *moving on, moving out,* and *moving up* are highly valued in American society. Yet because of the uncertainty and anxiety generated by the very values inherent in mobility—choice, tentativeness, change, progress, freedom, and individuality—one can as easily dig in and defend his constricted battlements as he can choose to pull up his roots and leave. As historian Nathan I. Huggins observes:

> While its absence [the Old-World community] could be a blessing in the way of fluidity, it could be a curse in the way of impermanence and in the relatively inconsequential character of interrelationships. Identity, status, and the nature of social responsibility all became open to question and doubt. Whatever advantages there were in freedom, the uncertainty made the quest for community and fixed, normal, social relationships a continuing part of American preoccupations. . . . The very qualities of American life that were attractive to most people—its dynamics, flux, and variety— caused chronic anxiety about disorder and social chaos, where all civilized values might be lost.[9]

Change, of course, goes both ways, and the ambivalence, as manifested in the swing between extremes, is the generic conflict. Just as lawlessness gives rise to the practice of overcontrol, too much security and too static a sense of community lead to a breaking loose from the tight reins.

The extended Elizabethan family, like the peasant family throughout Europe, had stressed obedience to elders, submission to authority, acceptance of social hierarchy, cooperation, duty and responsibility, religious piety, and loyalty to the group. Considerable social change in England, however, had loosened many of the traditional bonds; similar changes would also take place progressively eastward throughout Europe. What had been repressed and suppressed surfaced in the seventeenth century, and the "unoccupied" American continent profided the outlet for newly released energies, wishes, and ideals.

The lure of America was the opportunity to break with the rigid past, to leave behind the rules and obligations of extended family, most notably dependency and authority, and to fashion a new identity and community composed of self-made men. From the earliest colonist escapees of Elizabethan England to the great migration occurring between 1880 and 1920, through the present, the deep structural significance of immigration was the break with traditional constraints and the formation of a new identity based on freedom, aggressive independence, self-reliance, competition, and success through individual achievement. These terms, it will be noted, are dialectical opposites of traditional values.

The word *dialectical* is necessary because the identity change was not simply an exchange of one value for its opposite; rather, the transformation or reversal inverted the former positive identity (what one sought to be, the good person) into the negative identity (what one sought to avoid becoming, the bad person), and conversely, while the tension between them persisted. This tension, as we shall see, lies at the core of the dynamism of American culture history. The polarities of this conflict are expressed in Table 5, one class of which is *traditional* or *ethnic*, and the other, *American*. It must be kept in mind that this table expresses categories of overtly held values; the latent values which are the components of the negative identity are represented by the opposite of each pair. In American culture, to speak of "ethnicity as identity" is thus both accurate and incomplete because ethnicity is a part-identity, the dynamics of which is inseparable from that of the American identity. Moreover, "growing into ethnicity" is likewise inseparable from growing into an American identity.[10]

In his analysis of the Plains Indian equestrian-warrior culture, George Devereux provided a useful model that might be appropriately applied to American culture. He speaks of a "culture areal ethos" and "areal personality" in which an emergent value system and intrapsychic structuring gradually override tribal differentiations. We first quote his formulation at length and then discuss how the American Dream-Melting Pot imagery and ethos form the basis of the supraethnic American culture area and personality structure.

TABLE 5 Table of Values

Traditional/Ethnic	American
adult-centered	child and youth-centered
dependency	independence
obedience	self-reliance
non-aggressiveness	aggressive self-assertion
authoritarianism	egalitarianism
hierarchical	individual, collateral
group/cooperation	individual/competition
other	self
conservative	revolutionary
status quo	achievement and change
centripetal	centrifugal
closed	open and relentlessly expanding
settledness	mobility
present	future
submission to nature (acted upon)	mastery of nature (active)
image of "limited good"	image of limitless good(s)
(George Foster)	

The formation of a culture area entails more than the mere erosion of pre-existing, distinctive tribal or national culture *traits*. It implies primarily the evolving and/or acquisition of new, common areal traits and the rearrangement of both old and new traits and trait complexes into a distinctive areal pattern. What becomes constituted and crystallized is *primarily* a new areal culture pattern, which supersedes and reshapes the antecedent areal culture patterns of the groups which create or join the new culture area, more even than it supersedes and reshapes the antecedent *tribal* culture patterns and culture traits of the individual tribes in question.

Genuine—i.e., *relatively* heterogeneous—culture areas can and do result *only* from the meeting, blending, restructuring and reaffiliation of pre-existing culture, and from the high-level, pattern-forming innovations which result from such meetings between at least two discrete and distinct cultures which previously belonged to other culture areas. . . . the culture area—and particularly its areal culture pattern—can *initially* come into being *only* through contacts between adults who are, after all, the only immediately effective carriers of their respective, pre-existing cultures. Moreover, the very first germ of a—necessarily new—areal ethnic *personality* can come into being only after at least a trace, a shadowy seed, of the new areal culture pattern has already made its first appearance on the stage of history. At first this rudimentary areal ethnic personality is inculcated in childhood *by* adults whose areal ethnic personality is—and continues to be—that of the culture area to which they had previously belonged. In other words, psychologically non-acculturated, but culture-areally partially acculturated and areal-culture-inventing adults begin to raise culturally and psychologically more acculturated children. . . . In short, there exists a relationship of mutual induction between the areal culture pattern and the areal ethnic personality, which amplifies and perfects both, even though the very first impulse emanated from the former. This implies that:

(1) The initial formation of the areal culture pattern and its subsequent elaboration and stabilization is the work of *adults,*

(2) who, after the first generation, acquire in *childhood* an areal ethnic personality, which becomes more and more developed, stabilized and functionally operant as generation succeeds generation.[11]

As Fishman has recognized, the overarching framework of the American ethos is the supraethnic American Dream. Ideologically, it guaranteed freedom from the various constraints of one's past and one's native land, and claimed that reason and achievement, rather than ancient dogma and ascription, were the wave of the future and a wedge against the past. America meant freedom from the past. Franz Alexander observed: "The country was founded upon a protest against the old world, and this protest remained a characteristic feature of the new world."[12] Erik Erikson notes a similar relation between the Old World that one sought to repudiate and abandon, and the New World one sought to create. American history, at least in ideology, professed to be an end to the old history and the chronicle of a utopian age. The Declaration of Independence and similar documents are as eschatological as they are political. Erikson writes the following about American psychohistory:

Identity problems were in the mental baggage of generations of new Americans, who left their motherlands and fatherlands to merge their ancestral identities in the common one of self-made men. Emigration can be a hard and heartless matter, in terms of what is abandoned in the old country and what is usurped in the new one. . . . If something like an identity crisis gradually appeared to be a normative problem in adolescence and youth, there also seemed to be enough of an adolescent in every American to suggest that in this country's history, fate had chosen to highlight identity

questions together with a strangely adolescent style of adulthood—
that is, one remaining expansively open for new roles and
stances—in what at the time was called a "national character."

The American self-made man was one who had not been fashioned
by anyone else. He was to be "his own man," moving on whenever
he wished or, if necessary, digging in with a vengeance. The American woman was to be the helpmate of the self-made man on his way
up, deriving her sense of place from how high her husband (and
father, and children) could climb. This emphasis on the inviolable
individual underlies the special relation in American culture between
past, present, and future. The greatest obstacle to freedom was the
tyranny of the past. Hence the orientation to the future and the
American attitude that *time* is future tense: fleeing toward the future
from what was feared in the past—hence the relentlessness of change,
mobility, limitless growth and expansion, and the transitoriness of
relationships to anyone and anywhere. The *American* man is Robert
Jay Lifton's "Protean Man," described by Erikson as having "a
strangely adolescent style of adulthood—that is, one remaining expansively open for new roles and stances. . . ."[13] Fishman writes that
the American promise "held forth vistas of happiness in human affairs, limitless individual and collective advancement, and social inclusiveness in community affairs. In a very basic sense, each of these
ingredients is supra-ethnic, if not anti-ethnic. . . . cultural pluralism
was never explicitly 'covered' by the formulators of the American
Dream, nor has it been consciously and fully desired by the millions
who subsequently subscribed to the Dream. Indeed, the prime factor
leading most immigrants to our shores was the American Dream itself . . . and not any dream of cultural pluralism."[14]
The same is true of the search for religious freedom. The myth of
the Mayflower and New England Puritanism embodies the theme of
America as a haven from intolerance (ironically so, since the Puritans
denied to others the freedoms they sought for themselves). Nevertheless, the *status* of the Puritan legacy through its influence in American
culture from work to literature overshadows other cultural strands
that are at least as influential. It is perfectly true that Hawthorne and
his guilt-ridden fictional protagonists are generations removed from
their God-haunted Puritan forbears. Likewise, Melville's Promethean
self-made man, Ahab, destroys himself in the very process of destroy-
ing the object of his obsessive-compulsive quest. Even in its seeming
repudiation by post-seventeenth-century Americans, the Puritan legacy of virtue through consuming guilt apparently was pervasive.

Nevertheless, in an interesting study of frontier religion, historian Ross Phares writes: "The belief that America was settled mainly by church devotees seeking religious freedom appears to be based more on misinterpreted tradition than statistics. Indications are that the colonists may have been seeking freedom more than religion."[15] Even the dour, moralistic Puritans, who emigrated to worship freely in their own way, sought to escape persecution by conventional religion. While official history pictures the Mayflower emigrees as devout, virtuous, and hard-working pioneers seeking freedom *of* religion, it is closer to fact to say that many of the early immigrants were at least as eager to obtain freedom *from* religion. As with ethnicity, the first (and subsequent) Euro-Americans wanted to escape the limitations and controls that made religion more an agent of oppression than release. The American Dream, with its ideology of release from the past, offered in many ways a new religion expressing a new (proto-national) identity.[16]

The problem with all liberations and revolutions is what to do with the past that has been abandoned or repudiated. The past is not merely external and objective, hence readily disposable. It is part of oneself that must be coped with; it is an internalized sense of the past. As soon as we say *internalized,* we are confronted with the perennial Freudian riddle of manhood posed to us by the very fact of being a human animal: how to be a man without killing the father and without becoming the father—hence sacrificing one's own manhood. Our study of the American Dream and its discontents will tell us how well or how poorly we have succeeded navigating the dangers of the Scylla and Charybdis.

The "Melting Pot" was the compelling image and metaphor of the American Dream. This image of the age of industrialism was first employed by the French-born essayist St. Jean de Crèvecoeur in 1756: "Here in America individuals of all nations are melted into a new race of men." The metaphor was given its most elaborate expression in British playwright Israel Zangwill's play of 1908, *The Melting Pot.*[17] Into the crucible would go everyone to be reborn an American. Zangwill—like other cultural idealists and visionaries such as Locke, Goethe, Blake, Kafka, and Emerson—celebrated the ever uncompleted American as an amalgam of the best of the Old World with what was released in the New World, and a shedding of the oppressive dross that represented the worst of the Old World. As a vehicle of the American Dream, the Melting Pot encouraged the belief that one could choose the future and not be condemned to the past. Whatever else may be said about American culture, the existence of a core culture of aspiration and ambition cannot be denied. Its existence, not reducible to Anglo-conformism, attests to the efficacy of the myth of the Melting Pot. Likewise, the extent of intermarriage and cultural syncretism (in the case of America, the adoption of new elements into the mainstream) attests to the continued vigor of the American Dream in content and process as well as hope.

Freedom, Equality, and the Pursuit of Hierarchy

The historian Thomas C. Wheeler writes that "the America of freedom has been an America of sacrifice, and the cost of becoming American has been high. For every freedom won, a tradition lost."[18] The conclusion is inescapable, however, that it goes both ways. For every tradition that has been escaped, a new freedom is won. Freedom and tradition each exacts its own price, and every civilization, even a utopian one, has its own discontents. Indeed, unhappiness with the present is a chronic American cultural theme that is by no means limited to the current apocalyptic mood. Perpetual dissatisfaction is built into the very fabric and dynamism of America.

Over many waves and generations of immigrants, the American Dream was sustained despite frequent early disillusionment with the promise that it would be fulfilled immediately. Though the streets were not paved with gold, the hope and the promise sustained the immigrants' belief in the American Dream. It was a gamble on what was hoped would be a self-fulfilling prophecy: if the dream did not come true now, it was not rejected, but the timetable was extended. Given the open-ended nature of the dream itself, the fact that it was constantly being extended and revised, the reality which it would come to express would forever be incomplete, thus avoiding any intimations of finality. The Americans' faith in the dream created a perpetual sense of experimentation, creative insecurity, and a protean identity which were part of an endless cycle of anxiety and resolution that was tolerable so long as the dream could be sustained by the promise of unlimited opportunity.

Although in the early part of our history Americans made a dichotomy between the Old World that was decadent, tyrannical, and corrupt, and the New World that was youthful, free, and innocent of crimes of the past, what was physically abandoned was not so easily exorcised. One price of all human revolutions of consciousness and conscience is a fear of the past that has been palpably cast behind, that is, a fear of being overthrown and overwhelmed by that past. The American Revolution is no exception. Many current, and recurrent, conflicts in American culture reflect the influence of the past upon the present. It is as though America had two cultures. The conflicting themes of egalitarian democracy versus hierarchic autocracy, independence versus submission to authority, and the like, are endemic. The very emphasis on self-reliance, rugged individualism, and self-made men seeking to vanquish the claims and ties of the past suggests that the vehement self-uprooting and relentless escape are an inverse index of the haunting pull of the past that one sought so remorselessly to abandon and to forget. As is suggested by the mottoes "On guard for freedom" and "Eternal vigilance is the price of freedom," the defense of liberty is a full-time occupation. Little time remains to be free. Americans are so preoccupied with being *free from* enemy aliens, foreign influences, or being caught unprepared that there is little energy left to be *free for* other endeavors. The former is negative and aversive, as if one were in perpetual wait for an enemy who would surely come and take away what one had gained. The latter, could it be attained, is affirmative, self-actualizing, and does not need to insist on its freedom.

American freedom is usually defined in terms of its opposite, a form of unfreedom: fear of oppression, the dread of being tied down or "stuck," the fear of failure that would end one's mobility and progress, and the fear of being taken over by some authoritarian regime like communism. Reality, of course, does not always capitulate to one's wish; and it is realistic to expect people to be concerned about losing what they have struggled to obtain. But what makes this analysis of the "reality principle" inadequate is the enormity and chronicity of the fear. American history and ideology is one endless epic and heroic struggle against all enemies of freedom. Behind every phobic obsession and preoccupation that is insistently voiced in a myriad of ways and circumstances, there lies a *wish*—this we learned from Freud. To define something or oneself in terms of its opposite is to be possessed by that opposite even as one is combating it. It is as though Americans secretly wished to have undone all that they have wished to achieve. If a phobic fear is the symbolized inverse of an intense but repudiated wish, then there must exist a deep wish to surrender and renounce *American* freedoms to the potent forces of the *European* or traditional past, an example of what Erich Fromm has called "escape from freedom." In an interesting aphorism, Stephen Spender suggests that American and European images of each other are mirror images. "Americans fear the European past"; while "Europeans fear the

American future."[19] Americans recoil from this attraction to the dark
past through overcompensation in the defense of freedom, with special
emphasis placed on the protection of America, a vulnerable bastion of
freedom. Yet the ancient influences are present in the very personalities and institutions that defend against their insidious influence.

John Spiegel has noted "the tension between democratic slogans
and elitist practices," that is, "the chronic conflict between democratic and authoritarian values in our society," and the reciprocal
effects of cultural value orientations and social institutions upon each
other. Using Kluckhohn's "relational value category" and its three
subtypes, the individual, the collateral, and the lineal, Spiegel asks
how the overwhelming emphasis on the individual pattern, with its
antiauthoritarian implications, can be reconciled "with the authoritarian practices and the hierarchy of power."

> In accordance with Florence Kluckhohn's theory of variation in
> value orientations this [Relational] area is concerned with group
> structure and decision making. It is postulated that the ideal (domi-
> nantly preferred) decision-making pattern places Individualism in
> the first order or most preferred position; Collaterality—that is,
> horizontal, consensus decisions—in the second place; and Lineal-
> hierarchical, authoritarian structures—in the last or least preferred
> position. Although this is the ideal rank order of values in which all
> Americans are trained to believe and even though it fits well with
> the American middle-class family structure, still it does not corre-
> spond to the actual value patterns of many of our major American
> institutions. International relations, business, government, educa-
> tion, welfare, and many community organizations operate in accor-
> dance with a discordant pattern of preferences—that is, with the
> Lineal rather than the Collateral in the second order position. This
> means that behind our Individualism there is an intense but largely
> concealed emphasis on superior-inferior relationships—on "Who's
> on top?" or "Who is making it?" in terms of social position, power
> and income. The accent is on elitism and on power relations be-
> tween groups rather than the pluralism or equality between groups
> called for by our national ethos.[20]

Thus, while the individual-collateral-lineal pattern is the ideal ranking, the operative pattern is individual-lineal-collateral. From the days
of the revolutionary war, "the struggle was between tyranny—that is,
Lineality—and liberty—that is, Individualism." Not only was individualism elevated to a national value to rationalize the declaration of
independence from the Crown, but it has operated throughout Ameri-

can history as a value which provides constant vigilance against dependency and authority. Thus we are continuously warring with those (internally and externally) we fear would subjugate us; in the name of freedom we combat an enemy in whom we have located a repressed and "split-off" part of ourselves. Authoritarianism in our institutions perpetuates our ancient "identification with the oppressor," even as we vigilantly defend democracy (with autocratic means). According to Spiegel, "the Lineal principle, the unconscious or concealed endorsement of authoritarianism, persists behind the mask of Individualism."[21] We cannot create a democracy as long as we are consciously committed to undermining it with lineality.

This value conflict is one expression taken by the American structuring of the oedipal conflict. In *Childhood and Society,* Erikson writes the following:

> It is as if these American boys were balancing on a tightrope. Only if they are stronger than or different from the real father will they live up to their secret ideals, or indeed, to their mother's expectations; but only if they somehow demonstrate that they are weaker than the omnipotent father (or grandfather) image of their childhood will they be free of anxiety.[22]

Self-assertion and defiance of authority vie with self-abnegation and submission to a national lineage of authorities. Self-assurance of destiny is more manifest at some times than others. Boasting about the future contends with a brooding uncertainty, if not despair, over the future. In the American "family romance," the promise of self-madeness guarantees at least in fantasy that one is not the child of one's father and, simultaneously, that as the child of one's real parents one has the license to outdo them in every way. This side of American culture is a veritable oedipal paradise. The other side, the lineal, is a repudiation of the adolescent-oedipal and an unconscious restitution by reidentifying with the archaic superego introjections—with whom, in turn, one unabatedly contends. The historic struggles of the American Revolution are reenacted in the psychohistory and family history of generations far removed from the original scene of the battle.

In a sense, the American Dream is condemned to failure from the beginning, since the hierarchical subverts the individual and collateral, even as autonomy and cooperation are held as high ideals. The success of one (or of one group) is contingent on the failure of another. Here each *ethnic group* becomes an accomplice to the perpetuation of the above-mentioned cultural contradictions, as the oppressed of one generation or era become and join the oppressors of the next. Freedom for oneself is acquired by denying it to other "less worthy" aspirants. What Karen Horney called the drivenness toward "power, prestige, and possession" rests on a need for outward manifestations of success that are never adequate since they are all undermined by the dread of failure and sense of inner personal inadequacy. This sense of inner emptiness and the belief in the ultimate untrustworthiness of others (as well as oneself) are in turn compensated for by the anxious conquest of the outer, empirically verifiable, world, generating in turn a dread that what has been secured will be encroached upon. One is, therefore, on guard for freedom and all of its accumulated trappings.

With their cultural emphasis on social mobility, change, progress, and achievement, Americans constantly seek more and better and try to climb higher. While doing this, however, they compare themselves and their achievements (or those of their children, in whom they have invested their future), with those of others. The inner-directed man of David Riesman's "lonely crowd" is, in a sense, other-directed. His status is always changing, and he is never really sure of himself. The worst thing that can happen is to "get nowhere" and become a failure. Willy Loman, the protagonist of Arthur Miller's *Death of a Salesman,* is thus an archetypal American character at the opposite end of the spectrum from the myth of Horatio Alger and the self-made man. In order to safeguard what he has struggled to obtain, the self-made man becomes an unapproachable "boss." The American aspires to be "the best" because to be "second best" is to be no good at all.

Here the American core values of liberty, equality, and individuality are caught in the conflict between the American Dream and the prerevolutionary ideology that each new immigrant wave brings— including the founding fathers and mothers. On the one hand, there is the "cult of the average man" which does not reduce the individual to a group conformist, but which exalts him and urges him on. Clyde Kluckhohn wrote the following about American life:

> The American is not a passive automaton submitting to cultural compulsives like European provincials. The American voluntarily and consciously seeks to be like others of his age and sex—without in any way becoming an anonymous atom in the social molecule. On the contrary, all the devices of the society are mobilized to glamorize the individual woman and to dramatize every achievement of men and women that is unusual—but still within the range of approved aspirations of the conforming majority.

Earlier in the same essay he discussed American attitudes toward leadership.

The cult of the average man might seem to imply disapproval of outstanding individuals of every sort. Certainly it is true that a great deal of hostility is directed upward. However, under the influence of the dramatic and success aspects of the "romantic individualism" orientation, the typical attitude toward leaders may best be described as one of mixed feelings. On the one hand, there is a tendency to snipe at superior individuals with a view to reducing them to the level of their fellows. On the other hand, their very success is a dramatic vindication of the American way of life and an invitation to identification.[23]

But this is only half of the American reality, the revolutionary half. The antirevolutionary half is mercilessly lineal and (amounting to one expression of the same thing) socially leveling. Over a century and a half ago, Alexis de Tocqueville said that Americans preferred equality to liberty. He did not mean an equality that was conducive to liberty or individuality, but the quality of sameness or equality of condition.[24] Not only was no one better than anyone else in opportunity, but no one would be permitted to be different. An endemic insecurity about one's human dignity, a sense of inferiority, and anxiety over one's status and origins led on the one hand to a social leveling and the eradication of difference, and to a compensatory attempt to be the best in the world (from industrialism to the space race to symphony orchestras). While the former leads to the atrophy of genuine individuation (because it is so concerned with the opinions of others, and of becoming like others), the latter leads to "rugged individualism," the will to overcome all obstacles in the service of one's goal, no matter what the price.

In America great concern is given to the purity of identity and to fears of impurity. Such national founders as Washington, Adams, Franklin, and Jefferson feared the irreversible influence of potential immigrants on American law and civility. The Puritans, the original practitioners of the paradigm of freedom and intolerance, were also concerned with the purity and purification of identity and with the preservation of "blue bloods." The cult of the common man, as celebrated by poet Walt Whitman, is counterbalanced by a fascination with royalty, aristocracy, and lineage. While one's true ancestors may have been among the millions of "huddled masses yearning to breathe free," one does not want to be identified as a peasant, but as having an origin as noble as that of the putative American founders. Not only is one presently American, but those categories that express American identity are equally applicable to those who now seek to invert a sense of inferiority into one of equality, if not superiority. Our actual ragged, indeed, mongrelized maternity and paternity are not celebrated on national anniversaries.

The revolutionary-war patriots provided the original models. They are reluctant radicals comporting themselves as reasonable, well-tempered Whigs, certainly not "revolutionary" firebrands à la Robespierre or Lenin, aristocratic enough to look like Tories and comport themselves like monarchs. But the lineality must be modulated, even denied, as the leaders are seen as one of the people who must mix among them. Indeed, many of these leaders have risen from humble origins in order to occupy the sacred places of national leadership. Equality, then, both elevates and degrades, rewards the nonconformist and forces him or her to conform.

At its best, equality safeguards liberty and individuality because it is rooted in the belief in individual dignity and is untroubled by difference. This is the legacy of the American Dream. At its worst, however, equality operates remorselessly as a social equalizer to put everybody in their places. People begin to fear any otherness than that which is a loyal facsimile of themselves and are so insecure in their own identities that they must abort the individuation of others as they have had to repress it in themselves. The enemy they fight is an external representation of their own wishes, who, when defeated is forced to "shape up" and become a passionate defender of the American way of life. Anyone who points out the discrepancies and contradictions in American values and beliefs immediately arouses collective outrage at the airing of truths which Americans have good reason to deny. "Voluntary associations," from formal clubs such as the American Legion, the Elks, or the Eagles to suburban communities, become bastions of exclusiveness and conformism, transforming through rituals of inclusion impure identities into pure ones, while on the other hand, repelling violently any threat to their imagined solidarity. This is the legacy of the lineal, hierarchical system of values that is against the ideal American grain but which is as American as the dream itself.

We shall soon speak of this system as the doctrine of American-conformism. In concluding this section, however, let us recall Erikson's remarks about the essential adolescent quality of the American character or identity, one that thrives on choice, incompleteness, tentativeness, openness, inclusiveness, and change.[25] The present analysis of the American value and belief system suggests that Erikson is correct, but incomplete. The obverse side of the adolescent process is the fear of too much too soon, with the combination of physiological changes, the reawakening of childhood conflicts that require resolution anew, expectations of new social roles, and obligations as well as opportunities. Whether or not or even *how* a specific culture ritualizes this transition is one thing, but adolescence is universally recognized as a period of transition and of re-resolution. Particular resolutions depend on the particularities of the culture. While American culture encourages the continuation of adolescent styles of thinking and action, it insures not only progressive inclusion but also the possibility of groupish reactionary exclusion, having closed communities as well as closed minds. If the promising side of adolescence is that which is personified by the myth of the American Revolution and the American Dream, then the atavistic side indicates that the adult will abort his or her own adolescent rebellion in order to make restitution for the guilt and shame of abandonment and initiative. The inner representatives of dependency and authority come to dominate operant reality, while one even more ardently insists on the free will inherent in the American Dream. One forecloses the future while imagining it to be infinitely open.

The Dialectic of the American Dream and American Conformity

With each new wave of immigrants, indeed, with each new generation, the American psychological revolution is recapitulated. The vigilant doctrine of *American conformity* assures that *we* shall not become like *them* whom the immigrants and sons left behind and sought to escape through spatial and ideological separation. Conformity to *American* standards, not reducible to British or northwest European standards, would safeguard the future against the dangers of the past. American conformity, first severely practiced by the early generations on themselves and later by the subsequent immigrant generations, would guarantee a uniform American defense against the erosion of the future by the past. American conformity became a defense of the *American* way of life, in part constituted by the Melting Pot that accumulated the American mainstream culture.

It is thus incorrect to equate American conformity, much less the whole of Americanization, with Anglo-conformity, even when the culture content was explicitly Anglo-Saxon in origin. The "cultural amnesia" and flight from the past was not simply a product of Anglo-Saxon *Kulturkampf* which rendered the Americanized ethnics passive victims of a process they unwillingly underwent. Rather, the embracing of Anglo-Saxon culture was an active symbolico-ritual process of Americanization, a rite of passage by which one became naturalized. The immigrants and their descendants had a deep enough investment in the American Dream and a powerful enough motivation to overcome the past not to need the generations of Know-Nothings, ethnophobic and xenophobic Americanizing educators such as Elwood P. Clubberly or anti-Melting Pot sociological rationalizers of Americanization such as Henry Pratt Fairchild to convince them to become "good Americans."[26] Yet, as American culture history has repeatedly proven, though not to the satisfaction of the mistrustful new natives, there is nothing to fear from the immigrants who are eager enough on their own to become good Americans. The wish to escape from the past, to build a new life and a new future—which the New Ethnicity today mistakenly calls "self-rejection" and "self-hatred"—was an inwardly motivated process based on dissatisfaction with the old way of life, and was not the product of brainwashing and intimidation by American conformists.

Although Americanization is not reducible to American conformity in process (dynamics), it does involve the adoption of much of American cultural *content* (that itself changes, reflecting the interpenetration of the Melting Pot). American cultural items, from ideals to artifacts, become symbolic of separating oneself from the past. The Melting Pot theory from Crèvecoeur to Zangwill embodied in its contents the northwest European rebel-escapee model of the new man, which each succeeding wave of immigrants sought to replicate. The discrepancy between what one sought to be and what one actually was underlay the crisis of self-esteem and self-doubt which potentially could be overcome through "naturalized" membership in the group with which one compared oneself.

As Theodore Schwartz has demonstrated in his analysis of Melanesian millenarian movements called "Cargo Cults," the direct experience of oppression or exploitation is not necessary to the experience of acute deprivation that underlies cult activity; rather, it is the self-comparison that results in extreme self-devaluation and the quest for self-esteem in which one comes out favorably with the object of comparison. Such cult activity reflects the limiting case of a crisis of status anxiety, of self-esteem, and powerlessness in the absence of a direct relationship with a superior and oppressive outside force. In other areas of Melanesia which were studied by Kenelm Burridge, the sense of deprivation from within as well as nonreciprocal, exploitative relations with a colonial power were present.[27] In American culture, both internal expectations and discrepancies, and external relationships with those who were expected (and who promised) to help overcome the discrepancies, but only exacerbated them, were present.

Here the conflict between the American Dream-Melting Pot model and the American-conformity model is most visible. The Melting Pot model is the highest cultural ideal which has become real for much of American culture, despite the force of the opposing model. The American-conformity model, conversely, is an overt and a covert model held to be the ideal and regarded as, in a sense, "un-American." Yet it is a powerful operant model. While the American Dream is an *unconditional* invitation for the wretched of the earth to have a second chance at life, American conformity is ultimately an endless and exhausting list of *conditions* that can never be completely fulfilled. In the American Dream, all people are accepted; in American conformism, all people are inspected—and open to continual inspection. In oedipal imagery, the American Dream is personified by the beneficent and bountiful mother who will provide for lost and orphaned children, and who will protect them from evil and distant fathers, even as they in turn protect her. The American-conformist image is that of the demanding father (and, often enough, mother as well), authoritarian, restrictive, and forever dissatisfied with the child's performance. One grows up becoming—and internalizing—both kinds of Americans: open and closed, inclusive and exclusive, generous and withholding, accepting and rejecting, permissive and restrictive, expressive and inhibitive, and loving and demanding. The child is given an abundance of double messages, one of which is to obey the American Dream, the other, to obey American conformity. This is precisely the "double-bind" predicament (Bateson) which causes severe individual conflict in identity (Erikson).

It is important to realize that the conflict between the American Dream and American conformity is as much an *intergenerational* one within the family as it is between one cohort of immigrants and their descendants and another. Thus the child is encouraged to be autonomous, separate, and self-reliant, but also to do as he or she is told. Children must perform tasks to gain the approval of others and live as much according to an inner clock as to an outer schedule. The parents want their offspring to have it better than they, although they envy and resent such achievement and efforts of success. The parents overtly encourage their offspring to succeed, while warning them of failure, often seeming to hope for it. Children or adolescents are urged to be on their own, but are accused of being rebellious and unloyal when an attempt is made to live independently.

On the one hand, the Melting Pot image of American culture is that of a continuously improving amalgam. On the other hand, the conformist image is ever fearful of the mongrelization, contamination, and alteration of the purified American character. There is always a *peril* to be looked out for. Whether it is American Indian, Irish Catholic, Slavic, Jewish, black, Communist, red, or yellow depends on the era. In the conformist Melting Pot, all "foreign elements" must be eradicated in order to protect the integrity of the American culture. In the American Dream image, the ordeal of the Melting Pot is an actively chosen self-rite of passage; in the conformist image, it is a coerced rite of passage, passively endured, and supervised by another who stands outside the process and judges one's success.

Education provides a good example of where the two models and images clash, where the Melting Pot often does its work despite the explicit emphasis on conformism, and where the impossible-to-satisfy demands of the conformist model have their early casualties. Horace Mann, in the mid-nineteenth century, urged universal education in the United States to rid the nation of class and caste distinctions, and their concomitant advantages and disadvantages for those who happen to be fortunate or unfortunate by birth. Horace Mann saw "education as a great equalizer," the basis of hope for the future—clearly in the tradition of the American Dream, which later John Dewey would personify in education. Conversely, however, much of official, formal education inculcated the conformist model and was more an agent of homogenization out of fear than individuation out of hope. Through education, the immigrant and his or her children would be resocialized to the ideals of American democracy (assuming that these ideals had to be taught) and would prevent the corruption of civic life. If education based on the American Dream cast its lot with a hope for the future, instruction based on American conformism feared that the future would irreparably pollute the invaluable gifts from the American past—although that very American past was based on a repudiation of many Anglo-Saxon values. Education has continued to be a battlefield for the identities and loyalties of the next generation as teachers fear the disruptive potential of individualism and differences, while lauding individuality, creativity, and difference as something sacredly American. (The New Ethnicity, incidentally, is no exception.)

While the American Dream-Melting Pot model encourages and cultivates individuality and autonomy—indeed, nonconformism—by de-homogenizing the past, the American-conformity model has an abiding mistrust of individual difference (even as it overcompensates by stressing rugged individualism) and insists on uniformity in order to eradicate diversity and homogenize the future. Each succeeding wave of new Americans sees in the new immigrants a reminder of their own past, a world they prefer to leave behind and fear will overtake them. While the new immigrants look to the future as their salvation from the bondage of the past, the new Americans see in their *American* past their safety and security, while fearing for the very future they count on to help them evade the past. The Americans standardize the immigrants as an act of self-protection for their own identity ostensibly purified of the past. The Melting Pot, however, could never standardize, since its goal was the continuous creation and improvement of the New Man who was *protean* from the beginning and could not be completed. The American would constantly be renewed, during an individual lifetime and over the generations. The two competing models thus worked toward opposite goals, one a radical diversity, the other an unthreatening uniformity.

Thus what is most American is frequently suppressed and its expression reprimanded as virtually "un-American." Yet when the contradiction is pointed out, the discrepancy is denied, and one is expected to act as though the contradiction did not exist (i.e., setting up the "double bind"). It must be emphasized that the contradiction and the means of rationalizing and resolving it are not simply in the culture outside the personality. The two systems of values, indeed, the two Americas, are internalized within living people, which is what gives American culture its dynamism. Americanization would thus seem to involve the interaction of two force vectors, the American Dream-Melting Pot and American conformity, with the latter persistently undermining the former. We would go so far as to suggest that the conformity model is a powerful vestige of the European (not simply WASP) prerevolutionary ethos and personality that serves as a countervailing force to the American Dream, yet which invokes the dream to deny its true intentions.

The American Dream, as we have seen, is profoundly oedipal on the side of the *son*. For example, it encompasses such cultural themes as youth, limitlessness, success, autonomy, liberty, egalitarianism, self-reliance, opportunity, mobility, freedom, revolution, change, progress, and a fraternal-sororal-collateral image of coequals in cooperation and competition. These are the overt core values and ideals that are said to be at the heart of American culture, existing prior to the revolutionary period. The American-conformist model is also oedipal, but it is distinctly on the side of the *father*—not only of the father himself, but the father the son becomes. Former sons, in achieving power, status, and property, entrench themselves as bosses, autocrats, and bureaucrats, thus preventing the next generation—or wave of immigrants—from "making it" as they had, holding onto what they may have ruthlessly acquired for themselves. They recapitulate the repudiated European system, but justify themselves according to the American Dream with its system of "free enterprise" (which is license for opportunism rather than shared opportunity). The principle of hierarchy subverts that of individuality and collaterality. Inequality and severe restrictions on liberty are institutionalized, and social ladders and social distance scales become the measure of relationships.

In the struggle between father and son, one becomes the father one succeeded and defends against the next threatening wave of sons or immigrants. Although fathers envy the success of their own children, the oedipal conflict of sons and fathers is largely *displaced,* as fathers ambivalently encourage their own sons' success, while usurping the future of the sons of other fathers. Likewise, the competition of the sons is displaced from one's own father to other fathers. The conflict between father and son is no longer exclusively that of Europe versus America, respectively, but within America as well in the struggle between the recent natives (by naturalization and birth) and the new immigrants (e.g., blacks, Appalachians, Puerto Ricans, Mexican-Americans, and American Indians). A perennial source of fear is the immigrant who personifies the father who will limit, corrupt, or destroy all the freedoms and prerogatives of the sons. Newly native fathers and sons identify with one another as sons against the antagonist, the representation of the *ancien régime*. It is likewise a struggle of one son against another, those searching for the promised freedom in the promised land, and those who tenaciously cling to their freedoms and gains in the advance of new claimants.

From the early days of football in America (and derived from the English concept of fair play), the following slogan portrayed the ideal: "It's not whether you win or lose, but how you play the game." On the other hand, in the reality of the blood and guts of the gridiron and other games in American life that are played for keeps, the slogan and rule is coach Vince Lombardi's "Winning the game isn't everything; it's the only thing." The former applies to the American Dream and the latter, to the conformist model, according to which the stakes for freedom, success, and achievement are very high. It's all or nothing, for one is *either* a success *or* a failure. Recall Senator Barry Goldwater's 1964 aphorism that "extremism in the defense of liberty is no vice." If one is extreme in the defense of freedom, one is equally extreme in the attempt to attain it and other American goals as well.

Parents, teachers, and politicians of every era appeal to the American Dream and may firmly believe they are acting in accordance with its principles. What they frequently do, however, is in accordance with the antagonist of the Melting Pot, namely, conformism, though they would vehemently deny it. Similarly, the white ethnics today are the new nativists who are defending America as much as they are denouncing it for its failure to consummate the American Dream. The conformism model is implicit in the pithy slogan "America: Love it or Leave it," uttered by those who say in close succession that "You don't bite the hand that feeds you." In the operant ethos of hierarchy, lineality, and authority, the *European* past continues to subvert the *American* present and future; the revolution of the sons is undermined by the atavism of the fathers, not only between generations, but within each generation as well. The American Dream and American conformity are competing poles of American culture that have been in a dialectical relationship since the first ship sailed from England.

Throughout American culture history, every advance toward greater freedom, liberty, and egalitarianism is subverted before it can reach fruition. Invariably the conservative-hierarchic cancelled out whatever gains were made by individualism or collaterality. Indeed, the ideal of individuation and autonomy became distorted into the egoism of the self-made man, and voluntaristic groupism became a means of advancing the interests of one collectivity against those of another. In a revealing passage, David Danzig personified the *American Dilemma* which he was discussing; he succinctly articulated the dualistic pattern of American culture.

> In one set of circumstances, we strive to live up to the principle "regardless of race, color, and creed"; in other circumstances, *race, color, and creed* are the very principles by which human relationships are organized. Gunnar Myrdal in my view failed to understand American society when he assumed that this contradictory behavior reflected a moral dilemma. On the contrary, this is the accepted differentiated structure of our social order.[28]

The American Dilemma evaporates through nullification—that is, there is no dilemma, and anyone who says there is simply misunderstands American culture. Danzig's statement encapsulates the *compartmentalization* within American culture that nullifies the dilemma by saying that different rules apply to different situations. He is able to have it both ways and denies any ambivalence (read: dilemma). Race, color, and creed make no difference; yet they do make a difference: it is all a matter of context. Danzig ascribed to Myrdal the view that the dilemma is a matter of conscious contradiction that has become a moral issue. To Myrdal, however, the dilemma was a matter of unconscious contradictory patterns in the culture. The reason for the dilemma is that according to the *national creed,* the right to "life, liberty, and the pursuit of happiness" is unconditioned by categories of "race, color, and creed." That is, contrary to Danzig, the national ideal claims and promises to operate *for all sets of circumstances.* In the perspective of the national ideal, "race, color, and creed" are empty sets or empty symbols which do not serve as a basis for social differentiation—or discrimination. This inherently integrationist, or Melting Pot, creed transcends distinctions between *them* and *us; they* are one of *us,* and *we* together constitute the inclusive category *American.* These then are the explicit assumptions and promised consequences of the American ideology.

The dilemma persists because the national ideals can be neither consummated nor revoked, while the operant system of values opposes the idealized. Any conflict between the two is resolved (and repeatedly resolved) by denying the discrepancy, rationalizing any failure by "discovering" individual or group characteristics that contributed to it. The chronic ambivalence, anxiety, and guilt let one realize that any system of compartmentalization, rationalization, or physical segregation will constantly have to be shored up. The defenses are threatened by what they defend against, therefore requiring constant reinforcing. Precisely because the racial dilemma exists, the white American South has spent nearly three centuries—in everything from the insularity of family life to the self-justification of fundamentalist religion—trying to keep everyone in his place and rationalizing why, according to the laws of God and man, it should be so. Guilt, however, unerringly undermines protestations of innocence and makes them more necessary and frequent. Physical separation from the objects of ambivalence puts them "out of sight and mind," but it now becomes necessary to insure that boundaries will not be violated. Affective, cognitive, and physical separation go together.

Until 1965, the North was able to sustain an easy conscience by living off the bad conscience of the South. Defining itself by opposition, just as the South did, the North was everything that the South was *not:* liberal, open, inclusive, mobile, and untrammeled by doctrines and practices of racial purity. Many of our Polish- and Slovak-American informants insist they only "walked into a country that was already racist," emphasizing that as children they played with the black or "colored" children who lived near them and had lunch at their houses. The black and white children also had fights with each other and always made up, and took turns looking out for the police when crap games were played. But there were limits, and *everybody* knew what the limits were. As one of the informants stated: "What is wrong with America today is nobody knows their place any more." Thus interaction without integration was taking place, and everyone was free to compete in the same arena, creating the illusion of equality. Were it not for its own ambivalence and guilt, what would have motivated the North—with its generations of political, theological, and civil abolitionsts—to criticize continuously and stigmatize the South? Is not the South the "bad self" of the North, a displacement which has enabled the North to maintain its innocence and moral superiority? If the North did not also have the Black Dilemma, why did it have to protest its liberalism so doggedly? The white North and the white South are, therefore, intranational variations on the same theme of caste—*and* reciprocal phobic-psychopathic dissociation.

When the black integrationist apostle of militant nonviolence, Dr. Martin Luther King, Jr., said, "I have a dream," that dream was not shared by most white Americans, including white ethnics. When many black and white citizens sang "We Shall Overcome," most whites redoubled their efforts to make certain that the boundaries separating them would *not* be overcome. What is promised is not only not lived up to, but the nature of the promise is changed, and the original meaning denied. The double meaning makes it impossible to become an *American* although becoming an American is seen as the highest good—"free at last."

What the immigrant ethnics sought for themselves, they denied to the blacks. Equality, for them, meant becoming an American, and *American* meant *white*. The Melting Pot ideal of integration, unlike that of assimilation that implied Anglo-conformity, was not unidirectional, from ethnic to Anglo. For integration to work, mutual melting was necessary. More technically, cultural diffusion would have to flow considerably in both directions, and all social boundaries would have to be eliminated. For all immigrants to the United States, as well as for blacks, this is what the image, the promise, and the hope was. But the fact that universalist *and* particularist, achievement *and* ascriptive criteria were employed to determine eligibility meant that one could never do enough, even though one was told directly and through legend that by doing, one could achieve anything. Ascriptivist, particularist, hierarchical rules and values openly and subtly undermine and disqualify the more publicly heralded rules and values, while the latter deny that the former exist. The American Dilemma persists throughout the continuum of those who have succeeded in "passing," and constantly fear being found out; those who have "made it" to some degree, but could not pass; finally, to those who defend themselves against failure by lowering their ceiling of aspiration, seeking neither to make it nor to pass. But the wider process of "making it" involves more than passing, hiding, and imitation—although the apologists of the New Ethnicity would like to make the dynamics of Americanization appear that simple. Here, issues of status, initiative, power, mastery, and self-esteem all become intertwined; and the decision "to pass or not to pass" (with an infinite variety of gradations from clothing style to name change) becomes one among many means to an end occluded by the persistence of the outer dilemma and the inner self-doubt.

The problem was vividly present in the person of Thomas Jefferson, who, in helping to write the new rules for the nation of the New Man, also sought to pass as an enlightened, far-sighted social reformer. Passing, in this sense, did not require an external reference group, nor was it simply a matter of fooling himself; rather, it denotes Jefferson's new self-representation of himself *as American.* He was one of the creators of the new reference group. He combined the new American identity with the old English identity and was much troubled about the presence of the old identity in himself, since he was one of the articulators of the new identity and a prime mover of cultural transformation. Jefferson wanted to throw off the vestiges of the past in the service of the future, but was unable to be wholeheartedly committed to either. He personifies in many ways the contradictions that have pervaded the American identity from the outset: Democrat and aristocrat; restrained Whig and passionate revolutionary; slaveholder and polemicist against slavery; conservative and ideologue of the Enlightenment and Age of Reason.

In a brilliant review essay Alfred Kazin writes of Jefferson "not as a hypocrite, but as a self-defeating Virginian who wanted to do better, but did not always know what he wanted."

> The contradictions of Jefferson's life and thought . . . have to do, as Winthrop Jordan suggested in "White over Black," with Jefferson's fixed belief in progress. The future would take care of itself. . . . He tried to be the super-rationalist of American history—and instead became its ideologist. Jefferson was not merely a Deist, rationalist, emancipationist, and total "progressive" in the

Enlightenment's sense of the word, who happened to become a leading actor in American history and contradicted himself. His mental insistency was severe and I suspect he saw his life as representative of his sacred thought, so that he viewed life everywhere in terms of certain imperatives that of course he could not fulfil. Jefferson fled from all tragedy, in his own way, by assuring himself that destiny was with Americans all the way. The Deist good . . . was as clear as a watch. . . . Jefferson escaped into the future.[29]

While there is much in the essay about Jefferson that at first glance seems specific to southern regionalism, it is a variant on the national identity and not restricted to the single region in which it reaches cultural climax. The dilemma which Kazin described is accentuated in the South, and this very emphasis serves as the basis for stereotyping, dissociation, and moralism from the non-South. It is, however, significant that many of the leading founding fathers of the Revolution and the Republic were southern aristocrats who were troubled about the legacy of slavery in the future of a democracy. The almost impersonal belief in reason, progress, destiny, and common sense removed both the guilt and the personal responsibility for bringing the new ideals into practice and eradicating the inconsistencies. Thus independence and freedom would always remain a declaration, a distant ideal, rather than the basis in value for operant reality. Reality, therefore, would remain recalcitrantly traditional, conservative, and, in eras of conflict, reactionary and atavistic. The revolutionary ideal would be proclaimed, recited, and even reenacted in the rituals of nationally sacred occasions. Despite revolutionary idealism, hierarchic archaisms undermined the ethos of "life, liberty, and the pursuit of happiness." They were at constant war with one another in a historical dialectic of progress, versus backlash, or reaction, or they were uneasily compartmentalized in the same personality and cultural historic era. It was not unusual for outspoken liberals to be crypto-conservatives, and vice versa, or for conversions from one extreme to the other to take place. The unresolved conflict pattern within the American ethos can be seen from the dilemma of Jefferson, through the Civil War Reconstruction and its "backlash" of Jim Crow, through the attempt at integration and the War on Poverty of the mid-1960s.

What we cannot live, we idealize by setting up icons, myths of noble origin and destiny. Liberations and revolutions reinstate what they have dethroned. The repressed recurrently return in each newly socialized generation of Americans. What was long ago banished becomes a secret, yet forbidden, attraction. Hence the American fascination with monarchy and royalty, social class and descent, father-hood and kingship, order and hierarchy. The American Dilemma of black, Jewish, Catholic, ethnic, and of any other socially classified group of whatever American historic period is a functional conse-quence of the radical ideology of freedom, competition, and self-reli-ance that was a means of nullifying the past, yet which generated the relentless search for the certainty and security of place, ancestry, order, and hierarchy. Consequently, Americans are as intolerant of human differences as their preimmigrant forebears were.

The phenomenon of suspicion toward the stranger or newcomer is a human universal. Human cultures determine how, and if, the distance is overcome. American culture is infinitely open, flexible, and expan-sively welcoming because of its revolutionary ideology and idealism; it is also closed, rigid, exclusive, and distrustful because of the uncer-tainties in the American identity. Each new immigrant lives out this conflict. In the unending succession of immigrants (now encompass-ing such internal migrants to the city as blacks, Chicanos, Puerto Ricans, and American Indians and such new immigrants as Bangla-deshis and Vietnamese), the reception accorded newcomers has re-mained remarkably unchanged. In a *New York Times Magazine* es-say, Michael Novak quotes the response of a resident of Rosedale, Queens, to Bill Moyers's question concerning why he wanted to keep blacks out of his neighborhood:

> If you really want to know, they're basically uncivilized. Wherever they go, the crime rate goes up, neighborhoods fall apart, whites have to leave. Well, we don't share their life-style and we're not going to live with them. Rosedale is the last white stronghold in this city and nobody's going to push us out. We're going to keep it crime-free, clean and white. If that's racism, make the most of it.

How *timelessly* American this remark is, applicable to every wave of "alien" and "foreigner." How reminiscent of the defiant siege-psy-chology of the earliest Puritans and frontiersmen who invented the myth of the invading savages who were out only to molest and murder them![30] And how such abiding myths insinuate themselves into foreign policy, so that, as Lyndon Johnson saw it, South Vietnam came out looking like the Alamo. In the remark of the Rosedale resident is expressed the language of the *generic* American Dilemma, directed at its most conspicuous outcasts.

Nowhere is this dilemma more clearly updated than in President Jimmy Carter's remark on ethnic purity, made in Indianapolis during April 1976 (immediately preceding the Pennsylvania primary). While supporting open-housing, he said he opposed government programs designed "to inject black families into a white neighborhood just to create some sort of integration. I have nothing against a community that is made up of people who are Polish, or who are Czechoslovakians, or who are French Canadians, or who are blacks trying to maintain the ethnic purity of their neighborhoods. This is a natural inclination." Subsequently, reporters pressed him to clarify what he meant by *ethnic purity*. His usual public calm and geniality gave way to profuse sweat, anger, and obstinate digging-in. He spoke of the "black intrusion," of "alien groups," and of a "diametrically opposite kind of family," presumably upsetting the integrity of a settled neighborhood.[31]

It would be unfair to speak of Carter as a racist and white supremacist in the style of a George Wallace. Rather, he personifies the American Dilemma in its southern Progressivist form. Unlike Wallace (who with consummate demagoguery appeals to people's fears, claiming to be the one who will magically dispel them by putting the bad guys in their places), Carter conveys a public image of a quiet person in whom evangelical spirituality and a compassionate political philosophy are fused. It is precisely the innocence and spontaneity of his remarks on ethnic purity that allow us to connect them with the ambivalent wellsprings of the American Dilemma, in the context of a cultural climate that encouraged the expression of seemingly unspeakable social doctrines.

On the one hand, Carter emphasizes the right of the individual to move and live wherever he wishes; a policy of open-housing would express (and presumably enforce) this right. On the other hand, neighborhoods based on some notion of ethnic homogeneity have the equal right to maintain their integrity, whose ultimate corporate expression is that of inclusion and exclusion. An American right vies with a seemingly "natural inclination." It is not difficult to predict which would prevail, given the word choice used in describing each side. We might question the degree of voluntarism that entered into the formation of such currently "natural" enclaves or ghettos—whether white ethnic, Catholic, Jewish, black, Chicano, or otherwise. Some groups are more eager to preserve their current homogeneity than others, whereas others are anxious to leave where they have not chosen to reside in the first place!

The American Dilemma concerning human dignity, equality, liberty, hierarchy, and status is thus posed anew. When it comes to priorities, groups—which curiously seem to be independent of the individuals that constitute them—have a greater power of choice than mere individuals. Groups—certain groups, to be sure—have more compelling rights than individuals. We wonder if it is possible to discriminate in favor of groups without discriminating against individuals. Or is the unspoken goal behind much of the pluralist cant perhaps to favor individuals of specified groups to the detriment of those belonging to less favored ones? Ultimately, it is the insistence on purity itself that is the greatest threat to individuality—and to the American Dream itself.

3 From Rising Expectations to Unfulfilled Ambitions

The New Ethnicity can be traced, almost without exception, to the failure and disillusionment with the American Dream by adherents to its ideology and by its analysts. In this chapter we explore the American Dream and the myth of the Melting Pot in the periods in which they were virtually assured of success, World War II, the New Frontier, and the Great Society. We ask how they almost succeeded and how, paradoxically, the roots of their failure lay in the hazards of success. We trace the unfolding of the culture historical process that links illusion with disillusionment and, in later chapters, explore the White Ethnic Movement as a response to this dissatisfaction.

The American Dream, as we know it and as it has always been, is something of a fugitive vision, a forbidden quest that must be defeated even as it is earnestly and ruthlessly sought. The American Dream seemingly cannot be permitted to succeed or to fail. In failure lie the seeds of the attempt to succeed by a new means; success generates the seeds of its own undoing and self-destruction. The era of World War I and the presidency of John F. Kennedy opened an abyss of freedom and liberation, from libidinal to political, whose promise could not be allowed to happen by the very persons who sought it. We shall argue that the onslaught of assassinations and other external dramatic and traumatic events provided justification for the inner psychological change whose personal motivation could be denied, and blame for failure could be projected and displaced onto outer sources and events. Near the conclusion of Jean-Paul Sartre's play *The Flies,* the condemned liberator Orestes exclaims: "A crime that its doer disowns becomes ownerless—no man's crime; that's how you see it, isn't it? More like an accident than a crime?" This insight captures better than any other we know the internal representation of events from the assassinations of American liberators to the twilight of the American Dream.

While many accept disillusionment as the key to the withdrawal of belief in the American Dream, our proposal that those who had dreamed the longest and worked the hardest were tacit accomplices in their own undoing may be thoroughly repulsive and disgusting—in the visceral sense. This hypothesis seems to contradict everything in our experience and at first was as unlikely to the writers as it may be to the reader. We ask only that the reader suspend his or her radical disbelief, just as we have had to do to consider the hypothesis plausible. As we noted in our Introduction, Otto von Mering once said: "Unwelcome truth is better than cherished error." We must, in the spirit of science rather than ideology, pursue what seems to be true rather than adhere to and rationalize what we may have wished to believe.

The Liberation of World War II
and the Pursuit of Happiness

The periods of the New Frontier and the Great Society represented the culmination or *culture climax* of a spirit released by World War II, a descendant of the American ethos that can be traced to the ideals of the Revolution. The Kennedy spirit seems totally unlikely without this preparation. The results of five years of research among white-ethnic Americans, combined with a careful reading of social history from "official" to "folk," impressed on us the fact that the war was the great opportunity to make a decisive break with the suffocating insularity of the ghetto. As novelist Mario Puzo wrote in *The Immigrant Experience: The Anguish of Becoming American:*

> I was delivered. When World War II broke out I was delighted. There is no other word, terrible as it may sound. My country called. I was delivered from my mother, my family, the girl I was loving but did not love. And delivered WITHOUT GUILT. Heroically. My country called, ordered me to defend it. I must have been one of millions, sons, husbands, fathers, lovers, making their innocent getaway from baffled loved ones. And what an escape it was. The war made all my dreams come true. I drove a jeep, toured Europe, had love affairs, found a wife, and lived the material for my first novel.[1]

One might say that World War II was to the urban ethnic ghetto in the United States what Napoleon and the French army were to the

Jewish ghetto in nineteenth-century Europe. The war provided the opportunity to escape, in one immense leap, the constraints and ties of family, neighborhood, religion, and ethnic group. In a sense, it meant instant mobility, and the ghetto-dweller seized the opportunity for rapid acculturation. The camaraderie of training camp, the commingling of blood shed on the battlefield, and the widening of human ties on the production line made the Melting Pot a reality. The war effort became the great crucible of amalgamation, in common defense of freedom, out of which the American would emerge. Fierce American patriotism was the prevailing ideology as ethnic group competed with ethnic group, and steel mill with steel mill, to buy more war bonds to make more armaments—in defense of American freedom and independence against a common authoritarian enemy. What one aspired to was to be an American. The eschatological drama of the Melting Pot became a personally sought, and culturally sanctioned, ritual of conversion whose final outcome would be the development of the New Man, the American. For those who grew up in the urban ethnic ghetto, the wartime experience was the opportunity to be self-made, autonomous, and independent. World War II functioned as an intense expression of this rite, a literal trial by fire out of which emerged the supraethnic American personality.

The war was decisive in changing the structure of the ethnic community and the personalities of its members who participated in the war effort. However, the war itself did not cause this change, rather it accelerated the *rate* and *direction* (i.e., Americanization) of the change. It acted as a catalyst upon elements that were already, though slowly, in reaction. Here the Great Depression and World War II can be seen as similar forces, which acted in opposite directions. With the end of World War I, and through the 1920s, the immigrants and their children had already begun purchasing homes no longer in the enclave on the flood plain and adjacent to the mill, but up on the hill. However, the depression retarded the process because of the immigrants' reliance upon minimal resources, which were in the common hands of the family. The ancient ethic of group reliance and dependence was rigorously adhered to. But when the depression began to subside, the old structures and strictures continued giving way, slowly. World War II had the opposite effect, beginning on the heels of the improving economy of the late 1930s.

The *liberating* effect—at least until the men returned home—of the war upon the escapees from the ethnic enclaves was conveyed in a conversation Stein had with a McKeesport, Pennsylvania, Protestant funeral director and a Presbyterian minister of Slavic ancestry.

Funeral Director: The war changed everything. When you were in the service, a rabbi might be in charge, or a preacher or a priest, but you all went. They discovered that all blood was the same color. They threw out all that crap they learned at home and from their priests. Before the war, they had grown up in their little groups, they were all clannish. The priests had them under strict control. His word was law, and you listened to him, and did what he said. It's only since the end of the war that things have changed. It used to be that when a Protestant married a Catholic girl, he had to convert to the Catholic church and sign a paper promising that the children would be brought up Catholic. . . . Those priests used to control their whole lives. . . . But things are changing quick now. . . . The older priests had to hold their people in check, keep them under strict control. That's easing a lot now because the people aren't taking that crap from them anymore. They've seen enough not to buy it. I went into the service in 1941 and came out in 1946, and there was a complete change in the church during this time.

Minister: Their attitudes changed during this experience. A lot of men (in their fifties) that I visit in the hospital are still working through some of the trauma of the war experience. They tell me that the war changed their life. They were all melted together. They became one solid group of men fighting.

Funeral Director: Sure, it brought people together who had never been together before. Before, everyone was in their own little group, held tight by the priests. During the war, everyone got to know everyone else, and the old barriers fell apart. They saw that everyone was human just like them, their blood was all red.

The war afforded a way of openly affirming (and asserting through proof) that one was an American. The Slavic-Americans sought eagerly to remove from the wider community's eyes (and from their own) the belief that they were foreigners and not Americans, still *they* and not *we*. Slavic-Americans, as well as all other immigrant groups and descendants of the new immigration, outdid themselves and sought to outdo everyone else. They were, in a way, "more American than the [native] Americans." Those on the war front and on the home front were valiant defenders of the nation and the ideal, proving their loyalty and patriotism through ceaseless effort and sacrifice. From the intense initiation rite of the war, they emerged tried and tested as Americans.

The armed services had provided another function long in the hands of the ethnic fraternals and clubs: that of exclusive men's groups, though now ethnically mixed. Such exclusiveness, especially in the context of the military, afforded the demonstration of traditional male virtues (hard work, endurance, dedication, and physical prowess) unencumbered by the threat of dependency-evoking, controlling, and ridiculing women. Many Slavic men who fought overseas recall lustily their sexual adventures and exploits; how in the theater of battle, unlike at home, they could "love 'em and leave 'em." At the front, at least they did not have to be dependent on mothers and wives. Here women did not dominate and ridicule them. The war context likewise afforded the displacement and acting out of hostile and rebellious fantasies *directed against an authoritarian enemy in the name of democracy and independence.* Furthermore, the male group-orientation afforded a simultaneous sense of independence and peer solidarity as individual conscience was willingly suspended and one's character *restructured* according to the demands of the situation. Yet the very situation not only imposed new discipline but facilitated the *expression* of dimensions of one's traditional personality that had been repressed and suppressed.

Many Slovak- and Polish-Americans nostalgically recount their wartime experiences, how and where they "counted coup" on enemy and woman alike (and in many respects, women too were there to be conquered). The virginal, Madonna-like women were back home. Women on the war front were "women of the evening" to whom the rules of church and pedestal did not apply. Discussions of sexual exploits invariably became wistful boasts and counterboasts (always with a twinkle in the eye). Those Slovak- and Polish-Americans with whom we discussed their wartime experiences spoke of the war years as the best periods of their lives, the freest, and the most exciting. We talked with them in their homes and in their current refuges—the ethnic fraternal clubs, the service-related clubs, and in other voluntary associations such as the Eagles, the Moose, and the Elks. In these male retreats, contemporary versions of the primitive "men's houses," they continue to relive the war by retelling stories of the "good old days." The tales are almost stereotypic: the war was liberating; the return home, much as it was longed for during the lonely days overseas, was a letdown. In a way, the memory of World War II, even Korea, keeps the veterans going as an antidote to the boredom and constriction of wife, family, and the respectability of their present lives. They only need to drink some beer or hard liquor in the company of their fellows to cast off temporarily the bondage of current reality (which, in other contexts, they would vehemently defend) and return to the rose-colored past when manhood ruled supreme.

They are devotees of television reruns of action movies and current serials—from Gary Cooper, John Wayne, and Erroll Flynn adventures to the tough, individualistic (and wistfully sentimental) Tennessee sheriff, Buford Pusser (*Walking Tall,* parts 1 and 2), General George Patton, Don Vito Corleone and son (*The Godfather,* parts 1 and 2), and a variety of television supercops such as "Kojak." The veterans' current preoccupation with militant blacks and the defiant New Left, and with crime and violence in general may be still another expression of their longing for *action* and their need to repress that wish, and oppress those who seemingly act upon what is forbidden.

At the conclusion of the war, to return to one's Slovak or Polish mother, parish, or enclave as though nothing had happened was impossible. The war had changed their outlook, widened their network of associations, and had given them a freedom that stood out in even greater contrast in comparison with the constrictions of the ethnic ghetto. The men could enjoy the forbidden because it was thrust on them. But when they came back, those who had tasted the fruit had to pay the price of additional shame and guilt. Those who atoned for what they had done still could not forget what they had once enjoyed. From the safety of their present-day neighborhoods, they talk of the war as though it were yesterday, wishing it would resume tomorrow.

A third-generation Polish-American in his mid-fifties spoke to Hill about the war and its aftermath:

I was with a communications outfit in Europe. They put me there because I had electronics at a trade school near here and because I could understand and speak Polish. I did some translating whenever I got the chance. You want to see my uniform? It's hanging right back there in the closet in a plastic bag. . . . It was really something [the war]. I got to see lots of things. It was the best time of my life. . . . [But] when I got back after the war [at age thirty] there was a recession, and I couldn't find a job in electronics. I finally found a job in a factory [within blocks of the natal residence] making boxes. Mother was still working at the mattress factory [his father had died when he was five]. So I told her, "Either I quit working or you quit. One of us has to be home." Besides the shifts were all screwed up. I was on the afternoon shift, and she was on the morning shift. [Later, as if in repudiation of his decision to return home to the enclave and his mother, and with a Where did I go wrong? sentiment, he reflected:] I should have left the Hill [Polish Hill] a long time ago. Things might have been better if I had gone to Carnegie [an industrial town about an hour's drive away].

In other words, he returned after the war, but regretted it. He wistfully offered to pull out his uniform to show that he had been elsewhere, and later he mentioned that he should have moved away from the enclave and his mother. In another session, the veteran spoke similarly of the breakaway from his mother afforded by his marriage, three years after the war, to a woman he met at the box factory: "My mother was against it, but I got married anyway, and my younger brother was left holding the bag." Yet he brought his new wife to live in his mother's home where they lived in a constant state of conflict until the mother's death a few years ago, at age eighty-one.

In some way, many who have returned from the war either changed the enclave itself (as agents of Americanization) or left. Some, by taking advantage of educational opportunities within the service or by utilizing the G. I. Bill, learned a trade or got an education and did not return to the enclave, save for visits. Many decided to make a career out of the services, while others, undecided whether to return home, deferred the decision by reenlisting. Those who did return became the vanguard of the demand for modernization and Americanization of all the institutions. It is not merely coincidental that the war and postwar periods marked the sharpest increase in out-marriage, including wives acquired in the various campaigns of the war.

It would appear that there are many types of compromise and different prices for each. Those who returned and stayed wished they could have left. Those who left look nostalgically, guilt-ridden, at what they had abandoned and at the roots they fear they have severed. There are many ways of returning and many ways of leaving. It is largely a question of *how* to return without going back and *how* to leave without going away. Earlier we quoted Italo-American novelist Mario Puzo who spoke of making his "innocent getaway" "WITHOUT GUILT." In the following passage from *The Immigrant Experience*, he tells of his return to civilian life:

> Then why five years later did I walk back into the trap with a wife and child and a civil service job I was glad to get? After five years of the life I had dreamed about, plenty of women, plenty of booze, hardly any work, interesting companions, travel, etc., why did I walk back into that cage of family and duty and a steady job?
>
> For the simple reason, of course, that I had never really escaped, not my mother, not my family, not the moral pressures of our society. Time again had done its work. I was back in my cage and I was, I think, happy.[2]

He had returned voluntarily—or, rather, involuntarily—to the *cage,*

not an insignificant metaphor seen in the context of the absolute freedom which Mario Puzo now needed to restrain and literally *confine*.
We shall discuss later the close relation between the return to the
ethnic *cage* and the search for security in the tribal *cave*.

The decision about returning was fraught with dissatisfaction and
conflict, and many who did return, bowing to their parents' pleas,
fears, and threats, today bitterly regret having "given in." What the
war had opened, the return promised to close. One second-generation
Slovak-American, now in his fifties, recalls having returned from
overseas to stay in New York City for two weeks, where he wrestled
in anguish with the decision of whether to return to make the service
a career. He spoke glowingly of the years spent in the service and
also described the numerous phone calls his father made to his hotel
in New York, alternating pleas with demands and accusations, evok-
ing pity for an aging father. He had spent an entire lifetime working
for his family—who would now dare desert him? The son "gave in,"
returned home, and has taken care of his parents ever since, hating
himself, and them, for his having submitted. The dialectic themes of
dependence and independence, authority and freedom can be dis-
cerned in the relevance of the war experience to the men's subsequent lives, and how the memory of the war is evoked to contrast
with their present lives.

The following interview fragment is from the second-eldest son in a
second-generation Slovak-American family. He lives in a rented
house about a block away from the home of his parents, now in their
late seventies, in one of the earlier Slovak neighborhoods just across
the river from the mill. A laborer in the mill, he takes pride in the fact
that his son is now in college, studying mathematics. He said: "My
children are not following in my footsteps." Embarrassed, turning his
face away, but denying the shame in the next firmly stated phrase, he
continued: "My boy is in college—it's up to him! He has to be on his
own." His account of how he was raised contrasted greatly with how
he raised his own children:

> Severe—oh yes, he [father] was, by God! Restricted to be home at
> suppertime. If he told you to work, you had better do it! There was
> no such thing as a talking to—always got the back of the hand.
> Which ever one was home—mother or father. If father was work-
> ing, mother was the boss. If you weren't in time for supper, you
> just went to bed after a snack. Equal everybody—no patsy in the
> family. We *respected* our parents no matter how many lickens we
> got. We always check to see if they need something. . . . Mother

was very gentle—which my father wasn't! He put the law down. No ifs. It's still his way, right or wrong, no in-between. If you got punished and it's not your fault, he never apologized. At home, love never was much—shown. I got interested in playing with friends of Slovak background. Today definitely not—I'm with people in the mill, mixed nationalities. We belong to the Swedish Club—there's a mixture there. Sign up to be a member, just apply.

[Stein asked him, if in his own children, one son and one daughter, there were any signs of rebellion.] No rebellion against the parents. I blame myself for the kids' rebellion. We try to make it easy on our children. It backfired. We tell them to do something, and they come back with "As soon as I have time." Back then, you did it when you was told! Our clothes were all hand-me-down. Now when the child want a "Barracuda"—a fancy sports jacket— you have to get it for them. My boy in high school wanted a "Barracuda." I first said no—he didn't need it. I gave in to him in a week. My wife said: "Let him have it—it's the style."

[Stein asked him what sort of label he would give himself—Slovak, American, American Slovak, Slovak-American, etc.] American Slovak. My wife is German. She isn't interested in Germany any more. We were married in 1948. I was in the service seven years, 1941–1948. In the Thirty-fifth Infantry. After the war, I enlisted three years. The war experience changed my life! Over there you had more responsibility. Family, parents didn't dominate you. You had to survive on your own. It would be the loss of your own life. When I grew up, they were dominant. The Slovak people all stick together. You had to marry a Slovak girl! [He proudly smiled and then said:] Nobody's going to dominate our life. We got together and decided. For fifty years if you didn't marry a Slovak girl, you were disinherited. My parents tried to arrange for my older brother. They didn't succeed. He still married a Croatian girl. We just told our mother—there was no use in feeling mad. She already lived her life. It might be a mistake, but do it yourself—I will take the responsibility.

Note in the above excerpt some important polarities which World War II set in bold relief. On the one hand, he has decisively broken with the family and with Slovak traditions by: marrying a German; sending his children to public school (he had been sent through all eight grades of Slovak Catholic School); encouraging his children to be independent and above all not to take after their father; being an indulgent parent (in contrast with his father's arbitrary authority and a mother who gave only what *she* wanted to give); setting no limits (in contrast with his experience of endless and severe restrictions as a boy); and never punishing his children (in contrast with the frequent, often unwarranted, punishment that he endured as a child). We might add that his rejection of the traditional severe male role—hence his father—is more radical than usual, since he takes great joy in cooking and imagines himself someday as a restaurant chef. As a boy, he recalled experimenting in the kitchen when no one was at home, being careful to clean up all traces of food before his parents arrived. Today he does most of the cooking at home for his family.

On the other side of this dialectic of polarities is the fact that the informant chose to live and raise his children in the same ethnic neighborhood where he grew up; he frequently visits his parents and tends to their slightest need; he continues to feel very positive about the annual Christmas Eve dinner that is held at his parents' home, symbolizing family unity and parental authority; he continues to attend the Slovak Catholic church, although he dropped out of the Slovak fraternals twenty years ago and joined the Swedish Club and a local American social club in the interim; and although he insists his children have never rebelled, he links rebellion with his indulgent behavior toward them, as if he were asking or expecting them to rebel, encouraging such behavior while condemning it. Uneasy about his own independence, the informant fostered in his children all that he wished to be but dared not become—the negative identity, in short. He is not particularly happy with the result, and he blames himself for having raised the children according to his wishes rather than his conscience. Through his wife, he has permitted his children to "get away with" more than he would have directly allowed, indicating that an aspect of his unconscious allows him to be lenient and to recoil from the effects of leniency. Restitution is paid for his own guilt by living within earshot of his parents, to whose every whim he now caters. He is not aware of the New Ethnicity, nor did he vote for George Wallace, although he more than agrees with the need to restore order, respect, and authority—to whose undermining he has more than contributed.

The Triumph of the Son

What the war effort had catalyzed was unleashed within the United States and globally. Humanitarian, ecumenical, and integrationist movements, at least for a time, prevailed, and the United States became a model for emulation. It is no coincidence that the Civil Rights Movement by blacks closely followed World War II (as did a "world integrationist movement," the United Nations, and interfaith ecumenism). The discrepancy between the ideal and the real became apparent in the war effort itself, leading to the riots in the service and the cities. The war had heightened idealism and expectancy; surely a nation that fought and defeated nazism and fascism ought to practice democracy and egalitarianism at home. The changes beginning in the 1950s were an attempt to translate the ideal into reality by transforming society itself and demanding that it live up to its promises. The postwar era, climaxing with the Kennedy frontier, promised the realization of the American Dream. The only limits were the imagination and the boundless will. The war had radically opened up an abyss of freedom, a freedom which many Americans later feared they could not contain.

Recalling the tumultuous movement of the 1960s, Michael Novak, then one of its participants and articulators (and now a leader of the White Ethnic Movement), wrote recently: "It is as though an abyss had opened up, as if many peered into it, and as if the prospect of chaos and struggles was too terrifying to sustain; all have drawn back. The struggle is unresolved as many reconsider, reassess, redefine themselves. The sixties were a fevered time, dreamlike, nightmarish to protagonists on every side."[3] The "abyss," we suggest, was the liberation and freedom that were released in the youthful zeal of the Kennedy era. The recoiling from that abyss is an escape from freedom and responsibility (in Erich Fromm's sense), and the erection of defenses that will close the abyss with finality. The aftermath of the 1960s is marked by the vengeance of repression and atavistic attempts at restitution by idealizing a time "before the fall," before guilt—before Americanization. The present period, exacerbated by the economic crisis but not reducible to it, is the historic return of the repressed. Dostoevski, radical socialist turned penitent, orthodox Slavophile, said through one of his revolutionaries in *The Brothers Karamazov*, "I started out with the idea of unrestricted freedom and I have arrived at unrestricted despotism." And such is the dynamic of this period of American history. Here we explore the broader context of the current reconsiderations, reassessments, and radical self-definitions.

It is our thesis that the present crisis of American culture is characterized by the return and the vengeance of the *father,* the second act of a drama whose first act was characterized by the rebellion and temporary triumph of the *son* over the father. The oedipal conflict, we are well aware, has been invoked to explain everything from psycho-history to culture history. Abuses should not, however, be confused with uses. That a tool of insight becomes adopted for magical purposes is not new. All we ask is that the reader suspend radical disbelief, which we, in turn, have had to suspend in order for the pattern to become clear.

Although the two acts of this first drama overlap considerably, we propose that the curtain opened on the first act with the experience of World War II, began its slow descent with the assassination of John F. Kennedy, and closed with the death of Robert Kennedy, bringing to a precipitous end the first act. Using the language of the times, we shall call the first act "hope," the second act "despair"; the first act "idealism," the second act "disillusionment"; the first act "intention," the second act "rage."

If the first half of the 1960s marked the exuberant heights to which this new burst of liberation could be taken, it also marked the dizzying distance downward one could topple—but this we leave to the second act of the drama and only note that it is presaged by the triumph of the first act. The Kennedy era that began with the presidency of John and ended with the candidacy and assassination of Robert was a period of hope and expectation. It released indefatigable commitment, zeal, youthful vigor (a favorite word of the period), and a sense of limitless possibility. It opened windows and brought in fresh air—as did Pope John in the Vatican.

President Kennedy personified the American future, the fruition of the hopes from the American past. Optimism, liberalism, hope, idealism, and reformation were all personified by this single individual. The American Kingdom was to be fulfilled, not only in America, but in the world. The American Dream kindled the imagination wherever Kennedy the magician went. He spellbound audiences eager to hear the new global gospel of peace, friendship, and progress. The dashing, ambitious son would rescue the masses from the peonage and patronage imposed on them by countless decadent fathers. (The Kennedy myth and reality do not, of course, coincide: e.g., the abortive Bay of Pigs invasion and the attempt to overthrow—if not assassinate—the revolutionary Fidel Castro; the covert manipulation of the South Vietnamese government, possibly including involvement in the assassination of President Diem; and support in general for authoritarian, reactionary regimes in Latin America [Chile] and elsewhere [Greece, Turkey].) Not only did the throngs identify with him and his dream, but he identified with them as well. In Latin America, Jacqueline Kennedy spoke in the native tongue, and her audiences were delighted. In Berlin, President Kennedy said in his Bostonian German: "Ich bin ein Berliner," identifying himself with the freedom of West Berlin. He became a *Berliner,* and in so doing, symbolically made West Germans *Americans.* He bestowed freely upon them the American Dream. They saw themselves in him, and he extended himself—and his America—to them. *They* were no longer *them,* but *us;* for each, the other became also oneself. (Later, Robert Kennedy would identify with blacks and white ethnics alike—and for the same reasons would be warmly received by them.)

The era of the two Kennedys, Martin Luther King, Jr., and Malcolm X (among others) was a period of *reformation;* the second act of the drama—the era of the 1968 Chicago Democratic National Convention, the 1970 invasion of Cambodia, the Kent State and Jackson State shootings, and the 1971 Attica prison riots—would be a period of *counterreformation.* Martin F. Nolan wrote that "the Kennedy family has meant to America: upward mobility, ethnic assimilation, the generational changing of the guard in politics, assassination and national trauma, Camelot and the hope that politics can be fun again."[4] If the second act of the drama, in which we live as participants, is characterized by disillusionment, the first act of the drama embodies the illusions and idealism that had elevated President Kennedy to such a mythic and eschatological status. To say that he was a "legend in his own time" is not to repeat a cliché, but to state a fact. He had been canonized long before his assassination.

Yet it is equally true that Kennedy and his admired liberating contemporaries all met the same fates. This requires some explanation, and in the spirit of an earlier inquiry into the "silent complicity at Watergate,"[5] we shall suggest that the so-called conspiracy theory of the Kennedy assassination is true at the psychological level, irrespective of whether it is true in the literal sense. Some writers have referred to a "Kennedy neurosis," akin to a death wish; if true, it is only in part a private or personal affair because leader and follower must find, complement, and fulfill one another. We cannot talk about Kennedy without talking about a *symbiosis* with him, one that includes shared meaning and destiny. Anticipating the transition from act one to act two, we are suggesting an inexorable progression from liberation to repression, with the lineage personified by Kennedy, Johnson, and Nixon. But for now, in focusing on the Kennedy era of the New Frontier, we only remind the reader that we cannot talk about Kennedy without saying also something about ourselves: our hopes, our ideals, our dreams—and our childhoods.

It should be remembered that President Kennedy won the 1960

presidential election against his Republican opponent by a narrow margin of some 100,000 votes. The victory of the optimism and social change effused by the New Frontier over the post-McCarthyist suspiciousness of Richard M. Nixon was far from overwhelming. In the wake of the multiple assassinations, grim mistrust arose triumphant over the ashes of Camelot like the phoenix. Nevertheless, in the 1960 election, the two poles of American identity were placed in clear-cut opposition, at least ideologically: rapid social change versus fear of change; openness and expansion versus closeness and preservation; trust versus mistrust; inclusion versus exclusion; egalitarianism versus special privilege; and hope versus fear. While those favoring one pole gained temporary dominance, the forces of reaction and restoration were at work against it from the outset.

Not insignificantly, the period of the rise and presidency of John Kennedy coincided with the papacy of John XXIII (1958–1963). Thus we must recognize this period as one of global—not merely national—reform, enlightenment, liberation, and ecumenism. The adventure of space exploration provided vivid imagery for this more expansive consciousness of what would later be called "spaceship earth." The leaders, though, merely catalyzed a restless spirit, a *zeitgeist* already present and waiting to burst the confines of convention and tradition. The spirit was inherently unorthodox. The leading Western theologians of that period were Paul Tillich (Lutheran), Martin Buber and Abraham J. Heschel (Jewish), and Pierre Teilhard de Chardin (Catholic), whose particularisms all transcended their origins and reached out toward a universalism. The Canadian scholar Marshall McLuhan proclaimed the advent of the Global Village in *Understanding Media* (1964): the communication-cybernetic-technological revolution had inaugurated a new era in which all humans would be members of a single tribe. The *American* youth movement—itself part of an international one, Russian, even Chinese, not uniquely Euro-American—would later call it the Age of Aquarius under whose beneficent sign would prevail peace, love, and brotherhood. Teilhard de Chardin's *Phenomenon of Man* (completed in 1949, published in French in 1955, and in English in 1959) offered a compelling and optimistic mystical vision of the convergence and consummation of the spiritual specieshood of humankind at the Omega Point.

It should be noted that Père Teilhard was regarded with suspicion and as a near-heretic by his church (like other similarly unorthodox influential thinkers such as Erik H. Erikson, Abraham Maslow, and Weston La Barre—to name but three—in their professions). A devout French Jesuit, Père Teilhard submitted to the Curia's demand for silence on all but strictly paleontological research. Only after his death were his theological, evolutionary, and philosophical writings—fortunately placed by him in the hands of relatives—published. The guardians of reaction could not countenance a God of process rather than stasis; alas, the open-window policy and theology of John XXIII was short lived, as his successor, Paul VI, warned of the dire consequences of heterodoxy, individual decision, and the lapse of papal authority. The Vatican, too, began with a short-lived internal reformation which was soon vigorously suppressed and reversed by a counterreformation under Paul VI. If the Catholic church could not accept the evolutionary theology of Pierre Teilhard de Chardin, an eagerly awaiting world beyond the Curia and the Index embraced it.

The presentation of Pope John's encyclical *Pacem in Terris* was complemented by the youthful American Peace Corps (not as yet perceived to be an imperialist plot) that spread as an apostle of the Global Village and modernization to all corners of the planet. A civil peace corps, VISTA, was established to convey the social gospel (with techniques to help others help themselves) on American soil. In 1954 the U.S. Supreme Court declared de jure segregation to be unconstitutional and inaugurated the era of integration, an undertaking designed to resolve the American Dilemma once and for all. "We Shall Overcome" became the reformationist hymn of the Civil Rights Movement. In 1955, psychoanalyst and social philosopher Erich Fromm published *The Sane Society,* which articulated a vision and program for a humanistic and rational (as opposed to irrational) social order. During the same period, id-psychologies and sociologies were articulated by Norman O. Brown in *Life Against Death* (1959) and Herbert Marcuse in *Eros and Civilization* (1956). And in 1958, as the star of the New Frontier began to rise on the horizon, ego psychoanalyst Erik H. Erikson completed and published his psychohistory of *Young Man Luther,* the study of the Protestant Reformation written on the eve of the American Reformation! We are surely talking about convergences, not coincidences.

The American Reformation

The Kennedy era of the New Frontier marked the quiet overthrow of the old order. It was the apotheosis of youthfulness, zest, vigor, idealism, and liberalism. What had been previously repressed was in the 1960s released, liberated, and openly *exhibited* from the libido to the body politic. It was an era of supreme confidence, of wide-ranging social experimentation (from the university to public policy), and of frenetic activity and commitment. Anything willed and imagined by "the best and the brightest" could be made to work. Any notion of doubt or finitude was heretical to the visionaries and practitioners of a frontier ideology whose sense of the possible was dominated by the certitude of omnipotence and omniscience. Every problem had a solution. There was nothing that could not be managed.

The Kennedy presidency marked a new direction in American cultural and political life. His youth, his dynamism, his openness, his charm, his education, and, not the least, the fact that he as a Catholic had "made it"—these all contrasted with past leadership, with past political style. But if he "captured the imagination" of an age, it was only because large numbers of people were ready to identify with him as he was able to identify with their ideals and aspirations. His mana, or charisma, lay in the needs of his constituency which he fulfilled and personified. In the oedipal drama, Kennedy represented the replacement of the father by the son. Not only nationally, but internationally as well, he won victories over the old and decadent. In the 1962 Cuban missile crisis, he was the young American Arthurian knight calling the bluff of the old, menacing Russian Premier Khrushchev and forcing him to back down. He personified the truth of the American Dream, and in identifying with him, Kennedy followers could believe in the imminent fulfillment of that dream for themselves. The American Dream, in turn, is the fantasy of eternal youth, change, choice, progress, equality, and liberty. No longer could there persist unchallenged what Gunnar Myrdal called in the 1940s the "American Dilemma," the discrepancy between the ideal and the caste status of American blacks. All such dilemmas would have to be resolved once and for all—now. The 1954 U.S. Supreme Court decision in *Brown* v. *Board of Education* was now pressed for. The liberal, integrationist, and ecumenical climate encouraged the openness of black expression, demonstration, and demand. There was no reason to wait or to be patient any longer, for one wanted "justice now!" The prior constraining atmosphere was removed, and the social gospel took religion to the streets. All the liberation and countercultural movements *must* trace their ancestries to the permissive atmosphere which encouraged expression and catharsis.

If the 1960s marked the triumph of the myth of the self-made man and identified strongly with the young (and young at heart), then we should expect some reflection of this culture change in religion and theology, since they are, to a large degree, projections of current social structure and human relationships onto the supernatural. What we feel the gods do is an expression of how we portray ourselves. The same iconoclasm, liberalization, defiance, and hubris that characterized the New Frontier ethos proceeded to radicalize and liberalize religion and theology. Moral and dogmatic absolutes were replaced by the *situational ethic*, which in its ultimate perversion meant "do as you please" (without the Augustinian grace). Harvey Cox's *Secular City* (1965), which was meant to be the Bonhofferian and Buberian intimation of the "beyond in the midst" and "God of the moment," readily became the desecrated church and abandoned city whose legacy later became crime, corruption, and pollution of a very earthly sort, now decreed "unlivable." The crowning achievement of the New Frontier theology was the Death of God Movement, which rendered unto God what the earthly son had rendered unto the corporeal father. As a historical note, the Death of God Movement (with its countermovement "God is alive and well") was the American version of the theological debate inaugurated by the bishop of Woolwich (England), John A. T. Robinson, with his 1963 book, *Honest to God*. The movement articulated an ideological struggle that acutely reflected American cultural concerns.

Absolute human freedom and absolute human responsibility were the core of the Death of God theologies, two of whose most influential proponents were the Protestant theologians William Hamilton and Thomas J. J. Altizer.[6] According to the new reformation, human freedom was impossible as long as the transcendent Judeo-Christian and Mosaic-Pauline God-the-Father continued to exist. The Divine monarchy must be overthrown if man is to be free. The independence of the son is contingent on the banishment and death of the father, and of the conscience and Law associated with the father. The patricide and deicide associated with repudiation suggest that a mighty compensation is necessary in order to rid oneself of the tenacious hold of authority figures.

The Death of God theology was a marvelous trick of the christological imagination, resolving the oedipal ambivalence of fathers and sons without the bloody confrontation which Freud first analyzed in *Totem and Taboo* (1913). God Himself willed His incarnation and offered His very existence as the condition for human freedom. The Crucifixion became the self-sacrifice *of* God for the sake of man, His son. Through Christ, God willed His own death so that man could be free. Through Christ, *God* came to die for us. The onus of deicide is thus removed from man. The son's participation in the oedipal conflict is herewith denied and placed (or displaced and projected) in the father's (Father's) hands. As the new myth continues, the son does not kill the father to gain dominion over all the (mother) earth: the father sacrifices himself to the son. Not only is the wish denied, but the event is placed long before the birth of the radical theologians. The Father kills Himself for the sake of His beloved son by becoming a Human-Divine son as self-sacrifice of the incarnate Father to the Transcendent Father. In becoming incarnate, the Transcendent Father no longer exists, and in His Crucifixion, not only Christ, but God Himself dies. Man himself takes on the legacy of God and becomes Divine, the measure of all things. The act of theological hubris, rationalizing absolute freedom from any authority, save oneself, enacted the ancient murder of the jealous father by the envious "primal horde" of sons, recapitulating the first part of *Totem and Taboo* but disguising and obscuring the deicide through rationalization.

Following God's beneficent act, all laws were null and void, and man would have to use his knowledge and cunning wisdom according to a situational ethic. On the surface this is quite liberating, but in American culture it readily became distorted into the narcissistic self-indulgence of "do your own thing"—now, a decade later, legitimated under the more respectable slogan, *pluralism*. The self-made American was now the self-willed pinnacle of creation who, God-like, would do His work, at least in theory. But in fact, God, sin, superego, and conscience were all transvalued. The only absolute was the self-will of man. This was all done during the high noon of the American Empire, where American will and technology could accomplish anything. With God out of the way, man could be truly "self-actualized" (a vulgarization, of course, of Abraham Maslow's humanist conception of freedom, relation, and responsibility). But now that man had freedom, now that man was existentially free, what could he do with his freedom? Man was free *from*, what could he be free *for?* The son had liberated himself by banishing and eliminating the father. What would the son do with his freedom and without the father? And what would those fathers who remained make of this new freedom?

The answer was swift and relentless in coming. President Kennedy's assassination in 1963 was the first in a long series of hammer blows that lasted for five years, until every major embodiment of the American Dream was extinguished. The death of Martin Luther King, Jr., was followed immediately be the eruption of "black rage," and Robert Kennedy's death is cited by many white ethnics and their leaders as the event that caused them to lose faith in American culture and seek roots and identities in their primordial ethnic heritage. The first response to President Kennedy's assassination was one of numbness, disbelief, disorientation, and revulsion. He soon joined the company of Christ and Lincoln as martyred heroes who personified the highest ideals and aspirations of American culture. He also joined the list of those legendary figures (from Fredrick Barbarossa to James Dean) who could not die—who could not be allowed to die. As the fantasies go, Kennedy was taken to some distant hospital where he is slowly recuperating; he is still alive, although enfeebled and disfigured. He is hiding and awaits the right time to come again. The aura of expectancy surrounding Senator Edward Kennedy reflects America's wish to be able to hope again and not surrender to despair. Perhaps the Kennedy era and charisma can be resurrected. The Kennedy magic reveals a vigorous, romantic, savior son whose return will rekindle and rescue the American spirit.

The utopian cult surrounding the television science-fiction series "Star Trek" and its characters attests to the tenacity of the Kennedy-New Frontier ethos. While the television series lasted only three seasons, 1966–1968, it has spawned some fourteen books on "Star Trek," an autobiographical account by one of its leading actors (Leonard Nimoy, *I Am Not Spock,* 1975), fan clubs, national newsletters, and in the last few years, almost monthly conventions held in major cities and attracting many thousands of participants at each. At the beginning of each episode, William Shatner, who plays Captain Kirk of the starship *Enterprise,* sets the stage: "Space—the final frontier . . . to boldly go where no man has gone before. . . ." This is the language of the unfinished New Frontier, and William Shatner and Leonard Nimoy (among others) are charismatic stars who keep the legend alive. So great has been the increasing enthusiasm that a "Star Trek" movie is being undertaken, and a collection of stories, created by writers inspired by the official first-generation science fiction, was published in March 1976: *Star Trek: The New Voyages,* edited by Sondra Marshak and Myrna Culbreath.[7] The editors subtitle their introduction "The Once and Future Voyage" (paralleling "the once and future king"), and in effect reevoke the spirit of the Kennedy frontier.

Man's most shining legends of heroes always seem to carry the dream that the heroes will return again. King Arthur will rise—the once and future king. Camelot will live again, and does, at least in the minds of men.

Star Trek was just such a shining legend, for one brief moment, for a few brief years—a living legend of heroes and high deeds, of courage, glorious quests, splendid loves found and lost.

It was the most shining legend of all—man's truest legend, seen at last: the legend not of a golden age lost, but of one yet to be found.

A golden age yet to be found, never to be forgotten, always to live again; those who saw *Star Trek* in that way could not let it die . . . and did not.

They were not content to live with the memory.

They wanted to see the legend live again, real and whole, in their own time and for years to come—new voyages, new quests, new loves, new windows into that golden future yet to be found.

They fought for that.

And they won.

Through the efforts of people who love it, in a real-life saga rivaling any legend of a quest for the Grail, *Star Trek* does live again.

It will live again on the screen.

And it lives here [in this book].

These are the new voyages.[8]

For those who are nostalgic for the Kennedian Camelot, the quest is for a past that recaptures the quest of the (American) future. "Star Trek" is a tale of the American Dream in the imagery of the space age. The cult surrounding the story is an attempt to preserve, at least in fantasy, those oedipal heroes who lived far too briefly.

The conspiracy theory has been an undercurrent since the assassination of President Kennedy and has recently seen renewed interest, the interest itself expressed in wider themes of astrology, supernatural influence, and demonology. The drama must match the figure. Thus the assassination could not have been a single-handed job by Lee Harvey Oswald, a sick, deranged, pathetic human being. It must be a CIA or FBI plot, perhaps involving Fidel Castro. The Warren Report *must* be wrong. Were the assassination a one-man monstrosity, it would be meaningless. Psychologically held beliefs have not been disconfirmed by official reports from reality. Beliefs generate their own reality and their own data. The single reality that confers believable meaning on the drama of the admired and slain son is the inversion of the oedipal myth: the persistent suspicion that the father has plotted against the son. Lyndon Johnson, after all, was a father figure (which Kennedy was not) and a seasoned senator who had to play the role of *junior* or *son* in relation to the younger Kennedy, the president. More was reversed than mere social role. The fathers envied their sons, ever fearful that the sons would displace them—this the sons have always known. The fathers envy as they jealously guard. Lyndon Johnson, succeeding to the presidency, immediately became the focus of suspicion. Political scientist Arnold A. Rogow perceptively wrote the following in 1971:

> In the case of LBJ, I suspect that some part of the intense dislike for him among the youth may derive from their unconscious suspicion the he *was*, in some part, responsible for the death of John F. Kennedy. For many of the young people I suspect that at the unconscious level the death of Kennedy at the hands of persons unknown but including LBJ was experienced as the murder of a younger, more virile son by an older, impotent father, a father jealous of the son's very youth and vigor and greater success—for until November, 1963, Kennedy had never failed in anything he had attempted. If this was the case, certainly it was easy to imagine, to want to believe, that LBJ was somehow implicated and believing this, easy to hate him, to mock him, to hold him in the deepest contempt. Certainly, the popularity of *Macbird!*, the anti-Johnson jingles and buttons, the posters mocking his masculinity, and the obscene slogans, support such interpretations.[9]

The perceptions of the youth (and the not so young) were not a simple matter of projecting their inner and familial conflicts and transferring them onto external authorities and institutions ("the establishment"). The caricatures drawn were rather accurate portraits of Johnson's own obsessions and exaggerations: e.g., masculinity, pride, authority, honor, and intractability. Johnson did not have to engineer the death of his younger superior, and, in a sense, usurper whom he envied, disliked, and felt inferior to (e.g., he spoke disdainfully of "those Harvards," referring to the northeastern intellectual establishment). His personal and political style "gave away" his readiness to exploit the solemn occasion of national tragedy. What the sons feared—the eagerness of the father to replace the son who had earlier ousted him—was what the father secretly wished. President Johnson did not have to "plot"; history provided the event, although it was psychologically well prepared for. He and the eager, moralistic fathers seized upon it and, over the next decade, reversed the forces of reformation, as those of counterreformation, restoration, and counterrevolution came to prevail.

The Johnson era, it should be noted, marks the beginning of the expansion of American involvement in the Southeast Asian war. Large numbers of American sons were sent off to fight and die gloriously for a cause which their leaders and fathers had invented and rationalized, but in which the sons who made the supreme sacrifice for their fathers had no ideological commitment. On the "home front," the conflict was expressed in the estrangement and combat between university students, faculty, and administration; in the confrontation between liberal demonstrators and the police; and in the "generation gap." All authority was suspect in the rage of students and youth. In his presidential candidacy of 1964 (and as we mentioned in chapter 2), Senator Barry Goldwater had said: "Extremism in defense of liberty is no vice." The sordid excesses of the Nixon Watergate era were the answers on the Right to the revolutionary extremists on the Left (old and new) who were certain they had God and democracy on *their* side.

Michael Novak is correct in noting the following: "By invading Cambodia . . . President Nixon gave the radical movement a new lease on life; the movement depended on him for its life force. For one of the most important features of the counter-culture is its volatility; it constantly takes new directions, abandons old heroes, seeks new excitement."[10] But his observation is incomplete: Nixon and the forces of reaction needed the counterculture to embody the repressed and dissociated youth and vigor in themselves, to agitate for its rebellion and sadomasochistic rage, and to smash it overwhelmingly. Both sides needed each other, were inextricably bound up with one another, and were poles of a thoroughly interdependent system. What we emphasize here is the *reciprocal* provocation, in particular, the need for the fathers to incite the volatility and excitement of the sons and then severely punish them for having acted out.

Adding further credence to the authors' oedipal interpretation, Philip Slater inquires into the significance of the multiple assassinations of liberal leaders in the 1960s, suggesting that

> many of the assassinations of recent years—the two Kennedys, Martin Luther King, Malcolm X—may be understood . . . as actions triggered by a sense of latent community approval. Probably there is always a sizable pool of potential assassins . . . men disturbed and desperate enough both to kill a public figure and to run a very high risk of capture. When a rash of assassinations occurs we must assume that the threshold between fantasy and action has been lowered somehow—that some restraining pressure has been removed.
>
> It is probably not accidental that these recent victims were all rather young men—not conservative father figures trying to retain power and preserve old ways, but young liberals or radicals trying

to effect social change. If we make the rather safe assumption that the potential assassin is conflicted about authority, the assassination of such men satisfies both their rebellious and submissive tendencies: the assassin does not really kill authority, he kills in the *name* of authority. To one in his state of mind the hate exuded by his elders is a kind of permission. Not that the act is suggested to the assassin—it is rather that the constraining atmosphere that might have prevented his seriously entertaining the idea in the case of a conservative leader is lacking in the case of one who himself represents a challenge to established ways. In the anger and hate of older people around him the assassin finds a fertile soil in which the idea can grow instead of being extinguished.[11]

If indeed there was a "Kennedy neurosis," the ultimate outcome of which was a masochistic death wish, perhaps we can with equal plausibility speak of a "collective neurosis" which could not endure the liberation it had opened and had to eliminate its symbolic representations and representatives. Those who dreamed—and worked hard to achieve—the American Dream seemed to be working to undermine its fulfillment. The very embodiment of the American Dream was killed. The new order, the New Frontier, was not allowed to succeed. It was measured in days. The youthful leader was killed, and the machinery was set in motion to restore the old order. The presidency of John Kennedy, it seems, was "illegitimate." The victory of the son was short lived. The multiple assassinations of leaders who represented vigor, change, reform, and newness brought an end to the reformation and set in motion the forces of counterreformation: political, theological, social, and cultural.

In the second act of the drama, the vengeance of the father, and Father, would be wrought on the son. Not only were the symbolic leaders killed, but many radical and liberal advocates of change on the Left found a new niche through a conversion experience to the Right. Many former social dropouts, demonstrators, and drug addicts have converted to a new religious or political "habit" and have gained a new, ideological "high," receiving their identities from Jesus Pentecostalism, Charismatics, Billy Graham, ethnic retribalization, regimented communal living, or from the political Right. Iconoclasm and newness are replaced by the quest for absolutes and certainties, moral and religious fundamentalisms, and traditional moorings. The anarchy of rebellion is supplanted by the search for an externally imposed "law and order." Atonement; restitution; guilt; sacrifice; the totemization of the fallen leader and of newer, sterner authority; restoration; the embracing of neo-orthodox beliefs and life-styles; the search for all-embracing answers and strict codes; the rejection of relativism and the quest for fundamentalism—these characterize the bewildering variety of decisions, gestures, and resolutions of the second act of this drama of fathers and sons. The ethos of the stern, grim, moralistic, uncompromising, and dominating father has gradually crystallized and seeks legal, political, cultural, and religious representation and representatives. It is an emergent ideology in search of a figure.

Those who committed assassination, like those who tacitly sanctioned it, needed to kill a part of themselves and to restore what they had earlier usurped and violated, to renounce what they had wished but could not attain or were denied. The young radicals of the 1960s represented something that those who had tacitly condoned the assassinations wished and needed to eliminate from within themselves. The students' persistence in reality reminded them of their own wishes, ideals, anxieties, conflicts, and failures. By removing the external representation, one could magically eliminate the inner struggle. The oedipal conflict would be resolved by the elimination of the son whom one would no longer have to fear—or envy, or emulate. The murdered leaders had appealed to the highest American ideals and ethics for the realization of the American Dream for all. Even Malcolm X, after returning from his pilgrimage to Mecca, could no longer accept the black exclusiveness he had earlier embraced and, like his counterparts, developed a genuine *world* view. Dr. King's evocation of these ideals in "I Have a Dream" parallels President Kennedy's inaugural address and his posthumous book, *A Nation of Immigrants* (1964).[12]

In a period when the American Dream *seemed* realizable, why did it fail or, more importantly, why did it have to fail? Paradoxically, these leaders *demanded* too much of the conscience and *liberated* too much as well. It is fine to have a culture's highest ideals and deepest wishes appealed to—and the function of much of religious and national ritual is to do precisely this at specified times (e.g., Christmas, the Fourth of July). Here, however, what is released is also contained; the function of ritual is to disguise while expressing, to control while freeing. To attempt actively to realize these ideals and wishes, thereby removing both disguise and control, is to render cultural conflict and compartmentalization transparent because these ideals are not intended to be lived up to, and wishes are to remain only partly fulfilled. The highest values and aspirations cannot be fulfilled because they conflict with even more fundamental values. Thus we subvert our egalitarian ethic with authoritarianism, despite our best intentions.

The greatest threat to psychological and cultural stability is to release nocturnal and mythic dreams into the daylight of consciousness. It would upset the delicate compromise; what had been compartmentalized is now juxtaposed, what has "belonged" apart is suddenly together, and the discrepancy induces acute stress that demands relief. Ideals can only live as ideals, and wishes must submit to reality. Such prophetic leaders as Jesus and Lincoln, and perhaps Moses, were also victims of this unspoken rule. What is out of place must be put in its place. To return to Slater's observation in *The Pursuit of Loneliness:* "Killing in the name of authority presupposes the belief that existing authority is not the legitimate authority and does not meet psychological needs"—which partly defines *legitimacy*.

The pan-historic paradox we are dealing with is the murder of the redeemer. Redemption is as feared as it is longed for. The very agent and incarnation of redemption (liberation) became the *sacrifice* to appease and atone for those (conservative) values that would be violated and those anxieties that would be reawakened, should redemption become a reality. The unattainable ideal had to be put and kept in its place. Unleashed wishes had to recontained. Impossible demands of conscience had to be repudiated. What began as salvation ended as perdition and the quest for a new salvation that restored the compromise. The hero-as-martyr is an archetypal theme in Judeo-Christian mythology, with specifically American variants and universal underpinnings. In the christological perspective, many see Presidents Lincoln and Kennedy as having come to die, which takes the responsibility out of human hands and makes their deaths literally "acts of God." That their followers need them and must also see them die is the tragedy of such leaders.

The martyrdom of the liberal leaders of the 1960s was the collective solution to the conflict over the American Dream. We have suggested that the most dangerous ideal and wish is the success of the (liberal = liberated) son, the very basis of the myth of the self-made man—and the very reason for the American Revolution. The assassinations of youthful liberal leaders served the collective need to destroy and repress the youth, the rebellious adolescents, in the electorate, as if through these youth and their even more enthusiastic followers the older members of society relived the lost opportunities of their own earlier years. We thus have an inversion of Freud's theme in *Totem and Taboo,* namely, a conspiracy of the fathers against the sons, and later, the sons against themselves as they, in turn, become fathers.

The Revenge of the Father

If the Kennedy era of the New Frontier could be called the "rise of the son," then the subsequent period might be called "the revenge of the father" (we borrow this phrase from Peter Gay, who applied it to the later phase of *Weimar Culture*) and the "rage of both fathers and sons."[13] The exuberant idealism of reformative youth became the ugly and violent nihilism of rageful radicalism, asking for punishment when it became clear that the reformationist intentions of their elders, from university teachers and administrators to politicians, were not "for real." The reform-preaching liberals were crypto-authoritarians who were only flirting with reform, inspiring cynicism and nihilism. The ambivalence and bad faith of those in authority who had seemed genuine transformed militant nonviolence into wanton fury, construction into destruction, hope into despair, and utopian expectation into demoralization. Now, fury spent, anger had become apathy, social consciousness had become self-centeredness (what is the point of investing in a perfidious world?), mind expansion had given way to withdrawal and depression, and the urgent need to uproot became the equally desperate need to put down roots.

The cultural identity crisis of the younger generation (the sons) is matched by a reawakened identity crisis among the older generation (the fathers). In looking with envy, resentment, and disgust at what their children and youth, in general, have done, they see in these youth a mirror of their own adolescence, repressing in themselves what they could not become and suppressing in the youth what they had to repress in themselves. The fathers now look with disbelieving horror at what they deny having had any part in creating, and begin to wonder whether their lives were really worth it. Then they recoil from such overwhelming self-doubt by embracing a totalistic nationalism, ethos, or religion. Their children, in turn, confused about their parents' ambivalence, seek a source of identification that is more consistent and—so they perceive—self-confident. A *strong* grandfather or *strong* uncle is frequently chosen, one who seems to possess all the virtues which one's own parents lack. The image of the strong grandfather and the weak father offers a compelling solution.

We are thinking of a seventy-five-year-old Slovak-American immigrant and former steelworker with whom Stein became a good friend during his fieldwork in the early 1970s. Throughout our research among white-ethnic Americans, we have been struck by the frequency of the presence of a portrait or statue of John F. Kennedy, or of the Kennedy brothers, in the family shrine on a living-room wall or on top of the television set. Here are juxtaposed crucifix, Madonna, rosary, a portrait of the Holy Family, singly or in various combinations—but nearby or enveloped in them is the Kennedy presence, from dime-store photograph to bronze medallion. (We remind the reader that the presence of Kennedy portraits or statues is not limited to white ethnics. Indeed, pictures of the globally messianic figure are displayed in homes throughout the Third World.) The home of this man is filled with Americana, but Stein was most moved by one display. In a corner of the living room, on the wall, stands a small crucifix next to which is a small engraving of President Kennedy's face, and some lines from one of his speeches; a rosary is lovingly draped around both of them. More than any discussion we had, this shrine poignantly expressed the belief in Kennedy's communion with the saints and that Kennedy and Christ share a common meaning.

This man's belief in America was absolute: that, too, was the message of the shrine, the union of God and country. Starting from nothing, he had made it on his own—American style. He gave to his parents and his children what he denied to himself, allowing for himself only after they had been provided for. He bought his mother a home before he bought one for himself. He reared his children permissively, occasionally shouting at them for their disobedience, independence, and lack of respect. A kinder, gentler, more polite and more hardworking man the writer had never met. Yet he resented what the blacks, the college students, the Hippies, and the Leftist rebels were doing to America. "America, love it or leave it," and "Don't bite the hand that feeds you" were two of his most frequent mottoes. America had given him so much—and he had worked and lost and worked again for what he now had. Ingratitude was unthinkable. America was an Eden in comparison to the barren Tatra and Carpathian mountains. He had overcome years of shame and ridicule, and was now a member of the Eagles, the Moose, and the Swedish and German clubs.

As an adolescent, he had rebelled against the authoritarian atmosphere of the home and the demands of dependency to mother, church, and political machine. As an adult and as a parent, however, he could be neither permissive nor strict; he was both at once or vacillated between them. He fumed at the corruption and demands of servitude in the church, the mill, politics, and in the cleric-dominated fraternal society. He venerated the idealism and youthfulness of President Kennedy and Senator Robert Kennedy. But he was horrified at the disrespect, the sense of permissiveness, and the insolence of the younger generation of the Kennedy era. He was repulsed by what he saw of himself as acted out by those of his children or grandchildren's age. He was his own enemy, an enemy he fought in those who dared express what he was forced to repress. He had to kill his beloved American Dream and deny the right of others to attain it. He mourned the death of the Kennedys and was bewildered at the senselessness of such acts. But he had silently condoned a deed to which complicity he could never admit. Kennedy, like Christ, would remain an ideal symbolized in a perpetual shrine. The informant did not revere President Nixon, but he did *respect* him—and "respect" for those occupying legitimate authority, for one's elders, was sadly lacking. Too much freedom had led to disorder and disrespect.

Many young people agree with him. On the rebound from anarchy, they look backward to the restoration of the innocent days before rebellion and guilt. The return of the father progresses further as the son identifies with the father and represses the son within himself. Yet the fathers who denounce the current disorder precipitated it in the lives of their children because of their confusion, contradiction, and ambivalence toward their own parents, values, and ideals. They could not consistently inculcate—and serve as models of emulation for—ideals they were not fully committed to. They contravened by their behavior and attitudes the very conservatism they enforced. A generation that does not believe in itself does not inspire in its children belief, loyalty, and commitment to its avowed ideals. The demand for respect cannot command abiding respect, only obedience—and rebellion, later still, restitution. The confusion of identity crosses generational lines in both directions as each generation exacerbates the ambivalence in itself and the other. Neither what was repressed prior to World War II nor what was released in its wake and aftermath are clearly transmitted as ideals.

The reactionary and the anarchic abide and contend in the same soul. Those who are looked to for the setting of standards flaunt their violations and rationalize their poor behavior as somehow fulfilling those standards. Hence the double standards are established. Little is done "on principle"; rather, those who exhort to idealism live by expediency. Equal opportunity readily becomes equal opportunism. The uncompromising advocates of law and order (Daley, Rizzo, Nixon, Agnew, Wallace, and Reagan) are publicly moralistic (clean) and privately unscrupulous (dirty). Those who are incapable of loyalty have no trouble rallying and exploiting the loyalty of others, as the larcenous are the greatest advocates of righteousness (and those who are their eager consumers are the first to be outraged). "Integrity" becomes the motto of the psychopathic, cunning man. Cynicism prevails because neither oneself nor others are trustworthy.

Watergate and Nixon, as discussed in an earlier essay, are a microcosm of the modern oedipal drama, a drama that is far from behind us despite our eager forgetfulness. Turning for a moment to the metaphor of the *Time of Troubles* that characterized sixteenth-century Russia, would it too greatly stretch the imagination to envision Lyndon Johnson as the American culture-historical equivalent of the tormented czar Boris Godunov (who gained his throne by the death of the rightful ruler, although not in the same way Johnson did), carrying the oppressive burden of national discord, economic and military disaster, reformative intentions, revolt and dissent, unfulfilled promises and personal guilt? And might Richard Nixon be the false Dimitri who, rising from obscurity and burning with ambition, managed with masterful planning and open ruthlessness to exploit social and economic chaos in order to gain a national "mandate" which he would exploit further?

Leadership, of course, expresses and reflects the popular consensus as much as it forms it. Garry Wills subtitled his book *Nixon Agonistes* "the crisis of the self-made man." Nixon's character defect, if it can be called that, thrived on the crisis of his electorate. They were, in an uncanny way, made for each other until Nixon and his plumbers became too open with their sociopathy, upsetting the delicate balance between democratic, egalitarian myth and authoritarian, hierarchical operant reality. In terms of the dominant pathology of narcissism, Nixon too openly *exhibited* his contempt for democracy, for anything that needed "due process." Even fathers had difficulty identifying with a father figure who was as arbitrary and tyrannical as he. Many Americans said that Nixon had no shame; they probably should also have said that his facade was transparent. Nixon embarrassed their own compartmentalized propriety. He had his own way of doing things and would allow nothing to interfere with his decisions. His parting words as he left the White House in August 1974 were an admonition which captures the pathos of the American time of troubles: "Others may hate you. But they don't win unless you hate them—and then you destroy yourself." He did not recognize his own self-portrait in that statement, a portrait of a career in which he would do anything for success (e.g., the son) but insured that he would end as a failure (e.g., the father). He had brought about his own *Götterdämmerung* (though as King Richard, not the wiser and sadder Wotan), his own disgrace and fall, part of the twilight of the American Dream.

But Nixon is as much reflection as he is cause. Those who felt the need to take the law into their own hands in the name of "law and order" were those who contravened the law and placed it with its inviolate "executive privileges" into his hands—hands not too unlike those of novelist Mario Puzo's historical, fictional *Godfather, Don Vito Corleone.* Those same hands could have been those of the self-willed General George Patton, whom Nixon idolized and whose biographical movie Nixon viewed repeatedly at the White House; or the hands could have been those of the television supercop "Kojak," who is a ruthless yet sentimental Superman who fights in his own dirty style for "truth, justice, and the American way." Ironically, Nixon may have been ahead of his time. It seems that Americans now can control their inner sense of lawlessness only by restoring outer order and by searching for figures who will do the restoration openly. No process is inexorable. The scenario of the second act of this oedipal drama, however, unmistakably contains two leading roles: the *Strong Man* and the *Mighty God.*

The nonelective presidency of Gerald R. Ford (who reached the White House in August 1974 upon the resignation of the disgraced Nixon) does not contradict this scenario. For President Ford to invoke the name of God in granting absolute pardon to the former president, while requiring that Vietnam "draft evaders" repent their error and earn their absolution, is to demonstrate continuity with his predecessor. The difference between Nixon and Ford is one of personal style more than of sociopolitical philosophy and policy. During the first few weeks of his presidency, Ford was constantly pressured by those who wanted to "get Watergate behind us," encouraging perhaps what we consider his grave misjudgment. Nixon was openly deceitful and mistrustful, doubting the intentions of everyone (while demanding their fanatical devotion). Ford was not so worried and self-conscious, and seemed more at peace with himself. What for Nixon apparently was a symptom of character disorder and personal fragmentation is integrated in Ford's personality. Also absent in Ford is that burning ambition that would stop at nothing to achieve success.

As Nixon's vice-presidential choice, Ford had to be someone with whom he could identify. And what better choice (in terms of Nixon's needs) could he have made than a comfortable, quiet, all-American man from Michigan—a paragon of all those virtues he lauded but could not live. Integrity is now "in," and Ford certainly merits praise for public saintliness. But integrity along with its concomitant self-righteousness is just as easily made into a marketable commodity as unscrupulousness. And the two need not be mutually exclusive in one personality or in a cultural era. It is a matter of appearance and compartmentalization. In the post-Watergate era of decency in which official acting-out is no longer publicly sanctioned, the godfathers must be more benign and discreet than in the recent past. The contract between the father-protector and the protected, however, remains the same.

For the remainder of this book we shall focus on the era of the father. The symbolic meaning of *father* is embodied in the identity and ideology of the White Ethnic Movement. But before discussing the specific dynamics of the New Ethnicity, we shall explore the generic conflict and the direction of its resolution. We must understand this new fatherhood in general before we can understand any fathers in particular.

The Search for a New
Stability and Security:
4 Taproots of the New Ethnicity

What we have discussed as the dialectic of sons and fathers can be stated in broader cultural terms; in fact they can be understood as antimonies. In the following characterization of the 1960s and 1970s, there is considerable overlap in the transitional and volatile period around the turn of the decade. We are, after all, looking at the *process* of culture change, and categories based on chronology are partially correct and also convenient for purposes of analysis.

The fundamental distinction between the spirit of the 1960s and the 1970s, is vividly expressed in parallel passages from the inaugural addresses of Presidents Kennedy and Nixon. In his 1961 inaugural address, President Kennedy appealed to the sense of national community and to the idealism of the American Dream as he stated: "Ask not what your country can do for you, ask what you can do for your country." It was a clarion call for social mobilization and participation in the realization of the dream. In his 1973 inaugural address, President Nixon, clearly taking the Kennedy motto as his model, altered its meaning to suit the new age of social divisiveness and segmentation. It was self-aggrandized *ego*, not *civitas*, that was appealed to; every man was to be for himself, not contributing to an ideologically unified nation, but taking the burden from the government (country and nation were not mentioned) and assuming it himself. "In our own lives, let each of us ask—not just what will government do for me, but what can I do for myself? In the challenges we face together, let each of us ask—not just how can government help, but how can I help?" Kennedy invoked a poetic national vision;

Nixon, the absence of any coherent vision—which is precisely the distinction by which the two men mirror the two decades.

In the domains of identity, religion, morality, aesthetics, and politics, we have witnessed a reformation in the 1960s, and since 1968, a counterreformation, that is, a liberation succeeded and superseded by the panic-ridden quest for law and order. First occurred the blurring of conventional categories, the mixing of the immiscible, followed by the search to reaffirm those categories, identities, and boundaries that had been broken and violated. The 1960s were concerned with integration, and the 1970s are interested in purification and resegregation. If the sixties can be called an age of experimentation, the period beginning with 1968 and climaxing in the seventies can be called an era of restoration. In the former, everything was taken out of its place; in the latter, the effort is to put things back in their place.

The sixties were a period of heresy, apostasy, cultural parricide and deicide; the seventies are an era of neo-orthodoxy, neo-Puritanism, and neo-Fundamentalism, the return of the prodigal son (and daughter). Irreverence typified the sixties; penitence describes the attitude of the seventies. Countercultures proliferated in the sixties; the seventies witness the proliferation of counter-countercultures. The sixties were a period of radical questioning and doubt; the seventies are a period in which a desperate search for answers and certainty is taking place. If nihilism and the pursuit of nothingness characterized much of the sixties, absolutism and the pursuit of the millennium typify much of the seventies. The sixties promised the fulfillment of the American Dream and the Melting Pot—one's quest for mobility, integration, and assimilation; the seventies are a period of dashed hopes and the quest for new dreams. In the early sixties Frank Sinatra sang of "High Hopes"; his hit of the seventies describes the dogged insistence on doing things "My Way." One now asks with Peggy Lee, "Is That All There Is?" and echoes with Don McLean the nostalgic dirge of "American Pie." The sixties were a period emblazoned with the vision of building a new future with limitless spatial and social frontiers; the seventies are preoccupied with the past and the uncertain present, dominated by a firm grip on spatial and ideological turf in fear that all will be undermined and lost.

The spirit of the sixties was one of hope, adventure, exploration, openness, zeal, optimism, and of indefatigable ambition and almost messianic expectation. The spirit of the seventies, by contrast, is one of pervasive mistrust, the unwillingness to take any chances, an uneasy and dreadful sense that the end (for some, the end of the world) has been reached, a conviction that there are no frontiers worth pursuing or any futures (save that of the past) worth investing in—hence the search for security and definiteness, the exhaustion with ambiguity and novelty, the sense of pessimism and despair, rage and apathy, and the withdrawal from a world not worth one's commitment. The sixties were a decade of engagement; the seventies are one of disengagement and withdrawal. The sixties were a decade of restlessness and unrest; the seventies are a time of respite and rest. The sixties were a period of abandon; the seventies are one of caution.

The psychedelic drugs may exemplify the sixties; certainly the opiates exemplify the seventies. Likewise, psychologically, elation characterized the sixties; depression, the seventies—and with it, the search for a new ideological "high" to overcome the depression. If shamelessness and guiltlessness represent the sixties; then a pervasive sense of shame and guilt represent the seventies—and lead, in turn, to new means of creating self-esteem and reducing the overwhelming feeling of guilt. The sixties were a period which revealed the idealism, radicalism, and moralism of the son; the seventies mark the return payment in kind by the vengeful father. The youthful leadership of the sixties was personified by the two Kennedys, Martin Luther King, Jr., and Malcolm X; the grim, self-righteous leadership of the seventies is personified by Nixon, Agnew, Wallace, Reagan, and Jackson. The sixties were marked by the radicalism of the Left, and the radicalism of the Right characterizes the seventies.

The sixties were a period in which the search for self-realization and self-esteem was accomplished through personal and social fulfillment by *doing;* the seventies are a decade of preoccupation with self-image and self-esteem, which together are expressions of a narcissistic fixation on *being*. It is appropriate that just as Abraham Maslow's concept of "self-actualization" was a motto of the sixties, Erik Erikson's concept of "identity" is a motto of the culture and politics of the seventies.[1] With the failure of the American Dream, each goes in his or her way in search of a new guardian spirit which will piece life anew into a sensible whole. Finally, only in the context of the collapse of a cultural consensus (identity) are we able to understand the simultaneous and acute eruptions of discontent that are frequently called "crises": the crisis of confidence, the crisis in the classroom, the crisis on the campus, the crisis in the cities, the crisis of identity, the crisis of idealism, and the "generation gap."

We spoke earlier of the nineteenth-century Russian novelist Dostoevski, who began as a socialist reformer in the 1840s, later became a radical revolutionary and a nihilist, and finally (although ambivalently) became a penitential absolutist and fundamentalist for Russophilism and orthodox piety, disavowing Western and secular influences with which he had earlier identified. Beginning with absolute freedom, he ended with absolute despotism (despite his mighty capacity for insight which was achieved by his fictional protagonists, not himself).[2] And such has been the cultural itinerary and sequence of American culture in the 1960s and 1970s, as middle-aging revolutionaries repudiate their earlier reformist positions and turn to the extremism of reaction, the ideologies and programs of which for one "final solution" or another are embraced by those whose identities are likewise threatened.

The Culture and Polity of Fear

In chapter 3 we explored a number of "convergences" or variations on the theme of liberation and universalism that were expressed between the mid-1950s and the mid-1960s—the era of rising expectations, the New Frontier, and the Great Society. Here we turn to those convergences which are expressive of the return of the father. These, in turn, constitute the *generic* wellsprings of diverse identities, ideologies, and polities of which the White Ethnic Movement is a *specific* case or class. Without comprehending the generic cultural conflicts, we unwittingly are led to accept the model offered by the new nativists and their activists who insist that it is ethnicity that is generic— namely, primordial. From the point of view of the generative grammar, the New Ethnicity constitutes one form taken by the surface structure (conscious), but whose roots lie, by definition, in the deep structure (unconscious). Thus, for instance, the dogma of *ethnic* identity as primordial and authentic will be analyzed as one form taken by the search for preambivalent roots, certitude, and security. The two are of different logical types, the latter being the meta-class that subsumes and generates individual classes. Our concern here is to outline those convergences expressing the underlying conflicts for which the New Ethnicity is one solution.

The year 1968 was a crucial year. In the spring, Dr. Martin Luther King, Jr., was assassinated. He had been the single black leader who was able to overcome the intense factionalism among blacks. He personified hope. With his slaying, however, hope was totally lost and was replaced by rage. Robert Kennedy was the last youthful leader with whom diverse and even mutually antagonistic factions could identify. As many white ethnic leaders and nonideologically mobilized mill workers agree, he was the last leader who identified himself with the working middle class, their hopes and aspirations. To him, they were no distant abstraction (as they were to Eugene McCarthy) to champion, but were real people just as the blacks were. In Robert Kennedy was united the symbol and actuality of an *integrated* nation. With his assassination during the summer of 1968, the symbolism of the American Dream literally *disintegrated*. The emphasis is not a mere play on words, but gets to the heart of what integration and its precipitous fragmentation mean. The dream was now in pieces; the idealism was now shattered; and the fragmented and rage-ridden American culture was ripe for exploitation by those who lived and led others by fear and hate. Many of those who would have voted for Kennedy voted for Wallace in the 1968 presidential campaign. Of course, 1968 is the year in which Richard Nixon and Spiro Agnew campaigned and won on a program of "law and order," only months after the disorders by police and youth alike occurred at the Democratic National Convention. Following 1968, social segmentation along racial and ethnic lines, the exuberance of sectarian movements, and social reorganization along parochial and localistic lines became the order of the day.

The emerging identity of defiance, opposition, localism, and segmentation became quickly expressed in a polity of "Balkanization," in what Isidore Silver, in a brilliant review of the film *The Godfather* (1972), called the "Sicilianization of American life." He suggests that the appeal of *The Godfather* "raises the question of whether large segments of the society have withdrawn from any belief in the possibilities of public action. . . ."[3] The withdrawal is accompanied by the assertion of every man (or woman), family, ethnic group, or other interest group, for itself. Achievement and merit are replaced by demands from an increasing number of groups for "affirmative action" (quotas) based on ascriptive criteria, inherent right, and reparations for past or present injustices. The cultural atmosphere becomes paranoid and psychopathic as one observes the manipulation and exploitation of loyalties and ideals, not the attempt to live up to them; the willingness to gain at any price; and a pervasive mistrust of everyone, including oneself. Watergate and Nixon are, of course, a microcosm of this modern drama.

As his review of *The Godfather* continues, Silver asks: "Do we feel ourselves to be members of a lawless community, a pre-modern or a pre-industrial primitive Ardrey-like society? To fend off the anarchy of competing units, do we seek local strong-points?" In his analysis of the godfather phenomenon, his answer is an unequivocal yes. As a synthesis of gangster and western genre movies, *The Godfather* exemplifies "the myth of the non-existence of civilized society," and its popularity affirms the conviction that we live in a Hobbesian society. Each local group legislates its own morality in the service of its own interest, imposing its own law where the law is felt to be too distant to be just. The romanticized *Volk*, "swearing allegiance to the person of a leader, will be served by an instinctive communion which needs (and even transcends) legal forms. . . ."[4] Silver, citing Eric Hobsbawm's classic study of *Primitive Rebels*, finds that the mystique of the Mafia, quite apart from whether or not it exists, is understandable in terms of the needs it fulfills: " 'The Mafia maintained public order by private means.' "[5] There is no room for ambiguity, complexity, or relativity; the "moral universe" of *The Godfather* is majestically simple and absolute.

On the movie and television screens, numerous ruggedly individualistic, self-made men abound in different guises: *Patton* (1970); *Joe* (1971); *The Godfather*, parts 1 and 2 (1972 and 1974); *Walking Tall*, parts 1 and 2 (the tough and sentimental story of a law-and-order Tennessee sheriff, 1973 and 1975); and on television there are supercop serials such as "Kojak," "S.W.A.T.," and "Hawaii Five-O." Other popular movies of the same period convey with traumatic immediacy the sense of a world possessed by evil, the fundamental insecurity of what is taken for granted, and the sheer terror of a world that is not one's friend but deadly adversary: *Airport* (1970); *The Exorcist* (1973); *The Poseidon Adventure* (1972); *The Towering Inferno* (1974); *Earthquake* (1974); *Jaws* (1975); and *The Omen* (1976). If one genre declares society irrelevant and makes men the self-willed rulers of their destiny through heightened action, the other genre reflects our sense of uncertainty and our fear that we may be victims of the universe, not masters.

The multiple Academy-Award-winning film *One Flew Over the Cuckoo's Nest* (1976) ingeniously combines these two themes. We might take a moment to examine them because of the light they shed on contemporary American life. On the one hand, the film offers an image of American society as a total institution: the social system of a state psychiatric hospital becomes a microcosm of the wider society. Its evil is "banal" in Hannah Arendt's sense, but it is nonetheless coercive, demonic, allowing no alternatives or deviation. Order, control, and routine circumscribe life. The dialectic opposite of the obsessive-compulsive Nurse Ratched is Randle Patrick McMurphy, a new patient, a friendly and beguilingly innocent psychopath. He is the liberating nemesis who is out to enjoy life to the hilt, whose presence encourages the self-assertiveness of other patients and who wages a private and public vendetta to destroy Nurse Ratched. McMurphy is in the American tradition of admired, antisocial tricksters who insist on having everything their own way, oblivious to the presence, needs, and threats of others; on the surface they are dauntless, but deep down invite their own doom. McMurphy is the child with whom the viewing public identifies; Nurse Ratched is the evil parent and the hated society that crush all independence and initiative. In the end, McMurphy is lobotomized and rendered will-less for having caused so much upheaval and disturbance. Nurse Ratched proceeds, with her usual aloofness, to restore the ward to monotonous, benevolently authoritarian normalcy. The catatonic patient Chief Bromden performs a mercy killing on McMurphy, heroically lifts and hurls the water-control panel through the hospital window, and escapes toward Canada. McMurphy, the patients insist, did not die (oedipal heroes never die). He too escaped. The legend must prevail at all costs in order to give hope to the dashed spirits of the inmates who must remain (for the most part voluntarily) behind in the cuckoo's nest. The legend is greater than the man and offers to those who believe in his escape the persistence of their own manhood, embattled though it be. The psychopath as hero, and the banality of evil, are the dual cornerstones of this modern folktale—a tale resplendent with the paranoid theme that there is no exit from the penal colony of American reality. Yet beneath the popular interpretation of simple *opposition* of good and evil lies the unconscious *symbiosis* of anarchy and overcontrol, of deviant hero and punitive "establishment," of victim and victimizer. Each side of the polarity brings out the worst in the other and is not independent of its adversary.

In addition to *hero* and *victim* is a third genre in the media, one we need not belabor. It is that of *nostalgia* for simplicity and repose, exemplified by such films as *The Last Picture Show* (1971), *American Grafitti* (1973), and *Summer of '42* (1972). The television serial "The Waltons" is a paragon of togetherness, gently resolved conflict, and the lost virtues and innocence of the "good old days." The serial "All in the Family" cleverly interweaves all these themes, and seems, both from the point of view of content and popularity, to be best expressive of contemporary American conflicts.[6]

Turning from the theater of "as if" to the real world of powerlessness, alienation, and patronage, the preoccupation with violence, security, and control is expressed through numerous local and nationally symbolic *new* strong points. With everything out of place, these ad hoc concentrations and organizations of power attempt to restore everything to its presumed place. Thus the once rural-southern Ku Klux Klan increased its visibility in urban-northern settings. White ethnic power organizations formed both locally and nationally: e.g., "Displaced White Ethnics" (in Newark) and "Ethnic Millions Political Action Committee" (in Bayville, New York). The Jewish Defense League established quasi-military training camps for the defense of inner-city ethnic turf. Vigilante groups set out to fight crime in their own way. On June 19, 1975, for example, three men were caught in the act of stealing a television set in California; a vigilante group led one of them to a cliff and threw him to his death. If in the movies Don Vito Corleone was the master of patronage, in political life, the Nixon-Agnew team masterfully offered protection to the embattled electorate, asking in return only loyalty and devotion. Now George Wallace offers his service to the American people with simplicity, as vicar of law and order, control, localism, and authority.

Disillusionment and demoralization paved the way for the casting of the ballot for apostles of vindictiveness and mistrust—and equivocation—who, with the lapse of national consensus, would become eager advocates of localism. Unable to believe in their ideals, yet unable to disavow them, the electorate became moralists and opportunists at once, sanctioning the leadership that would do as they do, only on a grander scale. In their turn, Nixon and Agnew, now Wallace and others, offer to protect the interests of the "little man" of the middle class against those forces that threaten him. The offer of protection, though, is bound up with the perpetuation of conditions that make protection necessary—and, in turn, become part of the threat one needs protection against. As Philip Slater observed in *Earthwalk:* "Every protection contract becomes a protection racket. 'Give me what I want and I will protect you against me.' "[7] From the attitude of the "warrior-aristocrat toward the peasant" of Slater's example, to Richard Nixon and the American public, the war against any defined social evil cannot be won because the most devoted combatants have a vested interest in the chaos and uncertainty they exploit while fighting.

Ethnicity is one salve for modern wounds of violated and vulnerable identities. The romanticized and idealized "idols of the tribe," as Harold Isaacs calls ethnicity, not only create security and safety from the hostile, alienating world outside, but instill deeper fear of that world. Hence the greater need for the mystical womb of ethnos. A vicious cycle is created wherein ego, self, family, neighborhood, and ethnic group become more withdrawn and fearful. The tribal cave, ideological and territorial, inspires the very dread it assuages. The feelings of belonging and loyalty on the inside are inseparable from the fears of isolation and vulnerability on the outside. The opposites are symbiotically linked with one another. Defense not only defends, but perpetuates the uncertainty and anxiety that require constant vigilance. Defense must maintain what it defends against. Ethnicity, though, is only one among increasingly diverse responses to a generalized cultural condition.

Danger and the Quest for Purity

The protection and defense that are sought are invariably associated with *strength* to combat weakness, *authority* to restore *order* and *control, moral vindictiveness* to retaliate for hurts suffered, and *self-righteousness* to invert the overwhelming sense of guilt and shame. Erikson writes cogently of

> the new punitiveness which is based on the grim old identity and promoted with a barely dissembled combination of vindictiveness and bad conscience—for you can always be sure that the loudest moralists have made deals with their own consciences—such punitiveness seems to be more satisfying to the vindicator and self-vindicator than helpful in the solution of lawlessness.
>
> Because man needs a disciplined conscience, he thinks he must have a bad one; and he assumes that he has a good conscience when, at times, he has an easy one.[8]

Vindication and vindictiveness, though, are part of the new liberation of consciousness and conscience. An overweening conscience becomes liberated and easy as the source of guilt and shame are projected and displaced onto convenient scapegoats—in the case of the New Ethnicity, onto the mythically homogenized and homogenizing WASPs, Jews, blacks, Puerto Ricans, recent immigrants from the South, Hippies, and others. A second-generation Croatian-American in his mid-forties, married to a Slovak-American woman, angrily stated the following (notes from Stein, March 5, 1971):

> I'd like to be president for just a few years—not president, but *dictator!* Like Hitler. I'll tell you, the worst mistake this country made was winning the Second World War. If Hitler would have won, he'd of cleaned this place out. There wouldn't be Communist parties. There wouldn't be Negroes demanding things. . . . I'll tell

you one thing—the Russian system is good. If you got the brains to go to college, you go to college and go as far as you can. But if you don't, you're put to work on their farms. The ones who don't want to work starve! Here, they send checks and food to you if you do nothing. They pay you to be lazy. Our money is going to those bums. And they laugh at us because we're a bunch of jerks for taking it. Every morning at five I walk to work (a local plant), and when I'm walking past those Skidders' house up the street, I know he's standing there at his window, laughing at me as I go by. . . . Those Communists are going to take over sooner or later—that you can be sure of. They know how to beat you—they beat you with your own rules. They've got lawyers so smart that they can twist the laws around to do the opposite they're meant to. So the way it ends up, I'm going to work for nothing, practically. The taxes are all up; I've got to support those lazy asses up the street.

As soon as the kids get to college, you got them lost. Even at homes where the parents raised them good the same thing happens once they hit college. Those professors are all Communists. Then your children turn against you and against the world. They're not smart as they think they are. They ain't sowed one blade of grass. All they can do is get up out of bed and breathe. They'd be better off to work and pay for their college. Let them *earn* that bread (*snarl*). I get so damned worked up, I feel like fighting (*laughing*). [Subsequently, he did have a fight with one of the white immigrants from the South—those he calls "Skidders," as in *Skid Row*.] I started out delivering paper—I had to *work* for everything I ever had. Then they give you that phoney baloney of telling you how you should live your life. Nobody's going to be running me. My kid wants to run me, I throw them out. [His eldest daughter, in her late teens, feeling unable to talk with her parents and feeling watched over and questioned about everything she has done, moved out of the house and took a separate apartment, while working at a job and going to college. Her father at first said, "Good riddance!" Several months later, however, he came to her apartment and pleaded with her to return. He tries to project the image of a tough man, yet he has invariably given in to demands and requests from his wife and children.]

Today, most kids threaten their parents: "I won't go to college if you don't buy me a car." Them damn Hippies! Go get a pick and shovel and *earn* a living. Don't give me this baloney: "Give me a car, or else I won't go to college." Don't go to college—see if I give a damn. If you want a real education, tend bar. [He tends bar regularly at the AmVets Club.] I'd say in two years you'll really know life. Professors don't know what it's like to get up every morning and earn your bread. . . . [A short time later, he talks about his youngest child, a boy of three:] I want to send this kid to be a welder, electrician, or plumber—that's where there's great wages. . . . They'll be making more than graduates of college, and there will be such a demand on them that they can name their figure! This work has to be done by somebody. I don't want nobody doing what I've had to do. [He then talked about the neighbor children who allegedly stripped his children's bike and put the tires on their own bike; still later he related incidents concerning the theft of his children's toys from his yard and the theft of a hammock the family had given him for Father's Day, and which disappeared before he had a chance to lie in it once.] Everybody in the neighborhood knows it's my kids' tires—they even come up to you and tell you: "Aren't those tires from your bike?" And there's nothing you can do about it. I talked to the chief of police here just the other day. He said to me: "All this is is another nigger situation." What he means is that you're stuck. You can't do anything to them. I'm going to work to feed that jerk! I'd like to see them dead. I never wish someone dead, but I'd really like to see them dead.

They're just lying around and draining the government. Get more and more relief—so have another baby. That's all they're good for. . . . That's one thing I'm teaching them [his children], to hate Skidders. You're supposed to hate Skidders, those no good bums. [He then daydreamed, staring off into space:] One day I'm going to get him out in the alley. I have it all figured out. Because I can't do it any other way. It'll be a dark night, and nobody else will be around. He'll be in the alley, and I'll come up behind him and clobber him on the head to put him out. Then I'll work him over good so that he'll have to stay six months in the hospital. Then I'll get my satisfaction. That's the only way (*pause*). But I'll end up having to pay for the hospital too, because that comes out of welfare. (*Painfully:*) So I'll never get any satisfaction out of him! I'm stuck, just stuck. I can't do nothing!

[Later in the discussion:] I've been at the plant twenty-eight years. I thought I was smart when I started out. I went there when I was sixteen because I wanted to work. One day my father came up there to take a tour of the place and see what kind of place I was working in. He came over to me and said: "I want you to get out of here. This is no place for you." I told him: "You dumb Hunkie,

what do you know about it? I want to work here, I'll work here."
Today, I know I wasn't so smart—it was me who was the dumb
Hunkie. I should have listened to him and finished school. Then I
could have gotten somewhere. I could have done different then.
But now—it's too late. What can I do now? Who will hire me? I'm
too old to start anything new. And I never even finished high
school. So I've got to stay where I am. At least one thing I can say:
My job is steady. I've never missed a day of work in my life—
excuse me, one day, when I was sick. It's better than in the mill,
when you work steady for a few months and then you're off for a
few months. I don't make as much as they do in an hour, but over
the year it averages out. I've been out of the service twenty-five
years (*sudden amazement*)—twenty-five years! Where's it gone?

You know [turning to the interviewer, Stein], life's not worth
much. When you get twenty-five, you only have the next ten years
as your peak, and after that, it's all downhill. You see where I'm
heading. You get married, raise a family. Where does it all go? It
seems that the best years are gone. We had it better when we were
kids than the kids have it now. We *really* lived. When those old-
timers came over to this country, they had the time of their lives. A
lot of them had a good time here. Their wives were over in their
villages, and the men over here could do as they pleased. Many of
them probably didn't want to send for their wives to come over and
spoil everything! [He laughs heartily, and his wife gives a put-on
look of chagrin.] My grandfather came over here and was really
living it up. He didn't know it, but my grandmother and my mother
were getting everything ready over there to come over here. My
grandmother went to work to earn the fare over here. You can
imagine the surprise my grandfather had one day meeting them
coming down Fifth Avenue looking for him! He didn't even know
they were coming—and maybe he hadn't planned on ever sending
for them (*mischievous smile*)!

The very lusty violations he now nostalgically celebrates he condemns in the youth and colleges. Feeling trapped, helpless, and on
the way downhill for having lived a life he wishes he had not
chosen—he lashes out with fury against those whose lives and life-
styles he envies but must, to justify his own life, despise. What he
could not have (e.g., education, carefree enjoyment, and mobility), he
resents others having and insists that he does not want such luxuries.
The stronger the reminder of what he once (and still) wanted but
could not have, the greater the denial of its worth. In a moment of

insight—when the defenses are down—he recognizes his own participation in missed opportunity. But he resiliently "recovers" and proceeds to blame the Hippies, the Communists, the blacks, and the
colleges for all the disappointments, failures, and threats he experiences. To defend and protect himself, the informant must locate the
fault outside himself; yet his ambivalence shows his fascination with
what he repudiates. Sensing that the whole world is coming apart, he
desperately invokes an outer authority (i.e., Hitler) who will come in
and clean everything up in one immense sweep. The establishment of
outer order is required to help organize his inner chaos.

"Ethnic Americans," writes Michael Novak, "respect strength and
despise weakness." (That this is Novak's positive stereotype of those
he champions is a separate issue which we shall take as a partial
truth.) In a terse essay titled "Why Wallace?" Novak writes of the
Restek brothers, who live in a Pennsylvania steel town: one owns a
gasoline station, another works in the mills, and the older brother is a
manager at a chain store. They all voted for Wallace in 1968. Andy,
the gas-station owner, "responded to Wallace, I suspect, because
Wallace put things exactly in the way Andy's experience has put
them. . . . Andy trusts his own experience. He knows what he
knows. And he likes his world, his home, his America. . . . The outrage he feels is so deep he can't understand how anyone in his right
mind would not scream out in anguish at what is happening to America. He wants authority to tighten up, in part to assuage his own guilt
for having been too soft with his kids." He worries about his daughter
Sally whose boyfriend has long hair, who likes to wear her own hair
long and straight, who talks back to him as he would never have
dared answer his parents. Andy fears what might happen if she gets
pregnant "and [he] strikes out in fury at every manifestation of the
kind of youth he despises."[9]

Likewise, in the family of the Croatian worker discussed previously, we might note that the mother and father are constantly afraid
that their eldest daughter will become pregnant; they watch her every
move, search her personal belongings, read her mail, and expect a full
report every time she returns from a date, virtually inviting what they
fear will happen. The father asks her: "Who do you belong to?"
Later she tells Stein: "They want me to feel that I belong to them.
But I would like to feel that I belong to myself." Any self-affirmation
is necessarily a threat to the parental need for her to be a part of
them.

Returning to Novak's essay, Andy's son Bob is majoring in business administration and finance, but Andy "watches with trepida-

tion" and suspicion whenever his son brings home books of poetry and novels, especially those with *humanism* on the jackets. For Andy, *humanism* means "soft-headed thinking, pornography, and the collapse of authority." His brothers bitterly agree: "It's just like the priests say. Secularism is the collapse of all decency and morals and authority. We need a man who talks sense and isn't softheaded about authority, to clean this country up from coast to coast. That way, we can all have the America we worked to hard to build, which gave us what success we have."[10]

Cultural Paranoia and the Plea for Authority

We cannot stress too strongly that the answer to the question "What happened to the American Dream?" is not to be found exclusively by exploring outer events, for inner meanings that interpret and, to some measure, help cause these outer events must also be explored. *Reality* takes on deeply personal meanings whose external representations or symbols support the unlikely hypothesis that the American Dream has been subverted from within, not eroded from without, by a variety of enemy aliens. The enemy is ourselves. The insight into this complicity, however, is repudiated. Any personal responsibility for failure at achievement is denied, and the *inwardly* directed self-blame and depression are turned *outward* and blamed on readily available scapegoats (analogous to "primitive" witchcraft accusations). Guilt and shame are reduced by the compromise wherein one denies having had anything to do with creating what America is now like (e.g., even the children of good parents, once the liberal professors get their hands on them, are lost to perdition).

One can go even further and deny ambition and earlier rebellion altogether by stating that the American Dream was never one's private dream. Accordingly, one was forceably uprooted in the process of Americanization and did not freely choose to forsake his roots. One is rather an innocent, naive victim of Anglo-conformity, or what many blacks now refer to as "internal-colonialism." The image of the Melting Pot has taken on the quality of a paranoid projection: others have lifted us up body and soul and pitched us into the infernal Melting Pot in order to melt us down to their (WASP) consistency, pouring off the slag that did not conform to their formula of what the final alloy should be like. The Melting Pot ethos, initially a personally sought means of identity transformation and transcendence, now is seen as a persecutory, ego-alien experience forceably imposed from without. As early as 1970, the Polish-American council-woman from Baltimore, Barbara Mikulski (who herself had once considered changing her name to McClosky, a proper Irish-Catholic name), declared that America was not a Melting Pot but a "sizzling cauldron." The new metaphor, instantly adopted, aptly conveys the image of "white rage." Such eruption of rage, if directed inward, is literally self-destructive; to defend one's self, therefore, rage must be turned outward. The demand for law and order, quite apart from the New Ethnicity which becomes a new means of *reordering* society along cultural lines, is fundamentally a plea for some external authority to bring the seething rage under control and to give it some direction.

In the white ethnic population, then, there has emerged the conviction that one of the basic problems of our time is the lapse of respect for authority, that permissiveness and liberalism have undermined wholesome values, that too much freedom has led to disorder, and that a restoration of tough-minded *realpolitik* is called for to reverse the errors made by the softheaded leaders who have neither nerve nor backbone.

In a world, not merely a nation, that has experienced a decade of war, violence, refeudalization, retribalization, and terrorism, witnessing the disillusionment with the possibility of self-fulfillment through some supracultural identity and political structure, it seemed timely, beginning with the mid-1960s, that aggression and territorialism were rationalized as innate and inevitable. Robert Ardrey's *African Genesis, The Territorial Imperative,* and *The Social Contract,* as well as Konrad Lorenz's *On Aggression,* were apologia for an age. We learned from Desmond Morris a further confirmation of the human species' essential animality (with a very specific meaning): despite our narcissistic pretensions, we are no more than a *Naked Ape.* From Lionel Tiger we are told that *Men in Groups* is an innate bonding, closely related to our hunting and predatory ancestry. From Lionel Tiger and Robin Fox we learn that we are *The Imperial Animal,* i.e., we conquer by instinct. During his stormy reign, President Nixon was frequently caricatured as "King Richard," and Arthur Schlesinger, Jr., did write a book called *The Imperial Presidency.* This was the same period in which the United States was being accused both from within and without of being imperialistic and colonialist. Presumably, however, there is nothing culture-historically specific or unique about this fact, since it is now rationalized pragmatically and without apology as being simply another expression of human nature. "They all do it" is a more earthy way of putting it.

Our fascination with neoprimitivism, biological instinctivism, and raw power finds justification and explanation in the "way of nature," beyond our immediate cause and control. The fault, one might say, lies in our genes and in the stars. Environmentalist explanations are increasingly rejected as too complex, just as environmentalist solutions are dissatisfying because they do not achieve the desired effect immediately—and what they do achieve cannot be tolerated. We are helpless before the fires that impel us: the belief creates unabated fear, but it also removes personal responsibility. Misfortune is impersonally "other." Our perception of the human condition fulfills our need to disavow responsibility while enabling us to indulge vicariously or directly. The intellectuals of the society provide the cognitive legitimation for commonly held beliefs and help assure their perpetuation by making them "official." War and violence, terrorism and factionalism, territorialism and group exclusivism, among others, are inevitable, inexorable, and natural. Since they are not of our doing, we can excitedly indulge in them without guilt. Movies, television serials, and novels allow the participant-observer to engage in nature red in tooth and claw. The sudden popularity of hockey suggests the need to experience, if only indirectly (and hence under some control), rugged individualism at its extreme, *A Clockwork Orange* on ice; behind the rules of the game is a deeper rule that attracts the crowds—*homo homini lupus*. More potent antidotes for the dead ends of unfulfilled initiative could not be prescribed.

These are but a few of the convergences that characterize the period since the mid-1960s. With humanity seen as naked, wild, aggressive, vicious, and imperial, it seems that the swing of the pendulum in the direction of *control strategy* was predictable, if not inevitable. In fact, the dialectic of *instinct* and *order* pervades American culture history and is expressed at both extremes. Those who would restore order would sanction doing so by extreme means. One longs for war and peace, adventure and quiet, nihilism and order.

Unable to repress the conflicts reawakened within us, and unable to influence the forces that accost us from without, we would gladly purge from ourselves and from our midst everything that seems to contribute to the malaise of ambiguity and complexity. Good and evil are polarized and, in their own way, clarified. There must be no uncertainty as to what is right and what is wrong. All skepticism and doubt must be resolved decisively—either/or. Theories of demonic possession emerge out of a morbid preoccupation with evil, and all ills become transformed into impingements from without (ego alien). The outer world comes to represent our inner experiences of danger and anarchy; the engulfing paranoia is a projection of our own rage and mistrust, confirmed by events and chronic conditions that evoke our wrath and suspicion. The attraction of the occult, astrology, mysticism, religious orthodoxy, and the demonic reflects the hysterically charged atmosphere of the quest for control and resolute certainty while celebrating the exhilaration of chaos. Some punishment must fit the unknown and disavowed crime.

What has been taken for granted can no longer be assumed; connections and links decompose into disjunctures and discontinuities. Experience becomes diffuse; the boundary between inner and outer, self and other, concept and percept, becomes less certain. The fascination with the magical and the mythical simultaneously celebrates and dreads chaos, reflecting the wish to restore order and predictability to experience, and definiteness to the ego. The world is surely not run by a whimsical fate, but by the stars from beyond, perhaps by a god of retribution, perhaps from below by Satan. The projection of the need for definition and control returns as a wish fulfilled. Both the inner chaos and the need for control are projected onto the outer world, and the struggle for psychic (and occasionally psychotic) security is waged there. Uncertain of ourselves and of the world upon which we depend, we look for signs, for warning signals of doom or hope.

When things seem to be coming apart, we cannot help them; when our former faith in education, science, technology, and medicine (traditional means of problem-solving) has given way to disparagement and to a great pluralistic search for alternatives, our security is shaken; therefore the indomitable arsenal of magical thinking helps put our broken Humpty Dumpty together and prevents the endless falling that is dreaded. The need for finalistic certitude allows no room for the doubt, tentativeness, and inherent incompleteness of science. *The Godfather* extolled the tough-hearted and unscrupulous (yet sentimental and "proper") leader who obeyed only his own law, legislating a personal order in the context of a social order that oppressed but did not protect. A year later, *The Exorcist* displayed terror, sex, violence, assorted body parts, and voracious evil all out of control, requiring a call "on high" for a restoration of order and normalcy that even a godfather could not summon. The demonic, the anarchic, and the disgusting are first indulged in—out of control—and then purged in monumental, supernatural catharsis.

The control strategy that has gathered momentum since the late 1960s is a neo-Puritanism and neo-Fundamentalism that resolves to toughen what has gone soft. Many Americans practice penance, make acts of contrition, and hope for absolution and communion through submission and confession. They seek new rigors and hardships, they impose self-discipline and severities on themselves, in order to undo and compensate for permissiveness and indulgence. They look for the restoration of symbols of outer control which will establish authority in the inner spaces. Many undertake idiosyncratic rites of passage to bring under control the boundless and potentially disruptive energy of youth and of reawakened adolescence.[11]

It is the common denominator quest for control and order, authority and respite, that allows (indeed compels) us to bring into a single cluster such names as B. F. Skinner, Stanley Milgram, Michael Novak, Robert Heilbroner, the Reverend Billy Graham, Richard Nixon, Spiro Agnew, Ronald Reagan, and George Wallace (a list that would be more complete by adding the disturbingly large number of academics and intellectuals who publicly endorsed Richard Nixon in 1972). In addition to such names are functionally related and equivalent movements, sects, and groups such as the Jesus People, *Chevurah* (a Jewish youth organization), neo-Pentecostalism, Outward Bound, the Black Muslims, Synanon, Jews for Jesus, the neo-Catholic Cult of Mary, Fascinating Womanhood, Total Woman, Expo '72, and the segmented units of the New Ethnicity. Each, with its own rigorous dogma and discipline, declares *Extra ecclesia nulla salus,* "Outside the Church there is no salvation."

In *Beyond Freedom and Dignity,* published in 1971, B. F. Skinner expressed in his own voice what he had uttered through one of his fictional alter egos, Frazier, in his 1948 novel, *Walden Two* (it should be noted that 1948 also marked the beginning of the repressive McCarthy era).[12] Frazier attempted to justify himself, as well as his utopia, to Burris, the more skeptical and wary side of Burrhus Frederic Skinner. Obsessed with an idée fixe all his life, Frazier explains:

> To put it as bluntly as possible—the idea of having my own way. "Control" expresses it, I think. The control of human behavior, Burris. In my early experimental days it was frenzied selfish desire to dominate. I remember the rage I used to feel when a prediction went awry. I could have shouted at the subject of one of my experiments "Behave, damn you!" Eventually, I realized that the subjects were always right. They always behaved as they should have behaved. . . . And what a strange discovery for a would-be tyrant . . . that the only effective control is unselfish.[13]

By 1971, the ambivalence had been given resolution, as Skinner became Frazier out in the open, arguing for the design of a culture through control and conformity. The primal scream of "Behave, damn you!"—the rage-ridden demand for control of what seemed, on the outside, out of his control—had been given a more subtle and more acceptable expression. He cannot believe that the subjects are right and behave as they should behave; for if he did, he would not have needed to design a utopia that effected control through a barely disguised tyrant.

The stern demand for the restoration of proper behavior, obedience to authority, and the tightening up of control were echoed by the Nixons, Agnews, Rizzos, Wallaces, Reagans, Daleys—and the "little men" of Gary, Pittsburgh, and Cleveland. Yet they could not renounce the "freedom and dignity" that is at the core of American ideal values. Vice-President Spiro Agnew, Nixon's "talking chief" who was the strident, uninhibited alter ego of the president, fanning the flames both of Right and Left, denounced Skinner's managerial utopia as un-American, as undermining political democracy and individual choice. Yet what he could not openly advocate, Agnew, like the other fathers of this period, deeply believed to be the only answer to the prevailing lawlessness (a lawlessness in which they too were accomplices): overcontrol. What Skinner expressed through Frazier in 1948 became an undisguised and socially prevailing belief by 1971: "Our civilization is running away like a frightened horse. As she runs, her speed and her panic increase together." The behaviorist strategy and social philosophy were a means of totalistically reorienting a society not so much through *thought reform* as through *behavior reform*—although the necessary belief or conviction in the new ritual of conversion was widespread enough to make investment in the new behavior produce the desired result. Despite the behaviorist position, the will to control was internally motivated.

The socially useless and decadent permissiveness, liberalism, sensuality, indolence, ambiguity, and secularism would all be eliminated by a return to the small-town *polis,* a renewed Consciousness I to overturn the Consciousness III. As Richard Sennett has demonstrated in his analysis of the hidden agendas of Skinner's utopia, work, conformity, neo-Puritan asceticism, simplicity, control, and the need to destroy the illusion of autonomy and individuation are the values that underlie Skinner's terminal objectives—and terminally fixed social order.[14] Like the Nixons and Agnews who are shocked by the audacity of this totalitarian vision, Skinner has, as Sennett notes, an agenda that is at great odds with his claims.

According to Skinner, "Freedom is an issue raised by aversive consequences of behavior"; and in a way, what we need is freedom from freedom. Skinner's methods, like his values, are, of course, deeply American. *Freedom from,* with all of its aversive connotations (the past, authority, dependence, religious or political persecution, status disparagement, and inequality) is inherently avoidant. The question of *freedom to* is never addressed. The genetically and epigenetically built-in freedoms such as approach, exploration, and relatedness are not considered. Skinner is obsessed with control of the (non-existent) instincts run wild. The univocal articulation of the need for control strategies, to limit the expression of cathartic strategies, came "out of the closet" with Skinner and American society simultaneously. Skinner provided the ideogram and plan for its implementation that coincided with socially expressed needs: to establish external control for what inner and outer authority could no longer do. Whatever else it might be, *Beyond Freedom and Dignity* is a personal solution to the problem of anarchy and order which Skinner offers to a culture whose unconscious agenda coincides with his. If it is accepted, it will give Skinner the external sense of order he needs, while it becomes the eagerly adopted charter that fulfills the identical needs of the community for which he is the shaman at a distance.

The Search for a New Order

In the same year in which *Beyond Freedom and Dignity* appeared, a group of youth in California, on the rebound from Hippiedom and drugs, found salvation through the neo-Fundamentalist Jesus People and joined en masse the Republican party. The year 1971 also marked the founding of the much publicized Farm, a conservative commune of several hundred members, in Lewis County, Tennessee. The opposite of licentious, the atmosphere of The Farm is ascetic. LSD is forbidden, and marijuana is used only ceremonially. Permissiveness is replaced by discipline, and individualism by collectivity. Daily life is thoroughly circumscribed. The ideology of The Farm is other-directed, with the collective providing the individual with security, discipline, and supervision, as the individual, in turn, becomes undifferentiated from the group. Under the professor-turned-guru Stephen Gaskin, its final authority and exemplary giver of the law, the commune is characterized as "friendly, generous, peaceful, hard-working, law-abiding and—in their own distinctive manner—pious, moralistic, and orthodox.[15] It is a social experiment aimed at tightening up what has become loose and getting away from the artificial and returning to nature (e.g., neither birth control nor abortion is permitted). The Farm's philosophy is orthodox and conservative, the dialectic opposite of the affluence-renouncing San Francisco Hippie scene from which the communards began their long search for home.

Not by chance, home was found in the South, paragon of stability, old-time virtue, and old-time religion. Not only American religion, but American culture is influenced increasingly by the South. More specifically, the American ethos is coming to embody what was once felt to be a regional one. The Reverend Billy Graham "has long since risen above Baptism and his North Carolina roots to become the nation's unofficial chaplain and a globetrotting messenger of the Lord." The Southern Baptist Convention "has moved beyond the borders of the South, expanding rapidly in the North and West, riding on the crest of a conservative wave that is packing the churches that incline in the direction of fundamentalism and emptying the ones that tend to be classified as liberal."[16]

Michael Novak, the Slovak-American white ethnic leader, asserts that "being before doing" is "an ancient Catholic theme"; and he contrasts Anglo-American Protestant artifice with ethnic-Catholic authenticity. He contrasts the "call from beyond" with "personal will" and views with opprobrium the "American myth of the agent, the doer, the initiator, the intervener," whose aim is to make history over.[17] Interestingly, the South, not at all Catholic, has been making similar contrasts and claims for itself for two centuries. The romanticized ethnic-Catholic ethos and the equally idealized southern ethos seem to have much in common: being before doing, the sense of place, order, quiet, belongingness, loyalty, tradition, roots, sanctity of family and home, honor, clear authority and durable hierarchy, a certain God-hauntedness, and, each in its own way, the expiation of guilt and the certainty of communion.

Country music—no longer regionally identified as *country* or *western*—has gained a national audience since the late 1960s, expressing and articulating as can no other music the white man's blues and troubles. Nashville is now a national music capital, and the "Nashville Sound" infuses old themes into new contexts (urban, industrial, northern, etc.). The appeal of such figures as George Wallace and Jimmy Carter is no longer regional. In the next chapter we shall discuss the relation between Wallace, the South, and the White Ethnic Movement with respect to black-white relations. Here it need only be noted that the ancient ethnic-Catholic virtues, coinciding with those of the Old South, are personified in Wallace and Carter, who aspire to national leadership. They are no longer sectarian (regional), but denominational (more mainstream American).

The newly named Sunbelt now denotes an emerging *national* ethos. The nation seeks to be "born again," as was Jimmy Carter in 1967, in evangelical submission to God. It might be noted that Charles Colson, a key Nixon advisor and strategist of the Watergate era, subsequently experienced a religious conversion and was also "born again"—the title of his 1976 book. Many formerly assertive and arrogant sons are returning to their fathers and to their Heavenly Father, repenting their sins and dissociating themselves from their former identities. The psychopathic self-legislators of law and violators of other men's laws now assume the burden of Christ and cannot be pious (and self-righteous) enough. (We may be forgiven if we trespass but for a moment on the territory of other scholars to note a close resemblance of current American conversions to religion and ethnos with those of such Russian literary giants as Dostoevski and Tolstoi.) The South and the southern ethos become a restoration of home for those who have left and seek to return to personal and cultural purity. H. Louis Patrick of Trinity Presbyterian Church in Charlotte, North Carolina, perceptively writes the following:

> The South is returning to the mainstream of the nation's life. More than that, in the preservation of a stable society . . . the South is leading the rest of the land. . . . People at large see in this region the reflection of that status-quo for which they long. Not too long ago the gospel according to Billy Graham was strictly a Southern product. . . . Now, that gospel of individual salvation . . . appeals to persons throughout the land who struggle with the torment of littleness, trying to gain some sense of instant worth and welcome from an indifferent civilization that is too complex for their coping.[18]

If the South has long been obsessed with authority, hierarchy, ritualized relationship, status, sin, and fatalism, Michael Novak in *Choosing Our King* (1974) articulates a new myth of presidential politics that embodies similar ultimate concerns. The president, the presidency, and the election of the president are aspects of a symbolic-ritual process, with the president as the symbolic and religious center of the nation. He personifies the national purpose; he is the vicar of the national ethos. In spirit, the president *is* the nation that elected him. For a nation whose origin traces to a revolution against monarchy, yet which has remained fascinated with royalty and aristocracy from the beginning, what is significant about Novak's personal document is its *open equation* of presidency with kingship—and as we shall see, virtually divine kingship. Novak's image of the American presidency is profoundly ethnic-Catholic in symbolism (as is his understanding of American sports, which he considers elaborate ritual; cf. his most recent book, *The Joy of Sport*). Indeed, an ethnic-Catholic ethos is offered as a form of salvation from the Anglo-American Protestant system of values—and stresses. For Novak, *Catholic* no longer denotes a church, religion, or denomination, but is now a universal symbol for moral, social, cultural, aesthetic, and political regeneration and reorganization. His dichotomy between Protestant-American optimism and progressivism, and ethnic-Catholic realism and wisdom, stresses the need for a painful "recognition of brokenness, of only partial victory, of the inevitability of betrayal, of the untrustworthiness of everything human."[19]

In a National Town Meeting broadcast of September 29, 1976, from Washington, D.C., Novak contrasted the "nice cynicism," true to ethnic style, with WASP perfectionism and progress. He cited the salutary effect of the television serial "Kojak," which demonstrates that in America, we're not so bad after all; "New York is no different from Constantinople." The idea that things are getting better is alien to the ethnic view of life. Zealously antievangelical, Novak mistrusts Jimmy Carter's evangelical style—apparently failing to notice his own attraction to the "ethnic purity" he denounces, or likewise not taking note of the burgeoning *Catholic* Charismatic Renewal Movement that parallels evangelical Protestant Pentecostalism.

For Novak, the tragic sense of life would receive its highest affirmation and noblest expression in the president of the United States. The presidency becomes nothing less than the religio-symbolic center of a "new, dark civil religion," where, in a sense, church and state, ultimate concern and polity, national purpose and Divine Purpose, are fused. In an earlier essay, Novak spoke of the possibility that the American people might be "swayed by the example of the closest thing the American religion has to a high priest: the President of the United States." In the essay "Politics as Witness" (in which he offered Senator Eugene McCarthy as the ideal embodiment of numerous Catholic themes), Novak saw in McCarthy "something priestly." McCarthy, like Robert Kennedy, Catholic, "knew the final end and absurdity of history." In a parenthesis Novak writes: "It is not by accident that he [McCarthy] speaks of himself as 'we,' a little like a pope, *a vicar of the people*" (italics added).[20] But "the American system was not ready for either man; it prefers artificial hearts." Wallace, whom Novak openly detests, possesses these very qualities that make him such an attractive claimant to the American throne.

It seems hardly coincidental that the expatriate *Russian* (not Soviet) novelist Alexander Solzhenitsyn has become an *American* hero, winning accolades for his courage and defense of human freedom. AFL-CIO leader George Meany and Senator Henry Jackson are among his staunchest supporters. Solzhenitsyn is the unmeltable Russian in the Soviet-Communist melting pot. As an orthodox Slavophile, he is an equivalent to Novak, who is the American Catholic ethnophile. Both in the Soviet Union and the West, Solzhenitsyn roundly condemns secularization, modernization, and urbanization; as with Dostoevski and Tolstoi, for Solzhenitsyn the paragon of virtue is the undefiled, pious, simple peasant. Even as he is an outspoken political dissident in his own country, he laments the lapse of strong authority and cannot understand, for instance, how the United States government could let Daniel Ellsberg go free following the disclosure that he had made the "Pentagon Papers" public in 1970. In his novels (e.g., *August 1914*) he celebrates individual moral responsibility and personal ethical choice; in public life, he clearly subordinates the individual to the collectivity and to hierarchical authority. The antidote for the sickness of modern, Western, urban life is a return to orthodox simplicity, wisdom, and order. It is precisely this freedom from freedom that many Americans are finding increasingly attractive. In Solzhenitsyn they find an exemplary prophet of freedom through nostalgia and reaction.

From Hippies to intellectuals and political activists, many earlier zealots of liberalism and radicalism have become converts to the Right. The imagery of North versus South, Anglo-American Protestant versus ethnic-Catholic is expressed as Prometheus versus Atlas in Robert Heilbroner's influential book *An Inquiry into the Human Prospect* (1974).[21] In this work, Heilbroner shifted from his prior Promethean optimism to the pessimism and grim endurance of Atlas, the bearer of burdens, as his guardian spirit or totem. The shift from son to father could not be more dramatically symbolized. Prometheus was the god of inextinguishable energy, the disrespectful youth who committed the theft of fire (potency, vigor, youth, and enlightenment) from the gods for the benefit of mankind and who was later severely punished (but forgiven) by Zeus the father-god. Atlas is not so much the symbol and principle of wisdom and maturity—although he is rationalized to represent them—as he represents a guilt-ridden older Prometheus who must carry the oppressive weight of atonement and restitution for having done and seen too much.

In *The Cultural Contradictions of Capitalism* (1976) and *The Social Philosophers: Community and Conflict in Western Thought* (1973), sociologists Daniel Bell and Robert Nisbet, respectively, diagnose *modernism* to be the scourge of Western life. While neither social physician has a good prognosis for his patient, for both the treatment of preference is the restoration of community. The past is worthy of more respect than the prospective future. Bell sees hedonistic individualism run rampant; Nisbet sees bureaucracy and centralism devouring personal identities. Both yearn for a restoration of personal continuity with a past that has been severed. For Bell, *civitas* is a personal loyalty to one's city, one's community, that involves a willingness to relinquish some personal aggrandizement in the service of the common good. This presupposes, however, an inherent antagonism between individual and group, and the need of the individual to sacrifice altruistically, if not repress, personal wishes. Nisbet would restore the "ecological" and "plural" community, thereby reinstating "kinship" as the basis of social relations. The New Ethnics are in full accord with his prescription: "Living as we do in a world grown increasingly more centralized and collectivized, with the roots of localism and cultural diversity seemingly cut by the forces of modernity, it is possible to see in the plural community man's last best hope."[22]

It is as though the malignant forces of modernity were imposed from without, never from within, as though their presence is that of an alien to a natural body. The image of a countrified city is of recent, romanticized, vintage. Our immigrants of every wave have a different story, and their vision of the open city is part of an ancient tradition that found early expression in the burgher aphorism *Stadtluft macht man frei,* "City air makes you free." For all their monumental erudition and civility, Bell and Nisbet number among the prophets of neoobscurantism, praising a *communitas, polis,* and pluralism whose motivations they fail to understand.

In the days of the best and the brightest, we lived according to the General Electric motto: "Progress is our most important product." Now we seem unable to do anything right. If in American culture the valuation of progress generates a progressive dissatisfaction with each new achievement, the progressive dissatisfaction with progress itself casts radical self-doubt on everything we are and have done. Renewal is through the repudiation of the technological monster and the embracing of simplicity. This deep current pessimism—to the point of fatalism and catastrophism—voiced by former optimists to whom despair was un-American, is quite American. René Dubos construes pessimism "as a perverted expression of national conceit. If the United States can no longer be regarded as the best among nations, then declaring it to be the worst is a way of giving it uniqueness and therefore a special quality," perhaps manifest destiny inverted.[23] First chosen to conquer, now chosen to repent. To that degree to which we have done excess, to that degree must we now constrict ourselves and atone. In Heilbroner's view, democracy and liberalism cannot meet the task. As he recommends with reluctance, perhaps we are in need of "iron governments capable of rallying obedience."

In a book published in 1973, *Obedience to Authority,* psychologist Stanley Milgram offered us the image of a humanity that readily surrenders its humanness for the sake of power and control, gaining sadistic pleasure by the infliction of suffering upon others.[24] In the last two or three years, over a score of books on Nazi Germany have been published, reflecting the fascination with the ruthless expression of force and what Hannah Arendt called "the banality of evil." Milgram's research, it may be recalled, was frequently referred to by nonadmirers as "the Eichmann experiment."

Most recently, the control strategy of restoration has been suggested by psychologist Donald T. Campbell in the presidential address to the 1975 meetings of the American Psychological Association. On the rebound from what he regards as individualistic, hedonistic psychologies, he sees in social systems "an underlying wisdom in the recipes for living that tradition has supplied us," recipes far "better tested than the best of psychology's and psychiatry's speculations on how lives should be lived." Psychology and psychiatry have only "speculations," while tradition has "wisdom."[25] Here, another expression of the malaise of self-doubt. Buttressed by a reading of evolutionary theory and the new discipline of sociobiology (which seeks the origin of social behavior in genetics), he offers an updated version of the dualism and antagonism between body/individual and mind/social. Biological drives make human beings "selfish," "self-seeking," "uninhibited," "anti-social," "hedonistic," and "individualistic." All of these tendencies must be controlled if a society is to survive: hence the necessity for strong systems of religion and morality, the sense of sin and guilt, to balance and bring order out of individualistic chaos. (If all human behavior is genetically determined, then why is the latter necessary? This question goes curiously unanswered. Evolutionary biology surely would have provided for altruism as well as competition.) Human biology and its emotional expressions are thus opposed to cultural traditions whose repression and inhibiting traditions provide a corrective to the excesses and dysfunctions of human nature.

What this all amounts to is the mistrust of human biology and the concomitant belief that humans are born inherently evil—or at least inclined toward evil, that human beings must be constrained to do good. Humans cannot be trusted to be free. Interestingly, Freud once wrote: "Where id is, there shall ego be," suggesting the gradual autonomy of the ego from the drives, and the ability of the ego to delay and channel gratification. The school of psychoanalytic *ego psychology* has systematically explored the relation of human intrapsychic process to the environment and has not only demonstrated the potential autonomy of the ego from the drives, but, following Freud's later suggestion of an undifferentiated id-ego, inquired into the specific origin of the very *drivenness* that is really the subject of Campbell's address. From Vietnam and Lieutenant Calley, to college and urban disturbances, to Richard Nixon and Watergate, everything is out of joint. It would seem that Campbell, and others as well, mistake what is literally a culture-bound syndrome to be the essence of human nature. Their remedy is far from the compromise Freud had in mind. It would read: Where id was, there shall *superego* be. The *drivenness* of moralism and religious orthodoxy can be as consuming as that of hedonic sensualism. Here again we can see the oppositional process at work in the service of conservatism and reaction—sanctioned by the priesthood of science which further confirms our basic mistrust of ourselves and convinces us that salvation is through control.

Together, these symbols, images, and myths provide external representations to us of what we feel and imagine ourselves to be, which we, in turn, come to think of as human nature. Since we feel incapable of managing our own lives, we are in desperate need of external management, a care-taking, supervision, and control that will provide all the answers, give all the directions, and generally tell us what to do, though benevolently. The feared stern father is more readily acceptable if he is more like a big brother. This is perhaps what many of the radical youth have in mind when they speak of "friendly fascism." For the restoration of order from the panic-ridden abyss of chaos, even freedom and dignity will be sacrificed—but not their illusion, especially in the year of the American Bicentennial celebration.

A cluster of images, then, intimates the cultural ethos of our age: father, South, Catholic, white ethnic, fundamentalism, orthodoxy, conservatism, order, security, hierarchy. The task of the remainder of this book is to elucidate the nature of the White Ethnic Movement as one variation on this wider cultural thematic cluster. In this chapter we related the South (and all it connotes) to Catholic and ethnic. Our discussion of the White Ethnic Movement takes as its point of departure the often bewildering question of the relation between black and white.

5 The Illusion of Pluralism and the Preservation of Caste

Neither scholars nor white ethnics themselves can discuss the White Ethnic Social Movement without invoking the blacks, either as a source of opposition or to deny their own racism. The term *white ethnic,* though manifestly pluralist, is implicitly a way of maintaining or restating the black-white (caste) boundary. For example, Andrew Greeley, an Irish-Catholic sociologist, scholar, priest, and participant in the White Ethnic Movement, searches for the Irish "soul" while tacitly implying black "soul." In the same way blacks deny that whites have "soul," Greeley infers from his Irish-Catholic perspective that those white ethnics who have become Americanized have lost their Catholic souls *and* their ethnic souls.

> What if one white immigrant group had been able—without the aid of sensitivity training—to keep alive some of the wild passion which surburban culture abhors but desperately needs? What in other words would have happened if the Irish had hung on to not only their souls but also their "Soul"? What if John Kennedy had not been shot? But, then, we Irish have always been good at sitting by the side of the bog, staring into the raining mist and dreaming lofty dreams of what might have been.[1]

Yet "what might have been," symbolized by Kennedy and the American Dream, had it been achieved, would not have necessitated the search for ethnic "soul," since American "soul" would have been sufficient. The black revolt became a model for the white ethnic counterreformation, here, in Greeley's sense, with religion and ethnicity coterminous. Elsewhere, Greeley makes explicit the tie between the New Ethnicity and racial opposition, even as he denies it.

As objects of "disrespect and contempt," he emphasizes that "the ethnics want to be respected."

> They are becoming more and more conscious that they have been cast in the role of scapegoat for certain social ills. There is no evidence that the ethnics are any more angry at black militancy than anyone else in the society, but there is substantial evidence that they are angry at being typecast as society's racists. . . . One thing seems clear: the white ethnic movement does not and cannot represent a political, economic, or social backlash. The social dynamic of economic deprivation and suffering among the white ethnics to make such a thrust possible does not exist.[2]

The backlash that Greeley ignores is the *status* backlash—a point implicit in testimony by the Polish-Catholic priest Father Jozef Kubic at the U.S. Congressional Hearings on Ethnic Heritage Studies Legislation in 1970:

> There is some fear expressed about alleged antagonism between Slavic ethnics and Blacks. Remember that both were equally exploited and suppressed. The ethnics worked as hard and died as frequently as any slave ever did. The slave in the fields, the ethnic in the mines, the steel mills, the forests, the farms. The ethnic lived and worked in harmony with the Black for decades in our cities. After the Second World War came the rapid use of "Black Power." The ethnic sees history passing him by. He worked hard to provide for himself and his children without aid or assistance from government agencies. Now a paternalistic government showers generous favors on the Blacks and continues to ignore him.

More explicitly, a Slovak-American steel worker summarizes the bitterness and "racial slurs thrown in out of a feeling of personal frustration." Prior to a regular USWA meeting, a member of "us minority people asked the staff man what about the injustices fostered on the white ethnics over the years? . . . I don't like to use slang names, but here goes. What are the Niggers, the government's Chosen People? They are getting everything, what about us? Hell, those lazy bastards won't work, why cater to them? . . . " (from a letter dated May 1974, to Howard Stein).

For our final and most poignant example, we discuss an experience which took place during a March 1971 meeting of the Pittsburgh Ethnic Heritage Studies Center Committee, attended by both writers. All the local white ethnic leaders were in attendance. During the formal proceedings, a significant unprogrammed event occurred. A Slavic-

American member had noticed an article in that day's *Pittsburgh Press*, reporting on an address given by a member of the government of the Union of South Africa in which apartheid was defended on cultural grounds, namely, that its cultural pluralistic foundation would be mutually beneficial to all groups. The expression *separate equality* summarized the government official's position. Throughout the meeting, this newspaper passed in and out of a dozen people's hands, and as the number increased, there emerged a consensus, via undertone, that this indeed was a model to rally behind for America as well. Apartheid was clearly the answer. Those present emphasized, as did the government official, how this solution of separate equality would prevent any group from rising against any other because all would be voluntarily equal on a cultural basis. Because all cultures within the political structure are equal, there would be no reason for a member of one cultural group to seek to become a member of another group. Furthermore, since social mobility by the various Bantu groups would be tantamount to attempting to cross over, this would of course be impossible because one belongs to and in one's own culture. The fact that the cultural argument supported the white supremacist position was never recognized, probably because those who came under its spell had similar intentions: to retain their precarious socioeconomic attainments and their piece of the American Dream; to assert the cultural relativity of ethnic identity, thus enabling them to claim that their ancestral culture is equal to that of any culture; to rationalize through the cultural argument that blacks are and inherently belong where they are because of the nature of their culture; and to prevent those of lower socioeconomic levels from challenging their right to their own levels of attainment (rationalized both by the cultural argument and by the ethic implicit in the American Dream that one can gain anything through hard work, whereas failure to advance is simply a sign that one is not working hard enough, or, as Archie Bunker puts it on its obverse side: "Them that works eats").

This last example is but an extreme case of a sentiment frequently expressed by many Slavic-Americans among whom we have done intensive research (Stein among Slovaks and Rusins, Hill among Poles). The apartheid model is simply a rationalized system of caste separatism under the illusion of ethnic (cultural) pluralism and is shared, though not so clearly articulated, by many white ethnics, whether or not they actively participate in the White Ethnic Cultural Movement. Everyone in their place, with a rigid boundary between black and white, is likewise what Glazer and Moynihan have called the "southern model," which in fact would appear to be a national model, more overt in the South, more covert and disguised in the North—at least until recently.[3]

White Is Not Black

The label "white ethnic" is a term of self-identification and self-definition by means of contrast and opposition. From the foregoing examples, and numerous others which they represent, it is clear that such labels as "white ethnic," "ethnic," and "minority" are interchangeable, with whiteness being implied or spelled out. Distinguishing one's kind from blacks is of paramount importance. An individual defines himself in terms of what he is *not*. The dichotomy black-white becomes a generative grammar.

Let us briefly put this in historical perspective. The black countercultural movement asserted that "black is beautiful," "one should be proud to be black," and blacks must take the initiative and claim or reclaim power that is rightfully theirs. On the one hand, blacks have embraced the caste-racial definition and claim that blackness is equal or superior to whiteness. On the other hand, much of the new black culture emphasizes "negritude" or "soul," which as a cultural feature is claimed to be superior to the soulless whites whose European civilization can produce only technology, artificiality, consumerism, alienation, cold reasoning, enslavement, and destruction.

Moreover, much of black culture, in its mythological reinvention of Africa, repudiates and denies the American *and* African heritage of slavery (as Queen Mother Moore, an early Garveyite, recently said, "We were not slaves, we were enslaved"), leaping backward four centuries to dignity and pride before their defeat at the hands of slave traders. Blacks became an ethnic group not only with culture, but with high culture (e.g., empires of Dahomey, Ashanti, and Songhai). The Black Panthers, symbolized by Huey Newton (the black man with the gun), directly confront, demand, and dare to openly threaten the white man—a behavior heretofore unimaginable. In the "good old days," blacks were quiet, unassuming, and did what they were told— so the half-truth goes. The very idea of a black man with a gun, potentially aimed at a white policeman, is a complete inversion of the stereotype and the event all too often repeated in real history: the black man hunted by the white man's gun and rope. This total, systematic inversion by blacks has required that whites come to terms with a new ordering of man, society, culture, and world. Those who were once told, who listened, and who had to obey now do the telling. As in the Sioux Indian Vine Deloria's recent book *We Talk You Listen,* the superiority that whites had always taken for granted was thoroughly repudiated and flaunted before them. The whites now, in turn, attempt to recapture the lost ground and to restore their position in the hierarchy.

If in the early period of the Black Power Movement, black visibility, demonstration, and voice were of paramount importance, whites are now taking the initiative. As Isaacs has noted: "Physical characteristics serve as a badge of identity" and "figure with high visibility and powerful glandular effect in relations between groups." With the downfall of the white supremacy system in the United States, changes in the meaning of color, race, and ethnicity accompanied the revision of power, status, and intergroup behavior. In the following passage, Isaacs continues his discussion of the black and white identity crisis.

> The experience of change has opened a period of acute group identity crisis for blacks who must transform their blackness from the crushing negative the white world made of it into an accepted fact in their lives. Similar pressure has come upon some whites—not only in the United States by any means—for whom "whiteness" remains a paramount identification and whose group identity behavior is shaped by their need to mainstream their myths about it.[4]

The perversion of the golden rule which reads "Do unto others as they have done unto you," first practiced with a vengeance by the black movement against white middle-class American culture, is returned in kind by the New White Ethnic Movement. Re-definition by ethnicity, according to De Vos,

> is a way to change relative status that works for the blacks who have now taken the initiative in defining themselves by mobilized confrontation and militancy. Whites of various ethnic backgrounds, especially on the working class level, are being forced either to fight back, or to find some accommodative re-definition which makes sense to them and which they can more or less accept without seeing blacks totally as in-group social participants. Retreating from overt racist positions some American urban groups are seeking defensive accommodations, if not launching counter-offensives on the level of ethnic groupings.

Technically speaking, the United States is a "mixed class-ethnic society with caste-race features."[5] Ethnic pluralism became for blacks a means of attempting to overcome caste self-perception. But in doing so, blacks explicitly declared themselves to be the equal of whites. The white ethnic counter-counterculture is an attempt to reinstate caste through the guise of ethnicity, or culture—thereby putting blacks again in their "place"—while being able to rationalize and deny that this motive has anything to do with racial exclusion. Yet, and this is of utmost importance: whether a discussion of white ethnics is by or with scholars, researchers, white ethnic intellectuals and apologists, or with those multi-generation Americans of south, central, and east European ancestry who may not even call themselves "white ethnics," the contrast set of whiteness versus blackness is never absent, is unavoidable, even when denied because it reflects a generic conflict.

Opposition and the Process of Black-White Segmentation

Many competing classificatory schemes currently abound: black and white; white ethnic and nonwhite ethnic; minorities and ethnics; white ethnics or ethnics as oppressed minorities, and nonwhite ethnics claiming equal or greater discrimination; white ethnics, nonwhite ethnics, the Woman's Movement, Gay Liberation, and Gray Power (the elderly) as minority groups; the black (Afro-), brown (Chicano), red (Native American), and yellow (Asian) oppressed minorities, and the white oppressors. Categories based on *ethnic groups* compete with, complement, and overlap with those based on *sex, age, race* or *color* (which are, nevertheless, also cultural-symbolic criteria), with religion having become over the last decade a less salient and emotionally valent basis of distinction and identification.[6]

The black-white dichotomy and process of differentiation is explicit and inherent in the category *white ethnic.* Many white ethnics use the terms *ethnic* and even *minority* to denote exclusively whites, or at least to assert that the white ethnics have been as oppressed, both in the feudal-serf past and in the American present, as the blacks and other "colored" minorities. It is for this reason that we include white southerners in a volume concerning the White Ethnic Movement. It is our belief that the issue of race is inseparable from the current ethnic resurgence and is in fact part of its deep structure, i.e., the renewed and simultaneous definition of self and definition of the excluded other, the differentiation of *me-us* and not *me-them.* White ethnics and white southerners share the fact that they are white Americans who believe and feel themselves to be oppressed minorities in their own right, who contrast themselves with the so-called colored minorities *and* with the liberal-dominated elites of the North. Both become equally vilified opprobrious outgroups. Broadly speaking, we can say that those who now choose to be called "white ethnics" literally occupy a *residual* category. They are neither the "haves" (e.g., the homogenized stereotype of the so-called WASP or Jew) nor the "have nots" (e.g., many of whom call themselves the "minorities," and some of whom go by the ethnic label).

Socioeconomically, the white-ethnic Americans are largely lower middle class, working class "hardly haves" and nearly "have nots." Until recently they were literally taken for granted by the American polity and by the economic system, and it was assumed that they would vote the right way and be the obedient, industrious urban peasantry for the industrial fiefdoms. They were the "silent majority," the "forgotten Americans," and "middle America."

The white ethnics are simultaneously non-nonwhites, nonaffluent, and nonassimilated (or, more specifically, those whose assimilation aspirations were not fulfilled). The white ethnics are a forgotten people, many of whom have become painfully and angrily self-conscious. Those who have been overlooked and forgotten now seek immediate redress and try to draw visible and vocal attention to themselves and to their plight of status deprivation and downward social mobility. *White ethnic* becomes a chosen (voluntary) category of self-definition, self-identification, status reversal, personal loyalty and belonging, and, literally, affirmative action (power). Yet it is essential to remember that this self-definition is one term, or member, or class of a contrast set of binary opposition which cannot be understood as existing independent of the opposition. Self and other, insider and outsider, are simply extreme poles of an interdependent system. Within this system, boundaries are maintained by the persistence of vigilance, exclusion, and the projection, displacement, and dissociation of repudiated attributes of one's self onto the outgroup—which is essential to one's definition of self and *kind*. The white ethnic counterposes himself and his *kind* against the WASP-Jewish establishment on the one hand, and the minorities on the other. The insistence on difference and the process of differentiation (creating and enhancing differences) go hand in hand. In summary: white ethnic is *not* WASP, Jewish, or minority, and its positive self-definition is inseparable from the negation of what it is not. It has converted the residual category from a necessity into a virtue.

The Black Pride and Power Movement of the 1960s was simultaneously catalyst, precipitant, object of admiration and envy, and hatred for the White Ethnic Movement. Through identification with the aggressor, blacks were to be modeled after, outdone, and, in a sinister way, "put in their place." With the repudiation by many blacks of the American Dream and everything white associated with it, the black movement claimed that only those of the black race possessed "soul" and that those of the homogenized white race were "soulless." The erstwhile source of identification and emulation was repudiated, and such new vindictive stereotypes as "white devils," "Honkie" (precariously close to "Hunkie"), "whitey," "white racist," "bigot," "pig," and "hardhat" were imposed on anything that looked white. Not only was the American Dream and the myth of the Melting Pot rejected, but many black leaders now insisted that the American Dream was evil from the beginning or that blacks had always dreamed a different dream—one associated with "soul," Africa, or Mecca. One's own participation in the process of dreaming was rejected and reinterpreted through projection.

The dream of integration had been externally imposed, brainwashed in a conspiracy to whitewash one's blackness. As black became beautiful, white became ugly; as Africa became the cradle of civilization and the embodiment of humanism, Europe and America simultaneously became life denying, dehumanizing, and barbarous. A black clinical psychologist, a researcher of black suicide, recently remarked on the issue of equality and the American Dream: "Maybe it wasn't ever meant for us to have these aspirations." Others, however, have repudiated these aspirations and must invent a new dream.

A black activist professional, directing a drug rehabilitation program, insisted that "in order for brothers in the community to have a positive self-image, the Whites will have to have a negative self-image." He thus seeks to replace the need for a drug high in the addiction process with an alternative high (i.e., the embracing of a new black identity). He emphasized: "We are not deprived. We never wanted their culture. Whose culture are we deprived of? What we need is cultural enrichment," by which he means "a corrective Afro-American culture . . . we have to keep the unity. A lot of people would like to take our unity away." In discussing the 1954 U.S. Supreme Court desegregation decision, the black activist said: "If you read the small print, it's saying 'when you are together among yourselves that creates a sense of inferiority'; that's the logic: the more integrated we became, the greater sense of personal inferiority was implanted. To associate with Blacks was negative. You have to un-brainwash yourself of the false belief . . . American Blacks stand in awe of others. What you need is to love yourself, to idolize who you are." After presenting a radical reinterpretation of history, he emphasized that "you should stand in awe of yourself. . . . We are practicing someone else's culture. It enhances their lifeline, not ours. . . . Language perpetuates our inferiority. Everytime we use the English language it reminds us of a personal inferiority. We should learn a second and third *African* language."

A frequent emphasis in black consciousness raising is the need to "divorce ourselves from European thought." A recent example of the decontamination and purging of alien white influence is the appearance of *The Death of White Sociology* whose purpose is to define by opposition the field of black sociology.[7] At approximately the same time, a black psychologist expressing his belief that he would soon be converting to the Nation of Islam and who is now a minister of that faith (rejecting Western psychology) remarked that: "American science is Jewish science. We need an African science to explain our experience. Who are the leaders of the field? Who are the best known American psychologists, sociologists, anthropologists? Jews. It is their image that we have believed for so long. We believed what they told us we are. We need to make our own image."

Why Jews? In embracing the Black Muslim faith, in identifying with the exploited and oppressed Third World, in exorcising from himself the Western traditions of Judeo-Christian religion and science, his outgroup necessarily became a symbol of all that his new identity must oppose. Lest we be misunderstood, he did not simply execrate "Jewish science." Rather, as the ego attempts to synthesize everything into a coherent whole, Jewish science came to symbolize all that he once was, now detests, and must purge from himself and those he seeks to convert.

Later we will show that the ideology of the White Ethnic Movement is virtually identical with this, having only a change in content; here we explore the reaction of the forgotten and abused white ethnics of the North *and* the South, who use their new pride to make others ashamed, whose self-esteem is based on the degradation of others, and whose claim to power through affirmative action renders their opponents impotent.

The new positive identity—and we would suggest by extension any new liberated revolutionary consciousness—lives parasitically on the negative identity that not long ago was positive and was the very measure of one's self-worth. Now in the radical revaluation and devaluation, the supreme good has suddenly become worthless. What was the response of the white ethnics even before they became self-conscious as white ethnics, before their malaise was rationalized for them in ethnic terms by writers like Michael Novak? Despite the current unpopularity of the term *backlash,* it accurately describes the clearly symmetrical and mutually escalating process that finally led to the White Ethnic Cultural and Political Movement. What began as a *reaction* to the fear of territorial invasion, economic threat (the quota system, inflation, increased taxes, and the threat of unemployment), status disparagement, and downward social mobility (not only for themselves, but for their children in whom their future was invested), later became systematized into an *explanation* for the acute and chronic distress and as a *means* and *direction* for its *relief* and *resolution.*

Everything was imputed to the blacks and to the federal government, which were too permissive and too controlling. From Cicero to Gary to Pittsburgh, the white ethnics were saying in essence: "They're cramming the blacks down our throats. They don't have any understanding of our local needs. We can take care of our own problems." The blacks, it seemed, had all the rights and all of the guilty white liberals on their side, while the white ethnics had no one of consequence to speak in their behalf, but many willing to denounce them. Having spent their entire lives—not to mention those of parents or immigrant grandparents—earning their way to the good life and acceptance by individual merit, they see not effort or achievement, but (so it would appear) the lack of effort and ascription, rewarded. Having devoted themselves to an American Dream that seemed attainable, they see its ceiling ever receding, while its availability to the blacks and the minorities is seemingly free for the asking. Now, because of inflation, a lifetime of savings cannot pay for a child's college education—the prime requisite for socialization for admission into the respected mainstream—if one is a white ethnic. A white ethnic is not of the "right" minority or is not quite "poor enough" to merit the apparently unlimited opportunities accorded to blacks (though a black degraded by various welfare programs would have a different story to tell). White ethnics have given their taxes and their blood subsidizing the American Dream, with the hope that America's countenance would shine favorably upon their good works. Yet they learn that their labor does not subsidize their future through the education of their own children. For white ethnics, the subsidy, taken from the daily toil in the steel mills of Pittsburgh, Cleveland, and Gary (and the other urban fiefdoms as well), seems to be for the future of children not their own.

Tragically, it was in such an atmosphere of alienation, powerlessness, despair, frustration, the undermining of ideals, and the unbridgeable gap between expectation and realization that made the white ethnics vulnerable to the exploits and appeals to hatred, fear, and divisiveness by Richard Nixon, Spiro Agnew, and George Wallace. Those leaders who had appealed to hope and who had symbolized the American Dream were, in rapid succession, all dead—Martin Luther King, Jr., and Robert Kennedy assassinated within five months of each other. Cynicism and despair became easily marketable, and 1968 was the pivotal year, though not unprepared for.

In an analysis of the support which 1968 presidential candidate George Wallace received in Cleveland, Gary, and Boston, social psychologist Thomas Pettigrew found that "The typical Gary voter for Wallace was a lower-middle-class male who had some high school education, and was highly identified with the 'working class.' He was generally below 40 years of age, a skilled craftsman, and making an annual family income between $7,500 and $10,000."[8] The Gary Wallaceites felt that their lot was getting worse, seemingly at the expense of blacks. Antiblack sentiment, mistrust, and "feelings of acute relative deprivation" distinguished them. "Like black-Americans, they have high aspirations without a sense of making progress toward their goals. Worse, they believe that Negroes and others are unjustly making rapid strides forward at their expense, helped out by a too-generous Federal government that has forgotten them."[9]

Both blacks and whites feel unable to achieve the American Dream and blame each other for their own failures. In a study of the emergence of ethnic interests among Irish and Italians in Providence, Rhode Island, in 1966, John Goering found that the emergence of ethnic consciousness is conditioned by growing skepticism about the American Dream, more present in the third, than in immigrant and second generations.

> The third generation returns to the seclusiveness of ethnicity in resentment against un-attained promise. A withdrawal from the principle of a universalistic ideology provides the rationale for a new more heuristic creed. The new beliefs of the third generation appear less tolerant than those of the first generation. . . . The third generation does indeed return to ethnicity, but less as a source of cultural or religious refreshment, than as the basis for organizing the skepticism associated with discontent and racial confrontation.[10]

In times of threatened identity, status, and self-esteem, white ethnics, like their lower-class counterpart in the American South, have recourse to a culturally validated excuse, inaccessible to blacks. The belief in inherent racial superiority, more explicit in the deep South, more implicit in the deep North, justifies to whites why they should be able to achieve and succeed more easily than blacks. Furthermore, they have a reservoir of precariously maintained self-esteem available if they are somehow merely equal to, or lower than blacks. Racism thus provides justification for resentment by white ethnics against blacks whose own assertions of African superiority or Afro-American "soul" threaten those who have taken their superiority for granted.

The New Ethnic consciousness and claims to inherent rights by white ethnics can, in part, be understood as an attempt by whites to regain their fragile superiority over blacks. Thus, by appealing to their own glorious distant history, the white ethnics are trying to overshadow the blacks. This of course is done in the name of a pluralist model, horizontal, and egalitarian on the surface; but in its deep structure the model is vertical, lineal, and exclusive. By making cultural relativism absolute the white ethnic can "keep the darkies out" of white society, saying, "they would never want in because they are happiest among their own." Behind the guise of pluralism is caste redefined. Pathetically, in the sense of the sacrifice of the human potential for relatedness, the white ethnic and white America may have their way, as blacks increasingly isolate and enclose themselves within ghetto walls of their own making. White ethnics, too, battle weary and worn from a decade and a half of strife, insult, and dashed hopes, withdraw anew into their ethnic havens of safety, whether in the cities or the suburbs. Ethnic boundaries arise anew and are consolidated; each cave dweller is afraid to venture out to meet the other that is himself. "Good fences make good neighbors," he will steadfastly insist, wishing it weren't true.

Conflict in the Academy as Symptomatic of Cultural Polarization

Academe has played a major role in the erection of exceedingly good fences and defenses. First, blacks sought to put whites "in their place," reinterpreting black history in perspectives and contexts that were relevant to their needs. Whites soon responded in kind. Both pure and applied research became a battleground of ideology as part of the oppositional process. Black racism and white counterracism are mirror images.

Black social science developed through a repudiation of white mainstream social science which had concluded (from Davis and Dollard to Liebow and Moynihan) that the black family was disorganized and matrifocal (even pathological), that there was no black culture, that blacks were a shadow version of white culture, and that the plantation and slavery, rather than Africa, were the foundations of black-American life. With the eruption of the black countercultural movement in the late 1960s, mainstream became anathema. For the new black scholars, the black family was seen as a source of adaptive strength which provided extended ties of mutual assistance—unlike the white, nuclear, economic, and alienated family. The white family, it would seem, was the one which was disorganized. Turning to West Africa (the primary source of American slaves) to find preslavery role models, some black scholars emphasized the power and authority of the father.

Far from seeing themselves as inferior versions of the white man, many new black scholars affirm and take pride in a flourishing black culture—although they may dispute exactly which culture to affiliate themselves with ("soul," West Africa, East Africa, Mecca, etc.). The black counterculture, in research which generated much of the new positive black self-imagery and origin myths, has now precipitated a counter-countercultural trend among white researchers and intellectuals, who undertake a thoroughgoing revisionism for their own purposes—purposes readily congruent with those of the bewildered white population. Environmental determinism (e.g., the culture of poverty) is jettisoned for genetic determinism. The phoenix rises again from the ashes in the renewed genetic arguments of Jensen, Eysenck, Shockley, and Herrnstein. In their introduction to the second edition of *Beyond the Melting Pot,* Glazer and Moynihan contrasted the northern model of openness, fluidity, opportunity, and competition with the southern model of closedness, caste, inflexibility, and exclusiveness. The North at least was redeemable and the authors lamented the increasing "southernization" of the North—similar to a recent analysis of the Attica riots by white ethnic intellectual Michael Novak.[11]

In the North, at least, racism is not quite racism, and if and when it is, it will be because the alien, radical, southern influences migrated North, upsetting the subtle traditional balance between intimacy and distance. ("When we were kids we played with them, we wouldn't want our children to marry one of them, and they are still them, not us.") Since racism is not racism, guilt or responsibility is removed. The denial of active participation in racial exclusiveness is further facilitated by rationalizations derived from distortions of the "culture of poverty" concept—first formulated by Oscar Lewis and later elaborated by Daniel P. Moynihan.[12] According to the preferred reading of *The Moynihan Report,* black culture is the way in which blacks like to live. "If Blacks are poor, it's their own fault, since their preferred way of living makes them that way. Why should we try to change their culture since they seem to like it the way it is?" In more acceptable terms, this attitude is called "cultural pluralism."

"Racism is not racism" went the first argument. "Poverty is not poverty" goes the second. Finally, white historic revisionism in the counter-counterculture says that "slavery was not slavery"—and was not crippling because it had redeeming features. Fogel and Engerman's recent volume *Time on the Cross,* based on interpretations of a computer analysis of slave records, can be seen as substituting one myth for another.[13] Not only was slavery not all that bad, but it provided models and experiences for later participation, efficiency, and mobility in American-Protestant capitalist culture. Further, contrary to the school of Elkins and Moynihan, slavery did not disorganize, but *organized* the black family and the black personality—serving as a source of positive enculturation. Slavery for the blacks was something like a trade school for Americanization, so the argument goes. Slavery taught the true meaning and reward of hard work, productivity, and efficiency. As role models, black supervisors and overseers were proto-capitalists, working on an incentive basis. Black women learned neither promiscuity nor matrifocality during slavery because the birth of first children was late, implying delayed sexual activity in anticipation of the traditional marital dyad. Masters were not really masters; slaves were actually apprentices; the master, the mammy, the butler, and the rebel slave were not only positive role models but they set the stage for later social mobility; *exploitation* is an interpretation imposed from without. In essence, whites need not feel guilty or selectively empathize because blacks neither suffered more nor were more disadvantaged than any other group aspiring to mainstream American life.

Consequences, of course, are entirely different from intentions. But it surely can be no coincidence that this revisionist interpretation of slavery is so culturally timely. Anthropologically speaking, we mean that this constitutes a variation of a dominant cultural theme or one expression of cultural pattern or ethos. First the pendulum swing of black revisionism; now the equal and opposite reaction by white revisionists. One can in a way choose the interpretation one prefers: genetic, economic, cultural, or historical—all and any of which remove through rationalization the responsibility of whites for the condition of blacks—whether in the past or in the present. We note all this to remind the reader that intellectual history is part of cultural history and is deeply imbedded in it. It is in the context of the opposi- tional formula, "black is not white, and white is not black," that each of these individual strands should be seen.

White Ethnics and White Southerners

Additional insight into the dynamics of the New Ethnicity can be gained by what we suggest is the white counterpart in the South. What led us even to consider the analogy is the persistent and vehe- ment denial by northern whites that black-white relations were any- thing like those in the South and that the ultimate putrefaction of the North is its increasing similarity to the South. Absolute dichotomies, like absolute boundaries, not only separate, but reflect the fear of what must be kept on the other side. In denying the reality of the South in the North, what is it that northern white intellectuals, white ethnic or not, do not wish to see? What is the analogy they refuse to allow to be made?

In an essay, "The South as a Counterculture," Sheldon Hackney begins by comparing southern history with the contemporary counter- culture of youth and argues that the South is "the nation's largest oldest counterculture." Specifically, "the key to the Southern past is that Southerners are Americans who have taken on an additional identity through conflict with the North." He discusses the "siege mentality" or "defensive mentality" of the South and also empha- sizes the "approach-avoidance relationship of South to North," re- sulting in "the co-existence of hyper-Americanism and cultural pecu- liarity."[14] Hackney traces the history of this ambivalence and its abortive attempts at resolution from the early nineteenth century to the present.

In an essay, "Beyond the Mainstream: The Ethnic Southerners," George B. Tindall makes explicit the ethnic analogy and emphasizes that "ethnicity affords . . . a strategic vantage point from which to reassess the Southern past" and present as well.[15] Like white ethnic culture, southern distinctiveness has not been allowed to disappear. Analyzing "the South as an American subculture," Tindall notes that the South has undergone nearly four centuries of change without disappearing. In trying to understand the "pattern of its thought," he urges that attention be focused on the mythology which has shaped the sense of southern identity.

The insistence on difference, defiance, and opposition is a key to understanding southern persistence. Tindall contrasts the model of southern cultural distinctiveness with that of the disappearance of the South, its absorption into the mainstream, and concludes that since the mid-1960s the legend of homogenization has been disproven throughout American society with the breakdown of consensus in American life. He succinctly reviews the culture history of the period and the literature and rhetoric it produced. He argues that immigrant ethnics and southerners share a common experience, bear a common stigma as the perpetual outsiders to the American maintstream, and tenaciously cling to their heritage, which reflects the need for roots and a usable past. Localism (the home), violence (the private use of force), and conservative religion (salvation, assurance, fundamentalism) are seen as adaptive responses by minority groups to the unresponsive, dominant, and hostile culture that surrounds them. The experience of southerners, both black and white, is seen as similar to that of immigrant ethnic groups.

Moreover, the symbols, rhetoric, and polity of the Black Power Movement are seen as mirror images of those of southern whites. As we have previously suggested, much of the White Ethnic Pride and Power Movement is likewise functionally a mirror image of the Black Power Movement, and with which it is closely bound up. Finally, although Lewis M. Killian does not discuss the White Ethnic Movement in his book *White Southerners,* his study allows a close analogy to be made between the new movement and the search among white southerners of minority status for regional identity and group solidarity. Killian's historical and sociological analysis allows the conclusion that, despite their heterogeneity of national, religious, and political background, white southerners perceive themselves to be members of an ethnic group. Their subjective sense of being a persecuted minority within American society pervades past and present culture history. Although white southerners have not suffered unequal treatment to the extent that blacks have, they have "reacted as a defensive, self-conscious minority, regarding themselves as the object of collective discrimination."[16]

The white South has responded to this stereotyping and status disparagement from the dominant and self-righteous North by vacillating between or simultaneously asserting defiant cultural regionalism and hyper-Americanism (i.e., insisting on differences and/or sameness). Although white southerners may exaggerate the extent of discrimination against them and minimize their own racism toward blacks, their defensive reaction as a minority group, emphasizing their difference from and superiority to the North, is a consequence of the belief that this discrimination is real.

A paradox in the Civil Rights Movement of the 1960s was that the "moral frontier" was the American South, to be conquered and liberated by the North, with the moral opprobrium on the heavier historical guilt of the South. It is *perhaps* no coincidence that President Kennedy was assassinated in the South, where superior northern morality was enthusiastically imposed on what was assumed to be the inferior southern conscience. Only late in the Civil Rights Movement were marches staged in the de facto segregated North where racism could not be so readily isolated and righteously singled out. In the southern campaign, at least, the acting out of "righteous indignation" and projective identification, assuaging the North's own guilt by eradicating it in their selected victims, this "war of liberation" did not differ much from its predecessors or successors in the amassing of heavy assaults by those "in the right" against those who were, most assuredly, "in the wrong."

The war of liberation by liberals and radicals precipitated a counter-revolution, a war of liberation from the liberators waged by conservatives and reactionaries of the Deep North and Deep South. As Killian notes, "Both national and local elections since the Johnson landslide of 1964 suggests that the majority of White Southerners cling to the belief that the United States is and should be a white man's society. They have new cause for hope that, instead of hypocritically castigating them, the rest of the nation will now join, follow them. . . ."[17]

The furious resentment which greeted the integrationist marchers with Dr. King and Father Groppi in Cicero, Illinois; the use of overwhelming force against the inmates of Attica in upstate New York; the violence and consuming hatred which greets desegregation and busing attempts from Detroit to Boston; the outrage which greeted the federal program of scatter site housing; and the subtle metropolitan rezoning, redistricting, and incorporation, all designed to circumvent the courts and the new laws—all reflected the intentions, throughout the frenetic period of Civil Rights legislation and court decisions, to keep blacks *out* in whatever way possible. The ideal and goal of the full integration of blacks with whites and whites with blacks, in the community, turned out to be a sham that was never intended to be lived up to. "Black rage" was a predictable response to this traumatic realization.[18]

The North was not much different from the South but needed the South to project upon and embody what it could not tolerate in itself. Howard Zinn, a white southerner and a member of SNCC observed:

"The South, far from being utterly different, is really the *essence* of the nation. . . . Those very qualities long attributed to the South as special possessions are, in truth, *American* qualities, and the nation reacts emotionally to the South precisely because it subconsciously recognizes itself there." And Killian concludes, "If [the] national trend toward angry white reaction to black desperation continues, white southerners, except for the forlorn liberals, may find a shortcut to their own integration into the larger American society. They may cease to be a minority in which white supremacy is an ideal as well as a fact."[19]

Enter George Wallace and, in the past, Richard Nixon or Spiro Agnew—voices and symbols for angry white Middle America. George Wallace, now that strong man in the wheel chair, offers another "New Deal" to the "little people" he would champion and whose bitterness he would exploit. In an essay concerning columnist Tom Wicker and the 1971 prison riot at Attica, Michael Novak expressed his anger over "the masses of white people [becoming] the new niggers of America."[20] Tom Wicker and Attica became for him symbols of a fundamentalist "southernized" liberal revolutionary ideology come North. Whites, that restless not-so-silent majority, are human too.

For the children and grandchildren of Austro-Hungarian serfs (of which there are fifty-seven nationalities) whose ancestors were greeted with the term *Hunkie,* now to be called "Honkie" by the descendants of black slaves, and "pigs" and "racists" by self-righteous college youth liberals, is to have ancient stigma and insult reawakened by contemporary injury. But this vicious stereotyping does not occur in a social or historical vacuum. In Novak's earlier *Rise of the Unmeltable Ethnics* (1971), the WASPs became the "new niggers" of *his* America.[21] Novak demands empathy and respect for white Americans, but cannot seem to identify in the slightest with Tom Wicker and his life history of wrestling for *his* liberation. When Wicker was called "brother" by a black inmate, and hugged him; when Wicker recalls the event using Martin Luther King, Jr.'s, phrase "free at last," Novak can only speak of a "mystique of blackness and whiteness . . . possibly Scotch-Irish and . . . certainly Southern." He cannot identify with a southern white man who feels suddenly and finally liberated from the burdens of the southern past. (We also have some difficulty in seeing everything reduced, or seemingly so, to ethnicity.) Yet Novak is *also* right in mistrusting this new freedom. Is this new liberation to be attained by repudiating, dehumanizing still another group, Wicker's erstwhile ancestors and contemporary northern whites? Genuine freedom or liberation is achieved only when there is no longer a need for an outgroup upon which one dumps all of one's opprobrium.

In emphasizing the differences in racial relations between the North and the South, Novak joins an ancient tradition that denies that the North is like the South, that *we* are not like *them*. Just as the white South could not tolerate the self-righteous abolitionists and carpetbaggers, the contemporary white North does not want southern liberals flogging it with its moral superiority. We get the feeling from Novak that he feels the North would be better off without the insidious influences from the South. We might add that since World War II, southern blacks and whites, largely rural, are the new immigrants to the northern urban utopia and have been largely welcomed and treated by the new native whites just as the ancestors of these whites had been treated when they came over in steerage. In the North, blacks are called "niggers" (though mostly when blacks cannot overhear), and Appalachian southern whites are called "Skidders" (as in *skid row*). Stereotyping is coped with by counterstereotyping.

At any rate, works such as Joel Kovel's *White Racism* and Lewis Killian's *White Southerners* carefully dispel the common belief that the North is radically different from the South in the extent of its racial beliefs: what differs is the form of expression, its openness or subtlety, and how these expressions have or have not been codified. As essentially *private* sentiments and attitudes about racism become more *public* in the North, the extent of these differences diminish. If the North is so different from the South, why, when George Wallace did his bidding, did he make such heavy inroads in the North? Northern and southern whites are far from being of different species, but are regional variants of a single cultural species, *American*.

If localism, violence, self-legislation of law and order, and conservative religion seem peculiarly southern, contemporary socioeconomic conditions are making the "strong man" phenomenon increasingly attractive in the North. In both cases they are adaptive responses by minority groups to the unresponsive dominant and hostile supraculture that surrounds them. White southerners have been treated as "niggers" by the North for three centuries. Novak accuses Wicker of "sentimentalizing the sufferings of blacks." By offering historical examples (themselves true) that whites and white ethnics have suffered too, perhaps even more, and that imprisonment in America is far better than its counterparts in other places with which Novak is familiar, Novak attempts, and perhaps to many he succeeds, in defining as *relative* the suffering of blacks—in Attica, in America at present, and perhaps during slavery. Many Slavic-Americans (of several ethnic groups) with whom we have conducted field research insist that serfdom under the Russians, Prussians, or Hungarians was a far more cruel experience than was slavery for blacks in America and that, after all, they or their parents did not enslave the blacks here, but immigrated to a society in which racism was practiced by others. Although they admit they *came* to a racist society, what they do not admit is that they absorbed the racist values of America. And when they admit their racism, they deny responsibility for it.

There seems to be taking place at present a nationwide contest, participated in by all ethnic, racial, age, and sex groups, each competing for "most oppressed minority" status. Surely, the solution to paternalization of blacks by liberal whites is not to relativize, and thereby diminish, the effect of historical and contemporary experience—and in the process virtually to exonerate northern whites from guilt that is properly southern, like grits.

Turning finally to Attica: perhaps (like poverty and slavery) it wasn't all that bad. Perhaps the guilt-conscious liberals have just fed us a line. Novak comments that the Attica prisoners wanted to be treated "as men"; yet "precisely because they had failed to act accordingly they had found themselves in Attica. They had shown by their proven crimes that they did not deserve the society of men." Crime and recidivism reflect a failure of the individual rather than the state. Nowhere does Novak (like the white ethnics for whom he purports to speak) entertain the possibility of a relation between social structure, economy, polity, ideology, and deviance. Criminals have a character disorder because they have a character disorder. Is that why individuals fail? Is it a moral flaw, a genetic defect? One might recall that in the period of the great southern and eastern European immigration to America, American prisons and asylums were increasingly filled with *these* social undesirables who had gone mad or turned to illegitimate means of "making it" in America. If some flaw is to be located within the individual, it must also be located in the social experiences that led to that flaw. Not only do Americans fight crime, but they are fascinated with it even as they combat it. Those who are white and "straight," it would seem, need their "niggers" to act for them (in the streets and on the television screen) and get punished. To ignore the hidden and embattled humanity of the inmates and say, as does Novak, that they "had shown by their crimes that they did not deserve the society of men" is to make of them "niggers," regardless of race or ethnicity. When we make another nonhuman or subhuman, we dehumanize ourselves as well.

This is precisely the attractiveness of George Wallace and of less charismatic, conservative, populist aspirants to national leadership. In a sense, Wallace is a barometer of the national mood whether or not he is able to win national office. The pervasiveness of white American consensus with what Wallace symbolizes is reflected by the association between Wallace and Archie Bunker, that White American "everyman" of "All in the Family."[22] Just as hope, disillusionment, outrage, and reaction are threads uniting all episodes of the television serial, a sense of demoralization and rage is at the core of the white backlash.

In the 1972 Wallace campaign for the Democratic presidential nomination, humorous slogans and demonstrations encouraging "Archie Bunker for President" pervaded the Wallace camp. This was a time when American commercial enterprise had already saturated the ready and waiting market with Archie Bunker buttons, posters, books, cups, ashtrays, and the like. *The Wit and Wisdom of Archie Bunker* became for a while the cynical American equivalent of the *Writings of Chairman Mao* of the People's Republic of China.

During the 1950s, in the name of states' rights in local self-determination, Wallace defied federal orders to integrate the University of Alabama. He dramatized his opposition by blocking the "schoolhouse door." In those days, what he stood for was not especially popular, except in the South. Today he is acclaimed nationally for his integrity, for "having had the guts to stand up" for what he believed. Today the man who can no longer walk because of the assassin's attempt on his life, doggedly "stands up for the little man" who feels paralyzed.

Wallace has changed his image considerably in recent years, from that of an open reactionary to that of a subtle one. Not needing to display his racism openly because his attitudes are already well known, he can broaden the base of his support by appearing somewhat conciliatory, tempered, and matured. He is no longer a regional demagogue and anachronism, but claims to be the nation's redeemer and harbinger of the future. He no longer needs to impose his racism on an unwilling electorate. All he asks is that the will of the people be done. They will do his racism for him. White is not black, and there is no gray. White ethnics are white southerners, only in the North. George Wallace, however, is merely symptomatic of a cultural mood that is looking for the restoration of order, authority, and status. What is clear is that the ethos must embody the egalitarian principle of cultural pluralism while tacitly perpetuating the hierarchical principle of caste separation. Cultural pluralism in America, it would seem, has the future of yet another illusion. The white South did not lose the Civil War; the white ethnics did not melt. Hysteric denial knows no Mason-Dixon line: neither the Old South nor the Old Ethnicity is "gone with the wind."

6 The New Ethnicity As Counterculture

In the previous chapter we discussed the self-categorizations *white* and *white ethnic* as one member of an interdependent set of binary opposites of which the contrastive member, *nonwhite,* is always present, explicitly or implicitly. Here we shall explore the White Ethnic Movement in terms of other equally significant contrasts, specifically *white ethnic* as *non-WASP.* The oppositional, dissociative dynamic of self-affirmation is through negation and repudiation of the "other" (who in turn embodies repudiated aspects of one's self). This constitutes the generative grammar that is expressed and the dynamic of which is represented in particular cultural content of the white ethnic identity and ideology.

The White Ethnic Movement emerges and consolidates as a "persistent identity system" based on the oppositional process. In contemporary American cultural terms, the New Ethnicity is a counterculture or, more accurately, a counter-counterculture, defining itself initially against the counterculture of the withdrawal-pacific "greening-of-America" movement on the one hand and the engagement-radicalist New Left on the other. The New Ethnicity defines itself as an identity, ideology, and polity in simultaneous contrast with and opposition to other countercultures, mainstream American culture (under the acronym WASP), Jews, blacks, and other minorities with which it comes in conflict.

Throughout this chapter we emphasize that (1) self-definition is done for purposes of contrast, namely, what is excluded from the personal and group boundary still defines that group boundary and is implicit within it by inversion; (2) the white ethnic identity and those identities it opposes constitute an interdependent system, such that the white ethnic identity requires its opponents for its self-definition; (3) the content of the white ethnic identity and ideology is predicated

on the emblematic (totemic) and ritualized symbolization of differentiation of itself from that which it opposes; (4) the understanding of
cultural differences (symbols) between the New Ethnicity and that
which it opposes is inseparable from understanding the process of
social differentiation (relationship) which the symbols, rituals, and
boundary-maintaining activities come to symbolize; (5) the conflict
between the New Ethnic nativism and Americanization/assimilation
ideology is not merely between ingroup and outgroup, but is a fundamental ambivalence within the nativist ingroup that is resolved
through the projection and displacement of rage and hostility into a
stereotyped outgroup (the WASP) who now bears all the opprobrium
of what was formerly self-hatred. As a liberationist movement, the
New Ethnicity is not, nor can it be, free of that from which it seeks to
liberate itself. The enemy, alas, is within. This chapter demonstrates
the validity of these propositions and forms the basis of a model that
we believe to be applicable to nativistic revitalization movements and
crisis cults.

While for the youth movement of the 1960s antimaterialism was the
rallying call, and for the black movement of the late 1960s racism was
the single prism through which American culture history was viewed,
now, for the White Ethnic Movement ethnicity and pluralism are the
points of departure for the analysis of American culture and history.
Ethnicity as the new positive identity is counterposed against all other
identities that are inherently negative. In an essay titled "A Fever of
Ethnicity," Robert Alter notes a number of distinctive features of the
New Ethnicity all of which systematically relate to the oppositional
process: the placing of feeling over mind or reason, past over present,
collectivity over individuality; the Balkanization of politics and culture (separately, Harold Isaacs and Nathan Glazer would add the
gerrymandering of ethnicity in education); a racist reinterpretation of
American culture history in which all social ills are traced to the
WASP; the rejection of American standards and their replacement
with ethnic standards; an extolling of the virtues of the organic ethnic
community without noticing its constrictions and coercions; the perception of modernization, urbanization, and future-orientation as
negative and destructive; and the mystique of *Volkstum*.

To these we would add the creation of a new origin myth according
to which the white ethnic past, in the place of origin and in terms of
contributions to American life, emerges as equal or superior to
American culture. The origin myth serves as a charter for social action, creating a symbolic language of *harmony* within the movement
and serving as a language of *argument* with the antagonistic world

beyond. It becomes the rationale for obtaining redress and for the demand that others capitulate to one's wishes. While the first phase of the White Ethnic Movement is concerned with the raising of consciousness, the formulation of a new myth of origin, and the development of an ideology that will be the basis of one's self and one's public image, the second phase of the movement involves the mobilization of social participation toward goals based on the new ideology. Theory and praxis are not, however, isolable. While the ideology justifies action; as the social movement develops, experience provides additional confirmation for the ideology—the oppositional process makes this virtually inevitable.

Moreover, the ideology is not static, but cumulative. The leaders, as well as followers, require constant reassurance of their rightness. Hence a considerable amount of energy devoted to praxis involves the accumulation and propagation of documentation and substantiation of the ideology. The basic themes and premises are constantly worked and reworked in such a way that the language of ideology becomes stereotypic and redundant—abundant yet simple. Insofar as doubt renders absolute faith impossible, the White Ethnic Movement can never sufficiently prove what it would like to assume. The achievement of socioeconomic goals is insufficient to satisfy the voracious identity needs or to fill the void of pervasive shame, guilt, rage, and the paralysis of self-doubt. Paradoxically, this very dilemma of the New Ethnicity recapitulates the drivenness of the American Dream it rejects.

The American Mosaic

Since approximately 1970, the image of the *mosaic* (and to a much lesser extent, the *stew*) has dominated the white ethnic pluralist ideology. In earlier years, the image of the Melting Pot associated with the American Dream represented the hope for the progressive *integration* of all diverse groups into the mainstream of American culture. Beginning in the mid-1960s, the traditional image decreasingly represented the inner experience which was no longer meaningful. With the sense of inner and outer *disintegration,* a new image was invented and adopted which was more consonant with lived experience. The image of the mosaic constitutes a compromise between the search for a new coherence and the feeling of personal and social fragmentation. The fragments, and the pluralist ideology and polity they express, are a key to a lost wholeness (just as Erikson has stressed that personal psychopathology is a key to lost personal wholeness). The larger mosaic is an attempt to forestall total fragmentation (fission) by assembling the separate pieces into a larger, more comprehensive whole. A semblance of the American Dream is thus retained, though devoid of its formerly compelling wholeness.

An analysis of pluralist imagery confirms this impression. The shattering of idealism and the undermining of ideals that were increasingly more difficult to fulfill culminated in an effort to pick up the pieces and formulate a dream that made sense of inner and outer reality. *Pieces of a Dream*, published in 1972, concerned ethnicity and American society. One of its editors, Monsignor Geno Baroni, is a leading advocate of the mosaic metaphor.[1] The pattern or Gestalt of the American Dream was the Melting Pot in which a fusion, an amalgam, would emerge of greater quality than the initial ingredients. The idea of a better life in America included the possibility of realizing a fuller self, one that transcended the constrictions, dependencies, factionalisms, deferences, and degradations of traditional preimmigrant life. In the American Dream, the Melting Pot did not envisage a completed product or final amalgam (although the Anglo-conformist ideologues certainly did), but an ever-improving alloy. It was the process that would lead to a continuously perfecting product. The Melting Pot was inherently dynamic and the process it represented was a continuous becoming.

The mosaic mythos, conversely, is static and expresses a yearning for completeness, finality. While the principle of *fusion* describes the dynamic of the Melting Pot, the principle of *fission* describes the process underlying the mosaic. Whereas the Melting Pot mythos suggests an open-ended process both in spatial and temporal representation, the mosaic mythos suggests spatial closure and a time-frozen, stagnant quality. American culture, according to the mosaic aesthetic, is the totality of the elements in the mosaic. But while the mosaic is not a mere random assortment of pieces, but a *composite* that forms a picture in which one's own piece constitutes a vital part, the ethnic pluralists place considerable emphasis on the boundaries that separate the components of the picture. They celebrate the separate integrity of the small, individual units. Fragmentation is thus a central social and aesthetic organizing principle of pluralist imagery, balanced through a compromise that equally emphasizes the necessary relation of the piece to the whole. While the Melting Pot was exclusively American, the mosaic is both ethnic and American. The new whole is thus by design fragmented. "Unity in diversity" is a motto which expresses the pluralist ethos.

Whether or not such insistence on diversity (rather than the fact of diversity) makes unity possible is another matter. The lapse of community interest has precipitated the insistence on self-interest, of which ethnic culture and politics is one expression. Nathan I. Huggins writes the following about ethnicity:

> Ethnic pluralism creates multiple refuges where persons can find a common identity when broader community is in doubt. But these retreats are ultimately narrow and fail to lift the person to participation in a higher unity of nation. . . .
>
> Ethnic histories are no answer. There is no fairy of laissez-faire who will, by waving a magic wand, create a new synthesis out of many parts. Ethnic history, like pluralism, may be more an expression of failure than of achievement. We may well need to see the need for a synthesis and community before we can transform diversity into unity.[2]

Precisely because the ability to synthesize has been reduced and the investment in a wider and widening community has been withdrawn, diversity (qua pluralism) has been reified. Affective ties, shared values and interests, and strategies of action are now understood by the participants to be within the ambience of the localistically conceived and/or idealized community. Community, like the other core concepts of the personal and social world, has acquired a new meaning, largely replacing the old.

Keeping in mind the integrative image of the mosaic, one can say that the conception of community (like that of ethos, identity, self, etc.) is no longer fluid, but static and relatively impermeable. Among theorists and apologists of the New Ethnicity, like those of the organic community since Sainte-Simon and Durkheim, there is a distinct preference for models based on equilibrium, closed systems. Both in sociology and its aesthetic, the mosaic model of American culture expresses this penchant for the static, the clearly demarcated, as opposed to process, dynamic models that envision life as an open system. We might take the image a step further and suggest that its compelling aesthetic is functionally related to many concepts (indeed, themselves images and metaphors) applied *from without* to the analysis of the New Ethnicity: separatism, resegregation, refeudalization, Balkanization, the "southern model," and so forth.

Talcott Parsons has recently referred to this process of de-differentiation partly in terms of the motivational dynamics of regression.

> Its nature and significance should be seen against the background of the very powerful incidence, in recent developments of social

structure, of universalistic standards of mobility and of the development of relatively enhanced freedoms, which, however, can easily turn over in anomic directions. Perhaps the most important focus, however, is the pluralization of modern social structure by virtue of which the typical individual plays multiple roles, no one of which can adequately characterize his identification as a "social" personality. The de-differentiating tendency is to select particular criteria and use these as identifying symbols for what the persons who constitute the group actually *are*.[3]

Moreover, much of the white ethnic ideology divides ethnicity from mainstream American culture with an endlessly variable set of binary opposites that conform precisely with Parsons's "pattern variables," a componential breakdown of Ferdinand Tonnies's dichotomous concepts of *Gemeinschaft* and *Gesellschaft*. The oppositional sets central to the white ethnic ideology are listed in Table 6. What is ethnic is clearly *Gemeinschaftslich* ("communal, organic, involuntary, primordial"—all idealized), while what is American is unmistakably *Gesellschaftslich* ("associational, voluntary"—all disparaged). Parsons's analytic components of Tonnies's conceptual ideal type are: "affectivity—affective neutrality," "diffuseness—specificity," "particularism—universalism," "collectivity orientation—ego orientation," and "ascription orientation—achievement orientation."[4]

A cursory inspection of the ethnic versus American "pattern variables" reveals that the left member of each pair corresponds by analogy to the left member of each pair of Parsons's "pattern variables," and conversely. However, the ethnic versus American contrast set is to be understood as ideological, while that of Parsons is analytical. The de-differentiation to which Parsons refers is a psychological and sociocultural evolutionary regression from more complex and individuated to simpler and more "primitive" personality and social organization. To return to the image of the mosaic: it functions as a condensation, analogous to the dream, of the multiple themes fundamental to the white ethnic ethos that, in turn, defines itself in opposition to the ethos associated with mainstream American culture. To change Parsons's terminology slightly, if one of the central organizing images of the American Dream-Melting Pot was integration, the corresponding image in the New Ethnicity is differentiation, a literal *dis-integration* of the former (corresponding, incidentally, to Levi-Strauss's principle of "transformation" and Erikson's principle of "the negative conversion").

We do not argue that, at least at present, most white ethnic Ameri-

TABLE 6 Differences Between Ethnic and Mainstream American
Culture

Ethnic	American
Natural, Real, Genuine	Artificial
Organic	Anomic
Being	Doing
Nature	History
Heart	Head
Imagination	Rationality
Feeling	Thinking
Rooted	Uprooted
Communality, Inseparability of Self from Group, Merge with Earth	Privacy, Individuality, Alienation, Separation
Personal, Subjective	Impersonal, Objective
Myth	Science
Visceral	Cerebral
Body, Natural	Machine
Personal Experience	Universal Standards
"Network People" (Novak)	"Atomic People" (Novak)

cans are embracing this new identity, ideology, and imagery exclusively. *Belief* in the New Ethnicity, and *action* according to its tenets, are two continua that range from utter devotion to irrelevance. For the white ethnic intelligentsia and activists, their very identities depend on a purified ideology. The vast majority of Slovak-, Polish-, and Ruthenian-Americans with whom we have worked do not even know that such an ideology or movement exists. For those relatively few to whom the New Ethnicity does make a difference—individuals of high aspiration to greater status—the image of the mosaic and the new personal and cultural identity associated with it function as a safety valve that supplements, rather than supplants, the ethos of the American Dream, offering temporary salve for the discontents of American civilization. These persons are consistently individuals of high aspiration to greater status and mobility, but throughout their life histories they have been thwarted—as much by constraints within the family as by obstacles in the wider community.

While the American Dream may be in pieces, much of local and national white ethnic political strategy is designed to assure, by achievement or ascription (quota), that the white ethnics get a piece of what the American Dream promised.

Defensive Identities: The Erection of Personal and Group Boundaries

The insistence on difference, closure, relativism, subjective absolutism, and self-determination, all symbolized by the mosaic, is expressed as well through the obsessive preoccupation with identity. And it is precisely this quality that compels us to speak of the New Ethnicity as a defensive identity. Identity, like pluralism, is a symbol of the fixation that many under its spell attempt to analyze and succeed only in rationalizing—and obfuscating. White ethnic intellectuals and their constituency commit the error—which is their special need—of mistaking identity consciousness-raising for the process of identity formation itself. Moreover, to justify the ideology of primordial ethnic attachment, they must make a caricature of Freudian developmental psychology, arguing that the genuine personality of a person is established (in the womb of family and neighborhood), say, by the age of five and that the individual is inseparable from the group. Any argument to the contrary is an illusion based on the ideology of Americanization.

Yet, as Erikson points out, to talk about the end point of identity is to misunderstand the dynamics of human development:

> It is exactly at this point where my ideas about identity are easily misunderstood as meaning once you have become identified with a particular role, then the process stops and you know where you are. That is why the most common way identity is represented is as an answer to the question "Who am I"—a definition of identity I have never and never would use, because the answer to the question "Who am I?" (if there really were one) would end the process of becoming itself. Real identity formation, of course, is a continuous process with a special crisis in youth—and, I would think, it is a dialectical process.[5]

In terms of a normative psychology of human development, we thoroughly agree. However, the very preoccupation with "self-identity," "self-image," "ethnic identity," "image identity," and "self-esteem" suggests the need for particularist identification, and with it the *curtailment* of the process of becoming. A total personal reorientation is to overcome the sense of disorientation with respect to the future. Perhaps a key to the urgency and persistence with which the question "Who am I?" is asked—and equally the key to the quest for comprehensive images, ideologies, and groups to close the question once and for all—lies in the uncertainty and fear of the process of becoming.

This, in turn, implies a dread of the future, with its alternatives and unknown boundaries. The New Ethnic withdraws from investment in the future, and from its most powerful symbol, the American Dream, to invest instead in the past and in the immediate present. Out of the fear of the future, a foreclosed identity is defensively chosen, one that guarantees a fixed, if constricted "being."

The New Ethnicity emphasizes the past, the continuity and vitality of the past in the present, and the mental health and sense of well-being derived from affiliation and membership in an ethnic group. The individual is a connected link in a tradition, not an isolated social atom. The New Ethnicity is reviving a *sense of the past*, synthesizing personal history with new identity, not the past per se. Being (ethnic) is often contrasted with doing and becoming (American). What the New Ethnics fail to say in their ideology, though confessing it elsewhere, is that it was conflict and uncertainty over the promise and prospect of the future that led them to attempt to conquer the future regressively. The New Ethnics look backward to regain what they lost and renounced by having aspired forward and failed, or having succeeded and still having feelings of failure. Links with the past are necessary when links with the future are broken. But the future is not renounced; rather its nature, one's goals, and one's means of attaining them are redefined. The future is to be mastered retrospectively and regressively.

This is the paradoxical, regressive-atavistic and progressive nature of the New Ethnicity. The new movement, renouncing the guilt-inducing and shame-inviting American Dream and Melting Pot, aspires to many of the American "good things in life" from within an ethnic ideology. Initiative and the wish to succeed, American style, have reawakened the oedipal conflict through the pervasive threat to their realization. The anxiety over the personal meaning of the American Dream is resolved through regression and the embracing of an ethnic ideology, symbolism, and actions that rely heavily on pre-oedipal psychological dynamics. The son is no longer in competition with the father, seeking to succeed and replace him—which the father and the American ideology may have encouraged, although the conflict is generically human despite culturally sanctioned channels of its resolution. From the regressed position, the son reidentifies with his father and reidentifies with the organic, primordial, enveloping (maternal) group, becoming absorbed in it, if not in fact, at least in ideology. Restitution and penance for his earlier sins are thereby made.

By merging his identity with the natal group and by reidentifying with and idealizing his parents, the New Ethnic is able to blame

American culture for every failure suffered and simultaneously claim innocence and victimization for himself, his parents, his ancestors, and his ethnic group. Therefore, he becomes absolved of all personal responsibility for having sought the forbidden fruit of the American Dream. Under the protective sway of pre-oedipal dependence, a narcissistic innocence, rather than a debilitating guilt, dominates the New Ethnic's conscious outlook as the oedipal conscience is repressed and displaced. He is no longer the son, but the archaic, vengeful father.

Oedipal competition is thus displaced from one's real father, outside the symbiotic orbit of the ethnic group-ego, to other groups—WASPs, blacks, Jews, etc.—who come to represent and embody the detested features of one's real father, while the real father is idealized. The external representation of the dissociated father becomes fair game for ridicule, hostility, rage, and sometimes violence. The ideology and camaraderie of the New Ethnicity allow the illusion that the son is not attempting to "make it" for himself, but for the good of the group of which he is an inseparable member. The son may thereby take initiative without inducing oedipal guilt, an inevitable result if he admitted that he was trying to make gains for himself as a separate, autonomous individual.

As many white ethnic converts point out, only WASPs, pushy Jews, arrogant blacks, and "Uncle Toms" would put themselves first; any self-respecting white ethnic puts his people before himself and is thus able to rationalize success or failure: success, because one is doing it for the good of the group; failure, because only *those* (American) people make it that way—furthermore, one would not want to be like them anyway. Moreover, the New Ethnic is now able to rationalize earlier attempts at personal initiative, social and spatial mobility, separation, and individuation: one did it not out of personal choice and wish but in compliance with coercive Americanization that demanded that one renounce one's ethnic ties.

In these terms, the search for identity is the search for finality, literally for a final solution which promises to put an end to anxiety once and for all. The host of identity-consciousness movements (that assure that some things remain in heightened conscious awareness while others are vigilantly repressed) that attempt to provide a definitive *who-ness* are rooted in life history, family history, and culture history that find becoming, change, and progress—all formerly valued—fraught with unbearable danger. The competing and complementary identities and ideologies of our time must be understood as attempting to offer compelling coherence to what is experienced simultaneously as a fragmented self and culture. Defensive identities simply cannot tolerate what open-ended identity process promises—or threatens.

Rigid closure, reflected in dichotomous thinking, is necessary to avert the dangers inherent in the openness of becoming. What Abraham Maslow has called the "hierarchical-integrative" way of thinking (both-and) is rejected for the safeties of polarization and dichotomization (either-or), expressions of the cognitive aspect of the oppositional process.[6] Researchers and theoreticians on human development from Freud to Erikson, from Jung to Maslow, have emphasized equally the retrospective and prospective dimensions, the extent to which the individual can regress, and the basis for maturity. The entire life span is seen as an epigenetic sequence of developmental tasks, crises, and potentialities that result either in integration and synthesis or in premature closure and fixation. Intellectuals of the New Ethnicity now define as normative what is in fact regressed: the short-circuiting of doing and becoming as a function of the impairment of higher integrative functions, and the restabilization of the personality on pure being. The inability to do and to become are not seen as failure; rather doing and becoming are repudiated as not worthy of human investment.

Those who emphasize that ethnic identity is fundamental, based on early socialization, say that Freud, Erikson, and others have taught us the overwhelming importance of the past in the present and in our plans for the future. Here language conventions obscure the deeper meaning of *overwhelming*. Freud indeed demonstrated the determining, multiple influences of the past in the present. But to be overwhelmed by the past is something different, suggesting the "return of the repressed," the inability of the ego to cope with the eruption of repressed materials. It is, we suggest, precisely the coping with the flood of repressed materials from a regressed position that has led to the formulation and embracing of ideologies of primordial bonds: corporate identity, roots, peoplehood, organic community, the search for the past, continuity, security, the use of metaphors such as *family, brothers, sisters,* and the like. From this psychologically regressed point of view, the world is seen in terms of undifferentiation, merger, or fusing with the maternal object, organic-bodily imagery, and idealization. Romantic, organismic theories of the individual, community, and the state attempt to deny the personal sense of autonomy and separation associated with "Enlightenment." The defensive identity of the New Ethnicity takes regression, fragmentation, and disintegration as its starting point and builds anew to defend against further regression. An inspection of the image of the mosaic, and especially how it is used, confirms the functional relation between cultural symbol and psychological reality.

Providing a New Group Image

Another form taken by the heightened self-consciousness of the New Ethnicity is an emphasis on personal or group image. If before, the outgroup took the active role in labeling (e.g., the disparaging stereotypes, together with the group epithet—"Mick," "Wop," "Hunkie"), now members of the ingroup actively display with pride their ethnic identity. It is a way of identifying one's self before another can do it to you. The erstwhile badge of shame now becomes a badge of pride. The recent appearance of lapel buttons with the inscription "Kiss me, I'm Polish" announces the wearer's need to be appreciated for what one *is* (ascriptive-ethnic), not for what one *does* (achievement-American). What began almost humorously is now taken in earnest.

A more serious example of the insistence on the public display and recognition of only positive aspects of ethnicity, or of an ethnic group, is the concerted effort by the Italian-American Defense League and the Italian-American Anti-Defamation League, as well as by individual Italian-American leaders and spokesmen, to prohibit the mention of the word *Mafia* in the film *The Godfather* (1972). The public self-image of Italian-Americans (like that of other corporate identities imposed from without and which became internalized) must have no trace of those stereotypes that the group must live down—yet protests and conspicuous deletions draw attention to what the image-makers would like to eliminate. Likewise, the Anti-Defamation League of B'Nai Brith and other Jewish leaders have outspokenly protested against the airing of Archie Bunker's anti-Semitic and anti-ethnic indignities on the long-running weekly television serial "All in the Family."

Any mention of despised group stereotypes will reveal a fatal flaw that the New Ethnic seeks to dissociate from the newly positive self-image. Derogatory expressions serve as reminders of deeply felt personal defects that are brought to the public attention and are interpreted as being aimed at members of a specific corporate identity. Thus those features of Italian culture and history that are compatible with ideal and accepted American cultural patterns are celebrated as the

real and official Italian identity: e.g., Verdi, Puccini, Dante, Columbus, Galileo, the struggle against papal and Austrian domination, and
Italian cuisine. Conversely, those aspects of traditional Italian culture
and history (and we refer primarily to southern Italy and Sicily) that
conflict with American ideals, and which have been the partial truth
behind the unflattering stereotypes, are denied and are obliterated as
far as possible from private and public consciousness: crime, violence, explosive passion, all of which are fused into the *American*
image of the Mafia/Cosa Nostra which for *Americans* hold a great
fascination. Likewise, many Slovak- and Polish-American informants
vehemently reject attributes of their peasant past associated with dependency, obedience to authority, factionalism, family rivalry, jeal-
ousy—all disliked by the American identity. They emphasize that the
Slavic people are hard working, patient, thrifty, freedom-loving, independent, God-fearing, and loyal, earning everything they receive—all
solidly American virtues. A denial of complex, ambivalent, aboriginal
ethnic reality is central to the revisionism and selectivity of an ideology and imagery of the ethnic identity, now purged of anything negative. From having to live down the stereotypes that portray a group as
"no good," sensitive members of that group, the gatekeepers of the
corporate identity, systematically attempt to eradicate the very
thought of those images and portray anew the group as "all good."

By examining the language and symbols of the New Ethnicity, we
can see how *American* it is despite its efforts to differentiate itself:
ethnic content is expressed in thoroughly American cultural forms.
Stated differently, what the New Ethnics have *encoded* into a crypto-
gram that is intended to obscure as much as is intended to be revealed,
must be *decoded* if we are to penetrate the inherent obscurantism.

The essay titled "We Do Have a Heritage," by John P. Kovalovsky, appearing in the July 1973 issue of *Jednota*, the official organ of
the First Catholic Slovak Union, clearly expresses the American cultural form that the ethnic content takes. Kovalovsky begins by noting
how little he had cared about ethnic heritage, but "with each passing
year I began to notice that when people talked about their heritage,
they spoke with pride that reflected an enthusiasm that seemed to
give them a halo of royalty." *Pride, royalty:* Slovaks are not illiterate
peasants, mere mill and mine workers; their culture and past are not
inferior but superior; they are not born of lowly origins but are of
royal blood. Kovalovsky discusses the people, nations, and empires
he had read about in school. Since national pride and self-determination are a major measure of self-esteem in the Western world—and
now universally—if it can be shown that the Slovak nation, and na-

tionality, has a long and venerable history, then surely one who is Slovak need take second place to no one. Indeed, much of contemporary historiography at the Slovak Institutes in Rome and Cleveland consists of attempts to document the antiquity and continuity of the Slovaks from the proud days of the Great Moravian Empire of the ninth century, to demonstrate that *Slovakia* is the cradle of Slavic civilization and that *Slovak* is the mother of all Slavic languages.

Kovalovsky asks: "Where were the Slovaks in history? Didn't we exist? Surely we had ancestors, but who were they? Surely we had some beginning, and the good Lord placed us here for some good purpose. . . . We do have a heritage, . . . and we did have a place in history, and, by the way, a heritage that is second to none." *Ancestors, beginning, and a proud heritage:* Slovak-Americans, like the other white-ethnic Americans, have been a Caucasian version of Ralph Ellison's *Invisible Man*, a fact not understood by other whites who at least *now* regard them as white, and by blacks who do not distinguish between one white and another. Having been convinced that their own history was second rate and had to be repressed in favor of identification with Anglo-American history (which was History), the New Ethnics now selectively restore and invent a history that confers on their origins and parenthood a legitimacy that had been previously questioned. The Slovaks, too, had nation, empire, kings, peoplehood, a literary tradition—standard measuring rods of Western civilization.

Next Kovalovsky turns his attention to Slovaks in America, and implicitly addresses himself to basic American values, which he insists Slovaks have represented from the outset. With respect to his Slovak ancestors: "It is true that they left their native land to seek their fortune in America. . . . They didn't come empty handed. They brought with them skills that contributed greatly in building this Nation." *Empty handed versus skilled:* if they came looking for their fortune they worked for it and didn't come for a handout. Behind this imagery is the self-contrast of the descendants of the European peasantry with the new immigrants in America who are seen as expecting to be given something for nothing (blacks, those on welfare). The Slovaks brought valuable skills with them, skills the young nation needed.

Kovalovsky continues: "You have heard of the so-called 'blue bloods' whose ancestors came across on the Mayflower. Well, I'd like to let you in on a little secret. Our Slovak ancestors were here a dozen years before Captain Miles Standish appeared on the scene with the Pilgrim Fathers." *A secret, "blue bloods," and the chronol-*

ogy of arrival in America: the secret is a vindictive exposure that the Anglo-Americans are not all there was and is to America. If the Pilgrim Fathers are the mythological ancestors of all that is genuinely American, then the Slovaks must be one hundred percent American as well, since they arrived in America even earlier. "Getting there first" is a major American obsession, and the Slovaks who helped establish the Jamestown Colony arrived even earlier than those who are the measure of what is American. In every culture origin myths are important, conferring nobility and good standing on one's own group. Not only were there two Slovaks in Jamestown in 1608, but they were among six skilled craftsmen and artisans who came in answer to Captain John Smith's plea to his London agents. English craftsmen were relatively well off in England and hence did not emigrate. Consequently, the Jamestown Colony was composed of nobles, sons of nobles, cavaliers, and adventurers—and no carpenters. Interestingly, Kovalovsky names the two Slovak craftsmen, but not the others. In a 1973 radio-broadcast commentary, the Polish-American councilwoman from Baltimore Barbara Mikulski gave the identical account but spoke only of *Polish* artisans who enabled the inept English to survive.[7] Surely this would put the Polish joke to rest, but it also demonstrates the use of a new ethnocentrism to overcome an old one (it was the *Anglos* who were inept) and shows how history is selectively read in the service of one's present needs.

Kovalovsky writes: "It was the Slovaks who struck the first blow for equal rights in America. Despite their great contributions to the maintenance of the Colonies, they were denied the right to vote. They rebelled against this injustice and organized for equal rights. They won their demands, and it is recorded in the Court Book of the Virginia Company of London under the date of July 31, 1618." Barbara Mikulski claims that the early Poles called the first strike of workers against management, demanding citizenship and the vote in Virginia; no vote, no work. Each group presses its special claims of history to give legitimacy to its present existence, self-image, and demands. *Equal rights, rebellion, freedom, and legitimate citizenship:* while the Puritans who had sought religious freedom practiced monumental intolerance for internal difference and for other religious sects, it was the non-Anglo, non-Protestant American Slavs who conducted the first American revolution for equal rights—their own. The emphasis on Slovak participation in the early struggle for civil rights and freedom reflects the effort to live down and reverse current stereotypes about white ethnics: that they are racists, antiblack, and that because their ancestral nations are under Communist domination, they must somehow be Communist sympathizers. The Slovaks were thus not only among the first *real* Americans (and have remained so down to the present), but are more American in spirit than the Anglo-Americans. The Slovak-American message is an attempt to set the record straight, as the proponents of the Slovak variant of the New Ethnicity press their need to consolidate their status and legitimate their claim to power.

The above example further reminds us of the extremely negative reaction in the mid-1960s of Italian-Americans (led by Judge Michael A. Musmano in Philadelphia) to the discovery of old maps showing that the Vikings had regularly visited the East Coast of North America and had called it "Vineland." The Italians had taken their primacy for granted. Now one of their most important status symbols was taken away. If "getting there first" is a major American obsession, then maintaining one's status is equally important. If symbols of an ethnic group's time-honored claim to genealogy and origins are challenged, then their very sense of legitimacy, and with it the fantasy of being descendants of noble birth, is undermined. If one cannot be a "blue-blood," or the descendant of one, one's very American identity is called into question.

The ultimate mystique of American nativity, of course, belongs to the American Indian. Guilty white liberals and romanticizing white ethnics—who live sufficiently remote from Indians not to be threatened by them—eagerly champion what they perceive to be their cause. What arrogance it is to suggest that Columbus *discovered* the Americas! What Columbus discovered was the outer fringe of a continent inhabited by *native* Americans for millennia. The latter are the *original* Americans; the former and their followers are merely usurpers and pretenders to cosmic significance. Many white ethnics extol not only their forebears' peasant virtues, but Indian virtues as well, such that native Americans come out looking remarkably east-central European. A number of Slavic-Americans we have known for several years, and who are active participants in the New Ethnic Movement, find a commonality between the Polish and Hopi (Pueblo) languages, which are alleged to share a similar sound (a phoneme, the so-called slashed or softened *l*). They emphasize that this means that Slavs and American Indians are closely related; thus, sharing a common descent and affiliation, they are *both native* Americans. In Europe, many educated Slavs sought French and German affiliation in order to validate a European identity; now in America, many new ethnophiles trace their ancestry to the American Indian in order to validate their status as Americans: more blue-blood than the blue-bloods.

The *new* revisionist history of the American movement west never speaks of pioneer virtues or of the vacillation between lawlessness and rigid social control. Rather, it sees westward expansion as an uninterrupted, remorseless destruction of the American Indian. Those who were rooted in nature were uprooted and slaughtered and herded by those who felt themselves to be the masters of nature. Did not Benjamin Franklin himself suggest that Providence had provided the white man rum "to extirpate these savages in order to make room for the cultivators of the earth"? *Migration* and *settlement* are not the appropriate terms to describe the process; *invasion, conquest, genocide,* and *internal colonialism* are far more apt. Christian missionaries were little more than the advance column for the cavalry. History thus distorted, partial truth becomes integrated into an exclusive whole. The white ethnic and the American Indian regain their human dignity through their dehumanization of the WASP. Identification with the Indian further expands the pan-ethnic alliance of oppressed minorities in common grievance against the spoilers of the earth.

The westward movement, however, was more than one of wanton slaughter of those who were in the way of the Anglos' self-assured progress. The frontier cowboy spirit was concerned with more than pillage and the displacement of Indians. The American *Drang nach Westen* was no more limited to the history of atrocity than was the German *Drang nach Osten* in European history. Revisionism obscures the complexity of the age and people it would either romanticize or vilify. To meet its identity needs, the New Ethnicity synthesizes an image to verify, as though from without, its own distortions. For instance, the American "western" movies are thematically inverted. Pioneers, frontiersmen, cowboys, and cavalry are no longer courageous heroes; nor are the American Indians (who are fused into the single image of *the* Plains Indian) villains; it is the other way around. American history is deemed a venal lie that sugarcoats its own deeds. Ethnic, minority, or racial histories, whether in accord or in competition with each other, offer themselves as the truth. *White man* (meaning Protestant Anglos) is incarnate evil. The American Indian symbolizes the eternally noble, innocent, and wise—natural man, murdered, desecrated, and heartlessly placed in human animal reserves by the white man on his ruthless path toward new frontiers. Indian goodness, generosity, and integrity are counterposed against Anglo evil, avarice, and deceit. Indians know the earth is their mother; Anglos think they are masters of fate itself, that God is on their side. Indians have no scourge of private property and personal accumulation; everyone shares what he has. Indians never seek private gains at the expense of others. They trusted the white man with whom they were willing to share the bounty of the continent. It is the white man who proved to be untrustworthy. Indian medicine, language, and religion are the Indian way; what is white is foreign and must be purged from the Indian's mind and culture. The Indian is celebrated for his *resistance:* he too, like Novak's "unmeltable ethnics," refused to melt or die or disappear. Vine Deloria, the Oglala Sioux writer, tells the white man, "We Talk, You Listen" and capitalizes on the white man's guilt in *Custer Died for Your Sins.*

Alas, not even the "Native American" is exempt from "American" standards by which a citizen claims his right through the selective use of the past to serve the present. Nor is the American Indian exempt from the white man's (including white ethnic) oedipal fantasies of innocence, purity, and contamination. Nativist American Indians betray their American cultural frame of reference in the very labels and values they invoke. Name designations of self-reference are not arbitrary. The change from *American Indian* or tribal self-reference to *native American* is congruent with the current American obsession with nativity, descent, paternity, and "getting there first" (as *primus inter pares*). What better way to legitimate one's self *as an American* than to assert one's genuine American nativity? The American Indians thus come out as more American than the whites who came later onto their land. By this origin myth, the American Indians can claim—and attempt to reclaim—everything because, after making the irretrievable past one's personal present, that past validates the present. Whites are the trespassers on a continent that belongs to the Indian. The American Indian who justifies his nativist claims by American means is applauded by the white ethnics who do the same.

The idealized Indian, paragon of traditionalist identity, is free from "original sin" and may even be the source of the white man's redemption, if he will only repent and learn. What romanticizing whites fail to see, however, is that this Indian is part of *his* myth, and this mystique is a subtle way of using *the* Indian—and is not a veneration of any real Indian, past or present. The idealized Indian is a projection of white men's (and ethnics') psyches and needs, whose stereotypes the Indians themselves have come to internalize, live out, and now nativistically act out. There is in this myth no less distortion of history and reality than before. Whites look at the Indians through the eyes of their own deficits and expect them to compensate for them by remaining Indians—perpetuating the paternalistic tradition of keeping them down by saying that they would want nothing to do with American life-denying civilization. What white romanticists and Indian nativists admire and wish to preserve is more a consequence of captivity, benign neglect, exclusion, and inconsistent governmental policy than aboriginal virtues. The Indianist culture of nostalgia is as far removed from its origins as the White Ethnic Movement is from its roots. White ethnophiles *cannot* realize that the answer to the double message of termination and reservation is not nativism (which only imposes the reservation psychology from within) but integration, more specifically the American Dream that *even* American Indians have dreamt! Thus ethnophiles mistake what they project onto *the* Indian for aboriginal Indianness. What they think they use as a paradigm is an idealized culture of their own invention. They visit on their presumed allies the very error they make toward their adversaries: the failure to distinguish between what they need to perceive and what is really there. Neither *WASP* nor *Indian* can be permitted an existence separate from or independent of ethnophile imagery.

There are certain realities of native American life of the seventeenth and eighteenth centuries (encompassing all the Americas) that are conspicuously absent from nativist Indian and ethnic celebrations: intertribal warfare (accelerated, not caused, by the presence of the horse and the gun); witchcraft hunts; the masculine sport of status accumulation by counting coup through courting and inflicting death; ritual cannibalism and sacrifice; enslavement of captives; and the very precariousness of aboriginal life. There is a certain dishonesty in pretending that the nativist selection of the Indian's virtues coincides with the *whole* of Indian life—which we suspect the New Ethnics of all persuasions would be loathe to preserve. And there is equal dishonesty in insisting that everything that has befallen American Indians is a consequence of the white man's intentional malice. (Much of the death-by-contagious disease that nearly wiped out Indian populations was an unintended and inevitable consequence of the fact of contact between one group that was immunized and another that was vulnerable.)

Are American Indians really the *network people* the New Ethnics claim them to be? Only a few years ago, the American Indian—specifically, Plains Indians whom white Americans take to personify all Indians—was admired for his individualism, his heroism, his displaced aggression, his self-reliance, and his competitiveness—all strangely *American* characteristics. These qualities would make Indians far more like *atomic people*. If one must choose among American Indians to personify communitarian virtue, cooperation, noncompetitiveness, and peacefulness (at least in value, if not in action), why not the Zuni, or Hopi, or Pueblo Indians in general? In choosing Plains Indians, the ethnophiles only show their ignorance. Not quite, however, because the pan-Indian movement, as a nativist movement, is in search of its own roots and attempts to project publicly an image of rootedness and connectedness and meets the needs of the ethnophile system of self-deception. Historical falsification makes for poor history and anthropology, though as myth it is superb. It makes of all immigrants natives and confers upon each the pride of being the first arrival in the family, the sibling with whom all *others* must contend.

The New Ethnicity and the Dynamics of Paranoia and Narcissism

Such dominant features of narcissism as shamelessness, exhibitionism, rage, delusions of omnipotence, and desire for vengeance play a major role underlying the ideology and behavior of the New Ethnicity. A considerable amount of time and energy in the ethnic liberation is expended on vindication and vindictiveness, one means of directing outward the boundless rage that the failure of the American Dream has awakened.

New Ethnics become ever vigilant of their people and of their categories, lest either be defiled by ambiguity and true diversity. In the process of epistemological and ontological revisionism (how we go about knowing, and the nature of reality, respectively), the facts must be made to comply with new psychological and cultural needs, and reality is reinterpreted in order to generate new facts (and old facts are cavalierly repudiated).

In an essay titled "A More Sober Look at Slovak Ethnicity in America," the Reverend Ivan Dornic writes:

> Slovaks lived under the Magyar boot for one thousand years and survived. And the feudalism in Hungary, as every place else, was cruel, tyrannical, oppressive. But in America, the land of democracy and freedom, even the prophets lost their hope and say this is "Kaputt." . . . Since no other ethnic community was spared by the flames of the melting pot . . . one could conclude that in America they made you loose [*sic*] your spirit and your soul.
>
> Yet, the conditions for the growth of the ethnic communities in America was much better than in Austro-Hungary or any other empire. Economic, educational, cultural, and social opportunities and standards were superior in America even for the immigrants. However, the superiority of *WASPs* was demonstrative in educa-

tion, lasting in technology and employment, and predominant in the social life. That caused the immigrants and their descendants to feel inferior culturally as well. The feeling of inferiority makes men ashamed of their background and that in turn makes him [*sic*] desire to be somebody else. Henceforth, immigrants stopped fighting for their natural rights, started changing their names and moved away from their neighborhood.[8]

Father Dornic's argument succinctly states many of the assumptions of the white ethnic identity and ideology. He notes that Slovak culture thrived under the oppressive yoke of the Magyars, but that in America, where the Slovaks *should* have been free to be Slovak, they became American instead. We are reminded of a remark made by social psychologist Peter Rose, who, in reviewing works by Novak and Greeley, noted "two leit motifs, 'alienation' and 'reassertion,'" running through both volumes. "Reading Novak and Greeley, I kept thinking of the convoluted hypothesis that the Jewish community is held together by the threat of anti-Semitism, that each time emancipation seems close to fulfillment, some new persecution 'saves' the Jews from total disappearance."[9] The increasingly popular Jewish philosopher-theologian Emil Fackenheim is even more explicit. According to him, for the Jews to disappear by assimilation would be to grant Hitler a posthumous victory. The very survival of the Jewish people is a conscious act of defiance to deny such a sinister victory; otherwise, the Jews would do to themselves what Hitler could not do to them.[10] Hitler has become the demonic god for whom the Jews survive.

The guilt and shame induced by freedom, emancipation, and liberty lead to an "escape from freedom" catalayzed by the traumata of the 1960s and early 1970s that reawakened them. Freedom now is called oppression, and oppression, freedom. Identity confusion leads to the quest for closure and absolutes. Through rationalization, one is able to deny active participation in the earlier liberation. Consuming guilt is eradicated through the projection and displacement of the source of one's conflicts onto American culture. One thereby becomes self-righteously innocent. With ethnicity now called the basis of genuine freedom, history is rewritten: *oppression* by the WASPs becomes analogous to oppression of the Slovaks by the Magyars in Europe. The *sense* of oppression in the United States becomes crucial to the alleviation of guilt and shame through the shoring up of the ego by the paranoid process.

It would seem that the feeling or sense of oppression is necessary to the revival of a New Ethnic's "consciousness of kind" and the defiant insistence on the perpetuation of his people. The threat is invented to conform to current needs and is justified as *identity* or *survival*. For the Reverend Dornic, like numerous other ethnophile apologists, the ethos of the Melting Pot is reinterpreted and is no longer a personally sought change of identity and culture, but an ordeal by coercion in which one's natural ethnic inclinations and loyalties were not spared by the flames of the Melting Pot. One did not choose, one was forced—and one's responsibility evaporates. The Reverend Dornic, like such white ethnic Catholic writers as Michael Novak, Monsignor Geno Baroni, and Andrew Greeley, emphasizes that with Americanization one's ethnic spirit, or "soul," and one's religious spirit, or "soul," are lost. It was the involuntary casting of the immigrant into the satanic Melting Pot, tended by insensitive Anglo-conformists, that made him into a "soulless" American. Americanization means loss, deculturation.

An additional impetus for Americanization was the sense of inferiority the immigrants felt when confronted by WASP superiority; the Slovaks threw off their traditional natural culture and embraced the artificial WASP culture as a means of avoiding feeling ashamed. The Reverend Dornic argues that "the inferiority complex of ethnics in general and the Slovaks in particular would not really be too hard to overcome if at least an attempt would be made in a unified and persistent manner."[11] That the natural condition of Slovaks or ethnics is preferable to the Americanized version is a major ideological tenet of the New Ethnicity. What Greeley calls the primordial bonds of "land," "religion," and "blood" are the trinitarian emblems of the New Ethnic identity. Allegiance to them confers on the believer a sense of purity and superiority in comparison with the now-alien impure and polluted American identity. No longer is the *alien* American culture (which persists in viewing one of ethnic ancestry as alien rather than native) the standard of comparison; it is now the *natural, authentic* white ethnic culture that measures American values and beliefs in its own terms.

If religious and ethnic "soul" coincide, and if to become American means to lose both, it follows not merely logically, but ethnographically that the Melting Pot is the symbol of a WASP anti-Christ, of the devil. The Communist-dominated ancestral lands are not the only ones to earn the epithet "God-less." The youth movement, the secularization of the 1960s, the New Left, the WASP, and the American Dream itself have become roundly accused of preaching and practicing immorality, atheism, Communist learnings, and of being against God-given life (e.g., birth control and abortion). In the ideological polarization, theologically oriented ethnicity (dominated by what Novak calls "humble charity," following Dostoevski) becomes the domain of the *sacred,* while the elitist, WASPist mainstream of technological American culture (in the spirit of binary opposition: life denying, dominated by efficiency, individualism, white bread and hamburgers) comes to embody the *profane.* Moreover, the return of the prodigal son or daughter to ethnicity is a means of salvation, while the path of Americanization and assimilation leads to perdition—one literally loses one's soul.

The American Dream which the New Ethnics had identified with earlier is now repudiated and seen as an alien force of oppression. As ethnic history is rewritten, so is American history. One combats in earnest what had been longed for. Ethnophiles are haunted and their single-minded efforts are subverted because of their secret longing for the forbidden fruits of the American Dream—success, autonomy, independence, despite their guilt for having wanted them. The fictitious WASPs thus cannot be sufficiently condemned and exposed for their crimes against the immigrants and their descendants.

It is thus comprehensible why the idea of *assimilation* is now repugnant and takes on an ego-alien, dissociated quality as a defense against the wish. First, we note that the common use of the word *assimilation* combines what anthropologists call "acculturation" (the learning of a new culture, an active process) and "assimilation" (the structural incorporation into the new culture, a largely passive process, but impossible without the personal desire to become a member of this new culture). Assimilation presupposes acculturation which does not automatically lead to assimilation. If before, despite ardent acculturation, New Ethnics were denied assimilation (citizenship in good standing, a status beyond mere passing), they now refuse to assimilate. They reject the criteria of assimilation (acculturation) by denying what they formerly idealized. Moreover, the New Ethnics cannot assimilate in the psychological sense: to include and to be open to further inclusiveness. Because they cannot afford to be open to such inclusion—because prior openness brought hurt and exclusion—they cannot afford to assimilate and defend themselves by a radical exclusion of what they once attempted to include and be included in.

The reciprocal process of inclusion is inverted into one of exclusion. Nevertheless, precisely because what is excluded has long ago been internalized, it is necessary to transform part of *me* into *not-me.* What is excluded comes to be perceived as ego alien, outside one's self, an external threat. Psychoanalytically speaking, a *dissociated concept,* under the dominance of paranoid thought process, is experienced as a *persecutory percept.* One becomes not an active participant in the process of Americanization, but an innocent victim of its ruthlessness. Such fears as the onslaught of "global culture," and the image of the Melting Pot as a hellish inferno tended by WASPs, are comprehensible as expressions of this dissociated experience of anything associated with *American.*

In an article titled "Stereotypes and the Perception of Group Differences," Donald Campbell writes:

> The native ingrouper [e.g., the white ethnophile] perceives the different characteristics of the outgroup as causing his hostility. He feels that were it not for these despicable traits, the outgroup would be loved. The outgroup's opprobrious characteristics seem to him to fully justify the hostility and rejection he shows toward it. The social scientist sees the opposite causal direction: causally, first is the hostility toward the outgrouper, generated perhaps by real threat, perhaps by ethnocentrism, perhaps by displacement. In the service of this hostility, all possible differences are opportunistically interpreted as despicable, and the most despicable traits are given most attention.[12]

The individual psychology of this process has been explored by Heinz Kohut in his formulation of the dynamics of narcissism and narcissistic rage. The failure of environmental compliance with expectation for fulfillment of self-esteem and initiative-mastery needs threatens to fragment the cohesion of the self by undermining one's idealizations, reawakening "feelings of inferiority," and challenging the "omnipotence of the [infantile] self." Shame and rage combine forces producing a narcissistic rage whose predominant features include an attempt to recapture omnipotence through the exercise of absolute control and the exhibitionistic insistence on being admired. At the group level, group regression produces chronic group narcissistic rage, which is resolved through the attempt to "re-establish control over a narcissistically experienced world."

Kohut speaks of "the readiness of the shame-prone individual to respond to a potentially shame-provoking situation by the employment of a simple remedy: the active (often anticipatory) infliction on others of those narcissistic injuries he is most afraid of suffering himself." Moreover, "the existence of heightened sadism, the adoption of a policy of preventive attack, the need for revenge, and the desire to turn a passive experience into an active one, do not, however, fully account for some of the most characteristic features of narcissistic rage. In its typical forms there is utter disregard for reasonable limitation and a boundless wish to redress an injury and to obtain revenge. The irrationality of the vengeful attitude becomes even more frightening in view of the fact that—in narcissistic personalities as in the paranoiac—the reasoning capacity, while totally under the domination and in the service of the emotion, is often not only intact, but even sharpened."[13]

Discussing the relationship between narcissistic rage and aggression, Kohut writes that "the enemy . . . who calls forth the archaic rage of the narcissistically vulnerable is seen by him not as an autonomous source of impulsions, but as a flaw in a narcissistically perceived reality. He is a recalcitrant part of an expanded self over which he expects to exercise full control and whose mere independence or otherness is an offense." Finally, in the consolidation of chronic narcissistic rage, "conscious and preconscious ideation, in particular as it concerns the aims and goals of the personality, becomes more and more subservient to the pervasive rage. The ego, furthermore, increasingly surrenders its reasoning capacity to the power of the grandiose self: it does not acknowledge the inherent limitations of the power of the self, but attributes its failures and weaknesses to the malevolence and corruption of the uncooperative archaic object" (e.g., those who personify the early parent; the reexperiencing in new circumstances of old injuries to the self).[14]

Coping with what Erik Erikson terms acute "identity-consciousness," a hallmark of identity confusion and narcissistic disturbance, is one of the central—and enduring—tasks of the New Ethnicity. Identity-consciousness is "a special form of painful self-consciousness which dwells on the discrepancies between one's self-esteem, the aggrandized self-image as an autonomous person, and one's appearance in the eyes of others." What Erikson discerns in pathology and in normal adolescent process can be recognized as endemic to the dynamics of the white ethnic identity: the contrast between "total obliteration of self-esteem" and "a narcissistic and snobbish disdain of the judgement of others"; and the alternation between "sensitivity" and a "defiant shamelessness in the face of criticism."[15] The shame of having been visible, exposed, and an object of public inspection (not to mention remorseless private introspection and perseveration) is compensated by arrogant displays, an emphasis on visibility in public life, and an offensive exposure of those who had made one feel ashamed.

The other side of *ethnic pride* is *ethnic power:* a concern that brings together conflicts over role, initiative, and guilt. Erikson contrasts adolescent "role fixation" with "free experimentation with available roles," with their earliest antecedent in the oedipal crisis. If free experimentation is a hallmark of the identity of the American self-made man who refuses to be tied down, then the undermining of the American identity of acculturated white ethnics (and *natives* as well) by the accompanying regressive pull will reawaken archaic guilts over succeeding one's father, abandoning one's mother, family, and neighborhood (or the wish to do so), moving upward and outward.

The current socioeconomic realistic threats to mobility and employment conspire with inner experience to make it appear to an individual that initiative and attempts at achievement and success are the cause of his guilt, confirming not only a sense of role fixation but a choice of self-constriction. The choice of a less self-fulfilling, individuated role becomes the only acceptable form of initiative, with its pathological, most regressed form expressed as "a complete denial of ambition as the only way of totally avoiding guilt."[16] In the ideology of the New Ethnicity, ethnic power is actively asserted, proclaimed, and sought. This is not a contradiction, but a compromise, such that ethnic initiative, as opposed to initiative based on the American ethos, can be expressed without guilt because the role in whose name ambition and success are undertaken is ethnic. New Ethnics can still aspire to the American good life as long as it is rationalized in the interest of ethnic identity, family, and group, and as long as the guilt-inducing American values of self-reliance, individualism, and autonomy are not their primary goals. With a new system of beliefs and values consolidated in and sanctioned by the New Ethnic cultural identity, the sense of helplessness and paralysis is at least in part overcome, and a new pride with its new ideals is able to mollify the conscience and release the will for new mastery—though within a reality that is narcissistically conceived.

Some of Erikson's recent observations on the Woman's Movement can be extrapolated to the dynamics of the New Ethnicity. "Many young women could face the suddenly heightened awareness of their having been implicitly treated as 'them' in such a variety of confining roles throughout history, only by vindictively lumping men together as 'them' and by mistrusting totally where a little trust might prove treacherous. But vindication is not yet liberation."[17] Later, he states that "a corollary to the attempt to raise consciousness is the determination to repress the awareness of unconscious motivation, especially where it contributed to the adaptation to what suddenly appear to be the physical 'stigmata' of sex, age, or race." Erikson discusses the influence of the "atavistic *superego* which mortgages all choices in life history," which "can permit a liberation only at the price of turning guiltiness into consuming righteousness, and an erstwhile negative self-image into blind accusations against newly appointed enemies."[18] The divided self-image remains divided, but reversed. As the unconscious conflicts remain repressed and are continually repressed, the new liberation and freedom remain a jealously guarded illusion.

The conversion to the identity of the New Ethnicity is a self-created rite of passage (withdrawal, transition, and reincorporation) that has an underlying theme of renewal through death and rebirth. The old self is purged; a new purified self is born. One undergoes a "loss of reality" and emerges with a regained sense of reality under, quite literally, an altered state of consciousness. A sense of disillusionment, betrayal, hopelessness, and helplessness leads to disparagement of the American mythos and is followed by cynicism and nihilism.

The new identity does not include the style of thought and life that led to the trauma in the first place. Thus Michael Novak rejects the legacy of the Enlightenment and counterposes rationalism against imagination, the richness of the Slavic soul and the "diversities of human stories." Legend, soul, and feeling fill the void of the unsatisfying WASP intellect. The pursuit of narcissism, whether by the New Ethnicity or by its numerous countercultural parallels, declares the whole of traditional American education—indeed, the whole of Western civilization—to be irrelevant, culturally biased, passionless, and life denying.

An embracing of some "cult of the irrational"—with its own rationale—makes considerable sense in terms of ego functioning. However, through regression and a shoring up of the ego at more "primitive" levels, the ego, though now well defended, becomes impoverished in its higher integrative function. Thus, in education, such traditional standards as scholastic aptitude, attention span, concentration, analysis and synthesis capacities are challenged as their function is impaired. New styles of feeling and thinking preclude earlier or alternative styles because they defend against them. Psychologically, a threat to the stability of the ego is experienced as a threat to survival itself. What is labeled as "defiance" or "rebellion" by those in authority is often a desperate attempt by an individual or a peer group to find a simplified and safely narrow identity that provides escape from the contradictions and ambivalences precipitated by those who claim authority. The New Ethnicity can be regarded similarly. Under new ego conditions and under a new conception of the self, American culture must be vilified.

The white ethnic's earlier sense of selfhood was bound up with the American ethos. In a sense, the distinction between self and nonself, what is one's *own* and what is *American,* has been a discontinuous and uncertain relationship, pervaded by ambivalence. The resolution of these conflicts results in a radical distinction between self and nonself, and, by extension, between the collective self—*we*—and the collective opponent—*they.* Where one had earlier lived with more permeable and flexible boundaries, the ego now shores itself up against vulnerability by adopting rigid, inflexible boundaries. This would seem to be one aspect of the origin and perpetuation of ethnic boundaries.

Personal and group boundary delineations become homologous processes. Emphases on common language, history, life-style, personality, character, and institutions serve as boundary and identity markers to insiders and outsiders alike. The perception of America as a "pluralistic society" and the demand for "the right to be different" emerge out of the manipulation of exploitable differences for the purposes of clarification and definition. Within the new order established by the New Ethnicity, a premium is placed on the enhancement of difference—differentiation of one's self from another, or one's kind from other kinds. Polarization and social segmentation become an inevitable product of this dynamic, often crystallizing into a new social structure—on both sides of the dividing line.

The White Ethnic Movement as a Pan-Ism

One of the most salient characteristics that defines the White Ethnic Movement is its *pan-ethnic* emphasis. The white ethnic ethnophilism has as obvious parallels American Slavophilism or Pan-Slavism, Judeophilism (encompassing, for instance, American, Soviet, and Israeli Jews), Afrophilism, Pan-Hispanism, Pan-Indianism, and so forth. Although particularistic group identity (Italian, Polish, Slovak) is retained and indeed insisted on, thus creating internal differentiation, the pan-ethnic identity, ideology, and political activism attempts to override these distinctions and forge a new entity. Thus, *white ethnic* or simply *ethnic* becomes an embracing self-reference category that supplements, if not supersedes, that of individual ethnic identification.

The meaning of *ethnic* changes in the process. One hears slogans such as "ethnic pride" and "ethnic power" much more frequently than Polish, Italian, or Slovak ones. Michael Novak, a leading intellectual of the White Ethnic Movement, and now a political organizer for it, coined the acronym PIGS (Poles-Italians-Greeks-Slavs) to designate the core coalition of the White Ethnic Movement. In fact, PIGS is the pan-ethnic equivalent of the crosscutting social class-occupational category *hardhats*. Flaunting stigmata is inherent in the choice of self-categorization, tranforming an emblem of shame (of course, the working-class whites were called "pigs" and "hardhats" by self-righteous white liberals, college students, and blacks) into one of defiant pride.

The white ethnic intellectuals emphasize affinities, ties, common ancestry, and bonds of collective exploitation as peasants in Europe and the United States. They usually designate the core grouping as immigrants and their descendants from south, central, and east Europe, largely Catholic and orthodox; other groups are related through some affinity, though more distantly, e.g., Spanish-surname Catholics, French Canadians, Orthodox Jews, Irish Catholics, German Catholics, Scandinavians, and Dutch. The main point is that a natural affinity is discovered (while in fact an elective affinity is created) between erstwhile strangers and enemies. Historical and contemporary social segmentation is dissolved and denied, at least ideologically, in the new collective. Differences are overcome in a harmonious *unity* in which all become siblings of one great extended family.

In a succinct formulation of the dynamics of *pan-isms*, Stephen Lukashevich writes:

> All Pan-isms, which sought union with one's racial brothers, were attempts at rolling back history to a common point of departure. By the same token, all Pan-isms repudiated as a historical mistake their dolorous national self-identity, which they wanted to replace with a new collective identity. In other words, all Pan-isms preached a collective rebirth. It can be said, therefore, if one would use a biological simile, that all Pan-isms, which promised national rebirth [or in the present instance, ethnic rebirth], had to start by returning to the womb together with all the tribes that sprang forth from it. . . . This neurotic aspect of Pan-isms played an undoubtedly important role in the formulation of Pan-ist ideologies. . . .

"All Pan-isms," he notes with a lengthy list, "have appeared in the wake of social or military catastrophes." Analyzing Polish Pan-Slavism, "which developed roughly between 1772 and 1830, in other words, from the first partition of Poland to the insurrection of 1830–

31,'' he writes: It "was a wish to recreate 'regressively' a new Polish self-identity by losing the old one in the anonymity of a Slavdom composed in its vast majority of Russians—hence their Russophilism.''
The dynamic of American pan-ethnicity is identical. The initial catastrophe is the crisis of self-esteem and guilt in the ambience of the late 1960s and early 1970s culminating in the radical doubting of the American Dream. The "devouring feeling of social inferiority'' and "feeling of social insignificance'' suffered by the Pan-Slavists is identical with the American white ethnic experience of being the "forgotten Americans'' and their own profound sense of inferiority, alienation, shame, and rage.[19] Analogously, the New Ethnicity is an attempt to recreate regressively a new ethnic identity by losing the erstwhile American identity in the anonymity and heightened self-consciousness of ethnitude. For the Pan-Slavic Poles, Russia was the big brother, father, and mother who would protect the vulnerable Poles who suddenly felt small. For the American white ethnics, ethnicity serves similar paternal and maternal functions of succorance and defense. Likewise, each ethnic group becomes a sibling in the great white ethnic family. The image of smallness and helplessness is also present: e.g., George Wallace's reference to Middle Americans as the "little men,'' an image readily adopted because it is deeply felt.

Lukashevich cautions against "an attempt at rationalizing an irrational situation'' in the case of the Polish Pan-Slavists who are often seen with hindsight as traitors or as farsighted politicians for having been pro-Russian.[20] The latter is totally irrelevant to what we would call the deep structure of pan-isms which Lukashevich clarifies. Cultural rejuvenation, political organization, and social activism are all seen to flow from *irrational premises* based on regression. The biological simile is in fact a psychodynamic process by which the individual and the collective group attempt to regain the symbiotic tie to the mother, to fuse in organic oneness prior to differentiation from her (individuation). The same holds for the White Ethnic Movement. Behavior, ideology, cognitive categories, action strategies, and the like, are readily mistaken for aspects of a rational calculus of decision-making and behavior if their premises and dynamics are ignored—hence the need by adherents of the movement to mystify its origins and claim that ethnicity is ipso facto one's origin.

Just as in psychological terms, one should avoid rationalizing an irrational situation, in anthropological terms, one should not succumb to the rationalization that argues that the White Ethnic Movement is an *adaptation* to the environment. Adaptation implies a cumulative response to outer circumstances that increase survival chances. In a sense, this confirms one of the premises of the New Ethnicity, namely, that outer circumstances are the determinant of the present crisis of American culture; and that as an affective bond and interest group, ethnicity is a tactic of survival (and enhances the *quality* of that survival). For the present, we note that culture is as much a projection upon the environment (hence Hallowell's phrase "behavioral environment") as it is an objective interpretation of the environment; and that cultures are notorious for expressing human overadaptation and stereotypy, whose rigid homeostasis assures survival in the short run and catastrophe in the long run. Success is often the basis for subsequent failure. And where global cooperation means survival, atavistic adaptation portends disaster. By calling something adaptive, we justify its value and give it a scientific nod of approval. If the White Ethnic Movement is in any sense adaptive, then it must be seen in relation to internal as well as external environments. *Adaptive* can make sense in this context only if it subsumes the concept of *defense*. One of the central insights of our discussion of the pan-ist bedrock for the understanding of the New Ethnicity is that we must not look at consequences to the neglect of underlying process, but must explore instead their systematic relationship.

Ideally at least, particularist differences, ancient and modern feuds and animosities, are overlooked as rival siblings become loyal fraternal and sororal devotees of the New Ethnicity. Thus, as we have observed from workshops and coalition-building meetings in McKees Rocks and McKeesport, Pennsylvania, and in Pittsburgh, Detroit, and Washington, D.C. (home of the National Center for Urban Ethnic Affairs at Catholic University under Monsignor Geno Baroni), "burying the hatchet" is a consciousness-raising enterprise of the highest priority. In some instances, it is effortless, in others, past differences pose an insurmountable problem.

In our experience, the Pan-Slavic umbrella is eagerly sought by groups ranging from the more militant Ukrainians, to the Poles and Slovaks and Croatians, to the relatively quietistic and numerically small group of Ruthenians. Many who are caught up with the ideology emphasize their common Slavic roots: "We're all Slavs. We're all part of one great Slavic family. It's now time for the Slavs to take their place on the great stage of history." Those who have become familiar with Herder's early nineteenth-century prophecy celebrate the present era as the decline of the Germanic-Nordic WASP West and the ascendancy of Slavdom. Slavic spirituality will outlive the collapse from within of the materialistic, secular, rational West. Another version of the same theme, one clearly articulated by Novak, walking in the footsteps of the Slavophile Dostoevski, is that Slavic (ethnic) spirituality and "humble charity" will redeem America. Novak, in a sense, becomes the Alexander Solzhenitsyn of the United States.

How do non-Slavs relate to the Pan-Slavic alliance? For example, Hungarians, whose nobility, central government, church, and intelligentsia waged a *Kulturkampf* against all non-Magyar peoples beginning with the Germanizing reforms of Joseph II in the late eighteenth century, are hardly remembered by those and their descendants from the Kingdom of Hungary as villains. Rather, it is the century of experience on American soil that has shaped their current ethnic identity. Some writers have gone so far as to say that the ethnic experience is entirely an American product. Although we do not concur completely, we recognize an elemental fact: that Hungarians, Croats, Slovaks, Rumanians, Ruthenians, Slovenians, Montenegrans, and to some extent Poles were all indiscriminately called "Hunkies." Although separate religious and fraternal voluntary associations developed early in the period of the New Immigration (1880–1920), neighborhood networks, common peasant origins, similar experiences in the mines and mills, shared religious beliefs (Latin Rite, Byzantine Rite, Orthodox Rites outside the Roman Catholic church), and finally intermarriage acted as leveling and acculturating influences which led to Americanization.

A likewise potentially overriding influence is that of social class, the source of the common experience of adversity, discontent, and frustration concerning mobility, status, and control over one's own life. While, as we shall note, ethnic factionalism and fission frequently override socioeconomic commonalities, the very *cultural* pan-ethnic universalism that attempts to transcend ethnic particularism is rooted in shared *social* experiences—even if the social does not become the bond of affiliation and loyalty. It is the *primordial* stress associated with the American class experience that leads to the search for stress reduction through the embracing of the alternate symbolic system of ethnicity that subsequently becomes experienced as primordial.

The search for common denominators, for a shared common culture—e.g., putative ancestors, glorious origins, and supraethnic religious ties—provides the basis for the *belief* that one is or deserves to be a member of the pan-ethnic family. Numerous workshops and seminars and consciousness-raising sessions are devoted to discovering how the white ethnics are all related. Although social class experience—and its precursor in the European peasantry—may be a shared experiential base, social class is no longer available as the basis of increased social status, since the working class and middle class alike are disparaged. Ethnicity is chosen in its place, providing a *family* in which all members are equal—and equally cared for. The past is selectively used to justify citizenship or siblingship.

Thus, Slavs try desperately to disassociate themselves from the Communists who rule their ancestral lands; Italians play down the fact that the papacy is Italian-dominated and that the Italian-American image is marred by its association with organized crime; Irish Catholics, both marginally mainstream and marginally ethnic, emphasize their plight at the hands of the British-Protestants and try to avoid the fact that they have heavy handedly dominated the American Catholic church (a fact which is brandished before them, as they become the Catholic WASPs). That the practical and delicate politics of "impression management" and painfully self-conscious other-directedness is a full-time occupation for those aspiring to legitimated ethnic status should be obvious. Ethnic siblings are capable not only of cooperation and accord, but of vicious rivalry and exclusiveness of claim to be *primus inter pares*. Ethnic solidarity is more a wish and an ideology than a fact.

The Reciprocal Influences of Ideology and Polity

The identity closure of the New Ethnicity clears the suspicion-laden air of ambiguity, relieves the paralysis of action, resolves ambivalence, and removes obstacles to decisiveness. The disruptiveness of contemporary socioeconomic and sociocultural events catalyzes and confirms feelings of malaise and marginality in American life by giving them a concrete referent. Reality confirms the ideological or "delusional" system of the New Ethnicity. Once the source of experience becomes ego-confirmed and integrated by a select group of peers— and not the whimsy of the recalcitrant and perfidious outer world—a sense of control over experience and destiny becomes possible and exercise of power becomes more than an exercise in futility.[21]

This formulation suggests why such movements as the New Ethnicity seem first to undergo a cultural identity phase of self-definition and symbol-ritual elaboration and then may proceed to a political phase of decision and action. The cultural phase is a necessary but not sufficient condition for the development of the political phase, which is far more dependent on the possibilities and coerciveness of outer events than the first phase. The will to act must first be mobilized, the inhibition to act must be overcome by a system of beliefs and values which frame the possibility and direction of action. "Power and innocence," to use Rollo May's recent title, emerge to overcome a sense of inferiority, powerlessness, and paralysis. Questions of *what, who,* and *why* belong predominantly to the first phase; questions of *how* and *where* dominate the second. Of course, the process becomes circular—in fact an open spiral—as belief, decision, and action enhance and support one another. The cultural and political merge into a systematic, and constantly systematizing, patterning of thought, feeling, and behavior that provides a complete meaning for one's life—and for those who are to be socialized, indoctrinated, and initiated into the new order by its vanguards.

This second phase of the movement is its institutionalization, what Max Weber referred to as the "routinization of charisma" in the formalization of what was amorphous. The *expressive* becomes channeled into the *instrumental,* and *ends* (of identity and ideology) are provided *means* by which they are achieved. The second phase does not so much replace the first as it subsumes it by channeling or directing the emotionally valent and the symbolically significant. While one could say, perhaps superficially, that the two phases overlap with one another, it is more correct to say that they are in a reciprocal, transactional feedback relationship. The formation and elaboration of the new identity does not stop with institutionalization; indeed, the institutionalization provides a support system for a thorough-going ideological revisionism which, in turn, becomes the rationale for future action—wherein events that are *made* to happen confirm and validate the prophecy. Charisma cannot be routinized to the extent that tension is once and for all reduced. The movement not only thrives but is dependent for its perpetuity on a cycle of constant heightening and reducing of stress. It must, in a sense, "corner the market" on salvation and maintains its adherents (as does the church) by brandishing the threat of damnation (in the case of the New Ethnicity, the loss of identity, estrangement, and alienation) if their loyalty should lapse.

It must instill through socialization what it claims is primordial. It sets out to replace self-identification with low status categories (e.g., worker, racist, and limited education) by offering ethnicity as a high status and self-esteem source of identification. Through the thought reform of the present and older generations, the New Ethnicity seeks its *converts.* Through the ideological socialization of the younger generation and of the yet unborn, the movement assures its hard-won identity of continuity and of vindication. Those uncertain of their paternity and maternity look not only to the past and their progenitors as a source of reassurance and stability, but to those whom they now make in their own image to give them a future. If, as many argue, intergenerational transmission is essential to the very definition of an ethnic group, then as a consequence of the socialization of a new generation, the New Ethnics fulfill the prophecy of the continued vigor and existence of such groups. As a result of socialization, the ideological assumption of the nature of the past and the future—i.e., the place of genealogy and progeny in identity—is confirmed. An ethnic group that has been created can now claim longevity and persistence—and can thus legitimate its demands in the cultural marketplace.

Institutions play a vital role in this process, especially in the reciprocal interaction of identity, ideology, and polity. Although one could enumerate at length, we suggest that at present the most productive and influential cultural centers and organizational bases of the White Ethnic Movement are the following:

National Project on Group Identity and Mental Health
    Institute of Human Relations, American Jewish Committee, New York City. Irving Levine, Director
Center for the Study of American Pluralism
    National Opinion Research Center, Chicago, Illinois. Reverend Andrew Greeley, Director
National Center for Urban Ethnic Affairs
    Affiliated with the U.S. Catholic Conference, Catholic University, Washington, D.C. Monsignor Geno Baroni, Director
Center for Immigration Studies
    St. Paul, Minnesota. Rudolph Vecoli, Director
Center for Migration Studies
    New York City. Reverend Silvano Tomasi, Director
New York Center for Ethnic Affairs
    New York City. Ralph Perotta, Director
Slavic-American Studies
    New York City. Peter Goy, Director
Italian-American Studies
    Queens College, Flushing, New York. Richard Gambino, Director
Multi-Culture Institute
    San Francisco, California. Frances Sussna, Director
Pennsylvania Ethnic Heritage Studies Center
    University of Pittsburgh, Pittsburgh, Pennsylvania.
Kent State University
    Kent, Ohio. Offering an Ethnic Heritage Major; Ethnic Studies

Certificate Programs in Hellenic, Jewish, and Lithuanian
Studies
St. Mary's College, Center for Polish Studies and Culture
Orchard Lake, Michigan. Reverend Leonard Chrobot, Academic
Dean
Programs of ethnic studies also are presented at the Joint Center on
Urban Studies of Harvard and M.I.T., Queens College (City Uni-
versity of New York), and other colleges and universities
EMPAC: Ethnic Millions Political Action Committee
Bayville, New York. Michael Novak, Director (formed 1974),
devoted to white ethnic impact on government, education, mass
media, and corporations
The Ford Foundation and the Rockefeller Foundation
E.g., a recent working paper by Richard Gambino, with an intro-
duction by Michael Novak, *Ethnic Studies* (1975) from the
Rockefeller Foundation, discussing the need for ethnic studies,
offering course descriptions, resource centers, and bibliography
by ethnic group[22]

An example of the cultural diffusion of the New Ethnicity into the
mainstream and "the establishment" of American society is the re-
cent appearance of the following advertisement in the *Ladies' Home
Journal* (September 1975): "This month's American Issues Forum
theme is "A Nation of Nations.' Write and tell us how the people of
your ethnic background have contributed uniquely to the richness of
American life. We'll pay $25 each for the 10 most compelling entries.
Keep them under 100 words and mail to Ethnic Origins Contest. . . .
We shall publish the winning entries in an upcoming issue."[23]
A much more comprehensive and concerted effort at directed cul-
ture change through diffusion and resocialization is the Ethnic Heritage Studies Programs Act passed by the United States Congress in
June 1972, following more than two years of intense lobbying and
Congressional hearings.[24] Representatives of most of the above institutions and others argued the case against the model of the Melting
Pot and for an institutionalized pluralist model in which the educational system would play a vital role for the validation of ethnicity
(e.g., preparation of materials on minority groups for use in public
schools, the training of teachers to be conscious of ethnic differences
and to teach the importance of ethnicity to their students, the rewrit-
ing of American history as ethnic history). The Department of Health,
Education and Welfare now has an Ethnic Studies branch of the
Office of Education. The successful passage of the act provided impe-

tus for much of the movement's subsequent development, just as the period of the hearings served to mobilize and organize amorphous interest from local to national workshops and study sessions on ethnicity and urban strategies. The Ethnic Studies act gave at least a semblance of *national* confirmation to the pluralist identity, ideology, and polity, validating localistic and particularistic tendencies as fundamental to American freedom and culture. This, in turn, confirmed the ethnophile traditionalists (in addition to the nontraditionalist major leaders) in the church and fraternal organizations, who only several decades ago were on the vanguard of Americanization and who now urge the strayed souls to return to the ethnic fold.

While the New Ethnics did not get the regional centers they wanted—edifices symbolic of diversity—and, while much of the money has gone to academics for the preparation of ethnic educational materials, the act gave the New Ethnicity national recognition. But why the need for national recognition? In the early decades of the twentieth century, the impoverished but thrifty white ethnics saved their money in order to build and support imposing churches and church-related schools (while at the same time they sent money home to families in Europe and paid regular dues at the fraternals). The guiding principle was self-help, or "We take care of our own." Today such appeals for the support of the New Ethnicity would go largely unheeded, despite far greater affluence. The gap between ethnic leaders and those for whom they presume to speak is enormous: for the most part ethnic Americans devote their financial resources toward ends and goals commensurate with their self-definition and identity. The New Ethnics, however, seek more than government subsidy. In attempting to redefine America as pluralistic, they simultaneously wish to raise their status as Americans. The New Ethnics must seek official governmental validation and sanction of their redefinition by having pluralism accepted and promoted as national policy. Unlike their progenitors two or three generations back, they cannot stand alone because the very basis of their self-esteem remains American.

As for the future—which is inherently indeterminate—two major factors would seem to influence whether the New Ethnicity will develop into a full-blown crisis cult: the extent of frustration and sense of stress generated from within and without by unfulfilled ideals, ambitions, and expectations; and the extent to which the charismatic white ethnic leaders are willing and able to exploit the vulnerabilities and frustrations of those for whom they claim to speak and whom they seek to serve. Moreover, increased funding by foundations and government, in addition to increased public exposure by the mass media, will have an effect similar to that of the New Ethnic socialization of the young and the resocialization of the old: the self-fulfilling prophecy that ethnicity is not only real, but vital and pervasive. It is an assumption that is made to come true, and once the movement becomes highly visible and audible, white ethnics will take for granted that it has always been real. Such is the possible future of this new illusion.

The Nature of Ethnic Leadership

In discussing leadership, Erik Erikson writes that "it frequently happens in history that an extreme and even atypical personal experience fits a universal latent conflict so well that a crisis lifts it to a representative position."[25] George Devereux suggests that the shaman shares a common personality core and conflicts with those he ceremonially cures, that he is like them only more so.[26] It is the fact that there exists an underlying shared conflict that makes it appear that the charismatic leader so uncannily *understands* those whom he serves and exploits by offering them his own solution. His public conviction of certainty over issues on which everyone else is desperately confused inspires identification and a remission of their own confusion so long as they adhere to his ideology.

As De Vos and Romanucci-Ross note, "In numerous instances the leader who personifies an ethnic group is an outsider. Such a leader often vehemently affirms his allegiance as the means of overcoming his questionable legitimacy of belonging."[27] They cite Ataturk, Hitler, Napoleon, De Gaulle, Malcolm X, and Valiers. We would add to this list Wagner, Lenin, Trotsky, Stalin, Chief Crazy Horse, Tolstoi, Herzl, Mickiewicz, Dostoevski, Moses, Handsome Lake, Kossuth, Wovoka, and so on. The acute sense of estrangement, illegitimacy, inferiority, and guilt leads to the personal search for a positive self-affirmation. The sense of being different is overcome by merging one's identity with that of the group. Through great effort, one demonstrates that he or she is not only the same as they, but exemplary, the paragon of ethnic identity.

It seems hardly coincidental that the New Ethnic Movement is led and represented by those who, only a decade ego, were on the vanguard of the integrationist movement, if not in what has come to be called "radical politics." At the zenith of the Kennedy New Frontier and during the early days of the Johnson Great Society, the social imperative was the fulfillment of the American Dream, not ethnic reentrenchment. Just as Diggins speaks of "the ex-Communist as conservative," we might speak of the ethnophile as ex-integrationist and Americanist, reflecting the conversion from one identity to its opposite.[28] To cite a few examples: Monsignor Geno Baroni, from an activist in the Civil Rights Movement to the leading political figure of the White Ethnic Movement; Michael Novak, from radical existentialist and celebrant of nothingness to philosopher and theologian of the mystique and mythos of ethnocentrism; the late Abraham J. Heschel, from ecumenicist and outspoken leader of the Civil Rights Movement to theological rationalist for the fusion of Jewish identity and the State of Israel; Herbert Gold, from novelist of hedonism and sensualism to a returned prodigal son merging himself with Jewish history. It is a paradox of the identity of the new pluralism and the new pluralists that what is sought is *integration without integration.* All leaders of the New Ethnicity firmly believe that theirs is a formula for social reconciliation: cultural pluralism and social coalition-building will produce the genuine American society. Yet their often strident particularism and exclusivism readily disqualify the message of reconciliation. Their ambivalence toward both the American and the New Ethnic identity is reflected in the contradictory imagery of integration by dis-integration.

The potential leader and the wider population that experience similar conflicts gravitate to one another. As Erikson documented in *Young Man Luther,* the aspirant leader solves for himself (or herself) and others what he could not solve for himself alone.[29] A cultural selection process takes place by which many prophets of differing ideologies and personalities offer their personal salvation to the multitudes. The masses, in turn, *select* the true or authentic prophets and declare the others to be *false prophets* or imposters, based on their ability or inability to offer acceptable resolutions of internal conflicts.

In this perspective, Michael Novak seems to be the chosen spokesman and the major prophet of the New Ethnicity. Important, though lesser, prophets include Geno Baroni, Richard Kolm, Andrew Greeley, Irving Levine, and Richard Gambino. Although innovators in their own right, they function largely as the systematizers, the routinizers, and organizers of belief and concerted action, based on assumptions, axioms, and fundamental propositions offered by the major prophet. Both devotees and opponents of Novak agree that he is not so much a disciplined thinker as a spontaneous, poetic one. It is precisely the articulation of his passions in words and compelling word images that makes his tune sound so right. Speaking from the "gut," his contradictions, ambivalences, and distortions do not work against him. To the contrary, the language of the "gut" (primary process) does not get filtered through the head; it does not get scrutinized, but accepted, because he is seeing things in the same way as those who follow him perceive the world.

The lesser prophets, perhaps themselves *priests,* whom we would describe, following Max Weber, as the routinizers and bureaucratizers of charisma, elaborate on the original ideas systematically, making them into an official creed, insuring that no heresies are incorporated, and—much as the New Ethnics despise the word—*rationalize* the spontaneous into the official. Novak is not absent from this process (having served as the director of EMPAC, formed in 1974, as a consultant to the Rockefeller Foundation, and as a "gatekeeper" for definitions, policies, and funding). However, his major function in the White Ethnic Movement is that of charismatic leader, shaman and prophet.

The coincidence of ethnic "soul" with religious "soul" (not necessarily denominational) revitalizes traditional or former white ethnic leaders. The handful of charismatic leaders, activists, and intellectuals of the White Ethnic Movement are not the old style ethnic-religious-fraternal leaders, but are, in a sense, establishment men, highly mobile, educated, acculturated, and assimilated, and who have, in a sense, precipitated out of the American solution. However, they have at their ready service the not yet extinct fraternal organizations, newspapers, and local-regional leadership and editors; likewise, the multitude of religious organizations are at their service (from church-affiliated fraternals to ethnically segmented monastic orders), the leaders of which have stood ready for more than two decades awaiting the opportunity to cry: "I told you so. Assimilation is not the answer." During the earlier decades of the twentieth century, aspirants to mobility and leadership frequently chose the clergy or fraternal route as a means of making it without having to compare themselves to the mainstream associations of American culture in which they were reluctant to compete. Ethnicity for them has always been a defended turf of self-protection and insulation which they Americanized *from within.* Now they have their vindication—and the national leaders have their cadre of apostles.

The paradox of ethnic consciousness-raising is that it involves not so much a drawing out of what is latently within, but a resocialization that draws very selectively on what is within an individual and organizes it from without, convincing the eager convert to the movement that ethnic awareness was there all along. As Peter Rose suggests, "Maybe because there has been more 'melting' than Novak admits," consciousness-raising is necessary.[30] Apparently, one's identity is flawed and false unless it is completely ethnic, and it is the task of the new ideology to remove the fatal flaw.

More generally, Lloyd A. Fallers writes: "Leaders who speak in terms of being 'on the side of history' do so in order to inspire their people to efforts which they recognize to be far from inevitable. . . . "[31] The inevitability of ethnicity lies in its persuasiveness and believability. And the problem of believability first lies in the urgency the belief has for those who aspire to lead. They must make ethnicity as urgent and fundamental a fact of existence for their constituency as it has become for themselves. The aspiring leader cannot, of course, simply impose his will and project his private conflicts onto a public stage. For a leader to be confirmed, his *will* and message must coincide and correspond with shared conflicts to which he offers a solution. The direction of the resolution, however, is not inevitable. The art of charismatic demagoguery consists of the manipulation of fears and the heightening of a sense of vulnerability that only the new ideology can alleviate, creating the fragile sense of strength and the gnawing threat of weakness. The alliance, while ostensibly one of mutual liberation, is in fact one of mutual exploitation. The symbiosis—and, in a way, fatal parasitism—of leader and follower begins with the leader's need to convert. To remain certain of his own convictions, he must convince others. And since pervasive doubt haunts the most self-confident of proselytizers, no effort is sufficient. The numbers must grow into the multitude, and the multitude itself must multiply in numbers, in symbols, and rituals.

The ethnics are to the white ethnic intelligentsia and leadership what the Russian *mujiik* ("peasant") was to Leo Tolstoi, or what the *Deutsches Volk* was to Hitler: an abstract object to be romanticized and idealized, venerated as *the* human beings. One paradox of ethnic leadership is that, while disavowing separateness and avant-garde status, and offering themselves humbly as speaking the will of the people, the white ethnic leadership must implant in the consciousness of its constituency a sense of identity—hence of utopian cause, of messianic zeal—that is far from generic to being an ethnic. The white ethnic leaders undertake to instruct their presumed constituency what it means to be an ethnic, and how to go about becoming one. Those who are alleged to possess soul must be taught it by the elite ethnic catechists who become for many a caricature of those they champion and imitate. If ethnicity *is* the most powerful and compelling feature of one's life, then why is the *ought*, the imperative, the endless consciousness-raising, necessary?

The ethnic leaders, far from being the spokesmen for the will of the masses, must first convince their constituency—who may or may not be receptive—to renounce their false consciousness (American) and must reform them so that they will want to embrace their true consciousness (ethnicity). If the leaders must first convince the people of their true will and identity, they are hardly their mere voice. The New Ethnic leaders do precisely what they claim not to do—and which thought reform they angrily ascribe to the *American* opposition.

Their *social-class* distance and their attention only to emblematically differentiating stage characteristics, which they can use to distinguish themselves from the opposition, often make them appear ridiculous in the eyes of those upon whom they model themselves. Several Polish and Slovak informants familiar with at least some of the writings of Novak, Baroni, and others, have told us that the New Ethnic spokesmen insult their intelligence, and that their heavy-handed emphasis on ethnicity would deprive them of the American identity they seek. Not that they do not have conflicts over the relation between their ethnicity and their Americanness, but that they would prefer to be able to work it out for themselves rather than be thrown into an *ethnic* melting pot tended by white ethnic zealots as narrow and intolerant as those WASPs who tended the American Melting Pot. For them, the New Ethnics are no improvement, but simply the old pot pouring them into a new mold. The tremendous diversity of Polish culture, the even greater diversity of Slovak culture, is to be eliminated by simplification. Anglo-conformity is simply replaced with ethno-conformity. Most Slovaks and Poles we have worked with would prefer to be ethnic on their own terms, dictated to neither by professional Anglicizer nor ethnic homogenizer. For them, the particularisms of family, neighborhoods, human networks, formal and informal associations ("institutionalized" or not), and least of all dreams and aspirations for themselves and their children—all these are parts of the cumulative definition of *self,* the syncretism and compartmentalization of different pasts, presents, and futures they wish to have the option to preserve *and* change at their own initiative. The self-conscious confessionals and plans of the white ethnic intelligentsia tell us more about them than about those whom they celebrate at a distance.

Participation in the White Ethnic Movement

The following is a brief profile of the dynamics of participation in the White Ethnic Movement in particular, and in crisis cults in general. What Eric Hoffer says of members of minority groups in general can be applied to the New Ethnicity as one means of overcoming this uncertainty and insecurity.

> With a minority bent on assimilation, the least and most successful (economically and culturally) are likely to be more frustrated than those in between. The man who fails sees himself as an outsider; and in the case of a member of a minority group who wants to blend with the majority, failure intensifies the feeling of not belonging. A similar feeling crops up at the other end of the economic cultural scale. Those of a minority who attain fortune and fame often find it difficult to gain entrance into the exclusive circles of the majority. They are thus made conscious of their foreignness. Furthermore, having evidence of their individual superiority, they resent the admission of inferiority implied in the process of assimilation. Thus, it is to be expected that the least and most successful of a minority bent on assimilation should be most responsive to the appeal of proselytizing mass movements.[32]

In chapter 5, we saw that, as Pettigrew has shown, those who are attracted to George Wallace are generally of high aspiration but low achievement, suffering a crisis of self-esteem or status; consequently, they see in Wallace a means of restoring that self-esteem. In his study of Melanesian millenarian movements, Theodore Schwartz (1968) arrives at the same conclusion about the motivation for cult participation and the composition of the membership.

> Another basis for the cult fixation of some individuals is the personal gratification derived from the temporary exaltation of status. There was often a status inversion . . . [that] was possible as long as the cult persisted. Some people were equally at home in both cult and secular [modern] movement. . . . Those who remained cult-oriented longer ["fixated on the cult experience"] invariably were individuals of lower status or individuals of potentially higher status who lacked complete legitimation—in other words, who lacked either traditional or modern support for leadership. This does not mean that all such persons became or remained cultists.[33]

What Schwartz observes of the millenarian-chiliastic "cargo cults" of Melanesia we would apply to the dynamics of the contemporary

ethnic consciousness and power movements in the United States, and
to nationalism and nativism generally.

Cultists not only recruit to build confirmation through numbers of
believers, they also exclude and elicit opposition to add the dissonance and oppositional segmentation necessary to their own morale
and the maintenance of solidarity. Through exclusion of some they
recruit others, forming the larger interdependent system of which
cult and opposition are both a part. Where the cults persist, there is
partial addiction to states of expressive feeling that contrast with the
depression or pallid lack of feeling found in plateau and drift phases.
For some, the cult fixation is a counterdepressant. Hostility, even
more than hope, may be the dominant feeling of the cult phases.[34]

Among the white ethnics, hostility is directed predominantly toward the WASPs, the blacks, and more distantly toward Jews, other
impoverished ethnic minorities (Chicanos, Puerto Ricans), and the
so-called sexual minorities. While white ethnic animosity toward
blacks and WASPs is universal, their degree of antipathy toward
these other groups is contingent on the experience of conflict with
them (e.g., the presence of a large Latino population in Chicago as
opposed to Pittsburgh). When they cannot unite against a common
adversary, the illusion of white ethnic unanimity and amity evaporates, and a volatile fission quickly takes place, as the Irish struggle to
be bona fide white ethnics, while the Italians and Poles accuse them
of ethno-religious persecution in the Roman Catholic church and in
the political ward; the Slovaks and Ukrainians each claim the Ruthenians to be their own; and the Slavs unite against the hated Magyars
who can say nothing good about the Germans.

Among cult-fixated Melanesians, Schwartz reports that government
attempts at amelioration are met with resistance or apathy. The same
is true for many blacks, Chicanos, Puerto Ricans, and white ethnics
in the United States, who greet governmental, industrial, union, or
commercial *opportunities* with apathy, mistrust, resistance, or indifference. Schwartz's analysis holds both for Melanesia and the United
States:

> The offers it does make would weaken the grievances and threaten
> the hostility that has greater value as feeling and that is, perhaps,
> the main basis for the maintenance of cult solidarity.[35]

Heinz Kohut analyzes the hostility and opposition in terms of acute
and chronic "narcissistic rage." "If the rage does not subside," he
states,

then the secondary processes tend to be pulled increasingly into the domain of the archaic aggressions which seek to re-establish control over a narcissistically experienced world. Conscious and preconscious ideation, in particular as it concerns the aims and goals of the personality, becomes more and more subservient to the pervasive rage. The ego, furthermore, increasingly surrenders its reasoning capacity to the task of rationalizing the persisting insistence on the limitlessness of the power of the grandiose self: it does not acknowledge the inherent limitations of the power of the self, but attributes its failures and weaknesses to the malevolence and corruption of the uncooperative archaic object [and, we would add, its contemporary representatives]. We are thus witnessing the gradual establishment of chronic narcissistic rage. . . .[36]

What Bruno Bettelheim writes in his psychograph of the uprooting radicalism of youthful revolutionaries in the America of the 1960s is applicable to the atavistic conservatism of those who seek to put down roots with a vengeance. The revolution and the counterrevolution, reformation and counterreformation are sustained (and perpetual revolutionary vigilance perpetuated) by the paranoid position. Bettelheim states that "political activity for such persons enables them to escape a complete break with reality. They may interpret reality in line with their delusions, but at least they remain in touch with isolated aspects of reality, and the support and admiration of the followers is another, though most tenuous, contact."

To embrace the extreme position . . . can actually be an ego defensive action. It proceeds because the discharge of rage and violence drains off the aggression that would destroy whatever paranoid defenses remained working. Typical of such persons is the quasi or openly delusional quality of their beliefs, their inaccessibility to reason while loudly complaining that nobody listens to them, the oversimplification of issues, and the preoccupation with violence and destruction (the imagined destruction of themselves, and the readiness to consider the destruction of their enemies). All this is combined with an absence of, or emotional paucity and flatness in, their personal relations.[37]

In their "overwhelming *ressentiment*" (Bettelheim's term for the process of opposition) the New Ethnics press for the creation of a new order—including strong figures of authority who can "bring order to their own inner chaos."[38] To salvage self-esteem and guard against the eruption of reawakened early conflicts, the overwhelming self-hate and feeling of helplessness is transformed and projected into a paranoid ideology and aggressive activism. Great energy is directed outward to shore up the inner defenses as a guardian against narcissistic vulnerability. Some variant of the cry "Never again!" is characteristic of such intense repudiation and affirmation. Inherent in this cry is the explanation for the "emotional paucity" in the ethnic cultists object relations, suggesting the need to defend against schizoid regression and dissolution. Whatever else it implies, "Never again!" is a vow to never again trust human beings. The autistic armor of ideology makes that trust unnecessary while providing the illusion of deep trust, connection, belonging, and continuity. Devotion to an ideology replaces or substitutes for actual object relations, while claiming, through idealization, to be the real thing. The sense of closeness and intimacy (rather, pseudo-intimacy) is achieved through a transfixing of all eyes on the ideal and devoting all of one's energies toward its realization.

In the New Ethnicity, the mark of adolescence is clearly present with its vacillations, excesses, entrenchments, earnest concern over the relation between past and future, depressions and elations, and multifold oppositions. The erstwhile choice of an American identity and the repudiation of the ethnic identity of one's parents illustrates how what Peter Blos calls "conflictual elaborations" of adolescence were avoided by "generation gap" maneuvers such as the rupture of dependencies (object relations). Ethnic Americans distanced themselves through "spatial and ideological separations" which "are substituted for inner conflicts and emotional disengagement," resulting in developmental arrest.[39] A rigid ego, bolstered by the ideology, defends against the reexperiencing of the conflicts by personal rigidity and the fear of ambiguity.

The past decade seriously challenged the ability of American symbols, ideology, rituals to provide stability through conflict avoidance. The old conflicts reawaken and force re-resolutions. The New Ethnics reexperience the ancient adolescent tug of war between regression and progression, and they must atone and make restitution for the adolescent solution of counterphobic liberation and emancipation. They undo the past errors through regression—liberating themselves from their earlier liberation—which, in the relief of guilt and shame in the overcoming of the sense of mutual abandonment and of having "gone too far" (in many ways), confers a sudden sense of freedom and relief. But the character of the regression confirms its adolescent dynamic. A new ideology of relation and primordiality still replaces either genuine object relation or the emotional confrontation with and working through the conflict, giving it resolution. Idealization replaces relationship in order to defend against "the deadly fear of regressive engulfment."[40] The New Ethnics are as removed from those they now idealize and venerate as they were when they feverishly separated from their parents through Americanization, radicalism, or by dropping out. The New Ethnicity still carefully defends against the past it venerates. Indeed, the new movement is as much a form of radicalism as those—such as Americanization, the New Left, and the youth Counterculture Movement—it opposes.

In any discussion concerning the nature and extent of participation in the White Ethnic Movement, or of crisis cults in general, it is necessary to address the problem of *variation*. One way is to construct a typology of the different kinds of participation, or the extent of involvement, intensity, or commitment. The problem with this approach is that the movement is treated as though it were static (which is quite a contradiction), and as though individuals were fixed in their roles and degree of being socially or politically mobilized. While the next chapter will deal with the New Ethnicity from the point of view of the life history, the more important general methodological point is that we cannot take personality structure as a fixed given, simply unfolding like personal orthogenesis. Indeed, the New Ethnicity makes sense only in terms of how an ideology—in fact selected aspects of that ideology—becomes integrated into one's psychodynamic process, interpersonal relations, and wider cultural life. The New Ethnic identity and ideology is not a changeless monolith even for the full-time ideologists, intelligentsia, and activist leadership.

However, one clear distinction between leader and follower is that for the leader the ideology and activism are virtually full-time occupations, roles, and, encompassing all of these, identities. The heightened identity-consciousness and emotionality, even when channeled into highly *rational* and instrumental schemes, are never absent from the leader whose calling is not only the innovator and creator, but guardian of the faith. The contemporary language calls such people, of whatever cause, "radicals," "extremists," etc., which the New Ethnic leaders would be the *last* to call themselves, since they perceive their identity and cause as opposing the radicalism, extremism, violence, and permanent unrest which they use to characterize the black and youth movements of the 1960s and early 1970s. They view themselves as conciliatory and reasonable, and use confrontation with great care. However, both in the normative and statistical sense, the leaders of such movements must be the most extreme and radical of their group: it is this sense of intensity and urgency that is the very basis of their charisma.

Mircea Eliade says of the shaman in general: What is for the group a "cosmological ideograph" is for the shaman a "mystical itinerary"; that the shaman plumbs the very depths of existence and is on intimate terms with the seething forces of the universe; and that out of this very personal relationship and experience an idiosyncratic "itinerary" is offered to and adopted by the group as the road to follow.[41] The extent to which the shaman's vision or message is acceptable to the group—literally sharpening, clarifying, and confirming the multisense perceptions of the group—is the extent to which the shaman will be regarded as a curer or a fraud. The shaman is not a seer alone: the group determines his sanity, role, and authority, and appoints him to speak in their behalf with forces and beings too powerful for them to cope with. He thus mediates, based on their confirmation. The phrase *full time* must be clarified, since in the so-called primitive societies the shaman was very much only a part-time denizen of the nether world and spent most of his time as husband, hunter, fisherman, horticulturist (or, if female, in her customary worldly roles). Sociocultural complexity facilitated the development of specialization: the contemporary full-time white ethnic could hardly make a career of identity-consciousness in the primordial-organic society he so dearly idealizes!

Returning to the problem of variation: the returnee from a vision quest (whether stylized Plains Indian or idiosyncratic white ethnic) must have his vision validated by the group if it is to be accepted as legitimate. And a vision that departs too far from the norm (e.g., ethnic versus American Dream) will be rejected unless there is a commensurate change in the group's experience which departs from the normal and expected, which would be receptive to a new vision. In turn, the vision would confirm in broad sweep the altered perception of the group.

The New Ethnicity ranges from those who totally reorganize their identities and priorities, to those for whom it serves as a supplement to assuage the uncertainties and insecurities of the American Dream, to those for whom it is peripheral if not irrelevant. In our experience, by far the latter two very general *types* are the most prevalent. The intensely romantic and pragmatic members of the first category—discussed in this section as the prophets and the priests—though the most vocal and visible, are in a decided minority and their attendance at the ethnic church is indeed spare.

Among the great masses of Americans, the influence of the New Ethnicity seems to largely follow and resemble that of the youth movement, the black movement, the Woman's Movement, and so forth: namely, diffusion of many of the diverse elements into the mainstream, and in the process *de-radicalizing* them, *de-ethnicizing* them. Thus men's hair, from Wall Street to the U.S. Senate, is considerably longer than before the Hippies insulted the cult of the crew cut; likewise with the increased colorfulness of men's shirts, we observe the influence of the flower children. Unisex and the Woman's Movement contributed the emergence of pantsuits for women, of leisure suits for men, greater color, variety, and expressiveness for both sexes. The Black Power Movement, like that of the other movements, resulted in a greater cultural receptivity to the creative use of aggression in conflict resolution (we do not neglect backlash, and other forms of viciousness). Its language (e.g., *rapping*) has become part of American English. The natural or Afro hair style and the *dashiki* as a loose outer garment have found their way into the hair and wig salons of mainstream America and into the style of looser, more ornate, men's shirts. In a way, all of this is proof of the vitality of the Melting Pot (not merely Madison Avenue), which "co-opts" ethnic and other particularist traits into the mainstream—just as ice skates were adopted from the Dutch and spaghetti from the Italians.

Another important source of variation is within the White Ethnic Movement itself. While the ideology may stress harmony and cooperation, the reality of interethnic relations runs rife with discord and competition. At numerous conferences and workshops we have attended, where the agenda was the formulation of a common identity and an abiding coalition, the pan-ethnic hymn frequently broke down into dissonance and nearly violent discord as accusation and counter-accusation escalated. Among the problems besetting white ethnic conferences are: Old World ethnic rivalries; New World status and power inequalities inside and outside the church; claims and counter-claims to the position of "most oppressed ethnic group"; disputes over who is to be included in the definition of "ethnic"; and chronic discord concerning the relation between ethnics, minorities, WASPs, and Jews. In the late 1960s and early 1970s, coalition meant bridge-building between white ethnics and blacks; today it is operationally white ethnic only, with lip service to wider and crosscutting ties.

Building an inner-city urban coalition based on idealism and origin myths of recent vintage does not work because it is often too abstract and distant from more immediately experienced realities. The issue of *life chances* (the so-called bread-and-butter issues) is felt to be far more primordial than ethnicity. As a number of discussants at these meetings have pointed out, mostly incurring apathy if not wrath for their temerity, organizing around such themes as human services, health, education, and the like, will improve the quality of life for white ethnics, but to organize around ethnicity will not and will moreover be divisive from within, defeating its own pragmatic goals.[42] This is not to judge all activities of the New Ethnicity as irrational; rather it is to suggest that much of the heightened identity-consciousness becomes so all-consuming a concern that the instrumental amelioration of the sources of insecurity becomes of secondary importance.

While repudiating any cultural ranking of ethnic groups within the movement (or of ethnic groups in general, including WASPs, Jews, blacks, and Chicanos), any semblance of egalitarianism or relativism quickly breaks down in practice. While ideally the White Ethnic Movement is inclusive, its boundaries blurring to all those who embrace its tenets, eligibility requirements are stringent. The most dominant groups, and those from which the major leaders come, seem to be the Italians, Poles, and Slovaks. While there are many Jewish participants and sponsors in white ethnic meetings, their status as white ethnics is precarious, if not peripheral. All the decades of anti-defamation, of self-protection by protecting the dignity of others, do not guarantee admission to the core. Orthodox Jews, especially those who are poor, are the most welcome.

Stratification and inequality in the Roman Catholic church make for endless vindictiveness; and much energy of the White Ethnic Movement is spent in personal vendetta of one ethnic Catholic against another. While many Irish Catholics aspire to assimilation in the ethnic movement, they are seen as the WASPs of the American Catholic church, oppressors, not belonging in the august company of the oppressed. As the stereotype goes, just as there are no poor Jews, there are no poor Irish Catholics. The Irish Catholics thus become thrice estranged: peripherally Catholic, American, and now ethnic.

While the Italians and everyone else are at the jugular veins of the Irish, among Czechs, Slovaks, and Ruthenians, animosities resurface. Ruthenians attempt in vain to convince Ukrainians that they are not Ukrainians, while the latter argue that Ruthenians never existed. Religion compounds the ethnic fratricide. The Byzantine and other oriental rites have never been regarded either by the Catholic church hierarchy or by the Latin-Rite Catholics themselves as authentic Catholicism; they have always been treated, and equally regarded themselves, as inferior, giving rise, in turn, to resistance and counterassertions of superiority. Eastern Orthodoxy is regarded as beyond the pale, tainted with orientalism, communism, and everything eastern and evil. Byzantine Slovaks attempt heroically to be accepted as Slovaks, but are regarded by Latin-Rite Slovaks as *Russnaks* ("Ruthenians"), by Ukrainians as western Ukrainians, and by Ruthenians as Ruthenians. One self-identified Byzantine Catholic Slovak-American described the feeling of being a rebel in the eyes of the Latin-Rite Slovak Catholics, who regarded themselves as being Yankees. Polish-American Catholics, fiercely loyal to the church (or to the Polish National Catholic church), are suspicious of any alliance with orthodoxy, whose name is associated with an adversary more timelessly menacing than the Germans. In exploring the dynamics and relevant parameters of white ethnicity, one must consider not only the "ancient feuds" of Europe, but equally the multiethnic Catholic and orthodox religious systems in the United States, their relation to American ethnic rankings, and the relation of all of these to the dominant Anglo-American cultural system.

White ethnicity is certainly not a monolithic *minority;* indeed it is composed of a hierarchy of minorities and minorities within minorities, each struggling for respectability and power. Our central point is that although the White Ethnic Movement is egalitarian and horizontal in its ideology, it implicitly rearranged the social-distance scale that it repudiated. The lineal or vertical system of social stratification, in terms of status and decision-making power, remains the primary principle of social organization. The traditional system in large measure is inverted, and, in accordance with the principle of opposition, the last become first, and the first, last.

We do not suggest that ethnicity alone is the invention of the mass media and a handful of intellectuals and traditionalists awaiting resurrection. Rather, the media turn their microphones and cameras on those whom American culture would *expect* to be the natural leaders: university professors, the clergy, and officials of venerable ethnic fraternals. (There is some irony to this observation, since Michael Novak and others have emphasized that the media have been most responsible for creating the illusion of American homogeneity and the denial of ethnicity.) It is assumed that they speak for the constituency they claim to have. The very sensationalist nature of much of media *news* (and what is defined as *news* is usually the extraordinary, the disruptive, etc.) requires that it seek out the self-proclaimed leaders. This does not deny that an ethnic movement exists, but, in the spirit of good ethnography, requires that one be at least as attentive to those for whom the leaders claim to speak as to the leaders themselves.

Postscript: "American" Nativism

American nativism and white ethnic nativism are two variants on the same theme. White ethnics, as we have seen, often vacillate between virulently asserting their loyalty to America and their Americanness, and denouncing American culture and embracing ethnicity. The ambivalence is neatly compartmentalized or is openly ambitendent—or one of the poles predominates while the other is repressed. For the American nativists who are of northwest-European Protestant descent, and who claim on the basis of pedigree that they arrived the earliest, ethnicity and American identity are fused. America is *their* country; everyone else is an unwelcome, or begrudgingly accepted, foreigner.

Just as the white ethnic nativists exclude WASPs, Jews, and blacks (and other "colored" minorities) from their new identity, and just as many Black Power and Pride advocates separate themselves from white ethnics, WASPs, and Jews, now the Anglo-Protestant, white, largely working-class *American* nativists see Catholics (white ethnics), Jews, and blacks as the invading outsiders who have destroyed their country. The Anglo-Protestant American nativism is characterized by the same attributes as the New Ethnicity: exclusiveness, parochialism, separatism, self-righteousness, authoritarianism and the need for decisive authority, the veneration of the idealized past, the condemnation of the present as decadent, and the wish for an order that will tighten up the looseness and restore values. The search for old virtues through "old-time religion" is found through Neo-Pentecostalism, evangelism, the Jesus Movement, and other forms of religious expression among Anglo-Protestants that are homologous to the white ethnic search for religious and moral orthodoxies and fundamentals.

The localistic, often violent, self-legislation of law and order, which, for example, has erupted among the Irish Catholics of South Boston against the blacks of Roxbury, has its American nativist parallel in the proliferation of vigilante posses, Citizens' Grand Juries, the formation of a National Association to Keep and Bear Arms, the increasing ranks of Young Americans for Freedom, the greater visibility of the American Party, and the spread of the *new* Ku Klux Klan to the urban-industrial North. All of these express a defensive and defended identity, ideology, and polity.

In chapter 4, we discussed this at greater length as part of the "godfather phenomenon." Here we note *American* nativism as an *ethnic* phenomenon, even though no self-identified or WASP movement has yet developed. But it is clearly an American-for-Americans opposition or backlash that is saying, ironically, much the same as the White Ethnic Movement. Indeed, what we discussed in the earlier chapter as a "southernization" of the American cultural style amounts to the cultural diffusion throughout American society of what were formerly dominant, regional, Anglo-Protestant *nativist* attitudes, values, beliefs, and action strategies. The diffusion itself is based on selection receptivity—not on some mysterious osmosis or alien imposition.

One might say that the Anglo-Protestant backlash is the most recent in the sequence of oppositional movements and ideologies that all differ from one another in content, but whose underlying psychocultural dynamics is identical. Moreover, the American nativists and white ethnics share a similar *racial* orientation sardonically expressed in a recent poem by a Ku Klux Klanswoman: "Black is Beautiful, / Tan is grand; / But white is the color / of the big boss man."[43] Race, nativism, status, and the all-consuming American obsession with hierarchy are present in this poem—an attitude that has been stated in different forms by white ethnics themselves.

7 Transformation of a Personal Identity

In this chapter we pursue the theme of the New Ethnicity as a counterculture; here, however, the focus changes to the dynamics of personal identity transformation. As before, our starting point is the dichotomous and compartmentalizing manner in which the New Ethnic identity perceives and conceives the world. The preoccupation with the definition of "Who am I?" is simultaneously a concern with delineating with equal finality "Who I am not."

Everyone is vigilant lest his personal boundaries be violated. Heightened consciousness of self and concern over the definition of one's kind (with whom New Ethnics feel bonds of affiliation or kinship, loyalty, belonging, and obligation) lead to a preoccupation with maintenance of boundaries, symbolic and concrete. Love for one's fellows is inseparable from hatred of the collective enemy. The basis for ingroup solidarity is the sense of oppression from and the direction of hostility toward the outgroup. Paradoxically, neither ingroup members nor those of the outgroup are related to as complex human beings, but rather as abstract members of categories. Those who are *we* are idealized; those who are *they* are disparaged. To totalistically synthesize a defensive identity is to make an effort to put everything in its place once and for all, to simplify reality by positing dichotomies (dissociation): either/or, we/them, clean/dirty, good/evil, and ethnic/WASP. Yet even as the identity is shored up, it is accompanied by the persistent fear of the loss of identity expressed by the fear of impurity and contamination. No amount of "decontamination" and the removal of "foreign influences" is sufficient because the now-externalized enemy is already internalized. So ritual is piled upon ritual, unable to relieve, except temporarily, the underlying anxiety. Defense ultimately necessitates offense, since the New Ethnic's self-definition and the maintenance of his boundaries depend on the perpetuation of enmity with the opposition. Not only can he not relax within the movement, but he provokes incidents and confrontations in order to preserve the tension by having the sense of opposition confirmed. The adversary must be made to act like one! Consciousness-raising to reaffirm the new positive identity is necessary to distinguish it from the erstwhile positive, now negative, identity. The reiteration of belief is necessary to reaffirm what doubt could easily undermine. The revolution of consciousness of the New Ethnic liberation becomes a perpetual revolution in order to confirm its own convictions and guard against the erosion of belief. Narcissistic, paranoid defenses protect against inroads from the outer world while consolidating a sense of self-esteem from within. Paradoxically, the very intellectuals of the New Ethnicity who detest the other-directedness of American culture and who celebrate the presumed inwardness and integrity of ethnicity are vigilantly other-directed and require the public stage to act out their belief in the new movement. Wilfred Sheed observes that "expatriate ethnics tend to forget the many varieties and nuances of their national character and to cultivate the ones everybody recognizes."[1] The literal staging of ethnicity for consumption by American—and potentially New Ethnic—audiences has been one way in which the fledgling movement is able to sustain itself. Without an audience it would perish. The New Ethnic needs the stage of the universal to enact the drama of the particular.

Michael Novak and the Unmelting of Ethnicity

An important clue to the oppositional identity of the White Ethnic Movement and the dynamics of identity transformation is offered by the work of Michael Novak, a Slovak-American who is the movement's most prominent intellectual. To understand Novak is not only to understand in large measure the movement he symbolizes and the similar needs of those whom he fulfills, but to understand as well the dynamics of identity transformation to the New Ethnicity. *The Rise of the Unmeltable Ethnics* was not only required reading by both political parties courting the "ethnic vote," but represents the first comprehensive ideological synthesis of the case against American culture and for the New Ethnicity.[2] It also clearly establishes that the conversion to the New Ethnicity is a form of what Erik Erikson calls "the choice of the negative identity." The semantics and symbolism of the movement celebrate emblems of identity that were only recently repressed and repudiated.

All that is negatively associated with the stereotype "Hunkie" or "Polak" is now flaunted as a badge of pride associated with being ethnic. Through this transformation or inversion of affective valence, attributes of "Hunkiness" (not Slovakness) are dramatized as positive and superior. The negative stereotypes are the basis of the inverted positive self-redefinition. It is as if the New Ethnic said: "If all I'm good for is being a Hunkie, then I'll be a super-Hunkie." Under the illusion of acting his natural self, he all the more intently stages himself for his erstwhile oppressors, displacing rage and gaining at least a semblance of revenge. Nothing is enjoyed for its own sake. Slavic foods such as *kolachki, pirohi,* or *halushki* are not good simply because one likes them, but because they are emblematic of Slovak or Slavic "soul" food, hence totems or insignias of difference and distinction for public display. They acquire personal significance as good *ethnic* food because they are not American-WASP food. The very imagery and slogans of denigration and opprobrium are transformed into symbols of pride—for instance, the dirt, the crudity and the vulgarity of the coal mines and steel mills; the bouts of drinking, gambling, cursing, and fighting. Yet active self-definition in terms of what one was passively condemned to be merely confirms what is vehemently denied, namely, fixation on the negative imagery. Others outside the ethnic boundary still define the New Ethnic's identity.

In the previous chapter we emphasized acceptability in terms of American standards; here we emphasize the obverse: self-definition in terms of what Americans are *not*. This is only a contradiction logically or cognitively; the contradiction is symptomatic of a pervasive ambivalence toward American culture that is expressed, on the one hand, by the heroic attempt to prove how American ethnicity is, and, on the other hand, to show that ethnicity opposes all that America stands for. The white ethnics are the salt of the earth now; and the former salt of the earth, the now-ridiculed Americans, are declared to have lost their savor, becoming insipid, if not poisonous.

At a 1971 conference on New Directions for Urban America, Monsignor Geno Baroni reflected that it had been the assassination of Robert Kennedy that had reawakened his awareness of the importance of his own ethnicity. He then recalled that as a schoolboy, he took Italian salami sandwiches to school, and the other students made fun of them—so much so that one day he came home to his mother crying about how ashamed the other students made him feel. Monsignor Baroni immediately launched into a tirade against "Safeway baloney," tasteless, odorless, typically American, comparing it with the virtues of the spicy, greasy, robustly odored Italian salami sandwich, which came to be valued not because it was enjoyed, but because it represented a symbolic act of retaliation for the humiliation endured earlier. "Safeway baloney"—like white bread—comes to symbolize everything readily ridiculed about America: packaging, technology, and blandness of taste. Like the American culture it represents, "Safeway baloney" is artificial; like the ethnicity it symbolizes, Italian salami is real.

What is the connection, however, between the assassination of Robert Kennedy, the painful and angry recollection of the Italian salami, and the vituperation against "Safeway baloney"? The question is partly answered by another Italian-American in his early forties who, at the same conference, reflected upon the dilemma and anguish seething beneath the pride of the New Ethnicity: "What has driven us to our ethnicity is rejection." For Baroni, as for countless other white ethnics, the assassination of Robert Kennedy was not only a trauma or cataclysm in its own right, but the "last" of a seemingly endless volley of assaults on the *integrationist* movement and on the American Dream itself. Kennedy's death symbolized the hopelessness and helplessness of the situation. Just as the death of Martin Luther King, Jr., had led to black rage, the death of Robert Kennedy precipitated white ethnic rage, and white rage in general. Monsignor Baroni turned from Civil Rights activism following his abruptly reawakened ethnic-consciousness and made ethnicity his calling. Renewed self-consciousness reminded him of a much earlier self-conscious shaming, which he now mastered by inverting a symbol of shame into one of defiant and strident pride. In the previous chapter, we discussed at length the regressive, often oral, imagery utilized in the New Ethnic Movement. Here too the emphasis on the contrast between spicy and tasteless, smelly and odorless, and greasy and greaseless reflects the attempt to resolve regressively old conflicts reawakened by concurrent ones associated with self-esteem. The reevaluation of ethnicity is simultaneously a reevaluation of the New Ethnic and his parents, the outcome of which is the idealization both of the ethnic self and the ethnic parents and ancestry. By the very regressive nature of the process, the dominance of oral, tactile, and kinesthetic imagery is predictable. Equally important, however, is the fact that "salami" does not exist independent of "Safeway baloney" in Baroni's account. Idealization and love are but one side of the oppositional process whose dialectic opposite is devaluation and hate. Boundless rage precipitated by disillusionment is coped with by the radical exclusion of what was included, and the embracing of negative elements that had been previously excluded.

Hence the bipolar system of good food and evil food, ethnic food and American food.

The following lists of ethnic-Catholic and American-Protestant cultural attributes as seen from the viewpoint of the New Ethnicity express comprehensively the *grammar* of opposition underlying the new identity—one which prides itself on being what Americans or WASPs are *not*. The items are taken from a careful reading of white ethnic writers and lecturers such as Michael Novak, Monsignor Geno Baroni, Richard Kolm, Andrew Greeley, Richard Gambino, Herbert Gold, the Reverend Leonard Chrobot, and Paul Wrobel, as well as from our own interviews with Slavic-American participants in the movement.

This Manichean dualism assures the distinct separation between white ethnics and their adversaries. Interestingly, the terms of positive self-estimation that the New Ethnicity sees itself as representing are remarkably like those of the youth counterculture (e.g., Charles Reich, Theodore Roszak) that white ethnics so detest; likewise, the American culture is disparagingly evaluated in quite similar terms by the two opposing countercultures. Despite considerable shared and borrowed cultural content, the disdain held by white ethnics for the youth culture attests to the extent of the New Ethnics' Americanness. Novak aphoristically remarks that "Ethnic Americans admire strength and despise weakness." While we agree that the strong/weak, healthy/fragile, and independent/dependent opposition is fundamental to the Slavic-American value system, it is simultaneously at the core of the Protestant-American ethic—which meant preadaptation by the immigrants and the facile adaptation to American life. Novak, and other ethnophiles, of course, want to have it both ways: to demonstrate how different they are from the Americans, and how American they are. Our point here is that the need for dichotomies and the fact of abundant contradiction are expressions of the ambivalence toward American culture and ethnicity. Compartmentalization, approach-avoidance, and the like, should be seen as symptoms of this process.

Novak writes: "I am born of PIGS—these Poles, Italians, Greeks, and Slavs, non-English-speaking immigrants, numbered so heavily among the workingmen of this nation. Not particularly liberal, nor radical, born into a history not white Anglo-Saxon and not Jewish; born outside what, in America, is considered the intellectual mainstream—and thus privy to neither power nor status nor intellectual voice."[3] To Novak white ethnics are more than a silent majority; they are portrayed, however, remarkably like the blacks of Ralph Ellison's

ETHNIC-CATHOLIC
"The Pluralistic Personality"

being, being before doing, reality, truth, witness, individuality inseparable from community, connectedness, roots, continuity, genuine, mystery, ritual, transcendence, soul, feeling, absurdity, tragedy, network people, communitarian, family-parish-neighborhood, land-blood-religion, harmony with nature, relatives and the world are part of the self, inseparability of self from others, feeling, natural, close family, heart, integrity, instincts, reflexes, appreciation, imagination, subjective, organic, pessimism, nonrational, complexity, biological connectedness with the earth, rhythmic, sensual, emotional, emotional preferences, biological urges, affective, communal eucharist, primordial attachments, corporate identity, basic affinities, solidarity with one's own kind

AMERICAN-PROTESTANT
"The Liberal (individualistic) Personality"

acting, doing, hoping, future, agent, doer, initiator, intervener, make history over, logical, analytical, machinelike, myth of the head, spurious, lonely, individual, marketplace, head, mind, rationality, impersonal logic, atomic people, power over others, enlightenment, bland (food), standardized, contempt for mystery, new, alone, modern, solitary, alienated, relations and the world as extrinsic, destructive, self-annihilation, artificial hearts, unmasking, better, liberated, advanced, mature, cognitive, bureaucratic, imitative, competitive, invidious comparison, position, optimism, comfortable pragmatism, gradual progress, democratic soundness, middle-class contentment, inhibition and control of impulses, mastery of the earth, value on productivity, success, mastery, conquest, history replaces nature, Nordic man replaces Mediterranean man, privacy and isolated individuality, control of body by the mind, analytic, reticence, distance, make-believe relationships, the metaphor of mechanism, functional analysis, cocktail party, independence, self-sufficiency, the body as foreign

Invisible Man. Novak begins his self-affirmation and builds his solidarity with a litany of negations. Yet, as we shall discuss below, all that he says the PIGS are not, he has either become or closely associates himself with. In "Confessions of a White Ethnic" he writes the following:

> Odd that I should have such shallow knowledge of my roots. Amazing to me that I do not know what my family suffered, endured, learned, and hoped these last six or seven generations. It is as though there were no project in which we all have been involved, as if history in some way began with my father and me. The estrangement I have come to feel derives not only from lack of family history. Early in life, I was made to feel a slight uneasiness when I said my name. Later, "Kim" helped. So did Robert. And "Mister Novak" on TV. The name must be one of the most Anglo-Saxon of the Slavic names.

Several pages later, he returns parenthetically to the theme of the meaning of name:

> Becoming modern . . . is a matter of learning to be solitary—assuming it is normal to be alone—and dreaming of reconstruction. "New", "alone", and "alienated" are words of moral status. Those to whom they apply are to be commended. (My own name, "Novak" means newcomer, stranger, the new man who comes alone; I do not think the ancient connotations were of commendation.)[4]

While he is ashamed and angered at how little he knows about his origin, in his choice of words Novak is abundantly clear about his sense of origin, which is anything but noble. The oedipal son never wants to be the offspring of his ordinary, fallible father, and one who is deeply ashamed of his past cannot tolerate the possibility that "history began with my father and with me." Noble history will redeem both oedipal guilt (since one's real father will become inconsequential) and the New Ethnic's abiding sense of inferiority. As for the name *Novak,* the significance Michael Novak attributes to it is deeply personal rather than generic. In our research, we have known families with the names *Novak, Nowak, Novotny, Novotniak, Nowicki;* and the associations Michael Novak makes were altogether absent. He writes bitterly of "the sheer ruthlessness the immigrants have encountered here . . . concerning the urban experience of immigration, it is as though our grandfathers did not live and did not count; as if they were only grains, ground to tastelessness, powdered meal. Consumed." Here is the Melting Pot in the industrial image of a voracious grinder, reducing all to a common meal and devoured; the external cause of all personal and social ills. Novak alludes to the search for a strong male figure to compensate for the real father's alleged weaknesses, among them, his Americanness. "The language of Spiro Agnew, the language of George Wallace, excepting its idiom, awakens childhood memories in me: of men arguing in the barbershop, of my uncle drinking so much beer he threatened to lay his dick upon the porch rail and wash the whole damn street with steaming piss. . . ."⁵ Novak, we should emphasize, is far from alone in the search for a strong grandfather, uncle, or ancestor remote in putative ethnic history—a figure who will represent the opposite of one's father's weakness, one who will not, or did not, "sell out," a New Ethnic who has not lost his "soul" to the Americans.

PIGS becomes the measure of humanity, and WASPs, blacks, and Jews, in different ways and to different degrees, outsiders to that humanity. A label of self-hate becomes a powerful tool of self-assertion and self-defense. PIGS is similar to "Italian salami": a symbol of the erstwhile negative identity is flaunted menacingly as the symbol of the new positive identity. The creation of absolute, immiscible types assures that one of *us* and *them* can be readily identified. Yet Novak hesitates to identify the enemy with the stereotype he has created; he does and then he retracts. "I do not even wish to assert that all WASPs show the characteristics I am going to mention. I do not even wish to assert that any WASP allows these characteristics to dominate his conduct." It is not adequate to say that his argument thereby evaporates. It is sustained by the need for the stereotype of the WASP—and of the noble ethnic as well—which cannot be challenged by exceptions to the rule because such exceptions are irrelevant to the need for the rule. The rule is a grid imposed on the world, a filter through which the world is interpreted. The inviolable imagination that animates the world with its own projections is unencumbered by actual human diversity and variability. Cognitive categories that newly order social reality represent a new emotional reorganization that generates its own logic. Novak's autobiographical data, which he provides, reflect the actuality of the past as experienced from within the new identity at present, rather than the reality of the past itself. It would be mistaken, however, to argue that it is simply consciously self-serving *facts* that he is offering. Facts are never separate from the system they validate, and the facts we are provided (as well as those omnipresently absent) tell us how the past is remembered under current ego conditions.

A major premise of this logic is conspicuous visibility without vulnerability. Prior passivity gives way to aggressive activity, assertion, and the public exhibition of the new identity. The New Ethnic is no longer exposed, but engages vindictively in exposing his adversaries. The new liberation vigilantly maintains its distance from its opponent, at the same time making certain that the enemy is constantly being engaged. To the self-ascribed insider, the meaning of the ethnic experience is forever inaccessible and incomprehensible to the excluded outsider. The category of *outsider* is essential to the maintenance of the mystery of the new identity—without which there could obviously be no secret. One keeps a secret *from* an excluded other. Cultural content of the New Ethnicity becomes a vehicle for the creation and maintenance of social and personal difference. The identity of ethnicity is thus now only an ineffable mystery; its guardians have much at stake in mystifying the nature of ethnicity—*Das Volk dichtet*—and everything is lost in "translation." By this means, the New Ethnic intellectuals are able to obscure personal and ethnic history while claiming to clarify it. Moreover, they are able to inflame and incite confrontation while quite innocently are convinced they offer ethnicity as a solution of social peace, alliance, and conflict avoidance—and are thus able to blame their adversaries for breaches of the peace. The sweet and innocent tune of the Pied Piper disqualifies his rage and destructive intent. So disarming is the tune, who would dare attack its player?

One means of lessening and preventing vulnerability is to convert potential adversaries into allies—New Ethnics. Thus, Novak and the other major leaders of the movement function as apostles unto the Gentiles. They safeguard their own identity by helping others to organize and to be ethnically liberated through consciousness-raising. By assuring that others maintain their own particularist identities, ideologies, and boundaries, as well as entering into alliance with kindred groups, the gatekeepers of the New Ethnicity are assured of their own security. For instance, in a passionate rejoinder to Daniel Berrigan's anti-Israel diatribe, Novak identifies with American Jews, knowing without doubt the overwhelming ethnic sentiment of American Jews—or what should be their sentiment. "Rabbi Abraham Heschel was the greatest Zionist in our midst, and, surely the groundswell of American Jewish identification with Zion is overwhelming. Zion is home, Zion is roots, Zion is identity. To be a Zionist is now virtually identical with being Jewish—and the difference between the two is not for a Christian to adjudicate."[6] But indeed a Christian does adjudicate it. Novak is telling others what *their* needs are in terms of what *his* are: home, roots, identity, like those of Father Greeley—land, religion, and blood. To affirm himself in his identity he must confirm and insist on that identity in others. Ethnicity *is* home, roots, identity. Part of the politics of the new identity is to make certain that everyone abides by the new myth. Hence Novak is ethnophile apostle to the Jews.

Furthermore, one of the consequences, if not intentions, of the Ethnic Heritage Programs Act, now funded under Title 9 of the Office of Education, is to prepare ethnic studies materials for the entire range of education for purposes of the socialization in *American* institutions of the new identity. Identity is expressed in polity, and in turn the political process sanctions the socialization of a particular identity.

It is a truism that one simultaneously organizes the world as he organizes himself. What differs are the premises and how the organization is done. Novak's use of the ethnic principle as the basis of his own personal reorganization does not stop with himself, but expands to include all of those network people willing to listen. He requires that the lives of others be organized along principles congruent with his own—thus the paradox that the new liberation and freedom of the New Ethnic identity is severely circumscribed and regimented. Although the subjective experience of ethnic identification is knowable only from within, the New Ethnic intelligentsia gladly imposes it from without. If those on the outside are reluctant to embrace the New Ethnic categories, then it is their flawed identity that creates the barrier to the truth. Novak deftly explains social reformer Michael Harrington as an Irish-Catholic trained Jesuit. And because Senator Edmund Muskie is not acting properly Polish, "There seems to be a war within Muskie, between assimilation and distinctiveness. Unresolved, that war blurs his identity." Presumably that identity would be unblurred if Muskie acted according to the New Ethnic stereotype of how a Polish-American should act, which, in turn, would make him more credible. In the final analysis, because the emphasis is on an exhibitionistic visibility that prevents vulnerability, defending against an anticipated discovery of flawed identity, the New Ethnicity must rigidly *prescribe* what an ethnic should act like. In the New Ethnic science, description follows prescription—and proscription.

Novak continues, "Growing up in America has been an assault upon my sense of worthiness. It has also been a kind of liberation and delight."[7] Elsewhere, "Where in American institutions, American literature, American education is our identity mirrored, objectified, rendered accessible to intelligent criticism, and confirmed? We are still, I think, persons without a public symbolic world, persons without a publicly verified culture to sustain us and our children."

Yet in the next paragraph he seems to wish the Melting Pot had come true and that public self-consciousness of ethnicity were not so necessary: "A sense of separate identity is, in part, induced from outside-in. I am made aware of being Catholic and Slovak by the actions of others. I would be sufficiently content were my identity to be so taken for granted, so utterly normal and real, that it would never have to be self-conscious."[8] On the one hand, Novak protests that the self-consciousness is forced upon him; on the other hand, he makes ethnic self-consciousness-raising one of the principal callings of his present life, emphasizes that ethnicity is the most important feature of life, and literally seeks to turn American culture around to this recognition. Is it possible that he has tacitly conspired with those who "force" the ethnic crown of thorns upon him, accepts the crown as his destiny, and then acclaims the new religion as salvation? To extend the metaphor: Was the crucifixion sought, or was it simply inevitable? Political scientist Harold Lasswell and the psychoanalytically oriented school that followed his pioneering work suggested that leaders project their personal pathology onto the public arena where it, in turn, may or may not be supported. The personality of the leader, however, is incomplete without the sustenance of his constituency that provides the halo and the sense of hallowed presence, and at the same time protects against the vulnerability of self-doubt.

But what about those Americans for whom Novak speaks, whose anguish he claims to articulate? We know how *he* thinks they feel, but what about *them*? Has growing up in America been an assault upon their sense of worthiness? What of the Greeks, Armenians, Jews, Japanese, Chinese, and even white ethnics who have succeeded— perhaps not spectacularly, but even modestly? The *null hypothesis* requires that we inquire why American education did not have to be ethnically "relevant," why teachers from the same ethnic group were not necessary as sources of identification, why those who were historically oppressed and exploited as much as those who today demand special dispensation were nevertheless able to "make it" without ethnic identity crutches of a publicly symbolized world. The publicly symbolic world with which they identified and eagerly sought confirmation by was that of the American Dream and Melting Pot. To become American was not to be rootless, but to put down new roots, to synthesize identity anew.

It is currently fashionable to say that only black can understand black, only Jew can understand Jew, only Pole can understand Pole, only woman can understand woman, and so on. But in the past and the present as well, many have felt capable of being understood by those other than certified denizens of the tribal cave. The cry that outsiders cannot understand or identify may well be a ploy that in-groupers use to avoid understanding or identifying with the excluded outsider. It is a way of actively excluding while claiming to be excluded. In his paean to the New Ethnicity, Novak cites Dostoevski's "humble charity" as its ideal: "Not pretending to be universal, to speak for all groups, it closes its heart against no group." Yet his ideology is indeed universal, speaking for what all groups should be, and closing the heart against those who do not choose the ethnic *Ortho-Doxos* ("right teaching").

There is a further paradox to Novak's complaint about the failure of American institutions and literature to mirror, objectify, and confirm the white ethnic identity. This paradox lies in the apparent failure of Novak to understand the values and personality structure of his own people. For instance, in our experience, Slovaks, Poles, and Ruthenes of all social classes value a life of order, quiet, respectability, and, in a sense, invisibility. At an early age, they learn about abiding respect for authority, sacred and secular. Slavic-Americans seek to do their jobs right, to avoid criticism and conflict. If in the "American" or Yankee socialization process, one seeks incremental rewards or merit badges for a job well done, in the Slavic-American child-rearing process, the child is expected to perform a task right and is severely reprimanded when it is imperfect. Thus the Slavic-American labors hard, tirelessly, unobtrusively to get something done in order to avoid ridicule or anger. A person who is "pushy," independent, openly mobile, or competitive is the object of scorn by family and community alike. Socialization for dependency is the core of the Slavic personality. Cooperation is highly valued; competition and open hostility are severely proscribed. A bitter and acrimonious social leveling process prevents members of the group not only from violating group standards, but from attempting to succeed beyond the group norm. Envy tends to keep most people in their place. Many Slovak mill foremen or aspirants to management positions related the identical response from their families: resentment, ridicule, envy. "Who do you think you are, better than we are?" "You're just a mill Hunkie like us." "Mr. Rich Guy, when are you going to give us some of your wealth?" Many men with whom we spoke turned down the offer in order to avoid harassment and estrangement at home and at work. This is not to say that parents, for instance, want nothing better than to keep their children "down."

In addition to telling their children they do not deserve to have a better life than their own, Slovak-American parents also try to give them what they did not have, and encourage means of attaining a better existence, American style. The children receive, and later transmit, a complex and contradictory set of messages from their parents. This is not to invert Novak's argument and simply blame the Slovak or Polish family and culture. We should recognize, however, the role played by traditional culture, with its bias toward physical work and against what we would call American "liberal" education, in adapting to a particular socioeconomic niche in American society.

Factors intrinsic to Slovak and Polish ethnicity, together with the opportunities and limitations within the environment of the American host culture, have shaped the Slovak and Polish adaptation. The congruence of *ethnic* psychocultural considerations with *American* socioeconomic structure has, in our opinion, enabled the greater part of Slovak- and Polish-Americans to be moderately successful, while at the same time limiting that success (whether measured in mobility, occupation, income, or status).

The nature and structure of authority and the importance attached to work by the European Slovaks played an important role in the creation of Slovak-American culture for at least three generations. The entire human and supernatural universe consists of an unbroken line of ascending authority from the lowly peasant—or mill worker—to God the Father. The omnipresent authorities are to be deferred to and obeyed. One submits to a host of legitimate authorities and bosses: older siblings, parents, wife to husband (and in a less overt way, vice versa), elder kinsmen, bosses at work, the priest or pastor, leaders of village or city, ward bosses, and the more diffuse rulers such as Fate and Circumstance and Nature. What is, is; Slovak-Americans do not look for ways to change things, so much as seek ways to creatively cope with them so they will be less burdensome. The Slovak and Polish languages give a further key to the pervasiveness of authority. The honorific title *Pan,* meaning "lord," "sir," "Mister," is one of deference and respect. The superintendent of the feudal estate was addressed *Pan;* the lord of the estate was called *Pan Graf* (*Graf,* from the German, meaning "lord" or "landgrave"); the priest or pastor was called *Pan Farar* ("lord pastor," literally); Jesus was called *Pan Ježis* ("Lord Jesus"); and God the Father was called *Pan Bog* or *Pan Boh* (with *-og* being more Polish-Russian, while *-oh* is more Slovak). A reflective second-generation Slovak-American Lutheran minister in his late thirties remarked:

As you grow up: respect. You never hid yourself in your room, if your parents had visitors. You had to be cordial with them. In

Slovak we have the expression: *"Ako si ti?"*—How are you? It's in the singular, the familiar. And: *"Ako ste vi?"*—How are you? In the plural. It's also a sign of respect to elders. If I said, *"Ako si ti?"* to an older person, I really heard about it from my mother. I wonder if this overindulgence on being polite doesn't have its adverse effects. Slovak people tend to be too acquiescent, passive. They will do anything to maintain peace in situations. . . . [Stein, field notes]

The supreme value placed on hard, persistent work—indeed, the association of work with the sacred, God's work—is closely related to the insistence on earning everything that is received as a means of denying dependency. A Slovak- or Polish-American refuses to be at the mercy of another's good will (which is expected to be ill will) as passive recipient and actively engages in *doing* in order to merit what is received. Without exception, our Polish and Slovak informants proudly and defiantly stated: "We work for everything we get. If you don't earn it, you don't deserve to have it." One Slovak-American in his thirties remarked: "Slovaks are gluttons for work." The word for "work" in Slovak (and Polish and Czech as well) is *robot* or *robota,* which was introduced into English as the noun "robot," a mechanical man, in a 1920 play by the Czech writer Karel Čapek. The denotation of "robot" and *robota* is an inexhaustible capacity for physical-mechanical work. The worker, human or machine, is usually reliable and obedient, showing great self-control, but is capable of becoming a rage-ridden monster, self-willed and wantonly destructive.

Work was literally redeeming value, both socially and religiously. It is the measure of a man and woman's worth. Significantly, many of the attributes associated with the Protestant ethic are part of the aboriginal Slavic Catholic (as well as Lutheran) repertoire, and this value congruence made the choice of a niche within American culture relatively easy. Acculturation in the domain of work dealt almost exclusively with content as opposed to motivation or preparedness. In our field research, we have marveled at the mechanical deftness and inventiveness, as well as the inexhaustible energy and patience, of both male and female Slavic-Americans in work on their homes and in their gardens. Skills required for functioning in the mills—and we do not mean simply brute strength, though this was not lacking— were readily acquired. Such values and attitudes as hard work, earning what is received, patience, persistence, thrift, sacrifice, planning for the future, obedience to superiors (though with "griping"), the creation of work even when there is none to do, the admiration of strength, and the functional relationship between work and religiosity all make the Protestant ethic quite Slavic Catholic, despite ostensible religious and ethnic differences. This work *configuration,* both in its traditional ethnic and adaptive American contexts, is described by a third-generation Slovak-Ukrainian-Polish-American who grew up in a traditional ethnic town in western Pennsylvania, whose first language was a mixture of three Slavic languages:

> The religious [meaning of] work says that everything that is not used—such as mental activity, physical capacity, and space—is wasted. And everything that is wasted is sinful. To waste anything is a grave sin. This causes a guilt-anxiety related to the examination of conscience, such as you must do before going to confession. In this way, the authoritarian principles are broken down by the guilt. [I interrupted, somewhat confused, suggesting that the authoritarian principles would be reinforced by the guilt. He continued:] The authority is there to make you feel guilty. The only way you overcome the feeling of guilt is by going to confession. After you confess, you are granted forgiveness. Therefore the authoritarian principles are broken down, since the guilt is relieved. You show God that you mean business. You come to confession as a tough man in the suffering sense. You don't come soft or crying. You come with hard guts and hard work, Slavic guts! You come and take your medicine. "Absolve me—this is what I did." And you are forgiven. With the Slovaks, work is the capacity for good. To not work is to let in bad, evil. Work is God's work, laziness is the Devil's work. This authority puts me in unity with all Slavs. Without this authority—from the father, to the priest, to the Pope himself, and finally to God—without this authority, the whole chain of authority would be broken. This is the chain that unites us with God. Without this chain, we wouldn't be united with God. . . . Of course, you couldn't take confession and absolution too far—because otherwise everybody would be lazy. Severe punishment would compensate for laziness. One who was lazy couldn't just get absolved for it. The threat of severe punishment was to prevent laziness from becoming so diffuse. . . . With the Slovaks and the Ukrainians—How much I suffer here, How much I won't have to suffer there, in the next world. Here I am the suffering peasant; there I'll be a superintendent. Here you have to suffer—so do it joyously. Enjoy your deprivation. [Stein, field notes, 1972]

Novak's insistence that "being before doing" is "an ancient Catholic theme" shows both his distance from those whom he champions and his effort to replace the image of the worker with that of the bearer of culture superior to the image of Protestant-Americans. White ethnic leaders long ago fled the neighborhoods and families they now champion and patronize at a distance—spatial and personal. They need those they romanticize in order to assuage their own guilt for having made it or attempting to, for having abandoned those who depended on their dependency.

Although Novak says that, contrary to the American myth, a New Ethnic can indeed go back home, he is almost silent about his real home, or about Slovakness itself. He talks much more generically about pan-white ethnicity. And when it comes to particulars, he seems to equate the stereotypic natural, expressive "Mediterranean man" with his ethnic ideal. And this is for good reason: much more of the head is expressed in the everyday life of Slovak- and Polish-Americans than is the heart. Indeed, Slavic-Americans pride themselves on their ability not to let their emotions show. Within the family, they keep busy doing things to avoid having to interact intimately with other people—who can let them down. Human relationships are largely avoided, even as Slavic-Americans seek elusive dependability, keeping out of another's way lest an angry word be spoken, lest they be ridiculed. Novak invokes Mediterranean man as though this were the archetypal ethnic, while hardly mentioning his own ethnic group. The proverbial closeness of the Slovak- and Polish-American families is not so simple as the image of network people Novak and others wish to convey.

It is true that in the east, central, and south European peasant family the child was not regarded as separate, as an individual, but as an extension of the parents. The growing child's needs were experienced through introjection as another's will, and his personal interests were defined by another's will. From infancy, many European children have learned that the fulfillment of their needs comes not by making demands, but by submitting to the will and rhythm of another. They have learned to "be patient," to "say please," and to have a high frustration tolerance. Superficially this should vindicate the organic-network-communitarian argument. But it does not, because the socialization for dependency, obedience to authority, etc., set up a dynamic not only for compliance and submission, but for rebellion as well—throughout the life cycle. The Slovak culture hero and trickster *Janošik* reflects the undercurrent rebelliousness and wish for autonomy. Janošik was a Slovak Robin Hood figure, who defied feudal authority and who, until he was treacherously killed, acted out the free spirit that the Slovak peasantry must repress. His opposite is the symbol of traditional authority and hierarchy: the priest and the feudal lord, who are obsequiously obeyed and revered.

Latent individualism, factionalism, independence, and self-reliance simultaneously were anti-ethnic and facilitated Americanization. Freedom is as much valued as is the network of reciprocal obligation. Communalism, neighborliness and close familial ties are valued, but resented as well. Many immigrant and second-generation Slavic-Americans insist on living separate from their children, if only a few houses or blocks away. A grown son or daughter with spouse and family may live in a house next to the parents, or just down the street, but values his or her—and the nuclear family's—privacy at least as much as the togetherness of the extended family. Many families have established *rules* for visiting times, so there is a minimum of "meddling." The same holds for neighbors of related ethnic groups. Many of our informants talk happily of frequent "porch parties" in the summer and interhousehold visitations (which we have had occasion to attend). But all draw a sharp line, emphasizing that "my house is your house" is no longer true. Each values personal and family privacy—and private property.

Another facet of the traditional conflict between individualism and communalism, further complicating any idyllic notion of ethnic network people, is the atomism, factionalism, localism, and banditry that have characterized the European peasantry, and not merely those of the South European Mediterranean whom Edward Banfield characterized by the term *amoral familism*. According to this concept, the individual holds a fierce nuclear family orientation in a Hobbesian competition with other such units, making virtually impossible any sense of community. It has also been argued that the sense of Italian community—and we would add Polish and Slovak as well—developed on American rather than European soil.[9] The emotional and moral frontier of the original ethnics extended only to their immediate kinfolk. These arguments, it would seem, go too far in the other extreme. While strong centrifugal forces existed within the family, there were also strong extended family ties of cooperation, mutual aid, and belonging; the institution of the church, much as it was hated for representing distant authority and charging wages for salvation, was a focus of the wider moral community, if tenuously. However, despite proscription against hostility, competition, envy, hatred, segmentation, rivalry, and divisiveness, these are as much a fact of the European and American white ethnic life as their valued opposites are. Surely this is not the sort of natural, "Mediterranean man" whom Novak would idealize.

What the New Ethnic intellectuals must do is rewrite ethnic history in the "old country," so that its whole way of life can be counterposed against the fragmented American-induced way of life that caused the white ethnics to develop those traits that are felt to be undesirable. Richard Gambino's *Blood of My Blood: The Dilemma of the Italian-Americans* is an encyclopedic attempt to do precisely this.[10] A more modest attempt is made by anthropologist Paul Wrobel, a Polish-American, who emphasizes that American culture is spurious and that it forces a discontinuity of learning between the ethnic home and neighborhood, and the American educational system and television. He invokes Edward Sapir's distinction between genuine and spurious cultures and interprets it as follows:

> A genuine culture is built as an expression of individual differences—individual cultures, if you will—while a spurious culture is one that is imposed on individuals as an inhibition of their own or their group's uniqueness. American culture is therefore a spurious one because we have failed to recognize ethnic diversity. . . . The child experiences . . . discontinuities as conflicts within himself, conflicts between what he knows he is and what he learns society wants him to be.

A genuine culture, for Wrobel, is one whose educational process "represents a continuous and integrated experience for every child." Later, discussing the three most important spheres of his early life, "family, parish, and neighborhood," he argues that it is not Polish-Americans who have failed in American society; rather, American society has failed to take into account cultural differences in values and attitudes between Poles and mainstream Americans.

> It has been argued, of course, that the close family so representative of Polish Americans and other ethnic groups hinders the ability of individual family members to succeed in our society. But when scholars argue this point, they are really saying that a traditional ethnic family does not fit in with what is desirable in dominant American culture, a culture that stresses the independence and self-reliance of the individual as criteria for his success. Individuals in our society make it; families don't.[11]

These readings of American and ethnic history are remarkable for both their logical unsoundness and their factual falsity. Wrobel invokes Sapir to justify the inviolable sanctity of personal cultures, and in the same sentence places individual and *group* uniqueness on the same level; ergo, the inviolability of ethnic identity. If we were to follow Sapir to *his* logical conclusion, one with which we are in accord, we must conclude that American culture is to be faulted for its emphasis on conformism and its denial of genuine individual diversity or difference. Even this is too strong, however, for as we noted earlier, American culture *both* celebrates and is suspicious of those who are different. The conformism of ethnic groups is at least as suffocating and "life denying" as that of American culture. For Sapir, genuine culture lies in a personal transcendence of *any* culture in which a person is born. If Wrobel wishes to justify ethnicity, or anything else, he might at least argue his case logically and render accurately what those whom he cites actually say—not what he would like them to have said.

Nowhere here do we get the impression that the Americanization of the ethnic psyche was something personally sought; rather, it was something done to the immigrants, a harrowing experience endured passively. Discontinuity and uprooting were imposed on the continuous, homogeneous, organic, communitarian ethnics by the Nordic Anglo-Americans. Yet within the Slovak- and Polish-American homes where we spent nearly five years, and from what we learned about life in Europe through interview and documentation, Slavic life was far from idyllic. For all their proverbial closeness and family orientation, despite their being surrounded and enveloped in family, parish, and neighborhood, they frequently complain of being profoundly lonely and isolated, of having received much food, but little love, of having felt well cared for, but unwanted. The Slovak-Americans could speak of closeness without intimacy. On the one hand, there is a socialization for dependency, inculcating a fear of venturing into the outer world beyond the watchful eye of mother. On the other hand, there is the resentment of dependency, of being eternally indebted to those who have given so much when they yearned to receive. There is the wish to remain safely within, and the opposing wish to escape, to break out.

American culture did not create the discontinuities that Wrobel, Novak, and others denounce. The immigrants sought the very discontinuities—and new American continuities—American culture facilitates. Beneath the family secrecy of respectability, togetherness, and cooperation—which are certainly vital forces—are resentments, rivalries, competitions, and tendencies toward atomism and discontinuity that are often given expression, if there are channels in the outer environment. Factionalism, segmentation, discontinuity, and atomism were part of the identities and cultures of generations of immigrants. American culture did not so much destroy or repress ethnic culture as it served as a releaser for the expression of aspects of traditional culture that were suppressed and repressed. Conflicts in traditional ethnic culture served as much as economics as a "push" factor in Americanization. While the overt ethnic values and attitudes may indeed have been communitarian, the covert—and potentially volatile—values and attitudes made the immigrants and their descendants candidates for being Americans long before they associated the label "American" with their identity.

The nature of the contradictions and ambivalences within Slovak culture is encapsulated by the remarks of a bitterly perceptive immigrant Byzantine Catholic Slovak-American in his mid-fifties, who came to America at age nine with his parents. In 1971 he said the following to Howard Stein:

> Whenever you get your dissertation written, I want you to answer for me two questions. What do you think is the best trait of the Slovak people, and what do you think is the worst? I'll tell you what I think—I think their worst trait is that they're envious, jealous, submissive . . . suppressed, typical peasants (*bitterly*), compliant, submissive. Tell them anything, they'll believe it. Their best trait, I'd say, is their fierce self-reliance (*emphatically*). The Slavs are an independent people. They stand on their own two feet. They don't go crying for help any time something goes wrong. They do things for themselves.

This man, whom the writer has known for some five years, embodies the divided soul of which he speaks. Both the best and the worst not only suggest how Slovak one is in his or her Americanness, but how American, in many respects, one is in one's Slovakness. As we have seen from a discussion of Spiegel's observations on American value orientations, although the ideal (best) is individuality, the real (worst) is lineality. The world of the boss subverts both liberty and equality. Contradictions and conflicts in the Slovak character or identity are simultaneously conflicts in the American character or identity, regardless of cultural origins. Moreover, not only was the impetus for Americanization both from within and without; the impediments to Americanization were imposed by characteristics of ethnic culture and personality as well as by those of the host society. Conversely, it was precisely traditional Slavic-peasant characteristics and antitraditional rebellion against them originating in the feudalist country of origin that facilitated adaptation to the contradictory American value system.

We have discussed at length the results of the identity transformation, as well as the discrepancy between the tenets of the new identity and ideology, and what we believe to represent ethno-American actuality. We have also dealt with the process of this transformation, though in general terms. Here we shall follow the work of Michael Novak and attempt to understand his identity transformation, thereby understanding something about the change of those white ethnics for whom he is the exemplary prophet. Our point of departure is the fact that Novak neither suddenly discovered ethnicity, nor does he feel comfortable with the label "Slovak-American" or "ethnic." Now in his mid-forties and having "made it" in American academe by *external* standards, he perceives his life not as a cumulative development but as a cumulative estrangement for which the WASP superculture is to blame.

Though in his voluminous writing Novak says relatively little about himself directly, what he does say tells us what he feels to be relevant to his subsequent identity transformation. He writes the following: "Under challenge in grammar school concerning my nationality, I had been instructed by my father to announce proudly: 'American.' When my family moved from the Slovak ghetto of Johnstown to the WASP suburb on the hill, my mother impressed upon us how well we must be dressed, and show good manners, and behave—people think of us as 'different' and we musn't give them any cause. 'Whatever you do, marry a Slovak girl,' was the other advice to a similar end: 'They cook. They clean. They take good care of you. For your own good. . . .' The fact that I was born a Catholic also complicated life. What is a Catholic but what everybody else is in reaction against?" "Nowhere in my schooling do I recall any attempt to put me in touch with my own history. The strategy was clearly to make an American out of me. . . . During crucial years I attended a public school. It is hard to grow up Catholic in America without becoming defensive, perhaps a little paranoid, feeling forced to divide the world between 'us' and 'them.' "[12] He writes that his family was the first Slovak family in Johnstown to move into the "American" suburbs on the hill away from the traditional neighborhood. From grades two to six he attended public school in which there were few Catholics. Moreover, Novak's parents did not teach their children Slovak, hoping it would facilitate Americanization.[13]

Earlier we discussed a brief remark Novak makes about the personal meaning of his name—"newcomer, stranger, the new man who comes alone"—and noted that this is juxtaposed with words he associated with being modern, American—*new, alone,* and *alienated.* While he may talk of the ethnic network people who have roots, he sees himself as cursed virtually by his name to a life of rootlessness, something of a Wandering Jew in search of the elusive Zion. (His identification with Jews and their causes, although ambivalent, is not coincidental.) The absence of a sense of rootedness is not, however, merely something that occurred passively. Rootlessness is a product of decisive and cumulative self-rooting. He became the *them* and largely parted ways with the *us*. In the traditional Slavic peasant value system, education and literary prowess are not disparaged per se, but are seen as proper to the aristocracy, the elite. Among the Slavic European and the urban American peasantry, to seek a university education, to become a professor, to be a writer and philosopher, is to be *different*, if not outright unmanly. (Novak also notes that his maternal grandmother had worked as a housecleaner and laundress at the "town home of a man known to my father only as 'the Professor' "—a source of urban as opposed to rural, intellectual as opposed to peasant, values.) " 'Harvard' and 'Yale' long meant 'them' to us," Novak writes; yet he became a member of that elite family which President Johnson scornfully called "those Harvards."[14]

During the 1960s he participated in the radical student movement and became a celebrant of existential and theological nothingness, stressing the need to accept despair (*Theology for Radical Politics*, 1969; *The Experience of Nothingness*, 1970). He married a non-Slovak, and his residence might be characterized from the outside as "WASP suburbia." Although the New England and New York Jewish and WASP intellectual spheres of influence represent *them*, Novak (like the other New Ethnic leaders) was and remains an active member in their circles. In his series of searching books, as he approached and stood at the abyss of existentialism, nothingness, despair, and political radicalism, he was testing and risking himself to the limits. Yet in the same period since the early 1960s, he assiduously read everything Reinhold Niebuhr had written, finding in him a theology, ideology, and polity for his own subsequent countercultural revolution in identity. In *Ascent of the Mountain, Flight of the Dove* (1970), he drew back from the existential chasm, stressing the need to fill the void of nothingness with one's personal rich and unique cultural "stories." Religion became a search for an autobiographically livable myth. Likewise, in *Politics: Realism and Imagination* (1971— mostly previously published essays) Novak praised the Catholic tradition for its ability to face nothingness and to give it form. In *The Rise of the Unmeltable Ethnics* (1971), he found and systematized his story and his mythos: *ethnicity*. From the pyre of American national culture would rise again the indestructible phoenix of ethnicity, the durable amid the transitory. In 1974, Novak's book *Choosing Our King: Powerful Symbols in Presidential Politics* translated his ethnic-Catholic ethos into an ideology for American presidential politics. The election of a president would be seen as a sacred national ritual. Finally (for our present discussion), in 1974 he formed and became director of EMPAC—Ethnic Millions Political Action Committee, which directed the ethos into sociopolitical and economic activism. Ethnic identity, with its corollaries of multiculturalism and pluralism, was now systematized and, largely under Novak's leadership, has become a vital political force in virtually every area of public life.

Novak the nihilist and existentialist became the mythicist and essentialist of the next decade. Dostoevski, whom Novak deeply admires, said through the mouth of a protagonist: "I began with the idea of unrestricted freedom, and I have arrived at unrestricted despotism." In a sense, this is the cultural itinerary of the past two decades and that of Novak himself. Looking back, we might speak of the ethnophile as ex-integrationst and Americanist, and of the conversion from one identity to its opposite.[15] If in the 1960s Novak could be called an apologist for the student Left (in which position he felt uneasy), he could now be identified as the spokesman for the white ethnic Right (in which role he feels equally uneasy).

Novak writes of the 1960s: "It is as though an abyss had opened up, as if many peered into it, and as if the prospect of chaos and struggle was too terrifying to sustain; all have drawn back. The struggle is unresolved as many reconsider, reassess, redefine themselves. The sixties were a fevered time, nightmarish to protagonists on every side." "Many discovered that they were more 'conservative' than they had thought; or more 'religious'—or less so. It is far easier in 1974 to raise hard questions about one another's standpoints than it was in 1961."[16] It is Novak's specific reconsideration, reassessment, and redefinition—communicated in an enchanting, seductive style that is almost fairy-tale-like in its simplicity—that resolves not only his identity conflict, but those whom he addresses and for whom he presumes to speak. Having been one of *them,* he now rejoices in his return to *us*—a return to the collectivity and communion he largely invented. The New Ethnicity and the network people that populate it are the products of an imagination brought to life. It is Novak's accomplishment to have formulated a sweeping new personal and cultural identity that simultaneously gives clear voice to all that is wrong and recommends the way to set it right. The New Ethnic identity offers in a single stroke to reduce radically the unabated stress induced by the very fact of being an American:

community, communion, order, authority, roots, continuity, purpose, initiative, faith, family—in a word, *identity*. For Novak, the sense of alienation and estrangement inherent in the meaning he attaches to his name is overcome; conflicts of personal history, too, are overcome now that history no longer begins "with my father and with me."

If for Novak the estrangement was cumulative, so was the return path to mythos and ethnicity. We noted that during the 1960s he sought in the writings of Reinhold Niebuhr the path he would eventually take. But Novak himself draws our attention to a series of "political events" as the key to his turning—events he sees in retrospect as having shaped his growing identification with ethnics and ethnicity. We cite him in detail:

We are becoming almost Jewish in our anticipation of disaster. When anything goes wrong, or dirty work needs doing, we're *it*.

I never intended to think this way. I never intended to begin writing—ye gods!—as an *ethnic*. I never intended to dig up old memories. What began to prod me were political events. The anomaly . . . of William F. Buckley, Jr., had long troubled me: a Catholic who was making a much-needed criticism of American "enlightenment," but from a curiously Anglo-Saxon and conservative point of view. I hoped he was not a dotted line which a larger Catholic movement would fill in.

By the time of the Goldwater campaign of 1964 and the Wallace campaign of 1968, I was alarmed by the cleavage between the old WASP and the new technological consciousness. Catholics might be driven to choose, and might choose the older ways. Worse still, I began to be irritated by the controlled, but felt, anti-Catholic bias among journalists and intellectuals. Despite myself, I disliked the general American desire to believe that ethnic groups do not exist, or if they do, should not. I had nothing to do with ethnic groups myself, and no intention of linking myself to them. I was neither ashamed of them nor hostile to them; it simply seemed to me important, even from their point of view, for me to live the fullest life and to do the best work I could.

But then interpretations of the Wallace vote among Catholics in Wisconsin and Maryland seemed to me grossly unfair. I wasn't about to *identify* with the pro-Wallace voters. But I felt increasingly uncomfortable with the condescension and disdain heaped upon them. So I found myself beginning to say "we," rather than "they," when I spoke of ethnics. It is not an entirely comfortable "we," for many ethnics have not been to college, or travelled, or shared the experiences I've had. I wasn't sure I wanted to defend them, or whether I was entitled to do so after too many years of separation from them.[17]

How does the disinterested outsider, who had nothing to do with ethnic groups and who did not link himself with them, become one of their staunchest advocates and defenders? As a radical intellectual and philosopher who had cosmopolitan education, travel, and experience, to think "this way," to write "as an ethnic," and to "dig up old memories" was to be what he was *not*. Through a thoroughgoing self-uprooting, Novak had placed a seemingly safe distance between his new identity as a radical intellectual and an insightful culture critic, and his old identity as a Slovak. In a later essay he writes:

When *Time* Magazine referred to me in 1972 as a "Slovak-American," I felt an inner shock; I had never referred to myself or been publicly referred to in that way. I wasn't certain how I felt about it.[18]

Yet what was being confirmed from without was something that had been so well repressed and dissociated within that the major intellectual of the New Ethnic Movement felt an inner shock of discrepancy when he was identified with what he had written. He is torn between being *us* and *them*, who are not only two mutually exclusive groups outside himself but, seemingly, two mutually exclusive and opposing parts of himself. On the one hand, Novak speaks as an ethnic for the ethnics; on the other hand, he speaks as a radical, still liberal, intellectual about the ethnics.

"Despite myself": one part of him did indeed harbor the American desire that ethnic groups not exist, while another part of him disliked this wish. Ostensibly, until the political events of the late 1960s, especially those involving George Wallace, the ethnics were irrelevant to Novak's life. Radical politics, radical theology, radical philosophy were important means of *eradicating* the influence of the past. The ethnics were decidedly *them*. The primordial bond then lay elsewhere. Thinking and writing as an ethnic, together with the active search for old memories and relationships: here Novak rejects his earlier repudiation, and the *them* becomes *us*, and conversely. The return of the repressed overcame quickly the distance he had put between himself and the ethnics.

So long as ethnic groups, or ethnics as a group, did not exist, he did not need to feel guilty for having abandoned them. Their anonymity was crucial to his ability to "live the fullest life and to do the best work. . . ." While Novak had put the lived Catholicism of the Slovak and ethnic parish far behind him, he became a radical Catholic idealist, celebrating those who love the night, the mystic recesses of the universalist Church—one that would be later reethnicized and highly particularized. Absorbed in the radical, the mystical, and the universal, he was able to overcome the intolerable situation of history beginning with his father and himself. His father had sold out his ethnic-Catholic "soul" to the mammon of America; Novak the son became a devout adversary of that (American) culture and an apostle of the incorruptible universal Church.

The Wallace campaign of 1968 was the decisive event—with much precedent—that marked the turning toward mythos and culminating in the ethos and identity of ethnos. The uprooter and uprooted would subsequently try to sink new roots; the estranged would become the passionate nativist. Once the white ethnics surfaced, once they were *identified* as a group, the history Novak had abandoned engulfed him. As a radical Catholic liberal figure, he could not "*identify* with the pro-Wallace voters." To reidentify with the white ethnics, Novak had to assimilate them to his identity. They had to be like him; he could speak of *them* as *us* only if they were as he needed and wished them to be: more liberal than conservative, far less racist than the WASP, etc. To return to the white ethnics and champion their cause, he had to deny or at least equivocate about what they were accused of being. Novak redefined their reality to suit his own. Hence the need for romanticization, idealization, stereotypy, and distortion. It is as though he were saying: I am *not;* and they are *not.* Yet he chooses the acronym "PIGS" to symbolize the defiant, resistant, and resilient identity of the "unmeltable ethnics." For all of Novak's repeated emphasis that the ethnics are traditionally more liberal than conservative, that the WASPs rather than the Catholic ethnics invented and perfected slavery, and that ethnics are *not* Wallaceites, we have the uneasy feeling that Novak doth protest too much. Novak is justly disturbed, as are we, that the white ethnics have come to be regarded as the "new niggers of America," the butt of everyone's jokes and righteous indignation, the scapegoat for every social ill. However, the fact that the white ethnics did not enslave the blacks does not exonerate them from racism; the alibi of history does not work and is not convincing (though it works for those who invoke it) because it is what is practiced currently that counts. In a recent essay about Tom Wicker and the Attica Prison riots of 1971, Novak is quick to point out journalist Wicker is a racist against the white guards despite his liberal pretensions; yet, for Novak, the Attica guards emerge morally unscathed.[19] We wonder if the mote that Novak scrutinizes in Wicker's eye might not have been more difficult to detect were it not for the beam in Novak's. Novak's outrage at the "failure of nerve" at Attica and in America in general is not far removed from the idiom of George Wallace and Ronald Reagan—those who champion the "little man," and tacitly mean only *white*. Is it possible that Wallace can express for Novak things that Novak would like to say but cannot because they would be dissonant with his conciliatory, still universalistic, identity?[20] Is it further possible that Novak's ideological appeal is largely based on his overt liberalism, progressivism, and compassion, beneath which simmers a discernible rage and crypto-conservatism (which is disqualified by his disarmingly genuine and innocent style)? On the one hand, "Ethnic Americans respect strength and despise weakness"; on the other hand, those with whom he now identifies cannot possess those attributes contrary to the image of the radical philosopher—racist, conservative, authoritarian, not given to dissent. What is so convincing about Novak's personal and written style is that he can "tell it like it is" without telling it offensively. His politeness and simple grace convey the Dostoevskian "humble charity" of harmless, decent white ethnicity that only the depraved could attack.

The renewed visibility of ethnic groups, then, was the prod that reawakened Novak's ethnic self-consciousness. To assuage the guilt and shame of having abandoned and uprooted himself from his history, he reidentified with it, though not with the ethnicity of reality, but with an idealized ideology of ethnicity that merged with the thing itself. From a rupture of ties, he sought a restoration of ties. Reawakened guilt was resolved by remorse and restitution, of which the White Ethnic Movement is the symbolic and ritual progeny. From one who "had nothing to do with ethnic groups myself, and no intention of linking myself to them," Novak not only became their champion, but was identified from without as the personal embodiment of the New Ethnic identity.

One question, however, still remains unanswered: if he did not identify or associate with ethnic groups, why, when the ethnics were singled out as Wallaceites, did he feel compelled to rally to their defense? In a personal communication to Howard Stein, Novak stated that he wrote *The Rise of the Unmeltable Ethnics* not out of personal or autobiographic need, but because the misunderstood ethnics needed to be understood. But there is a legion of misunderstandings and injustices that need correction. Why *this* man for the task?— especially one who felt unsure he could defend the ethnics because of years of separation from them. The only psychologically defensible answer is that Novak felt the accusation applied to himself, not to a remote *them*. The need to defend himself became simultaneously a defense of the *us* with whom he identified and became identified. He rallied to his and to the ethnics' defense with a defiant "Ethnics are *not* . . . " and from that point began to formulate what it is that ethnics *are*.

In *Civilization and Its Discontents*, Freud wrote: "As long as things go well with a man, his conscience is lenient and lets him do all sorts of things; but when misfortune befalls him, he searches his soul, acknowledges his sinfulness, heightens the demands of his conscience, imposes abstinences upon himself and punishes himself with penances. Whole people have behaved in this way, and still do."[21] Misfortune triggers the return of the repressed that had been counter-cathected or defended against in times of well-being. Freud wrote in *Moses and Monotheism:*

> The repressed retains its upward urge, its effort to force its way to consciousness. It achieves its aim under three conditions: (1) if the strength of the anticathexis is diminished by pathological processes which overtake the other part (of the mind), what we call the ego, or by a different distribution of the cathectic energies in that ego as happens regularly in the state of sleep; (2) if the instinctual elements attaching to the repressed receive a special reinforcement (of which the best example is the processes during puberty); and (3) if at any time in recent experience impressions or experiences occur which resemble the repressed so closely that they are able to awaken it. In the last case the recent experience is reinforced by the latent energy of the repressed, and the repressed comes into operation behind the recent experience and with its help.[22]

Having fled from the father and mother who did not live up to his idealistic expectations, Novak became a radical Catholic, the prophet of an abstract Mother Church and Father God, who, unlike his real parents, would "be all in all." But even during those frenetic days of stability maintained by constant movement, he pored over the works of Niebuhr in search of a more *concrete, immanent* identity.[23] Novak approvingly concludes his essay with a quotation from Niebuhr. " 'To such faith the generations are bound to return after they have pursued the mirages in the desert to which they are tempted from time to time by the illusions of particular eras.' " Novak's vatic conscience, though never "lenient," was nevertheless consumed and channeled by radical theology and politics. Things went well, and

Novak led a markedly individualistic life until events of the late 1960s reawakened his tie to an ethnic-parental past that he had repressed and virtually severed. The path from misfortune to restitution was quick in coming.

The "strength of the anticathexis"—the strength of his radicalism—was diminished by the force due to the sudden feeling that the *them* from whom he had put such spatial and ideological distance was *us*. The dissociated *not-me* that was formerly ego-dystonic was increasingly experienced as *me*, reawakening guilt and shame that had to be subsequently coped with through projection. Guilt was transformed, through a paranoid-narcissistic process, into a sense of persecution. The unmeltable ethnics, whom Novak now championed, needed to be defended against the oppressive WASPs. Personal history and American ethno-history became the same story: denationalization, an assault on self-worth, etc. What, though, was "the instinctual element attaching to the repressed" that was reinforced? Through his earlier radicalism, Novak was able to resolve the intolerable oedipal situation of history beginning "with my father and with me." He had indeed become a part of a grand project of social reform and reformation. The reawakened association of ethnicity with personal identity desublimated and reinstinctualized the problem of personal history—hence the problem-laden relation of father and son. The father with whom Novak could not identify in the flesh, and with whom he had unsuccessfully tried to identify in the spirit, returns to haunt and persecute him. Now he must defend his father, but at the same time free himself of him. The new ethos of ethnicity enables him to be the prophet of white ethnics, including his father, in the abstract, while avoiding the terrors of relation in the concrete. Thus Novak is able to avoid his father while seemingly becoming reconciled with him. White ethnics in general, his very masculine Uncle George, and those of the grandparental and ancestral generations, become the *real* ethnics in whose myth and great cosmic lineage and project he is able to immerse himself and serve as prophet and spokesman. Still unable to identify with his father in the concrete, Novak defends himself against him by transforming his father into the embodiment of an abstract principle that has been defiled by Americanization. Freud's third criterion would thus seem to be satisfied, since the recent experience of the *not-me* suddenly becoming *me* closely resembled what was repressed and reawakened it, as we discussed earlier. At the same time as *not-me* became *me*, it had to be disguised and idealized in order to defend against the real relation with his father: in the concrete, his father remains *not-me*.

We should say a few words about Novak's use of christological symbolism. In chapter 4 we discussed his fusion of religion and politics: Senator Eugene McCarthy possessed "something priestly," a little like a pope, a vicar of the people; the presidency, the closest thing to priesthood in American culture, is a sacred symbolic office, and the election of a president is a sacred rite. In a 1971 essay which appeared in the *National Catholic Reporter* Novak writes:

> What price is exacted by America, when it sucks the raw material of the other cultures of the world to make them shape up? What do people have to lose, before they can qualify as true Americans? . . . You proved you loved America by dying for it in the military. [white ethnics] . . . pride themselves on "fighting for America". When my father saw my youngest brother in officer's uniform, ready to go to Vietnam, it was one of the proudest days of his life. . . . There is, then, a blood test. "Die for us and we'll give you a chance."[24]

Novak dedicated his 1971 book *Politics: Realism and Imagination* to his brother Richard (a priest who died in 1964) and to Brother David Darst, who was killed in an automobile accident in 1969: "WHO . . . IN COURAGE AND WITNESS DIED FOR US." Two of Novak's essays had influenced Darst to take an anti-Vietnam position, and Darst along with eight others burned about six hundred draft files. Sentenced to two years' imprisonment, he and two others were killed while out on bail. They were on their way to discuss, among other things, two of Novak's essays, one from *A Theology for Radical Politics*. In the Preface to *Politics: Realism and Imagination,* Novak writes: "Sometimes as I write, I see images of that burning automobile and strewn copies of my work. . . ." Novak's sense of responsibility is overwhelming. So is his identification with Christ the Son "who died for us," "who died for our sins," "who came to die. . . ."[25]

On the one hand, the only way for an ethnic to qualify as an American is to sacrifice his life for his country, if not in defense of it, then by perishing in the merciless fires of the Melting Pot. On the other hand, Novak influenced and participated in the antiwar movement, which revolted against the sacrifice of sons for the pride of the fathers—quite unethnic and un-American. Haunted by the image of the car wreckage, he seems to associate the accident with the consequences of his own radicalism. Brothers David and Dick are also martyr-sons who "died for us." America itself takes on the characteristics of God the Father who mercilessly demands the loss or self-sacrifice of the son in order that the son *qualify* for salvation or redemption. America is deeply intertwined with personal christological symbolism. Novak the philosopher-theologian, formerly identifying with the son, is in search of the good father who will not demand as appeasement the death of the son as the price of acceptance. Perhaps ethnicity will exact less of a price. He looks to the presidency of the United States for the leader who will bear witness, a vicar, not a self-willed doer.

Novak himself possesses the quality of the priestly, the fatherly, even the prophetic, whether as radical theologian or as white ethnic leader. As leader of the New Ethnicity, however, he has reidentified with the father and Father, and perhaps may not have to give his life since he is no longer a rebellious son. The only way he can avert martyrdom is by becoming the father. In embracing ethnicity, Novak has indeed returned to the father and the Father. In becoming the one he has feared, he need no longer fear the father because he is now his witness, his agent, and voice. His conscience will now have its vengeance, and restitution to the father which he has reintrojected is accompanied by the re-repression of the autonomous *son* within himself. He is now the obedient, dutiful, repentant son who renounces competition with the father, while displacing such conduct and combating the assertiveness, initiative, and pugnacity in other rebellious sons. If there was a terrible price for becoming American, then there is an equally terrible price for becoming ethnic: paradoxically, becoming ethnic is as much a sacrifice of the son to the father as becoming American was. In becoming the prophet and priest of his ethnic father, Novak loses not only his own voice but his manhood as well.

A passage by Weston La Barre clarifies not only Novak and other white ethnic leaders, but the psychodynamics of prophets in general who vacillate between being the mouthpiece of their God or group, and seeming to claim the dispensation or authority of God and Father himself.

If the male child relinquishes neither his own fantasied omnipotence nor the fantasied omnipotence of his father, and if he cannot enter into his male heritage of limited and contingent potency, he can become locked lifelong in the phallic "paranoid" stance. Who has the omnipotence—prophet-mouthpiece of male mana, or God! In the paranoid state, these ego boundaries are quite fluid and precarious, the prophet and his god often indiscernible clinically, and the same individual may at one time insist only on his oracular function, and at another claim godhood for himself. In longing for identity with the father, the paranoid self often merges with the

Self, omnipotence regained. For in paranoia neither has the psychological boy grown in potency nor has the father diminished in omnipotence, the attempted identity thus being of child with god, and not man with man.

The paranoid precariously possesses "omnipotence", but only at the price of potency, real and symbolical as a man. The paranoid *can not* identify with his father as the lover of his mother, except at the cost of madness. Nor, in a non-abstract (sexualized but really narcissistic) love of his father's maleness can he escape other terrors. Feminized, he seeks his father's love and is persecuted by it as well. In winning the fantasy battle for phallic omnipotence, he has lost the whole war. . . .

Institutionally, the paranoid is the *vatic personality,* the priest of his father's godhood, condemned to a child's poverty, chastity and obedience—or he is himself spuriously a paranoid omnipotent god. This is not the proud outcome of a man's struggle for potency!

The vatic personality is only the seer or humble witness of an external omnipotence, the oracle his "utterance" of the words of the god, his inspiration a being passively inspired or "breathed into" by the god. The prophet is not one who predicts, but literally one who "speaks forth" as the mouthpiece of omniscience, which latter it is that knows all, including the future. The vatic personality, in sum, is the individual driven by inner need and conviction to speak with the voice of god, as if the voice were not his own. Hence the prophet is psychologically parasitic upon a supposed external omnipotence that is really an equally fictive internal one. Every paranoiac is a god in person, every god a paranoiac projected into space.[26]

Through the identity and ideology of the New Ethnicity, Novak has once again become the priest of his father's godhood, this time not by fleeing but by returning. This New Ethnic god *in abstractu* has now attached not only to family, neighborhood, and the network people of concrete ethnic associations, but is the principle of redefining the very identity of America and Americanness, extending the ethnic-Catholic *principle* or ethos even into the now-sacral domain of presidential politics. While American culture is ethnicized, the office of the president is to approximate that of divine kingship—vicarship and stewardship, to be sure, not incarnation. Nothing is untouched by the deep structural transformation and transvaluation: ethos, family, lineage, ancestry, religion, philosophy, national politics, intergroup relations, and international relations. Just as, for instance, the idea of a small

Germany gave way to the concept of *Grossdeutschland* under the impact of nationalism, with its *Anschluss* and irredentism of territory, population, and identity, likewise the New Ethnic Movement is driven by the limitlessness and expansiveness of the need for omnipotence and exhibitionism. On the one hand, the boundaries of the movement, like those of the personalities they express, are expansionistically fluid, seeking to devour the entire world into the *me*. On the other hand, the paranoid-narcissistic ego of leader and led alike surrounds the new movement's identity with a protective autistic shell to create definite and safe boundaries within which the ego withdraws. The dissociated self-other is kept radically outside of personal and new group boundaries. For this reason the paranoid-narcissistic personality restructuring serves as the psychological underpinning of the oppositional process.

It is the accomplishment of the vatic personality, whether of the White Ethnic Movement or similar ethno-national movements, to be able to deftly offer illusion, prohibition, and taboo, and make their prescription and proscription more inviting, more liberating, than anything reality could offer. *Reality* is regained regressively through the magic of the glorified imagination, whose thought is the basis for instrumental or goal-seeking behavior. The paranoiac-narcissism of magical thinking is translated into public policy and polity, with the public support of those who commit their spirit into the hands of *He Who Knows*.

The New Ethnicity claims to restore dignity, initiative, and manhood, while in fact it sets up only another idol in the wilderness, a false god and prophet, jealous of all others. In inducing other men to submit to his active masculinity, Novak, as well as other New Ethnic leaders, feminizes them while deluding them into believing that they have renewed their initiative, potency. Ultimately, the vatic personality, with the consent of the exploitable, deprives those whom he promises potency of a sense of genuine strength and manhood: The New Ethnics' collective desperation and need to maintain the narcosis of the ideological "high" attests to the fragility of the indomitable veneer, and to the dread of depression and feminization that the illusory "high" defends against. Exploiting the prevailing rage and sense of helplessness, the vatic prophet serves as the medium of collective regression in the service of the *regressed* ego. The potency he offers his people is that of infantilization—and under the self-aggrandizing power of magical thinking, the New Ethnics cannot help but feel proud and competent.

If, as La Barre notes, the prophet-shaman is psychologically parasitic upon an external omnipotence that is a projection of his internalized omnipotent father, we might add that he is equally parasitic upon those to whom he restores and bestows the gift of manhood. But the parasitism is reciprocal—symbiotic in a perverse sense, in which the desperation and pathology of each lives off and confirms the other. It is in this regressive way that mutual deception and exploitation can be experienced as exhilarating insight and liberation. Novak has succeeded in overcoming the terrible flaw of history beginning with his father and himself, but the price of the New Ethnic *imagination* and *internal history* is to dehumanize one's parent and one's self in the service of a greater ideal that purports to elevate both. The price of gaining a New Ethnic identity is the sacrifice of the follower's human identity.

The Ingathering: The New Ethnicity and "Becoming a Jew"

Because of its special relation to the White Ethnic Movement, we cannot omit a discussion of contemporary American Judaism.[27] On the one hand, there is a simple parallel between the two: identity revitalization; pan-Ethnophilism in the former, pan-Judeophilism in the latter; etc. On the other hand, a number of influential Jewish leaders and intellectuals act as entrepreneurs, culture brokers, and coalition builders between American Jews and the non-Jewish white ethnics as a means of "self-defense." Just as Michael Novak is the white ethnic apostle to the Jews, many Jewish leaders are apostles to the White Ethnic gentiles—urging that the particularistic be universalized, emphasizing that the Jews are an *ethnic group* (with their own nation, Israel) rather than merely a *religion*.

Universalism, Americanism, and assimilation are becoming less attractive to American Jews as well as to largely Catholic white ethnics. Both share the identical identity transformation, although the status of Jews in relation to the White Ethnic Movement is still problematic. White ethnics admire and try to emulate the Jewish organizational acumen as evinced in the concerted effort to "Save Soviet Jewry" and in the seemingly instant reflex action in defense of the State of Israel. White ethnic intellectuals not only extol the ability of Jews to preserve a traditional identity, but see in what they formerly regarded as clannishness a model for themselves. White ethnophiles and Judeophiles identify ambivalently with one another, alternately including and excluding one another, seeing each other as potential ally and as adversary. The myth of rich, influential Jews in secret conspiracy to control everything still must be combated—and there is a decided effort to demonstrate that impoverished, disappointed Jews abound, as though to prove that an invisible population of Jews whose lives are proof of the falsity of the stereotype share identical socioeconomic life chances with the silent majority of white ethnics. Thus American Jews can claim not only to be a *minority* but to number substantially among the *American poor*.

Many American Jews agree with the white ethnophiles that to be Americanized is to be uprooted and alienated, to invest in a promise that can be only a mirage. If baptism was the price of admission of the Jew to European civilization in centuries past, then estrangement, guilt, and shame are the price of admission for the immigrant and his or her descendants, Jewish and otherwise, to American culture. In becoming American, the New Ethnics say, you do not gain an identity, but lose one. With the strident attack on Western science, and the perception that Jews are either "overrepresented" in this field or dominate it, Jews, with their traditional emphasis on education and rationalism, feel increasingly vulnerable. The withdrawal from "rootless cosmopolitanism" and the embracing of the ethno-religious attitude is an attempt by Jews to deny that they can indeed be trapped in this stereotype, thereby lessening their vulnerability to accusation. In a sense, it is a way of denying difference, of saying that "We are like everyone else, ethnic."

In past decades, Martin Buber and Abraham Joshua Heschel dominated Jewish theology and served as ecumenical bridges reaching out from Judaism to the world. Today, the increased interest in the writings of theologian-philosopher Emil Fackenheim is symptomatic of the inward-turning and nativism. Just as the white ethnics argue that to assimilate is to do to themselves what the *Americans* could not do, Fackenheim argues that to assimilate into the modern, secularist world would be for the Jews to do to themselves what Hitler and Nazism could not accomplish. It would be collective suicide. It is the duty of Judaism to defy history, as it has always done, by surviving. What emerges is a Judaism of defiance: the unassimilable Jews become the counterpart of Novak's "unmeltable ethnics." Here, too, as with the white ethnics, guilt plays a dominant role in the motivation to survive and to urge survival: to survive is not only to keep alive the memory of those who perished in the Holocaust and in the millennia of holocausts, but to appease the guilt for having survived the holocausts, and not perishing. Fackenheim stresses that Jewish universalism is not the true

Judaism, but a detour and dead end. Jewish particularism, devotion to the corporate covenant and identity, is counterposed against the anomic and individualistic legacy of the Enlightenment, Kant, and the erroneous assumption that personal authenticity is based on autonomy. Jews are a people, and any existence apart from that historical peoplehood is betrayal of the convenant. The continuity and authority of tradition are the expression and affirmation of authentic Jewish identity. The discontinuities of modernization, and the lapse of authority inherent in individual autonomy and choice, are to be overcome by a return to the covenant.[28] The ambiguities of alternatives and decisions are removed; a Jew no longer has to choose, because the law is both clear and enveloping.

White ethnic pan-ethnitude has a parallel in a pan-Jewish identity or pan-Judeophilism. In Judaism, the individual becomes inseparable from an even wider "group ego" than the ethnic group itself. One is united with one's brethren and sisters all over the world. The unbroken link is thus both historical and contemporary, temporal and spatial. The pressure and lobbying to "Save Soviet Jewry" is one current expression of the politicization of the symbiosis, a symbiosis that is further associated with the messianic significance of the State of Israel for Jews still in the Diaspora. Through the State of Israel, the Diaspora is overcome, at least psychologically, for those who remain outside the Homeland. Through identification with spiritual and political Zionism, and with the revolutionary ideology of the Kibbutz as well, the Diaspora Jew is able vicariously to dissociate himself or herself from the haunting stereotype of the mercantile, intellectualist, wandering Jews, and can become at least in fantasy the pre-Diaspora rooted, national, and militarily successful Jew. A compromise, however, based on compartmentalization, is made between local (American) and supralocal (e.g., with Israel) identification. Thus in America, there is a vigilant attempt to assure that group rights or quotas are not established, while American Jews working in behalf of Israel emphasize the group right or corporate identity of the Jewish State (i.e., an ethnically based nation-state). It might be noted that this compartmentalization has characterized Diaspora Jewry since the formulation of the Zionist ideology in the final decade of the nineteenth century: the corporate and legal status they zealously seek for those in Palestine or Israel, they bitterly oppose in their Diaspora homelands.

In general, however, pan-ethnicity or pan-nationalism, Jewish or white ethnic, provides a sense of greatness and invincibility that overcomes a sense of weakness and vulnerability, a sense of belonging that, however illusory, replaces isolation with connectedness. The connection, though, is invented, not discovered—although in order to maintain the illusion of primeval continuity that has only recently been broken, New Ethnics must speak of rediscovery. One *becomes* anew what he or she all along has *really* been, despite appearances or deviations.

The American Jewish novelist Herbert Gold wrote an essay in 1972 titled "On Becoming a Jew" and also published an autobiographical book, *My Last Two Thousand Years*.[29] The theme is of the Diaspora-Jew, who, like the Diaspora-ethnic, who has fled far from his nativity into primitivism, nihilism, and sensualism, now returns to the comforting and reordering fold of tradition, lineage, and corporate identity as a means of resolving guilt, shame, and alienation. The young anthropologist Paul Wrobel wrote an essay titled "Becoming a Polish-American," and English professor Richard Rodriguez wrote "On Becoming a Chicano."[30] Novak's *Rise of the Unmeltable Ethnics* (1971) is likewise a subjective confessional and report on the rejection of Diaspora American culture and an origin myth validating his becoming ethnic. The literary genre and personal itinerary are identical for each of these writers who attempt to *renew* their ties (and vows?) ideologically through the embracing of nativism, because they are so removed from the native experience they sought to escape. A rite of passage of withdrawal, transition, and reentry, symbolized by the death of the old identity and a rebirth into the new identity (being born again), is the underlying meaning of becoming a Jew or ethnic.

The return of the native is inseparable from the search for inner and outer order and authority. The influential philosopher and theologian Abraham Joshua Heschel, widely known in the non-Jewish American world for his participation in the Civil Rights Movements and for his mystical ecumenism, devoted a great part of his energy to the reconciliation of *Kabbalah* (mysticism), *Haggada* (legend), and *Halakah* (law) in Judaism. In the 1960s he wrote several widely acclaimed books, among them, *The Insecurity of Freedom* (1963) and *Who Is Man?* (1965). With the outbreak of the 1967 Arab-Israeli War, Heschel became reconverted to a more narrowly conceived Zionism and Jewish theology than he had before articulated. Religion, peoplehood, covenant, nation, soil, and the continuity of timeless sacred history became one and were hauntingly expressed in *Israel: An Echo of Eternity* (1967).[31] The refuge of group immortality had been threatened, and with it, the specter of the death of personal meaning. A personal reaffirmation of Judaism and Israel was simultaneously a prophetic call for a return to the covenant.

A 1971 article in *Time* noted that Rabbi Steven Riskin of New

York, age thirty-one, had sought out Martin Buber while attending the Hebrew University in Jerusalem, but had left unsatisfied. "Buber could not understand a God of Love giving a Law. . . . I respectfully differ. A God who loves must give commands, must be concerned about the way his people live. Buber gave us a theology, but not a life style." Riskin returned to New York determined to become an Orthodox rabbi. Significantly, Rabbi Riskin's early experience was in a family that was nominally Jewish, and he repeatedly sought out authorities that would give him what his family did not. In the ethno-religious sense, he became more Jewish than the Jews. His Orthodox synagogue services are filled with increasing numbers of young American Jews who need the authority and covenant that he now preaches and personifies. Here again the oppositional process is at work intergenerationally: assimilationist versus nativist; Reformed (Unitarian, or *Konfessionsloss*) versus Orthodox; American versus Zionist-Israeli ideology, etc. "Jews today have passed the age of rationalism and are giving the soul its due."[32] The opposition between "reason" and "soul" is at the core of the New Ethnicity. But "reason" is far from absent in the passions of ethnic "soul." Indeed those advocating the liberation of "soul" from rationalism are the mightiest and busiest rationalizers and legitimators of ethnophile spontaneity.

In the summer of 1966, Howard Stein was enrolled in several courses at the Jewish Theological Seminary of America, in preparation for study for the rabbinate (which he later abandoned). During a lengthy interview before the admissions committee, he was asked to present his own philosophical and theological views. He discussed Whitehead, Tillich, Buber, Heschel, Teilhard de Chardin, Jaspers, and others whose work had been (and remain) influential in his thinking. At the end of his presentation, the head of the committee said something like the following: "You know, Howard, I read Buber and all those philosophers. I knew Martin Buber personally. But you know, he always left me dissatisfied. He never told me what I should do. . . ."

The essence of the new Jewish identity, and ethnic neo-orthodoxy of all varieties, is the need for order, for unambiguous guidelines, for authority (e.g., as embodied in Judaic Law, and absent in the unconditioned meeting of *I* and *Thou* of Martin Buber's philosophical anthropology). Hence the need to be told what to do, and how to live. It is no longer necessary to think, to decide between difficult choices (and to cope with the ambivalences they largely represent): Jews can, almost impersonally, though with utmost personal commitment, follow the rules.

For many American Jews who had ventured into existentialism, assimilationism, radicalism, nihilism, and the like, the search for a renewed Jewish meaning and identity consisted of the often obsessive concern with having the right thoughts together with the compulsive search for the right deeds to perform. The new Judaism and the New Ethnicity share an underlying *Ortho-doxos* and *Ortho-praxis,* whose intention and consequence is to undo all previous violations. Just as Novak, Greeley, Baroni, and others had *become* ethnic, many Jews became twice born in their Jewishness, restoring for themselves what they had earlier breached and rebelled against: law, order, simplicity, and a community that was a haven of safety that would serve as an external control to bring order to inner and outer anarchy. The ghetto and the *shtetl,* the awesome magnificence of the Law and of rabbinic leadership, suddenly took on a comfortably romantic hue—not at all the ancient terrors and constrictions the original immigrants fled.

The ambivalence and the direction of the resolution among new American Jews is identical with that of participants in the Catholic White Ethnic Movement. A central message of the generic New Ethnicity is that a closely circumscribed order creates its own sense of freedom (from many choices, responsibilities, insecurities, guilts, solitariness, etc.), while exacting its own price. New Ethnics surrender freedoms of one kind to secure freedoms of another. The new freedoms, however, possess some new—yet remarkably ancient—dangers.

An example of the American Jewish "New Ethnicity" comes from some comments by Rabbi Benjamin Z. Kreitman. It is noteworthy that in the following passage, the reaffirmation of ethnic Jewishness is synonymous with a reaffirmation of an identification with the father and the patristic deity. The *re-binding* of the son to the tradition transparently expresses the Jewish oedipal paradigm—one whose resemblance to the New Ethnic model is unmistakable. While Rabbi Kreitman bases his reaffirmation on sacred text, it should be kept in mind how the secular dramas of everyday life closely follow and give meaning to the larger-than-life archetypal dramas enacted in sacred text. Rabbi Kreitman writes the following:

> Many have let their ardors of Jewish loyalty be cooled by indifference and unconcern. Others, more sensitive, have begun to give expression to their doubts and fears about the reasons for Jewish survival and fears over what perils may be imposed on their children, bearing a Jewish identity.

The issue over which the American Jew agonizes now is not

alone whether he should continue to be a Jew but over the question whether he has the right to impose this frightful choice on his descendants.

In Biblical terms the question is: Must we respond affirmatively to the command of destiny: "Take your son, your favored one, Isaac, whom you love and go to the land of Moriah and offer him there as a burnt offering." (Genesis 22:2)

We are the precipitates of centuries of suffering, of pain and heroism. Unlike other areas and other centuries, the American Jew living in an open society has a choice and an option. His position is akin to that of the first Jew, Abraham, whose decision to be a Jew was free from the coercion of fate, birth and the shame of betrayal. Our response at this juncture bears an extraordinary historic character.

To remain silent to the demand of "Take your son" in this hour is to surrender to the demonic in life. Not only will the Jew be diminished but humanity will be diminished as well. Even to the most secular-minded, the stubbornness of the Jew in continuing to exist and be a creative force gives faith for tomorrow.

Emil Fackenheim, who has given much thought to the theology after the Holocaust, writes: "To be a Jew after Auschwitz, and to bear witness against them in all their guises. It is to believe that they will not prevail and to stake on that belief one's life and that of one's children."

Given the nature of human evil, the choice of not being a Jew for the sake of the future security of one's children becomes an even more frightening decision. Fackenheim uncovers the dreadful possibilities of such a choice: "*By choosing for our children not to be victims* (read *Akedah,* BZK) may be exposing them to the possibility, or the likelihood that they will be murderers."[33]

We are reminded here that in 1918, when U.S. Ambassador to Turkey Henry Morgenthau protested the slaughter of Armenians, including women and children, the Turkish Interior Minister replied: "Those who were innocent today might be guilty tomorrow." Then, of course, Abraham was spared his deed, and Isaac his life, since the Angel of the Lord provided a ram to be offered in Isaac's place. It is the readiness, indeed eagerness, to bind over the next generation that troubles us. To be a Jew after the Holocaust—not merely Auschwitz, but the cumulative holocaust that makes a continuity of Jewish history—is not only to defy *them* but to fear that future generations of *us* will become *them,* the demonic adversary. Jews must bind over their children as potential victims or sacrifices to insure that they will not join the enemy. This does not reflect a faith in tomorrow or in their children, but the dread of both. To save one's self and one's children, Jews must sacrifice them! Without this, so goes the unerring logic, both Jews and the remainder of humanity will be diminished. The future security of Jewish children lies with their maximum vulnerability, which is subsequently transformed into an identification with the father who so graciously spared his son (and, more generally, offspring). Vulnerability becomes security, as son becomes father, and all become the children of the God of Israel. Such is the substrate of the creative force that gives faith for tomorrow, that makes for stubborn persistence, that makes Jews so valuable to humanity.

This interpretation of Rabbi Kreitman's passage—a passage representative of much modern Jewish thinking—makes explicit the grave doubts that underlie the prescription for security. Just as the white ethnics have their ethnic melting pot to resurrect and perpetuate the New Ethnic identity, likewise do American Jews have theirs. We would suggest that to succumb to Emil Fackenheim's prescription is to surrender to the demonic in life, not to transcend it. It would be to rationalize the irrational. In the act of protecting Jewish children and safeguarding their future, one condemns them to the very vulnerability and fate one would consciously (and conscientiously) avert. One constantly dares fate, and when Holocaust comes (or, read: assimilation, Anglo-conformity, etc.), one is able to protest one's innocence. It is *they* who are persecuting *us*. One is able to be the innocent son, awaiting a ram in the brush and rescue from above. In choosing to bind over their sons, however, Jews place them in peril. Survival becomes a way of inviting self-destruction. Placing in jeopardy is a means of preparation for coping with danger.

We are posing the ethical question of an individual's right to impose the burden of the past, with its seduction of a future already presaged, on his children. But an *ethical* question of such choice is absorbed in an *ethnic* question of continuity. The burden must be transmitted as part of the self-chosenness (quite apart from God's) of being a Jew. But the issue of ethics is overshadowed by the rationalization of concern for the future of Jewish children, which covers an individual's deeper mistrust of what his children may do in that future. Parents protect themselves, claiming to have only the best interest of their children in mind. There are, it seems, only two alternatives: victim or victimizer; none other is considered. Moreover, the entire process of assuring Jewish continuity is based on contradictions that should not be perceived, and if perceived, denied, with the entire process shrouded in sacred mystery and duty.

What is the deeper reality that revitalized tradition attempts to obscure? Why, for instance, is the father so frightened of his son? It is a fact of human development that parents see the child, toddler, adolescent, or offspring of whatever developmental stage not only as *it* (the child, etc.) is, but as *re-experienced* by the parents. The parents see themselves *in* their child. The father that sees in his son the potential man who might challenge, displace, and kill him has had his own childhood oedipal conflict reawakened, and must now cope with it—and does so partly through the child. He, the father, is now his son, challenging *his* father. But he is also the father, envious of his son, wishing to destroy him, preventing later challenge by preemptive attack. We have learned from the Freudian method of psychoanalytic investigation that when a fear is voiced seemingly in excess, behind it lies a wish that has been inverted and projected in order to defend against the conscious recognition of it. The wish to murder one's son, and, through identification with the son, the wish to murder the father, are, in fact, the deeper sources of the fright and dread. (We remind ourselves that we are not speaking of Jews in abstract, but of *American* Jews. Keep in mind how the revolutionary *American* oedipal paradigm relates to the Jewish one.)

In binding his son on the altar, the father is saying: "Unless we (fathers) subdue them (the sons), they will kill us." The father must force the son to become like him, bound *together* in a tradition of reciprocal renunciations that protects each against the other and against the wishes of each. Through identification with the father borne of guilt, the father is able to avert a conspiracy of son(s) against him. The son's identification with the father is nonetheless uneasy because, as biblical example confirms his own private and familial fantasy, the father was prepared to go through with the murder and sacrifice of his son. Theologians would say that *God* had commanded Abraham to make the sacrifice to test his faith, and that in fact by providing a substitute offering (the ram), God thereby declared the older sacrifice of firstborn males null and void. We would suggest that God's voice was Abraham's own—repeated in every generation of Abraham through the present—and that the substitute nevertheless represented and symbolized the son. The paradox of Jewish or white ethnic revitalization is that the very movement that attempts to remove the specter of victimization (Holocaust, Americanization, genocide, ethnic disappearance, etc.) bases its ideology of liberation on the victimization of the group members from within.

The socialization of the next generation and of subsequent generations assures the New Ethnics that their sorely won liberation is not lost; the future guarantees their own future and link with a timeless past. Neither the Jewish nor the Catholic white ethnic preoccupation with the past can obscure their concurrent concern for the future: the generation of the New Ethnics secures its place in the great chain of being through its progeny. Here culture and biology join. The Black Power Movement of the late 1960s and early 1970s regarded population control, abortion, and the ecology movement in general as a plot of white genocide against blacks, and argued that more, not fewer, children was the way of securing racial and cultural survival. Now a number of Jewish leaders are beginning to have second thoughts about the merits of planned parenthood and a no-growth strategy, since it would deplete the already small Jewish population and increase its vulnerability.

Withdrawing from an earlier global ecology to a particularist ethnic one, the greater concern becomes the survival of the ethnic group. The threat of extinction, whether by genocide or simple attrition, catalyzes a counteroffensive to preserve the endangered ethnic species by increased fecundity. During Stein's brief study in seminary, one of the rabbis passionately insisted that it was the duty of every Jewish couple to have one child more than they plan, in order to make up for those Jews slaughtered by Hitler. The horrors of the past would be reversed in some small way by pious acts of the present. What is at issue for blacks, Jews, and white ethnics alike is certainly not mere *survival*, but the survival and revitalization of an *identity*. In the present crisis cults, the future is *replenished* both culturally and biologically. Since mere existence without the support of the new defensive identity is unthinkable, all former universalist schemes become dangers to the species. But the real danger to the real species becomes ethnicity and nationalism itself—Jewish, white ethnic, or otherwise—whose short-term victories promise not a new florescence but extinction. Paradoxically, the New Ethnic solutions to the psychological fear of annihilation and loss hasten and accelerate what they claim to impede. Through the ingathering of the New Ethnics' tribal kinfolk, those very others who are necessary to their survival are declared to be unrelated.*

---

*In January 1977, Alex Haley's autobiographical odyssey *Roots* appeared as an eight-part television epic, attracting some eighty million viewers to the final episode. Its immense popularity suggests that *Roots* is a nodal cultural "event" that can inform us as much about ourselves as about Haley's identity. In the aftermath of the TV series, there occurred sporadic racial incidents. Through identification with past injustices,

Models of the White Ethnic Movement: Summing Up

In this section we present an encapsulation of our preceding analysis of the White Ethnic Cultural Movement. Figure 1 is a tabular paradigm of segmentary oppositional cults (or movements) in contemporary American culture, highlighting the wider context within which the White Ethnic Movement must be viewed. It seeks to describe some of the similarities and dissimilarities between groups, their internal segmentation, and the thematic relation which each shares with all the others and the American mainstream in time of crisis. By virtue of the very dynamism and unrest of both mainstream and sectarian American culture, this paradigm is necessarily incomplete. The student of American culture should attend as much to cultism generically as to any cult in particular. Figure 2 is simply the addition of a dimension not contained in Figure 1, highlighting more clearly the white ethnic group and its opposition to other cultural groups.

Figure 3 is a tabular paradigm of the process of nativist-militancy

---

some blacks sought retribution through name-calling and physical conflict, while, through identification with the masters, some whites insisted on continued superiority, telling blacks they once owned them. *Roots* also produced a tidal wave of personal genealogical searches. After all, if Alex Haley could trace *his* past through the labyrinths of slavery (with its built-in uprooting and forced name changing), couldn't *anyone* trace his lineage, claim noble pedigree, find out who he is?

Roots was adopted by many in the service of the New Ethnicity—encouraged, to some degree, by traces of us-them, either-or stereotyping in Haley's new black history. However, unlike most of the New Ethnic histories, Haley's is not affixed on the past. We suggest that *Roots'* deeper and wider appeal lies in the paradoxical fact that while Haley's book is about ethnicity, it also transcends it. It begins with the African past and moves toward the Afro-American present and future. *Roots* is not simply indulgence in a glorious past; it is *process,* from origins to destiny. The protagonist is not Kunta Kinte, the romanticized warrior-ancestor with whom Haley begins; the protagonist is the unfolding of the family history itself, one with deepening *American* roots. From the beginning in Gambia, to the triumphant march under patriarch Chicken George to farmland purchased in Tennessee, *freedom* is the metaphor of rootedness. Finally, *Roots* is profoundly American in its odyssey: the immigrant-pioneer spirit, the vow not to give up, the keeping of the faith, the passing on of the dream of freedom from one generation to the next. *Roots* is not a rite of ancestor worship, but, oddly enough, a crescendo of cumulative rootedness whose destiny is the fulfillment of the *American Dream.* It portrays anything but the retreat into the tribal cave. Unlike the New Ethnicity, which is based on fixation and regression, Haley's central theme, ever unfinished, is transcendence. (For a fuller discussion of *Roots,* see Howard F. Stein, "In Search of 'Roots': An Epic of Origins and Destiny," *Journal of Popular Culture,* 1977.)

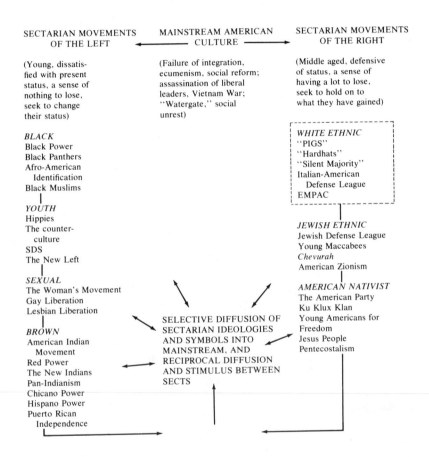

Figure 1   Paradigm of Segmentary Opposition Cults in Relation to Contemporary American Culture

formation at both the individual and group levels. It shows the dynamic and temporal relationship between cultural ideology, socioeconomic crisis, and militant-nativist identity formation. Following each column vertically, the reader can see how ethnic identity resynthesis precipitates out of a particular cultural ideal, is catalyzed by crisis, and emerges in rigid totalistic form (personal and group boundaries) through opposition and polarization.

In Figure 4, we present a transformational schema for the psychodynamics of the ethnic imperative (and cognate nativist movements). It shows how the distinctive features of primary narcissism are transformed, leading through regression to shame and rage, culminating in chronic narcissistic rage and its systematization in a new identity.[34]

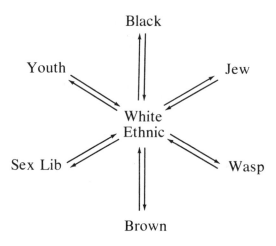

Figure 2   Oppositional Sociogram of the White Ethnic Movement

Group Level		*Individual Level*
(Sociocultural)	-----	(Psychological)
Dominant Cultural Ideology	-----	Personality Ideal
Socioeconomic Crisis (Status Denigration)	-----	Identity Crisis (Heightened Self-Consciousness)

Identity Resynthesis

		Affirmation of the Negative
Reactive Oppositional Process (Polarization)	-----	Identity as Positive and Repudiation of the Former Positive Identity as Negative (Polarization)
Emergence and Consolidation of Persistent Cultural Identity System: Totalistic Cultural Configuration with Fixed, Exclusive Social Boundaries	-----	Emergence and Consolidation of the Militant Ethnic Personality: Totalistic Personality Configuration with Rigid Ego Boundary

Figure 3   Nativist-Militancy Formation at the Individual and Group Levels

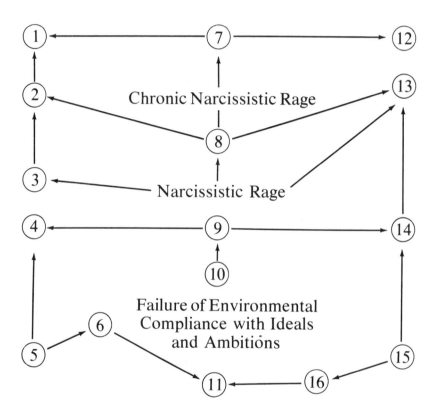

Figure 4   Transformational Schema for the Psychodynamics of
Nativist Movements

1. LIMITLESSNESS, Ego Expansion of Sense of Power, Failures projected onto the Repudiated Self Object, FANATICISM, AGGRESSION, and VENGEANCE, Projecting all Dissociated Negative Attributes onto Adversary, Destructive Impulses Directed (Displaced) outward rather than against Ego, Heightened Sadism, Preventive Attack, Turning Passive into Active, Sharpening Cognitive Apparatus into Service of Narcissistic Rage

2. Attempt to Reestablish CONTROL over a Narcissistically Experienced World, Guilt experienced as PERSECUTION, NEW AMBITION

3. SELF-RIGHTEOUSNESS, Omnipotence, Grandiosity, INNOCENCE, Persistent Grudge, Need for Omniscience and Total Control

4. RAGE, Reawakened GUILT, Helplessness, Hopelessness, Disturbance in the Omnipotence of Grandiose Self

5. OMNIPOTENCE of the Grandiose Self (Power) (Primary Narcissism)

6. Mastery, Initiative, Competence ("doing")

7. Narcissistic PARANOID Position Underlying the "OPPOSITIONAL PROCESS" Expressed in Personal and Cultural Symbolism and Relations

8. NEW IDENTITY: Simultaneous Liberation and Repression, Narcissistic-Paranoid Configuration; Choice of NEGATIVE IDENTITY

9. REGRESSION: Deneutralization, Desublimation, Reprimitivization of Archaic Conflicts, Returning of Repressed, Oedipal and Pre-Oedipal

10. DISILLUSIONMENT, Demoralization, Alienation, Crisis of Identity, Sense of Absolute Relative Deprivation, Identity Confusion

11. Culturally Based COUNTERCATHEXIS (Defense) and TRANSFORMATION of Narcissism into Self-Esteem

12. EXPOSURE of the ENEMY, Idealized, Purified Conception of the Innocent and Perfect Self, STEREOTYPING of the ENEMY as Inhuman, Division of the Good Self/Evil Other

13. Preoccupation with "Identity" Inviolability and Consolidation of PERSONAL BOUNDARIES, Concern over "Pollution," Protection, Merger with Idealized Self-Other, NEW IDEALS, Need for approval through mirroring, Defiant SHAMELESSNESS, PRIDE, EXHIBITIONISM, Insistence on Being Admired, Superiority, Withdrawal from Comparisons, Active Comparisons with Others, Overestimation of self, Underestimation of other, Search for IDEALIZED FIGURES, Desire to Merge with Overarchaic Omnipotent Self Object

14. SHAME, Vulnerability, Exposure, Feelings of Inferiority, Emptiness, Loss of Self-Esteem, Disturbance in the Exhibition of the Grandiose Self

15. EXHIBITIONISM of the Grandiose Self (Primary Narcissism)

16. Basic Trust, Acceptance, Worth, Personal Uniqueness ("Being")

8 Beyond the Ethnic Imperative

Any alternative to the magical thinking of the New Ethnicity cannot itself promise magic. While the New Ethnicity can afford the luxury of easy, total, and final solutions, we cannot. Science proceeds from uncertainty to tentativeness. Magic proceeds with omniscience and omnipotence. Our reflections in this chapter attempt to take note of human realities and possibilities that transcend the ethnic imperative and embrace what may be called a human imperative. We approach this through categories or themes most central to the New Ethnicity itself: pluralism, nationalism, education, cultural therapy, community, racism, and identity. We now discuss each in turn.

Ethnicity and Pluralism

The ultimate consequence of the New Ethnicity is to eradicate the very diversity it idealizes. The individual is conceptualized and treated as representing a single category or "class" (in the logical or mathematical sense). While claiming to enhance individual freedom and diversity, the New Ethnicity constricts freedom, seeks to organize diversity because it fears ambiguity, and tries to create conformity and uniformity so that it is not threatened by those very human differences it celebrates. While claiming to respect the individual, the New Ethnicity's goal and consequence is to destroy the individual by offering him or her the freedom of a one-dimensional identity.[1] While promising to create an open and fluid social system, pluralism is in fact a static and vigilantly defended closed system. It fixes hierarchy while idealizing egalitarianism or collaterality; it closes alternatives while claiming to open them up.

Admittedly, human life begins with the experience of inequality, which is present, in various forms, from the most primitive to the most modern society. The question, however, is whether inequality is mitigated and overcome by mutuality, mobility, fluidity, achievement by merit, or the inclusiveness of personal networks. By an ingenious sleight of hand—or ideology—the New Ethnic pluralism is able to re-order and maximize social hierarchy while offering itself as a cultural therapy that abolishes hierarchy. Yet, the New Ethnicity freezes while it claims to thaw, and it refeudalizes while claiming to modernize.

Demands for group rights, "affirmative action," "quotas," and the hiring of personnel on the basis of ascriptive criteria are an extension of the pluralist principle of treating the individual as a corporate entity, as a representative of a taxonomic class. It is an example of the relationship between a unit within the mosaic (or a bloc of units) and the total mosaic. In 1975, Slavic-American leaders and organizations in the Pittsburgh area applied pressure on the University of Pittsburgh to hire a Slav as chairman of the Slavic department. After all, they claimed, a majority of the Pittsburgh-area population was Slavic-American (a dubious assertion), and this should be reflected in such a symbolic position. And, moreover, who is more qualified to direct a Slavic Studies program than a Slav? That many non sequiturs abound in this logic is beside the point. The point is that equality of opportunity is dubiously defined to mean special privilege. In 1976, under pressure from the Illinois division of the Polish-American Congress, the midwestern regional office of the U.S. Department of Housing and Urban Development (HUD) extended affirmative action policies to Polish-Americans— marking the first time a federal agency has agreed to proportionate representation among its employees. It seems that in this region (as reported in the *Oklahoma Journal,* April 27, 1976), while the Polish-American population is 19.8 percent, only 9.8 percent of HUD employees are Polish-Americans. Thus Polish-Americans are "under-represented." It is only a few more steps until civil service, private industry, and so forth, are likewise besieged. But what, we might pause to ask, is a Polish-American? What criteria of "full bloods," "half bloods," "quarter bloods," and the like, should be used to determine a genuine Polish-American? And is culture to be determined from without (or for that matter from within) by *genealogy?* (Many New Ethnics go so far as to insist that ethnic culture is an entirely subjective experience; by extension, it would seem that one could imagine himself to be a member of any group!) And of course demographic statistics can be deftly manipulated to inflate any wish into reality. American Indians, we understand, are eligible for affirmative action only if they are one-fourth Indian or more. Paradoxically, no matter how one discriminates positively, the criteria chosen will also have the effect of discriminating negatively for members of the same "group." Why not affirmative action on the basis of a Polish surname? This would discriminate against those with Polish or half-Polish mothers. But what if the father is half-Polish and half-German and identifies with his Germanness: How Polish shall we say he is, even if he has a Polish surname? The assumption is inevitable that (perpetuating the stereotype) all Poles are alike in experience, origin, aspiration, discrimination, and underrepresentation. Is a Polish-American in, say, San Diego, the *same* as one in Cleveland, Gary, or Pittsburgh? And on what basis did those 9.8 percent who are HUD employees obtain *their* jobs? And should we expect the quality of HUD operations to improve if hiring is more heavily weighted toward the applicant's origins than to his or her acquired and proven competence?

It is probably only a matter of time until every self-defined and politically powerful *minority* is able to apply pressure from its lobby for a reparative and remedial quota, thereby making the American mosaic a collectivity of fragmented islands united only by a sea of discontent and animosity. We would also predict that less visible and politically influential (and exploitable) minorities will be less fortunate in their demands for proportional representation—although the bandwagon is certain to be crowded. With the prevalence of ethno-political opportunism, the gerrymandering of equality is certain to make some more equal than others on the tranquil American animal farm. At worst this should lead to open competition in the name of multicultural pluralism, and to personal, corporate, and governmental manipulation of quotas, thereby corrupting its original intent. Or, if we awaken quickly enough to the prospect ahead, it may demonstrate the absurdity of the quota system and lead to its dismantling rather than proliferation. The Nuremberg laws in pluralist guise are the last things a democracy needs.

We believe that racial (or such similar *we-they* taxonomic systems as ethnic, religious, gender, age) classifications cannot be "benign," whatever be their authority or precedent, legal or moral.[2] Discrimination from within or without, direct or reverse, personal or institutional, now is to be the paradoxical means of eradicating discrimination and its effects. Can one inequality plus one inequality make two equalities? Can you undo the effects of history by repeating it with different victims or casualties? Whatever your mathematics, you cannot get rid of discrimination by discriminating! Yet pluralism in its many guises commits this very error of epistemology and praxis (using the cause of the dis-ease as its remedy). After all, an ideological system of redistribution based on a psychology of retribution or guilt-riddenness (rationalized, to be sure) can only be one-sided. And with it, the pursuit of excellence is sacrificed to the pursuit of percentages. Standards based on competence are replaced by standards that are *functionally* irrelevant (at best).

With the individual self-identified and merged with the group, individual interests become an expression of group interests (creating conflict as often as accord). The New Ethnic demands and is often accorded mobility, social honor (status), occupational niches, and justice on the basis of ascriptive criteria. One is in a way able to succeed by individual achievement once he or she is forcibly accepted on the basis of group membership, although both success and stability in the newly opened niche are tenuous. Psychoculturally, we suggest that rewards and opportunities bestowed on the basis of what one *is* perpetuate the very problem the movement attempts to resolve—both for the giver and the receiver. The gift is necessarily in bad faith; and the recipients do not feel that they are valued for being themselves, but because of the preferential category to which they now belong. A person is still treated as a *class* rather than as an individual—though now by choice instead of passive condemnation and endurance. The category (*ethnic, black, Slav, female*) is asserted from within rather than imposed from without. The negative stereotype, now transformed into positive through inversion (reaction formation), is the basis of the New Ethnic's self-concept and subsumes those other categories salient to the class. If before, one *failed* because he or she was evaluated ascriptively, now one *succeeds* for identical reasons. The lack of a sense of initiative, accomplishment, mastery, and competence pervades both conditions, not merely the one preceding the New Ethnic Movement. One is still not one's self, but another's category (even if it is a newly internalized ethnic category), and continues to see himself or herself through another's eyes despite the ego-bolstering effect of new personal and cultural boundaries. It is in part the function of belief in the new pluralist ideology to eradicate self-doubt by putting a distance between the New Ethnic and the outer source of shame and guilt. The persistence of the internalized feelings, however, is attested to by the need for reassurance by the ideology. The merger of individual identity into corporate-group identity, the fusion of self-interest with group-interest, is both a means of combating the negative stereotype and of assuring that outsiders will continue to perceive members of the group in terms of the stereotype.

Affirmative action and similar pluralist affirmations lock the individual (while rewarding him or her) into the very straitjacket he or she may want to escape.[3] One is rewarded not for competence, but for being black, Polish, or female, not for being an individual, but for representing a group. The New Ethnic is never real, but only a symbol. There can be no individual justice where group or corporate justice prevails because the individual must be sacrificed in the guise of being saved.

Ethnicity and Nationalism

In this book we have argued that the crisis cult is the *fons et origo* of nationalistic movements and that the New Ethnicity is a crisis cult. Such doctrines as pluralism, self-determination, liberation, restoration, autonomy and such psychological traits as xenophobia, radical inclusion and exclusion, rigid delineation of group and ego boundaries, the search for the past, romanticism, idealization, and haughty pride are expressions of the common denominator linking all such movements. To ask, however, "What kind of nationalistic movement is the New Ethnicity?" or "Is the New Ethnicity a genuine nationalism?" (since its goal is not the formation of a nation-state) is to ask the wrong kind of question.

Likewise, to distinguish between the "nationalism of majorities" and the "opposition nationalism" of subjected peoples, to contrast primitive and modern, dividing between "history" and "prehistory," is, we suggest, to commit the fallacy of misplaced concreteness. To subdivide *nationalism* etymologically into *great* and *small, majority* and *minority,* and the like, is to engage in intellectual scholasticism that severely limits ethnographic and cross-historic comparison because it mistakes age-specific and social organization-specific content for the underlying dynamic and structure.[4]

We suggest, moreover, that it is fruitless scientifically to attempt to salvage the humanism of nationalistic movements by insisting that they are at root "part-ideologies" directed toward securing justice and freedom—"unity" and "self-determination"—while they may subsequently be appropriated toward irrational *völkisch* and authoritarian ends.[5] Intense love and devotion to one's own kind is intrinsically bound up with equal and opposite displacement and projection of hatred onto the outgroup(s). This is true on psychodynamic and comparative grounds. *We-they* bifurcation of humans and less-than-humans operates from a cult's inception and is essential to its self-definition.

The pioneering studies of nationalism by Hans Kohn, Carleton Hayes, and Boyd Shafer propose that nationalism proper belongs to the period following the French Revolution, and that those sects and primitive movements somewhat analogous to them belong to prehistory. G. D. Kerr, however, has clearly described patriotic-nationalistic sentiments and attitudes among the fifteenth-century French deriving from conflict with the English.[6] The dividing line would therefore seem to be pushed further back, calling into question the notion of medieval universalism. Nevertheless, the preoccupation is still with the culture- and time-bound notion of the nation-state.

Several scholars have recently distinguished between the nationalisms of the great and of the small, regarding *small* as "the opposition nationalism" of subjected peoples.[7] We would suggest that opposition (whose psychodynamic root is the narcissistic-paranoid position) is inherent in all crisis cult-nativist-revitalization movements throughout the spectrum of peoples *large* and *small*, peoples whose political, territorial, or religious autonomy is recently or remotely removed; and although in political-territorial-ideological form and symbolism, nationalism can be said to pertain to post-1789 nation-building movements, its psychocultural substratum is identical for movements throughout history and at all levels of social organization. It is the continuity of nationalism, pervading all sociocultural forms it takes, that we emphasize—while recognizing that for other purposes time periods and forms of social organization may be useful units for controlled comparison. All we ask is that what in fact unites them all not be omitted. The *genus* is everywhere and always "crisis cult"; the *species* may be nation-state, ethnic group, religion, or aesthetics.

In dynastic Egypt, the shamanistic Mosaic rebellion of the enslaved Semites eventually led to the establishment of a Hebrew theocratic nation-state. Some centuries before the Mosaic-Semitic cult occurred a rebellion of the Hamitic "natives" against the Semitic "foreigners," resulting in the expulsion of the former ethnic elite by the formerly oppressed Hamitic minority. Who, we might ask, was the majority and the minority in this and similar cases? Oppressors of one generation or era frequently become the oppressed of another, and conversely. And what shall we label such movements as this: "ethnic," "national," "religious," "proto-political," or "proletarian"? Here we get into epistemic trouble because we are looking from the *outside* through our own categories and thus cannot include movements such as the Hamitic-Semitic in our conceptualizations. And specialization in one historic era or culture area is no legitimate excuse for ignoring what is outside our chosen focus or for requiring similarity in external form, in order to meet our aesthetic criteria for relevance or for inclusion in classifications with which we are familiar.

A brief example should reveal how what on first inspection seems different is at a deeper level the same. Take the distinction between nationalisms of the *great* and *small*. Every majority group was once, or remains, a minority within the wider social framework with respect to which they compare themselves. What counts is the subjective feeling of the population participating in the cult or movement. It can be argued that all crisis cults involve a profound sense of inferiority, leading to the heroic and often sinister attempt to reverse it to one of superiority (never mere parity). Status deprivation—the anxiety a New Ethnic experiences when comparing himself with another and finding himself wanting—is a common denominator to crisis cults. How people subjectively perceive and define their situation becomes their reality, their sense of the objective nature of the world. Real territorial size, real economic advances, and the like are simply not experienced as *real* from within. Whatever the size of the territory or the population involved, all peoples swept up into crisis cult movements feel and perceive themselves to be small, vulnerable, exploited, oppressed, captive, and in mortal danger of annihilation. All cultists feel themselves to be subjugated members of a minority group that seeks release—and revenge. What seems to count most is not so much political or economic oppression as status deprivation, the discrepancy between a minority's perception of himself and his perception of the other who is, or has been, the standard of measure. One thereafter seeks to reduce the anxiety by overcoming the overbearing sense of self-diminution. While the sense of such deprivation is always relative (in terms of one's current status and what one aspires to), the experience of this deprivation is *absolute:* the New Ethnic feels depleted, empty, separated by an unbridgeable chasm between his wishes and current realities. Through regression to a narcissistic-paranoid position, fantasy performs the impossible and conquers the chasm.

The common experience of infancy provides the body imagery and the relative sense of absolute powerlessness which, together with rage, infuses whatever be the real geography, population size, or level of political organization. Thus such a gargantuan geopolitical entity as Russia felt closed in, surrounded, and sought warm water ports whose symbolism was as important as its obvious economic significance. Likewise, the German desperation for *Lebensraum* was an attempt to be free of those internal and external enemies (parent imagoes) who had surrounded, defiled, and conspired against German manhood and womanhood. Finally, we clearly discern in the so-called primitive cults of prehistory (even if contemporary or nearly so) both the dynamic of opposition and the world-body-ego imagery of powerlessness transformed through regression into omnipotence and omniscience (e.g., the American Indian Ghost Dance of the 1890s, the Melanesian "Cargo Cults" of the 1940s and 1950s). As movements of simultaneous modernization and atavistic reaction, they sought the immediate removal of the enemy aliens (white man), the end to acculturation (anti-Westernizing), the restoration (or return) of the status of ancestors (a new origin myth), and the like. The primitive and modern are essentially the identical movement, but at different levels of social organization and with different cultural markers.

Psychodynamically, all are equally primitive, in the sense of being regressed. In the narcissistic-paranoid position, the individual is simultaneously preoccupied with shoring up permeable ego boundaries and extending them to the limits of the universe. Such expansiveness of the body-ego, leading to a confusion of self and world, and to a suffusion of world with the hallucinosis of self, provides the ontogeny of the universal need for *Lebensraum* in all crisis cults. The adult who has regressed to the psychology of the pregenital narcissist has voracious and limitless demands on the world, knows not the meaning of "no," and magically exercises his self-deluded omnipotence and omniscience in his own impotent behalf—and *as* an adult he can appropriate the whole arsenal of rational technique to implement his irrational needs and premises. Weston La Barre believes that "the propensity to magic cults and religions derives . . . from the psychobiological neoteny . . . of the human animal, since each individual has passed through a magical (patterned on talking and walking) and a religious (nuclear-familial) stage of ego-differentiation to which, under stress, he may regress. World view is thus a function of ego differentiation and consequent psychosexual maturation. Similarly, cultural institutions roughly manifest *degrees of hallucinosis* in their epistemological grounds."[8]

Crisis cults, of which the New Ethnicity and the species of nationalism are expressions, would seem to be the most extreme cultural institutionalization of fantasy. Such cults know nothing of the Reality Principle and, as new Gods, make over the world in their own image. A "successful" cult, both routinized and sustained in fanaticism, is able to accomplish through self-deception what is impossible to the diurnally nourished mind: destroy critical faculties and coerce reality to assume the form and content of fantasy, thereby providing confirmation of reality testing. The paranoid, true enough, cannot accept cognitive feedback dissonant with his own projective system. But he can deftly arrange for the social and natural world to re-present to him what he wishes to see—and in fact placed in the field of vision. It is this that is most dangerous about the paranoid and the cultist, that with consummate skill he can make his dream come true (with obdurate disregard for the nightmare it may inflict on others). The politically mobilized escapism of the New Utopians invariably creates in its wake a mass of refugees and casualties. A sensitive observer of the New Ethnicity can sense behind the beguiling protestation of innocence *only* a hysteric denial of what is really going on. The ethnic cultist, the nationalist, the religionist, and the nativist share a common world: the loss of vexatious reality in order to regain the primeval unity of childhood. As La Barre asks: "What advantage is it to gain one's soul in eternal dream, yet lose the whole waking world?"

Ethnicity and Racism

To argue that ethnicity often functions as a ploy for racial exclusion, or that the principle of hierarchy insures group stratification and inequality, is *not* to simplify American culture history into a history of racism. Rather, it is a history of ambivalence and contradictions of values and motivations. Racism is but one expression of this. But it is woefully incorrect to say that anyone who has succeeded has necessarily done so unfairly, that one person's gain is another's loss— although the myth of the self-made man without the restraint of civility certainly has examples in life, and in fact is the basis of many admired legendary American heroes. American culture, however, is bipolar, not unipolar, in its values; and to see from only one pole is to have an unbalanced picture of the whole. This whole is in fact dialectic: between open and closed, internationalist and isolationist, cosmopolitan and localistic, melting pot and Anglo-conformist, inclusive and exclusive, cooperative and competitive, revolutionary and anachronistic, egalitarian and authoritarian.

Moreover, the process of "ethnic succession," mobility, and the like, cannot be seen as wholly imposed by external (American) forces. Such factors as ethno-cultural values, attitudes, beliefs, interpersonal relations, and intraethnic class structure function to inhibit, retard, encourage, or accelerate the rate and kind of acculturation. They act and have acted over generations to select for an ecological niche in the American sociocultural system. *Success* and *achievement* do not everywhere have a common meaning. Poles and Slovaks, for instance, placing a premium on security, stability, and dependency, may see many of their own aspirations as being fulfilled, although from without they may be seen as less mobile, less successful, or less achievement-oriented. This is not to minimize the conflict between dependency and independence in Polish- and Slovak-American culture, but to point to the predominant direction and structure of its resolution. Racial and ethnic exclusion and discrimination play an important role in American opportunity structure, but, as we have seen, limitation comes from within as well as without.

The New Ethnicity, perceiving the world in paranoid-narcissistic terms, rationalizes the suffering and failure of white ethnics by insisting that the only way others succeeded was at their expense. While in terms of social reality, the New Ethnics see themselves on the periphery, in terms of their psychodynamics they occupy the center of the world. Through such ideas of reference, they are able to deny their own envy, by denying that those who have achieved some goal or made something of themselves really did it on their own—a way of bringing them down to the New Ethnic's own level, in fantasy if not in fact. A follower of the New Ethnicity does not see himself separate from the other who has succeeded: thus, if another made it, one feels depleted, a failure at the other's expense. Envy and narcissism—and genuine racism—notwithstanding, many have made achievements great and small that are based purely and simply on hard work, patience, thrift, tenacity, and a faith in the future, that the effort was worth the sacrifice, if not for immediate realization in one's life, then for the ethnics' own children. This is equally true for the Wallaceites of Gary and Milwaukee, the so-called racists of South Boston, and the still silent majority of white ethnics throughout the urban-industrial east and central United States. This does not deny voting patterns, prejudice, or urban-peasant conservatism, but emphasizes that people are not unidimensional.

For those who have a vested interest in the all-inclusive explanation of racism, it will be a blow to self-esteem to have to admit that in many circumstances an individual is simply irrelevant in the life of another. South Bostonians do not have Roxbury on their minds twenty-four hours a day. White mill workers, heavily unemployed in the North, do not have blacks or Wallace perpetually on their minds. For the white ethnics who imagine the WASP as the ever-menacing threat to identity, dignity, and opportunity, it is hard to imagine the dehumanized enemy living the semblance of a normal life, not even thinking about, let alone plotting against, vulnerable white ethnic humanity. Moreover, if one admits to factors besides racism affecting achievement, one must consider the influence of cultural values, roles, attitudes, and beliefs; personality organization that varies from group to group; culture-specific patterns of family interaction and socialization; the nature of peer group influence within the ethnic group; the socioeconomic or "class" stratification *within* the group— in sum, intrinsic, endogenous variables brought to the social situation, brought to the host society, and which cannot be reduced to external, macrosocial influences.

Many blacks and white ethnics assert that the only way WASPs and Jews and others have made it is by keeping them down—equally a projection of what they would do if they had the opportunity. Oppression and exploitation explain both another's achievement and one's own failure. Those who have not, deserve; those who have, do not deserve what they have. Those who insist that in America the only way you gain is at someone else's expense, seek to gain at another's expense—only these New Ethnics claim to merit success by moral or historic right (to correct ancient or contemporary injustices and inequities). To redress the imbalance, they practice the same opportunism and moralism, under the guise of opportunity and idealism, that they attribute to the historic adversary. The invocation of racism, exploitation, and oppression becomes a means of rationalizing why members of some groups who are presumably overrepresented and who have disproportionately too much wealth, status, or power, should be deprived of what they have achieved, while members of the oppressed groups should take their place to make restitution and reparation for past and present inequities. This legitimation for "making it" is a barely disguised variant on the American theme of making it at someone else's expense. Only here the justification is not the (amoral?) myth of the self-made man, but deprivation and the moral obligation to make amends. The intention and consequences are identical: superiority, not equality. The criteria for deserving or meriting are simply inverted: from having made it on one's own, to having failed to make it. The American principles of hierarchy and opportunism again prevail, only rationalized to sound much more high minded than they are. After all, to be explicit about the intentions of the New Ethnicity would be "un-American"!

Ethnicity and Education

Ethnic resocialization under the aegis of ethnic studies, and likewise, the hurried re-search for ethnicity on the part of professionals, is another expression of the corporate pluralistic identity model that makes a mockery of diversity while championing its cause. Accordingly, ethnic education is not a matter of drawing out the ethnicity that is within, but of force feeding it from without. Being Hungarian or Slovak or Jewish is no longer a private matter, but becomes a publicly induced self-disclosure. New Ethnics are constantly inspecting others and themselves, lest either not live up to the new stereotype. Ethnic studies curricula provide the most up-to-date methods of thought reform, insisting that those under its influence are really becoming themselves. While the white ethnics accuse past American education of trying to erase ethnic awareness, ethnic studies stands ready to homogenize and de-Americanize ethnicity—in the name of enhancing difference. Pluralistic education does not so much recognize difference as create it and institutionalize it. The goal of ethnic studies programs is the recognition, appreciation, and tolerance of difference, creating the one out of the many. Pluralistic ethnophiles will not leave to parents, neighbors, peers, time, and chance the dangers of differences taking care of themselves. They must insist on the primordiality and ineradicability of differences that are *then* to be appreciated and tolerated.

There is a great gap between the simplistic differences the new pluralists need and the subtle and infinite variety of differences, similarities, overlaps, and changes in the real ethno-American world—from which the spokesmen are ideologically remote. We might take a few cues from children (rather than parents) who, not forced by their better knowing adult benefactors to act out parental categories, will resolve their differences rather than insist on them. Just as the new pluralists claim to abolish hierarchical evaluation through a horizontal model that does not culturally rank, so in education they would emphasize that the socialization of categories are identities based on ethnic differences need not be disparaging. The effect, however, is the same as that discussed earlier. As Edmund Leach notes, discussing ethnic studies, "to be different is to be odd; to be odd, is to be inferior." He later writes:

> "Our customs are different" is a claim for autonomy from external control; "Their customs are different" is a claim for the exclusion of newcomers. But in either case the assertion that we (or they) have customs which are different and by which we (or they) can be

readily distinguished *as a group* is a matter of belief rather than fact. My worry about the use of ethnographic film and other devices of visual reality in schools (or television or elsewhere) is that they provide (ready made) a set of images about "their customs which are different", and these images can be attached to any group of "others" that happen to be available."[9]

We would extend this observation generically to ethnic studies whose intellectual framework and business is to research, discover, package, distribute, and sell ready-made images, sounds, tastes, and styles that show how *we* are different from *them*. Because the individual is assumed to be a member of a category, he or she is treated as indistinguishable from that category. In the process of simplifying ethnic reality, ethnic studies will ironically be unable to describe or explain anyone in particular. What Michael Novak has made of the WASPs, ethnic studies will make of the PIGS.

An extension of the organic pluralist model is that one not only needs to be confirmed by the curricula of ethnic studies, but by a representative of the ethnic group with which he can identify. After all, identification is the basis for a healthy identity, and what could be healthier for a New Ethnic than identification with a teacher of one's own kind, who surely shares the same primordial experience? Since "only an insider can know," "only an insider can teach." All of this ignores, of course, the fact that education for individuation, mobility, fluidity, achievement, and inclusiveness has been successfully imparted, not by primordialists and nativists, but by objects of identification who represented to one degree or another success and acculturation into the wider American identity. It was not merely a matter of force feeding. Identification was on the basis of what the children and youth themselves wanted to be, seeing in their American elders, the promise of their own future. We might also note that too much attention is placed on the school and formal education, and too little on the home, the neighborhood, the peer group, the work group, and other similar networks—who teach the lived-in hopes and reality of American history, civics, and political science before one ever enters the classroom, and perhaps in spite of whatever is taught.

Ethnicity and Cultural Therapy

The proponents of pluralism, from "the right to be different" to those who demand "secession" (resegregation), seem to argue that American culture is especially culpable because of its insistence on homogeneity and homogenization; that is, insistence on acculturation toward uniformity has been a traditional sickness of American culture. The proliferation of heterogeneity is presumably a sign of the emergence of American cultural health. The New Ethnicity is to perform a major curative function for the estrangements and anxieties of American life.

At the 1973 annual meetings of the American Anthropological Association, Oliver Osborne, in a paper on "Social Processes and Symptom Patterns," argued that there had occurred considerable changes in psychiatric symptomatology and difficulties in applying traditional diagnostic classes to current clinical problems.[10] The image of America as Melting Pot was changing to the image of a pluralist society. What was once called deviant behavior is now normal, legitimate behavior. What was once controlled is now expressed, what Osborne calls the "cathartic strategy." Standardized goals, definitions of appropriateness, and the normal, have given way from a single uniform model to multiple models (in street talk, it's called "different strokes for different folks," each of whom "lets it all hang out"). Institutional change has led to new images of self and society, leading in turn to new meanings, and in turn to multiple definitions of the situation.

From his study of the changes in presenting symptomatology in first admissions over twenty-five years in Seattle, Osborne notes that there is an increase and diversification of symptoms. Earlier there had been socialization for work in the context of a national ideology; now emphasis is on socialization for idiosyncratic qualities. Traditionally, mental illness is conceptualized as a thought disorder. Yet there has been a decrease in the symptom that is recognized as mental illness. There has been a break from traditional images and an increase in the diversity of symptoms. This in turn relates to the availability of individual alternatives and expression. Deviant behavior formerly labeled as abnormal is now normal.

This, of course, is all very positively valued and is seen as a sign of the emergence of cultural health. The twilight of coercive American uniformitarianism is celebrated, but it can also be recognized as a simple inversion of standards, of norms, of values, expressions of such psychological ego defenses as denial, repression, rationalization. It is yet another expression of the oppositional process. The exuberance of alternatives and diversity of symptoms can be seen as symptomatic of cultural breakdown rather than stability. In her pioneering paper titled "The Concept of Culture and the Psychosomatic Approach" (1947), Margaret Mead wrote of:

the possibility that there is a correlation between concentration of deviant attitudes in specific somatic symptoms and the lack of homogeneity of the culture. In most homogeneous cultures [note that homogeneity is not a peculiar affliction of American culture] we may expect to find consistent slight pathologies, as well as consistent and systematic somatic modifications. Furthermore, we may expect to find a certain amount of aggravation of the consistent pathology in individuals with greater constitutional vulnerability or among those who have been subjected to unusually severe pressures. But the extent to which we find an exuberance of somatic expressions of varieties of psychic conflict or persistent character strain may well be correlated with cultural heterogeneity. In a heterogeneous culture, individual life experiences differ so markedly from one another that almost every individual may find the existing cultural forms of expression inadequate to express his peculiar bent, and so be driven into more and more special forms of psychosomatic expression. It is well known that mass hysterias tend to occur among primitive people during periods of rapid cultural change when individuals are extremely disoriented. Movements like the Ghost Dance, or the Vailala Madness, simply swept through a whole district. It is quite possible that the speed with which a disturbed population seizes upon one of these standard hysterias is a function of the extent to which large numbers of individuals have been using divergent idiosyncratic symptoms to express disorientation, all of which will be replaced by the new socially acceptable form of behavior.[11]

The reader will, of course, recognize that the New Ethnicity and its more generic form, identity revitalization, performs precisely this last function, that of a complete reorientation to overcome the idiosyncratically expressed disorientation, but in the name of pluralism, alternatives, and diversity. Within the movement itself, deviation from the sectarian norm is heresy (e.g., to show anything but contempt for the WASP outgroup) as the new values and ideological elements become systematized and standardized, as the new True Believers become the newly faithful, and as a uniform dogma and homogeneous community of the faithful emerge. Pluralism and diversity become an ideologic means of maintaining the boundary between separate groups and maintaining uniformity within each of the boundaries. To rejoice in the exuberance of symptomatology is, to say the least, misplaced; to accept the native definition of the situation is to embrace and rationalize the native delusion, not to understand it. It is to mistake the cure for the disease.

Ethnic studies is one such social medicament—and palliative. According to the ethnophiles, if the schools and universities were to implement ethnic studies, a whole assortment of chronic social problems would evaporate: students' short attention span and lapse of interest in school; the eruptions of violence and negativism; the lack of discipline and respect for authority; the omnipresence of depression, despair, and drugs; the often unbridgeable "generation gap." The young will be saved before they have a chance to stray too far, and will be spared the conflicts of the preceding generation so eager to teach them. The future will be redeemed. Provided with a neatly and comprehensively packaged answer to the question "Who am I?," students will then be liberated of their burdensome identity crisis. The problem, surely, is one of identity. If only young people knew exactly who they were and who everyone else was, problems associated with identity would vanish. There would be no identity confusion, for everyone would know exactly where he stood—and where everyone else belonged. Ethnicity stands eagerly available to bind up the nation's wounds of identity. Perhaps the developmental crisis of identity could even be averted if a rite of passage is intense enough to prohibit and repress any normal questioning, doubt, or rebellion.

Pluralistic education is the proposed treatment of preference. There is, of course, some question as to which minorities and differences are fundable, noticeable, and relevant. The institutionalization of difference offers little choice of alternative, since the New Ethnic is taught to choose what he *is*. He is offered identification (and identity) by ascription and is zealously informed that he should be happy with his new self-stereotype. Whose pluralism shall be tolerated, for instance? If some ideologically privileged ethnic minorities emphasize their historical role as an oppressed people, what are their children to think of their classmates who are identified as the sons and daughters of oppressors? Guilt by association, or by birthright? And what are these non-ethnic youngsters to do to defend their self-esteem? Perhaps retaliate, further excluding the others; perhaps attempt to discover some way that proves that they too can trace *their* ancestry to an oppressed minority. After all, the original Puritan dissenters were a persecuted minority in their homeland and were compelled to emigrate to practice their religious freedom (which they denied subsequent dissenters). Teaching mutual respect through a value-loaded comparative history is hardly conducive to a sense of mutuality and equality of dignity. If all are claimants to minority status, seemingly the best way for an ethnic to insist on his superiority is to prove that he is from the lowest of the low. Quite apart from ethnic considerations, we know that for many disturbed or delinquent youngsters, to be a "big zero" is quite an accomplishment!

In contemporary America, addiction to drugs (i.e., opiates) has become for many a way of life by which an underlying depression, dependency, despair, and absence of self-worth are masked. Drugs temporarily offer the individual escape from reality, while making that very reality more difficult and menacing to deal with. The defense offers protection and greater vulnerability. Escapist magical unreality holds the addict under its spell. The New Ethnicity, in effect, substitutes for a drug-induced "high" an ideological "high" of ethnic identity which is presumed to be a superior antidepressant. It is an *ideological* hallucinogen that induces a culturally sanctioned altered state of consciousness by the cheap omniscience and omnipotent suggestion of guru-teachers who stand ready to exploit the uncertainties and ambivalences of those who credulously look to them for their future.[12] Ironically, such ideological addiction ultimately deadens, rather than heightens, awareness and insight, either into one's own personality or into reality. But since *reality* is now autism, what counts is the content of projection, not the careful scrutiny of percept and concept. As cultural hallucinosis becomes the measure of reality, the ability to assess accurately any separate reality is impoverished, and with it, the ability to cope realistically. A vicious circle is created whereby the drug is all the more needed the closer reality makes its incursion.

In substituting one habit for another, one (culturally prescribed) symptom for another (culturally proscribed), the need for addiction is perpetuated and the underlying character disorder or identity conflict never comprehended. Both teacher and student now have a vested interest in their shared self-deception. Teacher and student (doctor-shaman and patient?) are in constant need of a new fix—one that includes the other member of the pair. And if passivity and dependency are the terrible plight of the addict, the habit of ethnicity renders the person no less passively dependent on the certainty of his ethnic identity. In the attempt to forestall the dread depression, the identity addict who fears ideological withdrawal must continuously seek renewed affirmation. Self-doubt and vulnerability can never be fully removed, and serve to undermine whatever temporary false security the habit may confer—and urge the addict to search for a new fix. It is ironic that such cultural ideological drugs should be "pushed" (or dispensed) under Title 9 of the Office of Education, DHEW, as a seemingly innocent "opiate of the masses."

It seems to us particularly tragic that pluralistic education should be a form of suggestion-induced addiction. Children and youth need to feel secure enough to develop creative and critical faculties in order to *edit* independently the heritage of their elders. They need the encouragement to *think* rather than the compulsion to *accept*. The implicit paternalism and foreclosure of the New Ethnicity emphasize being precisely at the developmental phases in which doing, becoming, mobility, initiative, and exploration are at their peak. The New Ethnic ideology counts on the individual's mistrust of himself and his need to find the answers in another. Adolescence becomes no longer a developmental phase for potential social questioning and renewal, but one of subtly rigorous compliance with the ethnic categorization of teachers, revisionist texts, intellectuals, and an all-too-willing government for whom self-esteem sells cheaply (much more cheaply than social reform). Pluralistic education as social therapy does not help youth voice its uncertainty and master it through painful insight, but exploits the uncertainty and pain of adolescence, promising to *remove* it, making the choice of a foreclosed identity not only respectable and genuine, but necessary to reduce anxiety. If the future is presented as not real or worth investing in, what better solution than an emphasis on multilingualism and multiculturalism, which prepare the individual for an idealized past in a narcotized present? The social therapy of ethnic education makes of the schools nothing less than an intellectual reservation.

Ethnicity and Community

In its research for a purified identity, unblemished roots, and a program for the repluralization of America, the New Ethnicity cannot ignore the theme of community. The residential ethnic community is portrayed as a natural, homogeneous, organic whole, where face-to-face relationships predominate and network people take care of their own in the spirit of brotherly and sisterly love. This image of course bears no resemblance to the real American community of the present (ethnic or not); thus the New Ethnicity must conclude that it did exist in the past (their past) and has only been cumulatively corrupted by WASP materialization, depersonalization, and ethnic deculturation. Re-search of sociologists and anthropologists has played no small part in all of this. Building on the "collective consciousness" organic model of Emile Durkheim in the nineteenth century, and augmented by Robert Redfield's study of the "little community" in peasant society in the early twentieth century, numerous social scientists have documented the rise and fall of the inner-city ethnic community. The latest of these, and in the same philosophical tradition, is a work by Gerald Suttles, *The Social Construction of Communities.* Suttles offers a new typology which fits in very well with the ideological needs of the New Ethnicity:[13]

1. the "natural community" ascribed to turn of the century industrial America, where topography, geography, political ward, parish boundary, occupation, social class, and nationality background all coincided and assisted in the construction of an organic "we-ness".
2. the "defended neighborhood" of the inner-city present, where those who have been left behind by flight to the suburbs, threatened by urban renewal and the "new immigrants", desperately cling to what is theirs; and
3. the "community of limited liability", of the urban present and future, where anonymous residential units are tied together only by the invidious collusion between urban planners, zoners, and politicians, segmented by newly overlapping school, parish and ward boundaries, and mobilized only by the commonalities inherent in what another social scientist calls, "the inner-city impact": crime, taxes, pollution, garbage, busing, and political corruption.[14]

The problems with the organic community model, so naively embraced by the New Ethnicity, are manifold. First of all, there is little evidence that the so-called natural community ever existed in the past of any industrialized Western society, despite its continuous appeal from the period of classical sociology in the eighteeenth century to the present. In a review of *The Sociological Tradition* by Robert A. Nisbet, Lewis Coser offers the following observation:

Nisbet shows how disillusionment with the atomistic individualism inherent in the philosophy of enlightenment led congeries of otherwise divergent 19th century thinkers to emphasize the importance and the primacy of the social matrix in which individuals were variously embedded. . . . The vision of modern society that these scholars variously evoke is one of the loss of community, of atomization, bureaucratization and imperative centralized control. As the roots of the community dry up and are replaced by external and ephemeral relationships, as the organizational revolution undermines the appeals of tradition and transcendental values, modern man, in the plenitude of all his newly won freedom, suffers from the lack of the primordial ties with which his ancestors were bound to their fellows.[15]

Wishful thinking to the contrary, the American urban industrial ethnic communities of the late nineteenth and early twentieth centuries were anything but primordial and homogeneous.[16] The inner-city, immigrant ethnic enclave was never the romanticized natural community; and from its earliest day it vacillated between being a "defended turf" and a "community of limited liability." Even kinsmen who were the "blood of each other's blood" did not exclusively associate with one another, feel unambivalently bound to one another, or even know each other. Here, moreover, as we discussed at length earlier, even the personality structure, family structure, and village structure of peasant Europe was as much centrifugal as it was centripetal. Ethnic network people, with ineradicable roots, are the product of Novak's imagination.

If this is true, then the model used by social scientists inspired by the New Ethnicity is hopelessly inadequate. As we proposed in chapter 1, if the static equilibrium of the "little community" is inappropriate for the study of primitives or peasants, how can it possibly account for the lived reality of complex modern, urban, technological settings? If research is undertaken by those in need of a natural, primordial community, they will, through transference to their data, surely find it—especially if they are estranged natives studying their own, as a compromise means of recommitting themselves. Through the magical thinking of regression, they are certain to find what they are seeking; armed with professional schemata of analysis and interpretation, they will be unencumbered in validating and legitimating their premises.

We have said that one of the premises of the New Ethnicity is that "only a native (or nativist) can know." Ethnic studies legislation, community control, and gatekeeping by ethnic leaders and nativist researchers will assure that the manner in which ethnics want to be known will be the basis of future social scientific knowledge of white ethnics. The insistence that only an "insider" is privy to a deep understanding of the "inside," however, is a radical departure from the anthropological tradition. Anthropology based on nativism would repudiate the *disciplined* subjectivity of participant observation and interview and supplant it with unbridled obscurantist subjectivism as the methodology for arriving at truth. Tradition, of course, should not be adhered to simply because it is traditional to do so. It requires a foreigner, someone with distance—very frequently one who is an alien to his own tradition, and not necessarily one outside it—to be able to distinguish between native insight and rationalization, or to be able to identify culturally shared resistances. The "insider," or New Ethnic, is caught up in a system of transferences and countertransferences that are taken for granted. It requires an "outsider" to discern how he or she is enveloped in the native transference, avoid being trapped in that relationship, and understand the intrapsychic and interpersonal processes that are involved. Crudely stated, while the "native" can afford to live by unexamined unconscious process, for the scientist to do so would be suicidal, unless the scientist seeks to kill the scientist in himself and embrace the irrational. Just as it takes a lifetime for the "native" to live by his or her unexamined premises, it takes a lifetime for the scientist (Sigmund Freud, for example) to even begin to recognize that what is, is not as it seems to be. "Going native" was, until recently, what every anthropologist held up before his or her students as the most heinous of sins. Anthropology, of course, has had its own obsessions, a major one being a staunch commitment to remaining a perpetual outsider; a defense, perhaps, against the wish to belong and make commitment somewhere. Nevertheless, the injunction against "going native" contains a powerful grain of truth, that although it is our ethnographic task to try to see from within how the inhabitants of the native world understand themselves, our ethnologic task is to understand *how* and *why* they understand themselves in the way that they do. Any kind of nativist anthropology sounds the death knell for anthropology as a science, and would make it into yet another cult.

Ethnicity and Identity

The New Ethnics take as their premise that ethnicity is the only genuine identity because it is primordial—if not in the genes, then at least in the mother's milk. We have emphasized that the doctrine of primordiality as well as other major tenets of the New Ethnicity are expressions of an oppositional dialectic at the level of regressed, paranoid, narcissistic ego defense, on the one hand, and culturally symbolized group boundedness, on the other. The vicissitudes of the New Ethnicity are inseparable from the American identity and the American Dream it expresses. In his world-wide travels, and as former ambassador to India, Daniel P. Moynihan noted the presence of pictures of John F. Kennedy in virtually every corner of the world—from Latin America to India. Other revolutions and a multitude of constitutions are based on the American model. The contempt with which America is currently held derives from the fact that this nation has not lived up to its own ideals, which are universal ideals. The American Dream after all is a universal dream whose appearance in the United States is merely a culture climax, in the Kroeberian sense. Such values as autonomy, individuation, achievement, reason, and enlightenment are not mere impositions from the United States, but represent an undercurrent of human aspiration.

In his celebrated 1784 essay, *What Is Enlightenment?*, Immanuel Kant wrote: "Enlightenment is man's leaving his self-caused immaturity. Immaturity is the incapacity to use one's intelligence without the guidance of another. Such immaturity is self-caused if it is not caused by lack of intelligence, but by lack of determination and courage to use one's intelligence without being guided by another. . . . Have the courage to use one's own intelligence, is therefore the motto of the Enlightenment." (Freud had a similar motto: "The truth shall set you free.") Man was to embody his own manhood and not need to derive his pseudo-identity and illusory potency by merger with another. Man would always seek to learn from others, but would learn critically, not awestruck by the cheap omnipotence and omniscience of the authoritarian guru.

Neither Kant nor the American founding fathers meant that reason should be disembodied ("heartless"). Rather, what the German theologian and martyr Dietrich Bonhöffer spoke of as the "coming of age" of modern man meant that humankind would be freed of its unknowing drivenness through understanding, through insight, through bringing light to that which dwells stumblingly in the darkness. Reason without emotion is schizoid and is not authentic understanding at all. Genuine insight is, as it were, a psychosomatic experience, not an exclusively cerebral one. Likewise, freedom or independence based on schizoid flight is no real liberation; while dependence or safety based on depressive anxiety makes for no permanent security. Individuation and individualism preclude one another. Genuine independence and interdependence presuppose one another; one is not cause and the other effect, but both are expressions of the capacity to be alone and to enter into intimate relationship.[17]

Genuine freedom must mean freedom for, not an avoidant freedom from. The ego-alien, the "foreign" and "uncanny," must become ego-syntonic, a part of one's self. Freedom is never won once and for all. And revolutions of liberation that depose the father (or mother) only live to repent and restore him (or her) in one guise or another. Fathers and sons must painfully learn to include one another in their dreams, to identify with one another and affirm one another's identity. Erikson reminds us, following Thomas Jefferson, that it is the task of an enlightened generation not to burden the next generation with its conflicts—which means that it must first resolve them for itself. Only then does the possibility of a psychodynamically genuine (as opposed to idealized) free will emerge. Erikson writes that "a choice is free when it can be made with a minimum of denial and of guilt and with a maximum of insight and conviction."[18]

And it is precisely this free choice that is rendered impossible by the psychological dynamics underlying the New Ethnicity, for denial, repression, and guilt give it its locomotive force. The New Ethnicity *forecloses* the possibility of freedom while convincing itself that it possesses the genuine article. What is especially disturbing to us—though predictable—is how concepts and data from developmental psychology, cultural anthropology, and sociology are appropriated by evangelists and scholars of the New Ethnicity as *resistances* to insight into the nature of the human animal in general, and American culture in particular. Novak and others become part of the same intellectual tradition as Ardrey, Lorenz, and Morris, all of whom indulge in tendentious disquisitions, selectively garnering their evidence to demonstrate an a priori ideology. Novak can write that as human beings "we live and move and have our being in social symbolic worlds." True enough. Who would argue? What matters is what Novak—or any other scholar—means by his statements. As we have shown, Novak's "privatization" and mystique of ethno-cultural worlds make his statements ineffable even as he insists on communicating them, in "passing over" between cultural worlds while being the resident of one. Symbols are symbols *of* something, and the insistence on their ineffability functions as a defense against making conscious (let alone public) their deeper meanings. Novak's concept of "the pluralistic personality" is a ploy for the self-deceiver to deny his essentially *authoritarian personality*.[19]

In this book we have tried to show why the New Ethnicity cannot tolerate insight, but must rely on anger and paranoia to produce an aborted identity that defends against the riskiness of identity itself. Paradoxically, and tragically, the very maneuvers taken to resolve the conflicts and alleviate the anxiety generate a vicious circle that perpetually requires repair; namely, reaffirmation. The New Ethnicity is one among numerous movements pan-historically and cross-culturally built upon what Erikson has called "identity foreclosure," a defensive rigidification of ego identity, producing a self-image based on the inability of further structural integration to take place. Openness is replaced by a tight closeness. As a consequence of this foreclosure, a rigidly elaborated depressive strategy of defense is adopted to avoid subsequent failure, yet it confirms the sense of inferiority, exposure, and shame through the very choice of the negative identity. In choosing to be what one was enjoined to repudiate, the New Ethnic chooses failure as a desperate avoidance of risking future vulnerability. Ego and environment together "conspire" to perpetuate the cycle of self-doubt, against which the arrogance of power must ever more defiantly assert itself. Without a sense of competence, without the ability to affirm one's self, to confirm others and be confirmed by them, and without the inner sense of dignity that derives from an authenticity of being and doing, pride is empty, an arrogance that fills an insatiably expanding void.

Genuine identity presupposes and fosters an individual's "coming of age." Any other identity is based on the infant's and later adult's infinite exploitability. It is the achievement of the New Ethnicity to make its devotees more terrified while keeping them safe. Paradoxically, independence is not an adversary of the true expression of community, which is interdependence. One who has come of age can be independent without fleeing from relationships, and interdependent without being parasitically dependent. A genuine community can be built only of those who are capable of dialogue, who are capable of reaching out to otherness. Genuine self-actualization partakes neither of the caricatured self-made man nor the equally caricatured primordial ethnic withdrawn in fright peering out of the tribal cave. Rather it implies the capacity for close interpersonal relationship and commitment. Heinz Ansbacher, an Adlerian psychologist, defines Adler's concept of *Gemeinschaftsgefühl* ("social interest") as "an interest in the interests of others."[20]

The new collectivities, such as the New Ethnicity, are the antithesis of genuine community, are pseudo-*Gemeinschaftsgefühl* because the other does not and cannot exist independent of the self. The New Ethnic's self is parasitic on the other who is a projection of himself. Identities based on the bundling of collectivity are defensive identities, defending against their own humanity. Identities capable of community cannot defend against otherness because selfhood is simply an expression of an individual's otherness.

The New Ethnicity mistakes collectivity for community, seeing in the regressed and idealized symbiotic tie the only valid form of social organization. The inability to relate is held to be the highest form of relationship. The dialogue is replaced with the monologue of assertion. Martin Buber writes:

> Collectivity is not a binding but a bundling together: individuals packed together, armed and equipped in common, with only as much life from man to man as will inflame the marching step. But community, growing community (which is all we have known so far) is the being no longer side by side, but *with* one another of a multitude of persons. And this multitude, though it moves toward one goal, yet experiences everywhere a turning to, a dynamic facing of, the other, a flowing from I to Thou. Community is where community happens. Collectivity is based on an organized atrophy of personal existence, community on its increase and confirmation in life lived towards one another. The modern zeal for collectivity is a flight from community's testing and consecration of the person, a flight from the vital dialogic, demanding the staking of the self, which is in the heart of the world.[21]

Charles Rycroft writes similarly from a psychoanalytic point of view:

> Far from modern man having lost a true sense of identity, it may well be that as his external supply of idealized father-figures is being diminished by the disillusioning effect of scientific knowledge he is being forced to become aware of himself in terms of his capacity to love, without recourse to the supports of religion or morality, which . . . is ultimately a defense against infantile ambivalence. From this point of view the loss of identity . . . is really loss of defensive identifications, while the quest for identity is either the search for some new defensive organization or for access to the one value which is not culturally determined, the capacity to love.[22]

Likewise, Sapir writes:

> To say that individual and culture must needs grow organically out of the rich soil of a communal culture is far from saying that it must be forever tied to that culture by the leading strings of its own childhood. Once the individual self has grown strong enough to travel in the path most clearly illuminated by its own light, it not only can, but should discard much of the scaffolding by which it has made its ascent.[23]

Human identity it would seem, is meta-cultural, beyond culture, beyond the defenses that keep us from coming of age and preventing others as well. As Erikson has noted, repression, suppression, and oppression are found together. Genuine human identity begins where adolescent culture ends. It is not and cannot be simply another culture, or yet another counterculture. It is *beyond the culture principle*. Oddly enough, this is what the American Dream has been about since it was first dreamt before the continent was discovered. It is the same dream that fires, and fired, the imagination of blacks and whites, Berliners and Navahos, Latin American peons, and South Asians, not to mention four centuries of Europeans. The American Dream is a dream of what humankind can be and would not have been so readily imported abroad, if a foreign dream were not native already. It is not self-aggrandizement to speak of America as the last best hope of mankind or a beacon unto the nations, for this is not only how Americans, under the spell of the American Dream, see themselves, but how the world wishes and needs America to be, in order to themselves become.[24]

The ethnic imperative is far from primordial. It is a choice of self-condemnation by those who feel condemned and let down. Anthropology, like American culture in general, is woefully misguided if it embraces ethnicity as the wave of the future. The meaning of anthropology, and of America, is ethnic identity and pluralism only if we wish to build the future from our fears, rather than our hopes and aspirations. The ideals both of this profession and this nation are openness, inclusiveness, and a reaching out to the alien whose humanity an American comes to see as his own. When the New Ethnic turns inward, he turns his face away and makes himself and others less than human. Hillel once said, "If I am not for myself, who am I? If I am only for myself, what am I? If not now, when?"[25]

Notes

Introduction

1. Robert Ardrey, *The Territorial Imperative* (New York: Atheneum, 1966); Konrad Lorenz, *On Aggression* (New York: Harcourt Brace Jovanovich, 1966); Lionel Tiger, *Men in Groups* (New York: Random House, 1969); Lionel Tiger and Robin Fox, *The Imperial Animal* (New York: Dell, 1972); Steven Goldberg, *The Inevitability of Patriarchy* (New York: Morrow, 1973).
2. Milton Himmelfarb, "Plural Establishment," *Commentary* 58, no. 6 (December 1974): 69–73.
3. See, for example, Abner Cohen, *Urban Ethnicity* (London: ASA Monographs, no. 12; New York: Barnes and Noble, 1974). See also *Ethnicity in the Americas,* ed. Frances Henry (Chicago: Aldine, 1976); *Ethnicity and Resource Competition in Plural Societies,* ed. Leo A. Despres (Chicago: Aldine, 1975).
4. Anthony F. C. Wallace, "Revitalization Movements," *American Anthropologist* 58 (1956): 264–281; Ralph Linton, "Nativistic Movements," *American Anthropologist* 45 (1943): 230–240; Weston La Barre, *The Ghost Dance: The Origins of Religion* (New York: Dell, 1972), p. 41. See also "Materials for a History of Studies of Crisis Cults: A Bibliographic Essay," *Current Anthropology* 12 (1971): 3–43.
5. Peter Gay, *Weimar Culture: The Outsider as Insider* (New York: Harper and Row, 1968), pp. 79, 84.
6. George De Vos and Lola Romanucci-Ross, eds., *Ethnic Identity: Cultural Continuities and Change* (Palo Alto: Mayfield, 1975), p. 366.
7. George Devereux, "Ethnic Identity: Its Logical Foundations and Its Dysfunctions," in *Ethnic Identity,* eds. De Vos and Romanucci-Ross, pp. 66–68, p. 65.
8. Devereux, "Ethnic Identity," p. 68.
9. Harold R. Isaacs, "The New Pluralists," rejoinder to Letters to the Editor, *Commentary* 53, no. 6 (1972): 14.
10. Weston La Barre, *The Peyote Cult,* 4th ed. enl. (New York: Schocken, 1975), p. xvi.
11. Howard F. Stein, *An Ethno-Historic Study of Slovak-American Identity* (Ph.D. diss., University of Pittsburgh, 1972); Robert F. Hill, *Exploring the Dimensions of Ethnicity: A Study of Status, Culture, and Identity among Polish-Americans* (Ph.D. diss., University of Pittsburgh, 1975).
12. See Konstantin Symmons-Symonolewicz, "Nationalist Movements: An Attempt at a Comparative Typology," *Comparative Studies in Society and History* 7 (1964–

1965): 221–230; "Studies in Nationalism: Old and New," *Canadian Review of Studies in Nationalism* 2, no. 1 (Fall 1974): 152–156; Holm Sundhausen, *Der Einfluss der Herderschen Ideen auf die Nationsbildung bei den Völkern der Habsburger Monarchie* (Munich: R. Oldenbourg Verlag, 1973); Miroslav Hroch, *Die Vorkämpfer der nationalen Bewegung bei den kleinen Völkern Europas. Eine vergleichende Analyse zur gesellschaftlichen Schichtung der patriotischen Gruppen* (Prague: Charles University, 1968).

Chapter 1

1. For a review of the literature on the New Ethnicity, we refer the reader to the following sources: Howard F. Stein and Sam H. J. Ramtu, "An Annotated Bibliography of White Ethnic Nationalism in the United States," *Canadian Review of Studies in Nationalism,* special issue, "Annotated Bibliography of Works on Nationalism," 2 (1975): 298–323; Robert F. Hill and Howard F. Stein, "Ethnic Stratification and Social Unrest in Contemporary Eastern Europe and America," *The Nationalities Papers of the Association for the Study of Nationalities, USSR and Eastern Europe* 1, no. 1 (Fall 1972): 1–28; Howard F. Stein and Robert F. Hill, "The New Ethnicity and the White Ethnic in the United States," *Canadian Review of Studies of Nationalism* 1, no. 1 (Fall 1973): 81–105; Howard F. Stein, "Ethnicity, Identity, and Ideology," *School Review* 83, no. 2 (February 1975): 273–300; Howard F. Stein and Robert F. Hill, "The Limits of Ethnicity," *American Scholar* (Spring 1977): 181–189.

2. Claude Levi-Strauss, "Social Structure," in *Anthropology Today: Selections,* ed. Sol Tax (Chicago: University of Chicago Press, 1962).

3. George Devereux, "Ethnic Identity: Its Logical Foundations and Its Dysfunctions," in *Ethnic Identity: Cultural Continuities and Change,* eds. George De Vos and Lola Romanucci-Ross (Palo Alto: Mayfield, 1975), pp. 42–70.

4. Noam Chomsky, *Language and Mind* (New York: Harcourt, Brace, and World, 1968).

5. Claude Levi-Strauss, *The Savage Mind* (Chicago: University of Chicago Press, 1966). See especially chapter 3, "Systems of Transformations," pp. 75–100.

6. Charles E. Osgood et al., *The Measurement of Meaning* (Urbana: University of Illinois Press, 1957).

7. Edward Spicer, "Persistent Cultural Systems," *Science* 174 (1971): 795–800; Eric Voegelin, "The Growth of the Race Idea," *Review of Politics* 2 (1940): 283–317; Erik Erikson, *Identity, Youth and Crisis* (New York: Norton, 1968).

8. Morris Opler, "Themes as Dynamic Forces in Culture," *American Journal of Sociology* 51 (1945): 198–206.

9. Howard F. Stein, *An Ethno-Historic Study of Slovak-American Identity* (Ph.D. diss., University of Pittsburgh, 1972); Robert F. Hill, *Exploring the Dimensions of Ethnicity: A Study of Status, Culture, and Identity Among Polish-Americans* (Ph.D. diss., University of Pittsburgh, 1975).

10. Wsevolod W. Isajiw, "Definitions of Ethnicity," *Ethnicity* 1 (1974): 111–124, citation p. 122. Harold R. Isaacs, *Idols of the Tribe: Group Identity and Political Change* (New York: Harper and Row, 1975), pp. 39–45.

11. Fredrik Barth, *Ethnic Groups and Boundaries: The Social Organization of Cultural Difference* (Boston: Little, Brown, 1969), pp. 9–10.

12. Joshua Fishman et al., *Language Loyalty in the United States* (The Hague: Mouton, 1966); Talcott Parsons, "Some Theoretical Considerations on the Nature and Trends of Change of Ethnicity," in *Ethnicity: Theory and Experience,* eds. Nathan Glazer and Daniel P. Moynihan (Cambridge: Harvard University Press, 1975), pp. 53–83, p. 65, p. 67.

13. Robert F. Hill and J. Thomas May, "Exploring Hidden Ethnicity: Problems and Methods" (Paper presented at the International Society for Ethno-History, Central State University, Edmond, Oklahoma, October 27, 1973).

14. Fishman et al., *Language Loyalty,* p. 345.

15. Janet M. Schreiber, "Ethnicity: Its Management among South Italian Migrants to Switzerland and Germany" (Paper presented at the American Anthropological Association Meetings: Symposium on Migration and Ethnicity, Mexico City, November 22, 1974, pp. 7–8).

16. Eric Hoffer, *The True Believer* (New York: Harper and Row, 1951), p. 95.

17. Joshua A. Fishman, "Childhood Indoctrination for Minority Group Membership," *Daedalus* 90 (Spring 1961): 329–349.

18. For a full discussion of the processes of continuity and change in Slovak and Polish-American institutions see Stein, *An Ethno-Historic Study,* chapter 5, pp. 195–288; and Hill, *Exploring the Dimensions of Ethnicity,* chapter 3, pp. 40–97.

19. Stein, *An Ethno-Historic Study,* pp. 225–227.

20. Stein, *An Ethno-Historic Study,* p. 255.

21. Hill, *Exploring the Dimensions of Ethnicity,* pp. 194–195.

22. Hill, *Exploring the Dimensions of Ethnicity,* pp. 126–127.

23. Lola Romanucci-Ross, "Italian Immigrants in the United States" (Paper presented at the American Anthropological Association Meetings: Symposium on Migration and Ethnicity, Mexico City, November 22, 1974).

24. Miguel Leon-Portilla, "Anthropology and the Endangered Cultures," Distinguished Lecture, 1974 (Washington, D.C.: American Anthropological Association *Annual Report,* 1974), pp. 9–10.

25. George De Vos and Lola Romanucci-Ross, "Ethnicity: Vessel of Meaning and Emblem of Contrast," in *Ethnic Identity: Cultural Continuities and Change,* eds. George De Vos and Lola Romanucci-Ross (Palo Alto: Mayfield, 1975), citation p. 398.

26. Franklin H. Giddings, *Inductive Sociology* (New York: Macmillan, 1901).

27. Edmund Leach, *Political Systems of Highland Burma* (Boston: Beacon Press, 1964).

28. Margaret Mead, *New Lives for Old* (New York: Mentor, 1956).

29. Lloyd A. Fallers, *The Social Anthropology of the Nation-State* (Chicago: Aldine, 1974), citation pp. 1–2.

30. Clifford Geertz, "The Integrated Revolution," in *Old Societies and New Nations* (Glencoe, Ill.: Free Press, 1963); Andrew M. Greeley, *Ethnicity in the United States* (New York: Wiley, 1974); Isaacs, *Idols of the Tribe;* Robert Redfield and Alfonso Villa Rojas, *Chan Kom: A Maya Village* (Washington, D.C.: Carnegie Institution of Washington Publication no. 448, 1934).

31. Oscar Lewis, *Anthropological Essays* (New York: Random House, 1970).

32. Gunnar Myrdal, "The Case Against Romantic Ethnicity," *Center Magazine* 7, no.

4 (July–August 1974): 26–30; see also George Kateb's review of Isaiah Berlin, *Vico and Herder* (1976), *American Scholar* (Winter 1976–77): 124–130.

Chapter 2

1. Melford E. Spiro, "The Acculturation of American Ethnic Groups," *American Anthropologist* 57 (1955): 1240–1252, citation p. 1250.

2. See, for example, Colin Greer, review of *Poor Jews*, eds. N. Levine and M. Hochbaum, *Social Policy* (May–June 1975): 63–64.

3. Erik H. Erikson, *Childhood and Society*, rev. ed. (New York: Norton, 1963), citation p. 341.

4. Carl Becker, *The Heavenly City of the Eighteenth-Century Philosophers* (New Haven: Yale University Press, 1932).

5. See H. N. Smith, *Virgin Land* (Cambridge: Harvard University Press, 1970).

6. See F. J. Turner, *The Frontier in American History* (New York: Holt, 1921).

7. Daniel Boorstin, *The Americans: The National Experience* (New York: Random House, 1965).

8. Vance Packard, *A Nation of Strangers* (New York: David McKay, 1972).

9. Nathan I. Huggins, "Afro-Americans: National Character and Community," *Center Magazine* 7, no. 4 (July–August 1974): 51–66, citation p. 61.

10. Otto von Mering, "The Question of Ethnic Identity," *Council on Anthropology and Education Newsletter* 3, no. 1 (February 1972): 1–5, citation p. 4.

11. George Devereux, *Reality and Dream: Psychotherapy of a Plains Indian*, rev. ed. (New York: Doubleday, 1969), citation p. 37, pp. 38–39.

12. Joshua Fishman et al., *Language Loyalty in the United States* (The Hague: Mouton, 1966); Franz Alexander, *Fundamentals of Psychoanalysis* (New York: Norton, 1948), citation p. 149. See also *Our Age of Unreason* (Philadelphia: Lippincott, 1951).

13. Erik H. Erikson, "Autobiographic Notes on the Identity Crisis," *Daedalus* 99, no. 4 (Fall 1970), citation p. 748.

14. Fishman et al., *Language Loyalty*, pp. 401–402.

15. Ross Phares, *Bible in Pocket, Gun in Hand: The Story of Frontier Religion* (Lincoln: University of Nebraska Press, 1964), citation p. 2.

16. Richard W. Van Alstyne, *Genesis of American Nationalism* (Waltham, Mass.: Blaisdell, 1970).

17. Israel Zangwill, *The Melting Pot* (New York: Macmillan, 1910).

18. Thomas C. Wheeler, ed., "Introduction," *The Immigrant Experience: The Anguish of Becoming American* (New York: Dial Press, 1971), citation p. 1.

19. Stephen Spender, *Love-Hate Relations: English and American Sensibilities* (New York: Random House, 1974).

20. John Spiegel, *Transactions: The Interplay Between Individual, Family, and Society*, ed. John Papajohn (New York: Science House, 1971), citation p. 352, pp. 359–360.

21. Spiegel, *Transactions*, pp. 352–353.

22. Erikson, *Childhood and Society*, p. 313.

23. Clyde Kluckhohn, *Mirror for Man* (New York: Fawcett, 1965), citation pp. 202–203.

24. Richard Sennett, *The Uses of Disorder: Personal Identity and City Life* (New York: Random House (Vintage), 1971).

25. Erik H. Erikson, *Identity, Youth and Crisis* (New York: Norton, 1968). See also "Reflections on the American Identity," *Childhood and Society*, pp. 285–325.

26. Elwood P. Clubberly, *Changing Conceptions of Education* (New York: Riverside Educational Monographs, 1909); Henry Pratt Fairchild, *The Melting Pot Mistake* (Boston: Little, Brown, 1926).

27. Theodore Schwartz, "Cargo Cult: Melanesian Response to Culture Contact," in *Responses to Change*, ed. George De Vos (New York: Van Nostrand, 1975); Kenelm Burridge, *Mambu: A Melanesian Millennium* (London: Methuen, 1960).

28. David Danzig, in *Overcoming Middle Class Rage*, ed. Murray Friedman (Philadelphia: Westminster Press, 1971). Quoted in Harold R. Isaacs, "The New Pluralists," *Commentary* 53, no. 3 (March 1972): 75–79, citation p. 77.

29. Alfred Kazin, review of *Thomas Jefferson: An Intimate History*, by Fawn M. Brodie (New York: Norton, 1974), *New York Times Book Review*, April 7, 1974, citation p. 2. See also Erik H. Erikson, *Dimensions of a New Identity* (New York: Norton, 1974); and Thomas Fleming, *1776: Year of Illusions* (New York: Norton, 1975).

30. Michael Novak, "Black and White in Catholic Eyes," *New York Times Magazine*, November 30, 1975, p. 108; see Michael J. Arlen, "Blood Marks in the Sylvan Glade," *New Yorker*, October 13, 1975, pp. 142–151.

31. *Time*, April 19, 1976, p. 14. See also *Time*, May 10, 1976, pp. 11–27.

Chapter 3

1. Mario Puzo, "Choosing a Dream: Italians in Hell's Kitchen," in *The Immigrant Experience: The Anguish of Becoming American*, ed. Thomas C. Wheeler (New York: Dial Press, 1971), pp. 35–49, citation p. 46.

2. Puzo, *The Immigrant Experience*, p. 47.

3. Michael Novak, "The One and the Many," *Daedalus* 103, no. 4 (Fall 1974): 203–211, citation p. 203.

4. Martin F. Nolan, review in *New York Times Book Review*, March 31, 1974.

5. Howard F. Stein, "The Silent Complicity at Watergate," *American Scholar* 43, no. 1 (Winter 1973–74): 21–37.

6. See William Hamilton, "Banished from the Land of Unity," in *Radical Theology and the Death of God*, by Thomas J. Altizer and William Hamilton (Indianapolis: Bobbs-Merrill, 1966); see also Thomas J. Altizer, ed., *Toward a New Christianity: Readings in the Death of God Theology* (New York: Harcourt Brace Jovanovich, 1969).

7. Leonard Nimoy, *I Am Not Spock* (Millbrae, Calif.: Celestial Arts, 1975); Sondra Marshak and Myrna Culbreath, eds., *Star Trek: The New Voyages* (New York: Bantam, 1976).

8. Marshak and Culbreath, *Star Trek*, p. xiii.

9. Arnold A. Rogow, "Some Psychiatric Aspects of Political Science and Political Life," in *Social Psychology and Political Behavior*, eds. G. Abcarian and J. W. Soule (Columbus, Ohio: Charles E. Merrill, 1971), pp. 185–209, citation p. 200.

10. Michael Novak, *Politics: Realism and Imagination* (New York: Herder and Herder, 1971), citation p. 140.

11. Philip Slater, *The Pursuit of Loneliness* (Boston: Beacon Press, 1970), citation pp. 49–50.

12. John F. Kennedy, *A Nation of Immigrants* (New York: Harper and Row, 1964).

13. Peter Gay, *Weimar Culture: The Outsider as Insider* (New York: Harper and Row, 1968).

Chapter 4

1. Abraham Maslow, *Toward a Psychology of Being*, 2d ed. (New York: Van Nostrand Reinhold, 1968); Erik H. Erikson, *Childhood and Society*, 2d ed. (New York: Norton, 1963); see also *Identity, Youth and Crisis* (New York: Norton, 1968).

2. Robert Langbaum, "Thoughts for Our Time: Three Novels on Anarchism," *American Scholar* 42, no. 2 (Spring 1973): 227–250.

3. Isidore Silver, "All in the Mafia Family," review of the 1972 movie *The Godfather*, *Society* 9, no. 8 (June 1972): 34–37, citation p. 37.

4. Silver, "All in the Mafia Family," pp. 34–36.

5. Eric Hobsbawm, *Primitive Rebels* (New York: Norton, 1965), quoted in Silver, "All in the Mafia Family," p. 36.

6. Howard F. Stein, "*All in the Family* as a Mirror of Contemporary American Culture," *Family Process* 13, no. 3 (September 1974): 279–315.

7. Philip Slater, *Earthwalk* (New York: Doubleday, 1973).

8. Erik H. Erikson, *Dimensions of a New Identity* (New York: Norton, 1974), p. 108; *Young Man Luther* (New York: Norton, 1958), p. 263.

9. Michael Novak, *The Rise of the Unmeltable Ethnics* (New York: Macmillan, 1971); "Why Wallace?," in *Politics: Realism and Imagination* (New York: Herder and Herder, 1971), pp. 58–59.

10. Novak, "Why Wallace?," p. 59.

11. Howard F. Stein, "American Nostalgia," *Columbia Forum* 3, no. 3 (Summer 1974): 20–23.

12. B. F. Skinner, *Beyond Freedom and Dignity* (New York: Knopf, 1971).

13. B. F. Skinner, *Walden Two* (New York: Macmillan, 1948).

14. Richard Sennett, review of B. F. Skinner, *Beyond Freedom and Dignity*, *New York Times Book Review*, October 24, 1971, pp. 1, 12, 14, 16, 18; see also Letters to the Editor, exchange between Skinner and Sennett, November 21, 1971. See also Michael Beldoch, "Science as Fiction," *Psychotherapy and Social Science Review* 6, no. 1 (January 7, 1972): 12–18; see also a review by Richard L. Rubenstein, *Psychology Today* 5, no. 4 (September 1971): 28–31, 95–96.

15. John Egerton, *The Americanization of Dixie: The Southernization of America* (New York: Harper and Row, 1974), pp. 188–192. Additional data on The Farm were obtained from a former member; see also Kirkpatrick Sale, *Power Shift: The Rise of the Southern Rim and Its Challenge to the Eastern Establishment* (New York: Random House, 1975).

16. Egerton, *The Americanization of Dixie*, pp. 194–195.

17. Michael Novak, "Politics as Witness," in *Politics: Realism and Imagination,* pp. 71–72.

18. Quoted in Egerton, *The Americanization of Dixie,* p. 198. Originally published in the *Forum for Contemporary History.*

19. Michael Novak, *Choosing Our King: Powerful Symbols in Presidential Politics* (New York: Macmillan, 1974); "If This Is the Green Wood," in *Politics: Realism and Imagination,* p. 157.

20. Michael Novak, "A Nation with the Soul of a Church," in *Politics: Realism and Imagination,* p. 69; "Politics as Witness," in *Politics,* pp. 71–73.

21. Robert L. Heilbroner, *An Inquiry into the Human Prospect* (New York: Norton, 1974).

22. Daniel Bell, *The Cultural Contradictions of Capitalism* (New York: Basic Books, 1976); Robert Nisbet, *The Social Philosophers: Community and Conflict in Western Thought* (New York: Thomas Crowell, 1973), p. 7.

23. René Dubos, "The Despairing Optimist," *American Scholar* 41, no. 2 (Spring 1972): 184–192, citation p. 185.

24. Stanley Milgram, *Obedience to Authority: An Experimental View* (New York: Harper and Row, 1973).

25. *Time,* September 15, 1975, p. 94. The present discussion is also based on conversation with psychologists who attended the APA meeting.

Chapter 5

1. Andrew Greeley, "The Last of the American Irish Fade Away," *New York Times Magazine,* March 14, 1971, pp. 32–58. citation p. 58.

2. Andrew Greeley, *Ethnicity in the United States: A Preliminary Reconnaissance* (New York: Wiley, 1974), pp. 286–287.

3. Nathan Glazer and Daniel P. Moynihan, *Beyond the Melting Pot,* 2d ed. (Cambridge: MIT Press, 1970); see Lewis M. Killian, *White Southerners* (New York: Random House, 1970); Joel Kovel, *White Racism: A Psychohistory* (New York: Random House, 1971); John Egerton, *The Americanization of Dixie: The Southernization of America* (New York: Harper and Row, 1974).

4. Harold R. Isaacs, "Basic Group Identity: Idols of the Tribe," in *Ethnicity: Theory and Experience,* eds. Nathan Glazer and Daniel P. Moynihan (Cambridge: Harvard University Press, 1975), p. 39. See also Isaacs, *Idols of the Tribe, Group Identity and Political Change* (New York: Harper and Row, 1975).

5. George A. De Vos, "Social Stratification and Ethnic Pluralism: An Overview from the Perspective of Psychological Anthropology," *Race* (The Institute of Race Relations, London) 13, no. 4 (1972): 435–460, pp. 446–447.

6. Glazer and Moynihan, *Beyond the Melting Pot.*

7. Joyce A. Ladner, ed., *The Death of White Sociology* (New York: Random House (Vintage), 1973).

8. Thomas F. Pettigrew, "Ethnicity in American Life: A Social Psychological Perspective," in *Ethnicity in American Life,* by John Hope Franklyn, Thomas F. Pettigrew, and Raymond W. Mack (New York: Anti-Defamation League of B'Nai B'rith, 1971), p. 31. See also *Ethnic Groups in the City,* ed. Otto Feinstein (Lexington, Mass.: Heath Lexington Books, 1971), pp. 29–37.

9. Pettigrew, "Ethnicity in American Life," p. 31.

10. John M. Goering, "The Emergence of Ethnic Interests: A Case of Serendipity," *Social Forces* 49, no. 3 (March 1971): 379–384, citation p. 383.

11. Michael Novak, "Tom Wicker's Attica," *Commentary* 59, no. 5 (May 1975): 49–56.

12. Daniel P. Moynihan, "The Negro Family: The Case for National Action," in *The Moynihan Report and the Politics of Controversy*, eds. Lee Rainwater and William L. Yancey (Cambridge: MIT Press, 1967). See Oscar Lewis, *Anthropological Essays* (New York: Random House, 1970); *Five Families: Mexican Case Studies in the Culture of Poverty* (New York: Basic Books, 1959); *La Vida: A Puerto Rican Family in the Culture of Poverty* (New York: Random House, 1966).

13. Robert W. Fogel and Stanley L. Engerman, *Time on the Cross*, 2 vols., *The Economics of American Negro Slavery*, vol. 1, *Evidence and Methods*, a supplement, vol. 2 (Boston: Little, Brown, 1974).

14. Sheldon Hackney, "The South as a Counterculture," *American Scholar* 42, no. 2 (Spring 1973): 283–293.

15. George B. Tindall, "Beyond the Mainstream: The Ethnic Southerners," *Journal of Southern History* 40, no. 1 (February 1974): 3–18; see also by Tindall, *The Ethnic Southerners* (Baton Rouge: Louisiana State University Press, 1976).

16. Lewis M. Killian, *White Southerners* (New York: Random House, 1970), p. 142.

17. Killian, *White Southerners*, p. 140.

18. William Grier and Price M. Cobbs, *Black Rage* (New York: Basic Books, 1968).

19. Quoted in Killian, *White Southerners*, p. 141. See also pp. 141–142.

20. Novak, "Attica," p. 56.

21. Michael Novak, *The Rise of the Unmeltable Ethnics* (New York: Macmillan, 1971). See also review by Howard F. Stein, *Society* (Trans-Action) 11, no. 6 (September–October 1974): 94–96.

22. Howard F. Stein, " 'All in the Family' as a Mirror of Contemporary American Life," *Family Process* 13, no. 3 (September 1974): 279–316. See also "The Silent Complicity at Watergate," *American Scholar* 43, no. 1 (Winter 1973–74): 21–37.

Chapter 6

1. M. Henk, S. M. Tomasi, and G. Baroni, eds., *Pieces of a Dream* (New York: Center for Migration Studies, 1972).

2. Nathan I. Huggins, "Afro-Americans: National Character and Community," *Center Magazine* 7, no. 4 (July–August 1974): 56, 66.

3. Talcott Parsons, "Some Theoretical Considerations on the Nature and Trends of Change of Ethnicity," in *Ethnicity: Theory and Experience*, eds. Nathan Glazer and Daniel P. Moynihan (Cambridge: Harvard University Press, 1975), pp. 53–85, citation p. 69.

4. Talcott Parsons and Edward Shils, *Toward a General Theory of Action* (Cambridge: Harvard University Press, 1951).

5. Erik H. Erikson and Huey P. Newton, *In Search of Common Ground* (New York: Norton, 1973), citation p. 109.

6. Abraham H. Maslow, "Health as a Transcendence of Environment," in *Toward a*

Psychology of Being, 2d ed. (New York: Van Nostrand Reinhold, 1968), citation, p. 180.

7. See Laura Pilarski, *They Came from Poland: The Stories of Famous Polish-Americans* (New York: Dodd, Mead, 1969); see also Sister Wobilis, "Sienkiewicz and the Poles in America," *Polish American Studies* 2 (1945): 34–37.

8. Rev. Ivan Dornic, "A More Sober Look at Slovak Ethnicity in America," *Ethnic American News* (American Slav), June 1975, p. 10.

9. Peter Rose, review essay of *The Rise of the Unmeltable Ethnics* by Michael Novak (New York: Macmillan, 1971) and *Why Can't They Be Like Us?* by Andrew Greeley (New York: Dutton, 1971), *Contemporary Sociology* 2, no. 1 (1973): 14–17, citation, p. 17.

10. Emil L. Fackenheim, *Encounters Between Judaism and Philosophy* (New York: Basic Books, 1972); *God's Presence in History: Jewish Affirmations and Philosophical Reflections* (New York: New York University Press, 1970).

11. Dornic, "Slovak Ethnicity," p. 10.

12. Donald Campbell, "Stereotypes and the Perception of Group Differences," *American Psychologist* 22 (1967): 817–829, citation p. 825.

13. Heinz Kohut, "Thoughts on Narcissism and Narcissistic Rage," in *The Psychoanalytic Study of the Child* (New York: Quadrangle, 1972), 27: 360–400, 381–382.

14. Kohut, "Thoughts on Narcissism," pp. 385–386, p. 396.

15. Erik H. Erikson, *Identity, Youth and Crisis* (New York: Norton, 1968), citation p. 183.

16. Erikson, *Identity,* p. 184.

17. Erik H. Erikson, "Once More the Inner Space," in *Women and Analysis,* ed. Jean Strouse (New York: Grossman Publishers, 1974), citation p. 321.

18. Erikson, "Once More the Inner Space," pp. 322, 334.

19. Stephen Lukashevich, review of Georges Luciani, *Panslavisme et Solidarité Slave au XIXᵉ Siècle: La Société des Slaves Unis (1823–1825)* (Université de Bordeaux, 1963), *Slavic and East European Journal* 12 (1968), citation p. 121.

20. Lukashevich, review of Georges Luciani, p. 121.

21. See Thomas Freeman, "Narcissism and Defensive Processes in Schizophrenic States," *International Journal of Psychoanalysis* 43 (1962): 415–425; Hazel H. Weidman, "Anthropological Theory and the Psychological Function of Belief in Witchcraft," in *Essays in Medical Anthropology,* ed. T. Weaver, Southern Anthropological Society Proceedings, no. 1 (Athens: University of Georgia Press, 1968); Robert A. Levine, *Culture, Behavior, and Personality* (Chicago: Aldine-Atherton, 1973).

22. Richard Gambino, Ethnic Studies Working Paper, Rockefeller Foundation, 1975.

23. *Ladies' Home Journal,* September 19, 1975, p. 74.

24. See Hearings Before the General Subcommittee on Education of the Committee on Education and Labor, House of Representatives, 91st Congress, Second Session on H.R. 15910, February 16, 17, 18, 24, 26; March 4, 5, 19; and May 6, 1970.

25. Erik Erikson, *Childhood and Society,* 2d ed. (New York: Norton, 1963), citation p. 336.

26. George Devereux, "Normal and Abnormal: The Key Concepts of Psychiatric Anthropology," in *Some Uses of Anthropology: Theoretical and Applied* (Washington, D.C.: The Anthropological Society of Washington, 1951), pp. 23–48.

27. George De Vos and Lola Romanucci-Ross, eds., *Ethnic Identity: Cultural Continuities and Change* (Palo Alto: Mayfield, 1975), citation p. 372.

28. John P. Diggins, "Buckley's Comrades: The Ex-Communist as Conservative," *Dissent* 22, no. 4 (Fall 1975): 370–381.

29. Erik Erikson, *Young Man Luther* (New York: Norton, 1958).

30. Rose, review essay of *Rise of the Unmeltable Ethnics,* citation p. 15.

31. Lloyd A. Fallers, *The Social Anthropology of the Nation-State* (Chicago: Aldine, 1974), citation p. 136.

32. Eric Hoffer, *The True Believer* (New York: Harper and Row, 1951), citation pp. 52–53.

33. Theodore Schwartz, "Cargo Cult: A Melanesian Type Response to Culture Contact" (Presented at De Vos Conference on Psychological Adjustment and Adaptation to Culture Change, Hakone, Japan, 1968), citation pp. 78–79.

34. Schwartz, "Cargo Cult," pp. 77–78.

35. Schwartz, "Cargo Cult," p. 78.

36. Kohut, "Thoughts on Narcissism and Narcissistic Rage," pp. 360–400, citation p. 396.

37. Bruno Bettelheim, "Obsolete Youth: Toward a Psychograph of Adolescent Rebellion," in *Adolescent Psychiatry,* vol. 1, eds. S. C. Feinstein, P. Giovacchini, and A. A. Miller (New York: Basic Books, 1971), pp. 14–39, pp. 28–29.

38. Bettelheim, "Obsolete Youth," p. 34.

39. Peter Blos, "The Generation Gap: Fact and Fiction," in *Adolescent Psychiatry,* citation p. 10.

40. "The Generation Gap," p. 11.

41. Mircea Eliade, *Shamanism: Archaic Techniques of Ecstasy* (New York: Pantheon, 1964), p. 265.

42. Edward Chambers, Presentation on "Inner City Community Organizing" based on his experience in Chicago with Saul Alinsky; Conference on Urban Ethnic Priorities, Msgr. Gino Baroni, director, Catholic University, Washington, D.C., June 8, 1971.

43. From an interview by Judy Klemesrud of the *New York Times,* May 22, 1975, quoted in an editorial "Ancient Malady," *Nation,* June 7, 1975.

Chapter 7

1. Wilfred Sheed, "Wasp-Wasting and Ethnic-Upping," *New York Times Book Review,* June 4, 1972, p. 2.

2. Michael Novak, *The Rise of the Unmeltable Ethnics* (New York: Macmillan, 1971).

3. Michael Novak, "Confessions of a White Ethnic," in *White Ethnics: Life in Working Class America,* ed. Joseph A. Ryan (Englewood Cliffs, N.J.: Prentice-Hall, 1973), p. 24.

4. Novak, "Confessions," pp. 25, 35.

5. Novak, "Confessions," p. 27.

6. Michael Novak, "The New Anti-Semitism," *Congress Bi-Weekly* (American Jewish Congress) 41, no. 1, (January 18, 1974): 6–7.

7. Novak, "Confessions," p. 24.

8. Michael Novak, "The New Ethnicity," *Center Magazine* 7, no. 4 (July–August 1974): 18–25, citation p. 21.

9. Edward Banfield and L. F. Banfield, *The Moral Basis of a Backward Society* (New York: Free Press, 1958); Joseph P. Fitzpatrick, "The Importance of 'Community' in the Process of Immigrant Assimilation," *International Migration Review* 1, no. 1 (Fall 1966): 5–16.

10. Richard Gambino, *Blood of My Blood: The Dilemma of the Italian-Americans* (New York: Doubleday, 1974).

11. Paul Wrobel, "Becoming a Polish American: A Personal Point of View," in *White Ethnics: Life in Working Class America*, ed. Joseph A. Ryan (Englewood Cliffs, N.J.: Prentice-Hall, 1973), pp. 52–58, citation pp. 55–56.

12. Novak, "Confessions," pp. 25–26.

13. Michael Novak, "The Price of Being Americanized," *National Catholic Reporter*, April 2, 1971, p. 17.

14. Novak, "The Price of Being Americanized," pp. 25, 27.

15. Cf. John P. Diggins, "Buckley's Comrades: The Ex-Communist as Conservative," *Dissent* 22, no. 4 (Fall 1975): 370–381.

16. Michael Novak, "The One and the Many," *Daedalus* 103, no. 4 (Fall 1974): 203–211.

17. Novak, "Confessions," p. 32.

18. Novak, "The New Ethnicity," pp. 18–19.

19. Michael Novak, "Tom Wicker's Attica" *Commentary* 59, no. 5 (May 1975): 49–56.

20. The current symbiosis between "radicals" and "conservatives" has recently been discussed by Howard F. Stein, "*All in the Family* as a Mirror of Contemporary American Culture," *Family Process* 13, no. 3 (September 1974): 279–315.

21. Sigmund Freud, *Civilization and Its Discontents*, standard edition, vol. 13, 1930 (London: Hogarth Press, 1961), p. 126.

22. Sigmund Freud, *Moses and Monotheism*, standard edition, vol. 23, 1939 (London: Hogarth Press, 1961), p. 95.

23. Michael Novak, "Needing Niebuhr Again," *Commentary* 54, no. 3 (September 1972): 52–62.

24. Novak, "The Price of Being Americanized," p. 17.

25. Michael Novak, *Politics: Realism and Imagination* (New York: Herder and Herder, 1971), p. 8.

26. Weston La Barre, *The Ghost Dance: The Origins of Religion* (New York: Dell, 1970), pp. 106–107.

27. Howard F. Stein, "American Judaism, Israel, and the New Ethnicity," *Cross Currents* 25 no. 1 (Spring 1975): 51–66; "The Binding of the Son," *Psychoanalytic Quarterly* (1977).

28. Emil Fackenheim, *God's Presence in History: Jewish Affirmations and Philosophical Reflections* (New York: New York University Press, 1970); *Encounters Between Judaism and Modern Philosophy* (New York: Basic Books, 1972).

29. Herbert Gold, "On Becoming a Jew," *Commentary* 53, no. 3 (March 1972): 60–65; *My Last Two Thousand Years* (New York: Random House, 1972).

30. Paul Wrobel, "Becoming a Polish American: A Personal Point of View," in *White Ethnics: Life in Working Class America*, ed. Joseph A. Ryan (Englewood Cliffs,

N.J.: Prentice-Hall, 1973), pp. 52–58; Richard Rodriguez, "On Becoming a Chicano," *Saturday Review,* February 8, 1975, pp. 46–48.

31. Abraham J. Heschel, *Israel: An Echo of Eternity* (New York: Farrar, Straus and Giroux), 1967.

32. *Time,* October 10, 1971, p. 69.

33. Quoted by Rabbi Joel S. Geffen in "A Question of Jewish Existence," *The Torch,* published by the National Federation of Jewish Men's Clubs (Fall 1975): 6–7.

34. In this chapter we have taken the *theoretical* position that it is possible to understand the dynamics of a social movement through the examination of the lives and works of its leaders, since cult-society and charismatic leader or prophet share the same conflicts, to which the leader offers a solution. Moreover, to the extent that the leader is able or unable to fulfill current social need, to know the dynamics and symbolic-ritual world of the successful or failed prophet is simultaneously to know the social ambience that finds him savior, fool, or psychotic. The extent of the acceptance of the prophet's personal solution is a measure of the extent of shared symptomatology (epidemiology) with the wider population (though we have stressed that consensus is not validity). As La Barre writes in *The Ghost Dance* (1972, p. 614), "In crisis situations, since impotence in the individual demands omnipotence in the savior, it is therefore to be expected that many charismatic leaders would be paranoid." For further discussion of this viewpoint which the present work substantiates, see the following: Weston La Barre, *The Ghost Dance;* George Devereux, "Charismatic Leadership and Crisis," *Psychoanalysis and the Social Sciences* 4 (1955): 145–157; "Shamans as Neurotics," *American Anthropologist* 63 (1961): 1088–1090; "Normal and Abnormal," in *Some Uses of Anthropology: Theoretical and Applied* (Washington, D.C.: The Anthropological Society of Washington, 1962).

The *methodological* orientation of the present chapter has been that of the life history and personal document as an instrument for gaining an understanding of the individual in his cultural-historical, psychodynamic, and psychogenetic context. Because the way one arranges and articulates his life and its meaning is itself a projective test, it is amenable to analysis akin to that of the Rorschach or Thematic Apperception Test. The advantage over the Rorschach is that the "stimulus situation" itself is naturalistic, that is, it is one that has been organized and invented by the native informant, either in a relationship with the ethnographer or totally independent of him (as, for instance, Novak as author). The stimulus situation consists of the informant's *Umwelt,* rather than a card placed before him to interpret. All of life consists of a projective-interpretation of the significant. What we have engaged in is an interpretation of a person's internal-cultural (phenomenological) world without the mediation of devices *alien* to that world. What Allport calls "introspective protocols" of the personal document reveal the patterning of a person's life in his own context. While other investigators utilize formal projective protocols to corroborate data from observation, interview, life history, and the like, we have chosen not to use them, but rather focus on those *protocols* developed by the informant himself. Indeed, we suspect that the introduction of traditional projective tests would have intruded on the relationships we established and created resistances against revealing further and deeper aspects of their personal lives—especially in the *American* context in which our informants are well aware of the use of projective tests for assessing clinical pathology! The essential references underlying the present methodology are as follows: Sigmund

Freud, *Psycho-Analytic Notes on an Autobiographical Account of a Case of Paranoia (Dementia Paranoides)*, standard edition, vol. 12, 1911; (London: Hogarth Press, 1958); Gordon W. Allport, *The Use of Personal Documents in Psychological Science*, Social Science Research Council Bulletin 49, 1942; John Dollard, *Criteria for the Life History* (New Haven: Yale University Press, 1935); Clyde Kluckhohn, "The Personal Document in Anthropological Science," in *The Use of Personal Documents in History, Anthropology, and Sociology*, eds. Louis Gottschalk, Clyde Kluckhohn, and Robert Angell, Social Science Research Council Bulletin 53, 1945; Erik H. Erikson, *Young Man Luther* (New York: Norton, 1958); Michael V. Angrosino, "The Use of Autobiography as 'Life History,' " *Ethos* 4, no. 2 (Summer 1976): 133–154; David G. Mandelbaum, "The Study of Life History: Gandhi," *Current Anthropology* 14, no. 3 (June 1973): 177–206.

Chapter 8

1. George Devereux, "Ethnic Identity: Its Logical Foundations and Its Dysfunctions," in *Ethnic Identity: Cultural Continuities and Change*, eds. George De Vos and Lola Romanucci-Ross (Palo Alto: Mayfield, 1975), pp. 42–70.

2. John Hart Ely, "The Constitutionality of Reverse Racial Discrimination," *University of Chicago Law Review* 41 (1974): 723–741.

3. See Nathan Glazer, *Affirmative Discrimination: Ethnic Inequality and Public Policy* (New York: Basic Books, 1976). See also Lloyd A. Fallers, *Inequality: Social Stratification Reconsidered* (Chicago: University of Chicago Press, 1973); John H. Bunzel, "Bakke vs. University of California," *Commentary* 63, no. 3 (March 1977): 59–64.

4. Miroslav Hroch, *Die Vorkämpfer der nationalen Bewegung bei den kleinen Völkern Europas. Eine vergleichende Analyse zur gesellschaftlichen Schichtung der patriotischen Gruppen* (Prague: Charles University, 1968); Konstantin Symmons-Symonolewicz, "Nationalist Movements: An Attempt at a Comparative Typology," *Comparative Studies in Society and History* 7 (1964–65): 221–230; Symmons-Symonolewicz, *Nationalistic Movements: A Comparative View* (Meadville, Pa.: Maplewood Press, 1970); Holm Sundhausen, *Der Einfluss der herderschen Ideen auf die Nationsbildung bei den Voelkern der Habsburger Monarchie* (Munich: R. Olderbourg Verlag, 1973). Konstantin Symmons-Symonolewicz, "Studies in Nationalism: Old and New," *Canadian Review of Studies of Nationalism* 2 (Fall 1974): 152–156. Sundhausen, *Der Einfluss der herderschen Ideen;* Hroch, *Die Vorkämpfer der nationalen Bewegung;* Symmons-Symonolewicz, "Nationalist Movements," *Nationalistic Movements.*

5. Symmons-Symonolewicz, *Nationalistic Movements, "Studies in Nationalism";* *Modern Nationalism: Toward a Consensus Theory* (New York: Polish Institute of Arts and Sciences in America, 1968).

6. G. D. Kerr, " 'Oyseaux de proye qui vivent de rapine': Opinions on the English in Fifteenth Century France," *Canadian Review of Studies in Nationalism* 1 (Fall 1973): 70–80.

7. Hroch, *Die Vorkämpfer der nationalen Bewegung;* Sundhausen, *Der Einfluss der herderschen Ideen.*

8. Weston La Barre, "Anthropological Perspectives on Hallucination and Hallucinogens," in *Hallucinations: Behavior, Experience and Theory*, eds. Ronald K. Siegel and Louis Jolyon West (New York: Wiley, 1975), pp. 11–52, 18, 22.

9. Edmund R. Leach, "Presidential Address: The Royal Anthropological Institute of Great Britain and Ireland," *Royal Anthropological Institute News* (September–October 1974), no. 4, p. 7.

10. Oliver H. Osborne et al., "Social Processes and Symptom Patterns: The King County Example" (Paper presented at the Meetings of the American Anthropological Association, New Orleans, 1973).

11. Margaret Mead, "The Concept of Culture and the Psychosomatic Approach," *Psychiatry* 10 (1947): 57–76, citation p. 72.

12. La Barre, "Anthropological Perspectives on Hallucination," p. 16.

13. Gerald Suttles, *The Social Construction of Communities* (Chicago: University of Chicago Press), 1972.

14. Zvi Maimon, "The Inner-City Impact," *Urban Affairs Quarterly* (December 1970): 233–248.

15. Robert A. Nisbet, *The Sociological Tradition* (New York: Basic Books, 1966), reviewed by Lewis A. Coser, "A Schism in Man's Soul," *New York Times Book Review*, August 20, 1967, p. 4.

16. Richard Sennett, *The Uses of Disorder: Personal Identity and City Life* (New York: Random House, 1970).

17. Howard F. Stein, "Freedom and Interdependence: American Culture and the Adlerian Ideal," *Journal of Individual Psychology* 30 (November 1974): 145–158.

18. Erik H. Erikson, "Once More the Inner Space," in *Women and Analysis,* ed. Jean Strouse (New York: Grossman, 1974), p. 336.

19. Michael Novak, "The Social World of Individuals," *Hastings Center Studies* 2 (September 1974): 37–44, citation pp. 43–44.

20. Ansbacher, in a personal communication with Stein.

21. Martin Buber, *Between Man and Man* (New York: Macmillan, 1965), pp. 31–32.

22. Charles Rycroft, review of *The Quest for Identity* by Allen Wheelis (London: Gallancz, 1959), *International Journal of Psycho-analysis* 41 (1960): 87.

23. Edward Sapir, "Culture, Genuine and Spurious," in *Culture, Language and Personality,* selected essays of Edward Sapir, ed. David Mandelbaum (Berkeley: University of California Press, 1966), pp. 78–119, citation p. 107.

24. Erik H. Erikson, *Dimensions of a New Identity: Jefferson Lectures, 1973* (New York: Norton, 1974).

25. Hillel, *Pirkei Aboth,* 1:14.

Index

Acculturation, 25–26, 32, 46–47, 182, 185, 199, 224–33, 275
Adams, John, 65
Adaptation, 189–90, 224–30, 255, 269–70, 282–87
Adler, Alfred, 285
Agnew, Spiro, 108, 114, 116, 119, 129–30, 149, 156
Alexander, Franz, 57
Alger, Horatio, 64
Alter, Robert, 161
American conformity (Anglo-conformity), 33, 47, 67–80, 125, 270
American Dilemma, 73–80
American Dream, 30–34, 43, 45–46, 48–60, 66, 70–72, 80–82, 90–105, 112, 114, 125, 141, 146, 163, 165, 168, 179, 182, 223, 282–83, 287
American Indian Movement, 5
American Indians, 55, 175–79
American nativism, 211–12
American value orientations, 31–32, 39, 48, 54–80, 185, 217–18, 230, 232, 271
Americanization, 20–21, 32–36, 39, 82–92, 161, 222
Ansbacher, Heinz, 285
Anthropology and Ethnicity, 40, 44, 281–82, 287
Apartheid, 141
Ardrey, Robert, 1, 284
Arendt, Hannah, 117, 137
Assassinations, 98–105, 115
Assimilation, 180, 182, 199, 222
Attica Prison, 93, 151, 156–58, 238
Authoritarianism, 30, 61–67, 72–73, 88–90, 115–17, 119–38, 224–32, 241, 284

Balkanization, 126, 161, 164
Banfield, Edward, 229
Barbarossa, Fredrick, 99
Baroni, Geno, 163, 181, 190, 194, 198, 201, 215–18, 251
Barth, Fredrik, 201
Basic group identity (Isaacs), 20
Bateson, Gregory, 69
Becker, Carl, 51
Bell, Daniel, 136
Berrigan, Daniel, 221
Bettelheim, Bruno, 204
Biological Instinctivism, 1, 126–27, 137–38
Black Panthers, 142–43
Black Power and Pride, 5, 43, 140, 142–43, 145–47, 150–51
Black rage, 98, 216
Black-white dichotomy, 11, 139–59
Blacks, 11, 75, 143, 146, 148, 150–52, 154–58, 160–61, 169, 173, 188, 203, 206–9, 211, 223, 238, 272, 287
Blake, William, 59
Blos, Peter, 205
Bonhöffer, Dietrich, 283
Brown, Norman O., 95
Buber, Martin, 94, 247, 250, 286
Buckley, William F., Jr., 236
Bunker, Archie, 141, 159, 171
Burridge, K. O. L., 68–69

Calley, William, 138
Campbell, Donald, 137–38, 183
Čapek, Karel, 226
Cargo cult (Melanesian), 42, 68–69, 269
Carter, Jimmy, 78–79, 132–34

Caste, 139, 143
Castro, Fidel, 92, 100
Chomsky, Noam, 14–15
Christology, 99, 105, 242
Chrobot, Leonard, 195, 217–18
Clubberly, Elwood P., 68
Colonialism, 125
Community, 3, 5, 54, 78–79, 82–83, 136, 161, 164, 170, 217–18, 230, 235, 279–82, 285–86
Conspiracy theory (Kennedy), 100–105
Corporate identities, 27, 172, 230, 262–66
Coser, Lewis, 280–81
"Counterreformation" of the 1970s, 101–11
Crèvecoeur, Jean de, 59, 68
Crisis cult (La Barre), 2, 196, 202, 267, 269–70
Culbreath, Myrna, 99–100
Cult of the average man, 64–65
Cultural Centers of the White Ethnic Movement, 194–95
Culture areal ethos (Devereux), 55–57

Daley, Richard, 108, 130
Danzig, David, 73–74
Dean, James, 99
Death of God theology, 97–98
Deep Structure (Chomsky), 14, 16
Defense, 7, 8, 11, 120, 124, 126, 135, 150, 167–71, 190, 199, 202–6, 213, 240, 242, 275, 284–85
Deloria, Vine, 143, 177
Descartes, René, 50–51
Devereux, George, xi, 7–8, 14, 55–57, 197
De Vos, George, 7, 40–41, 143, 197
Dewey, John, 70
Diaspora, 248–49
Diderot, Denis, 52
Differentiation, 5, 17, 165, 187, 262, 273–77, 281
Diggins, John P., 198
Displaced white ethnics, 119
Dornic, Ivan, 179–81
Dostoevski, Fëdor, 91, 114–15, 133, 182, 191, 197, 224, 239
Dubos, René, 136–37
Durkheim, Emil, 164, 279

Education, 186, 222–23, 273–74, 278
Ego boundaries, 7, 23, 167–71, 182–83, 187, 213, 245, 265, 269
Eliade, Mircea, 207
Elkins, Stanley, 152
Ellison, Ralph, 173, 217, 219
Ellsberg, Daniel, 135
Emerson, R. W., 59
EMPAC, 119, 199, 235
Engerman, Stanley, 152
Enlightenment, 50–52, 76, 170, 283
Erikson, Erik H., xi, 1, 4, 15, 41, 57–58, 63, 66–67, 69, 94–95, 114, 120, 163, 165, 167, 170, 184–86, 197–98, 214, 284, 287
Ethnic boundaries, 7, 19–21, 23–28, 74, 141–60, 162–71, 187, 214–57, 265, 276, 281
Ethnic Heritage Studies Programs Act, 195–96
Ethnic personality (Devereux), 14
Ethnic power, 184–85, 188
Ethnic pride, 6, 171–79, 184, 188
"Ethnic purity," 78–80, 177
Ethnic Studies, 194–97, 222, 273–74, 277–79, 281
Ethnic voluntarism, 21–22, 145
Ethnos, 15–16, 238
Exhibitionism, 5, 22, 171–79, 184
Existentialism, 95, 97–98, 234–35, 251
Extended family (peasant), 29–30, 54–55, 224–32

Fackenheim, Emil, 180, 247–48, 253
Fairchild, Henry Pratt, 68
Fallers, Lloyd A., 42, 200
Family imagery (New Ethnicity) 170, 188–92, 217, 218–55, 279–82
Farm, The (Tennessee), 131–32
Father figures (quest for), 106, 115–17, 119–38, 213–56
Feudalism, 50–51
Fishman, Joshua, 21, 23–24, 57–58
Fogel, Robert, 152
Ford, Gerald R., 110
Fox, Robin, 1, 126
Franklin, Benjamin, 65
Fraternal organizations (ethnic), 17–19, 26, 32–36, 199

Freud, Sigmund, 41, 61, 97–98, 105, 138, 170, 240–41, 282–83
Fromm, Erich, 61, 91, 95

Gambino, Richard, 194–95, 198, 217–18, 230
Gaskin, Stephen, 131
Gay, Peter, 3, 4, 106
Geertz, Clifford, 42
Gegenidee (contrast conception), 15
Glazer, Nathan, 141, 151, 161
Godfather, The, 110, 116–17, 128, 171
Godunov, Boris, 109
Goering, John M., 149
Gold, Herbert, 198, 217, 249
Goldberg, Steven, 1
Goldwater, Barry, 72, 102
Goy, Peter, 194
Graham, Billy, 103, 129, 132
Greeley, Andrew, 42, 139–40, 180–81, 194, 198, 217–18, 221–22, 251
Greeley, Horace, 54
Group rights, 72–73, 79–80, 116, 262–66
Guilt, 82, 125, 162, 180, 205, 219–46, 265

Hackney, Sheldon, 153
Haley, Alex, 255–56
Harrington, Michael, 48, 222
Hayes, Carleton, 267
Health-illness model, 5, 274–79
Heilbroner, Robert, 129, 135, 137
Herder, Johann Gottfried von, 190
Heschel, Abraham J., 94, 198, 221, 247, 249–50
Hill, Robert, 10, 86, 141
Hitler, Adolf, 120, 197, 200, 247
Hobsbawm, Eric, 117
Hoffer, Eric, 30, 202
Horney, Karen, 64
Huggins, Nathan I., 54, 164

Identity, 1, 3, 11, 57–58, 114, 167, 236, 277, 282–87
Identity confusion, 98, 106–11, 180, 282–87
Identity foreclosure, 279, 284–85
Immigration, 23–36, 71–72, 74–75, 120, 158, 219, 231
Integration Movement (Civil Rights), 96, 146, 162, 198, 216

Intermarriage, 36–39
Isaacs, Harold, 8, 20, 42, 119, 143, 161
Isajiw, Wsevolod, 19

Jackson, Henry, 114, 135
Janošik, 228
Jaspers, Karl, 250
Jefferson, Thomas, 65, 76–77, 284
Jews (American), 147, 171, 180, 221, 234, 246–57, 272
John XXIII (Pope), 92, 94–95
Johnson, Lyndon, 78, 93, 100–101, 109, 155
Jung, Carl, 170

Kafka, Franz, 59
Kant, Immanuel, 248, 283
Kazin, Alfred, 76–77
Kennedy, Edward M., 99
Kennedy, John F., 45, 81–82, 91–94, 96, 98, 100, 102–8, 112, 114, 139, 283
Kennedy, Robert F., 92, 102, 107–8, 114–16, 134, 149, 216
Kerr, G. D., 267
Khrushchev, Nikita, 96
Killian, Lewis M., 154–57
King, Martin Luther, Jr., 75, 93, 102, 114–15, 149, 155–56, 216
Kluckhohn, Clyde, 64–65
Kluckhohn, Florence, 62
Kohn, Hans, 267
Kohut, Heinz, 183–84, 203
Kolm, Richard, 198, 217–18
Kovalovsky, John, 172–75
Kovel, Joel, 157
Kreitman, Benjamin, 251–53
Kroeber, Alfred, 283
Ku Klux Klan, 119, 212
Kubic, Joseph, 140

La Barre, Weston, ix–x, xi, xiii, 9, 94, 243–46, 270
Lasswell, Harold, 223
Leach, Edmund, 42, 273–74
Lee, Peggy, 113
Lenin, 66
Leon-Portilla, Miguel, 40
Levine, Irving, 194, 198
Levi-Strauss, Claude, 14–15, 43–44, 165
Lewis, Oscar, 43, 151

"Liberal (individualistic) Personality,"
217–18
Lifton, Robert Jay, 58
Lincoln, Abraham, 99, 105
Localism, 126, 149, 160–212, 229, 236–55,
262–87
Locke, John, 59
Lombardi, Vince, 72
Lorenz, Konrad, 1, 126, 284
Lukashevich, Stephen, 188–89
Luther, Martin, 52

Malcolm X, 102, 104, 114, 197
Mann, Horace, 70
Marcuse, Herbert, 95
Marshak, Sondra, 99–100
Maslow, Abraham, 94, 98, 114, 170
May, Rollo, 193
McCarthy, Eugene, 116, 134, 242
McLean, Don, 113
McLuhan, Marshall, 94
Mead, Margaret, 42, 275–76
Meany, George, 135
Melting Pot, 27, 33, 55, 59, 67–68, 70–71,
125, 163, 168, 183, 201, 219, 223, 242,
275
Melville, Herman, 58
Mikulski, Barbara, 126, 174
Milgram, Stanley, 129, 137
Miller, Arthur, 64
Models of the White Ethnic Movement,
256–61
Montesquieu, Charles de, 52
Morgenthau, Henry, 252
Morris, Desmond, 126, 284
Mosaic image, 162–67, 264
Moses, 105, 197, 267
Moyers, Bill, 78
Moynihan, Daniel, 141, 151–52, 282–83
Muskie, Edmund, 222
Musmano, Michael A., 175
Myrdal, Gunnar, 73–74, 96

Nahirny, Vladimir, 23–24
Narcissism, 9, 179–90, 213–56, 271
Narcissistic rage (Kohut), 183–84, 214–46
Nationalism, 11, 266–70
Negative conversion, 15, 165
Negative identity, 55, 214
New Ethnicity and the Southern Ethos,
132–34

New Frontier, 11, 53, 91
New Left, 5, 181
New World, 29, 53, 59
Newton, Huey, 142
Niebuhr, Reinhold, 234, 236, 240
Nimoy, Leonard, 99
Nisbet, Robert A., 136, 280
Nixon, Richard M., 93–94, 102, 108–10,
112–14, 116, 119, 129–30, 138, 149,
156
Nolan, Martin F., 93
North, The (U.S.), 78, 151–52, 154–59
North-South relations, 74–77, 135, 147,
151
"Northern model" (Glazer and Moyni-
han), 151
Nostalgia, 4, 135–36, 168
Novak, Michael, 48, 78, 91, 102, 124–25,
129, 132–35, 148, 156–58, 166, 180–82,
186, 190–91, 195, 198–201, 210, 214,
217–25, 227–29, 233–43, 245–47, 249,
251, 274, 284

Oedipal conflict, 63, 69, 71–72, 90–111,
168–69, 219–55
Oedipal heroes, 90–101, 219–46
Old World, 29, 50, 53, 59
Omnipotence, 52, 179, 243–46, 269
One-Dimensional identity, 7, 8, 262
One Flew Over the Cuckoo's Nest, 117–
18
Oppositional process (Spicer), 15–16,
153, 160–61, 165, 180–81, 214–57, 266–
69, 275
Order and control, 11, 102–3, 112–38,
157, 248–55
Organic model of society, 168, 214–57,
262–87
Origin myth(s), 161–62, 171–79, 188, 191,
213–55, 269
Osborne, Oliver H., 275
Osgood, Charles, 15
Oswald, Lee Harvey, 100

Packard, Vance, 54
Pan-Ethnicity, 187–92, 248–49
Paranoid-narcissistic position, 4, 109–11,
115–29, 179–87, 214–57, 267–69, 271,
282
Parsons, Talcott, 21–22, 164–65

Patrick, H. Louis, 133
"Pattern variables" (Parsons), 165
Patton, George, 86, 110
Perotta, Ralph, 194
Pettigrew, Thomas F., 149, 202
Phares, Ross, 59
PIGS, 48, 188, 217–20, 238
Pluralism, 8–9, 139, 159, 161–64, 196, 198, 262–66, 273, 276–79
"Pluralistic Personality," 217–18
Polish-Americans, 10, 19, 23–39, 166, 172, 201, 222, 224–32, 263–64, 271
Polish Pan-Slavism, 188–89
Ponce de León, Juan, 53
Presidency (politics and symbolism), 132–34, 242
Primordiality, 20, 41–45, 167, 181, 191, 217–18, 281–82, 287
Projection, 155, 183, 214–55, 270
Psychopathy, 109–11, 116–18, 133, 213–55
Puritans, 58, 277
Pusser, Buford, 86
Puzo, Mario, 82, 87–88, 110

Queen Mother Moore, 142

Racism, 139–59, 161, 236–39, 270–73
Reagan, Ronald, 108, 114, 129–30, 239
Redfield, Robert, 43, 279
"Reformation" of the 1960s, 90–105
Regression, 8, 9, 164–65, 168, 170, 185, 188–89, 205, 213–55, 266, 268–70, 281, 285
Reich, Charles, 217
Religious revivalism, 103–4, 128–29, 132, 235, 248–55
Renaissance, 51–52
Repression, 77, 91, 106, 108, 169, 186, 211, 232, 240–41, 243
Retribalization (Isaacs), 126
Riesman, David, 64
Riskin, Steven, 249–50
Rizzo, Frank, 108, 130
Robinson, John A. T., 97
Rodriguez, Richard, 249
Rogow, Arnold A., 101
Romanticism, 3–4, 8, 44, 170, 177, 200, 216–18, 221, 235–46, 279–81
Romanucci-Ross, Lola, 7, 40–41, 147

Roots, 5, 216, 219, 221, 233, 236, 255–56, 281
Rose, Peter, 180, 200
Roszak, Theodore, 217
Rycroft, Charles, 286

Saint-Simon, Claude Henri de, 164
Sapir, Edward, 286
Sartre, Jean-Paul, 81
Schism (factionalism), 34–36, 190–92, 203, 208–10
Schlesinger, Arthur, Jr., 126
Schneider, David, 22
Schreiber, Janet M., 29
Schwartz, Theodore, 68, 202–3
Self-actualization, 98, 114, 285
Semantic differential, 15
Sennett, Richard, 130
Shafer, Boyd, 267
Shamanic leadership, 197–99, 243–45, 267, 278
Shame, 15, 125, 162, 171–79, 181, 183, 215–16, 219–46, 265
Shatner, William, 99
Sheed, Wilfred, 214
Silver, Isidore, 116–17
Sinatra, Frank, 113
Skinner, B. F., 129–31
Slater, Philip, 102–3, 105, 119
Slovak-Americans and Ruthene-Americans, 10, 19, 23–39, 166, 172–75, 179–80, 201, 224–33, 237, 271
Social class, 191, 201
Solzhenitsyn, Alexander, 135, 191
"Soul," 5, 6, 139, 142, 181–82, 186, 199, 217–18, 220
South, The (U.S.), 76–77, 132, 153–59
Southeast Asian war, 101–2, 242
"Southern model" (Glazer and Moynihan), 139, 164
Spender, Stephen, 61
Spicer, Edward, 15
Spiegel, John, 62–63, 232
Spiro, Melford, 46–47
"Star Trek," 99–100
Status anxiety, 68–69, 140, 143, 148–49, 188–89, 196, 219–46, 268
Stein, Howard, 1, 10, 21, 30, 33, 40, 83, 89, 106–7, 120–24, 140–41, 226–27, 232, 239, 250, 256

Stevenson, Adlai, 53
Surface structure (Chomsky), 14, 16
Sussna, Frances, 194
Suttles, Gerald, 280

Teilhard de Chardin, Pierre, 94–95, 250
Tiger, Lionel, 1, 126
Tillich, Paul, 94, 250
Tindall, George B., 153–54
Tocqueville, Alexis de, 65
Tolstoi, Leo, 133, 135, 197, 200
Tonnies, Ferdinand, 165
Totalism, 4, 167
Transformation (Levi-Strauss), 14, 165

Vecoli, Rudolph, 194
Visibility-exhibitionism, 6, 22, 160–212
Voegelin, Eric, 15
Volkstum, 3–4, 161, 221, 266
Von Mering, Otto, XIII, 12, 82

Wallace, George, 79, 90, 114, 116, 119,
    129–30, 132, 134, 149, 156–59, 189,
    202, 236–39, 272
Washington, George, 65

Watergate, 109–11, 116
Weber, Max, 193, 199
Wheeler, Thomas C., 60
White ethnic-black dichotomy, 139–59, 272
White ethnic leadership, 196–202, 213–55
White ethnic-WASP dichotomy, 132–35,
    160, 166, 169, 176, 178, 180–82, 201,
    214–57, 272
White ethnics and white southerners,
    149–50, 153–59
Whitehead, Alfred North, 250
Whitman, Walt, 65
Wicker, Tom, 156–57, 238–39
Wills, Gary, 109
Wilson, Woodrow, 28
Woman's Movement, 5, 144, 185–86
Work ethic, 224–27
World War II, 11, 82–92
Wrobel, Paul, 217–18, 230–31, 249

Youth Culture-Youth Movement, 90–111,
    135, 161, 218, 234

Zangwill, Israel, 59, 68
Zinn, Howard, 155–56